MY SLOVAKIA, MY FAMILY

One Family's Role
in the Birth of a Nation

JOHN PALKA

Kirk House Publishers
Minneapolis, Minnesota

MY SLOVAKIA, MY FAMILY
One Family's Role in the Birth of a Nation

by John Palka

Library of Congress Cataloging-in-Publication Data

Palka, John.
   My Slovakia, my family : one family's role in the birth of a nation / John Palka.
      pages cm
   Also published in Slovak: Bratislava : Kalligram, 2010.
   Includes bibliographical references and index.
   ISBN 978-1-933794-55-6 (alkaline paper) -- ISBN 1-933794-55-0 (alkaline paper)
   1. Hodža, Milan, 1878-1944. 2. Hodža, Milan, 1878-1944--Family. 3. Palka, John. 4. Palka, John--Family. 5. Slovakia--Biography. 6. Slovakia--Politics and government. 7. Slovakia--History. I. Palka, John. Moje Slovensko, moja rodina. II. Title.
   DB2191.H63P358 2012
   943.73'0320922--dc23
   [B]

2012039128

Kirk House Publishers, PO Box 390759, Minneapolis, MN 55439
Manufactured in the United States of America

I dedicate this book to the memory of my parents:
Ján Pálka of Liptovský Mikuláš,
whose love for his native place never dimmed,
no matter what danger, disappointment, or distance life put in his way;
and Irene Pálka, née Hodža,
who bequeathed to me a treasure chest
of language and poetry, song and history, that ties me forever
to the Slovak land I knew only briefly in my childhood.

By example and by teaching, they made sure that I would never forget.

Contents

Prologue

Aká si mi krásna, Ty rodná zem moja . . .
How beautiful you are, O land of my birth . . .

Deep in the inner spaces of many of us who are immigrants to the United States is a lingering link to the homeland left behind—a longing to be reunited, inner images of what life had once been like, a poignant craving to recover our roots.

I know these inner spaces well, for my family was driven into political exile not once but twice. In 1938, during the frenzied time leading up to World War II, Hitler engineered the break-up and subjugation of my home country, Czechoslovakia. My grandfather, Dr. Milan Hodža, was the prime minister of Czechoslovakia during the three turbulent years leading up to this pivotal event. The success of the Nazi strategy placed in danger the lives of not only my grandparents but also my parents. With the possibility of arrest and deportation to what would soon become concentration camps looming, they escaped to France, where I was born, and ultimately to the United States. Grandfather Hodža died in this country and was buried in Chicago. The rest of our family returned to Czechoslovakia as soon after the war as we could. In 1948, however, before hardly any time had passed, a Stalinist regime took power and the Iron Curtain descended. My father was imprisoned for some time, and our lives were once again threatened. My parents and I escaped a second time, carrying with us only memories of our homeland.

CZECHOSLOVAKIA WAS A COMPOSITE COUNTRY, formed in 1918 by the decision of two related but nonetheless distinct peoples living in two adjacent regions—Czechs in the west and Slovaks in the east—to form a single state. When my parents were born, there was as yet no Czechoslovakia, only the Austro-Hungarian Empire. The Czech lands, Bohemia and Moravia, were part of the Austrian half of the empire. Slovakia was a part of Hungary. Today there is again no Czechoslovakia. Czechs and Slovaks went their separate ways in 1993 to form the Czech Republic and the Slovak Republic or Slovakia. My family was Slovak—all branches of it for at least three hundred years. (For an overview of Slovak history see Appendix I; for maps, Appendix II.)

I grew up in America at ease with being Slovak and proud of my heritage. On the walls of our tiny apartment in New York City hung paintings that reached us by a circuitous route from home: Peasants working the fields under looming mountains, pastoral images that portrayed the age-old connection of Slovaks to the land. A demure village girl in her Sunday best, representing the traditional culture that Slovaks treasured even in the twentieth century. A thickly bundled-up couple driving their sleigh through the glistening snows of the bitter mountain winter, steam billowing from the nostrils of the horses, an evocative portrayal of my father's home region (Plates 1-3, Appendix VI). I understood that these were merely glimpses of the home my parents loved, captured by the brushes of painters during the early part of the twentieth century. I knew, too, that my family's life had not been like this at all. For generations they had been townspeople, not villagers, and had often moved in a high and even international society. Nonetheless, there was some sense in which their roots, like those of the people in the paintings, were deep in the place, in the land itself.

WHEN I WAS A BOY AND OUR FAMILY of three sat at our modest dinner table in New York, my mother would occasionally tell me bits of family narrative and national history. Her stories blended with the imagery of the paintings and, imperceptibly, I developed a felt sense of my original homeland—its natural beauty, the struggle of its people against domination by others, and my parents' profound feeling of rootedness there, derived not from mere nostalgia but from generations of service and sacrifice to the national cause.

I grew up with my own sense of connection to my Slovak homeland, as well as a collection of oft-repeated stories. Now, however, I have been able to go much further, to assemble a full-fledged family saga spanning eight lineages and seven generations over 300 years. Because so many of my ancestors were significant in Slovak history, this saga is interwoven with the story of the whole Slovak nation. I tell it here in two cycles of time. The first cycle tells of my immediate family and of our two journeys into exile. The second cycle starts as far back as I am able, in the late 1600s, and moves to the present. It tells of men and women in my broader family—peasants, pastors and poets; scholars and politicians; hard working craftsmen and savvy entrepreneurs—many of whom struggled against oppression, fought for freedom, and made a profound mark on their country.

THE LOSS OF HOME IS A RECURRING THEME in the lives of my family. Some, like my parents, died in foreign lands. Some, like I, were able to return to their homeland during their lifetimes. The return of yet others has been symbolic. The physical remains of two of Slovakia's greatest national leaders—my great-granduncle, Michal Miloslav Hodža, and his nephew, Grandfather Milan Hodža—were brought home from their resting place in foreign soil by a grateful nation. The ceremonial return of Grandfather Hodža's remains from Chicago to the National Cemetery of Slovakia was one of the great experiences of my own life, bringing into new and vivid relief the way in which my family's story and the nation's history are intertwined.

The event began with multiple ceremonies in Chicago. The one that touched me the most was the modest service at a small Lutheran church that still served the Slovak community there. The presiding bishop, who had himself grown up as an emigrant in Argentina, gave the sermon. The choir sang "Going Home," the moving song based on a theme from the New World Symphony written by Antonín Dvořák, the great Czech composer, while he spent time in America. And it sang, *"Aká si mi krásna, Ty rodná zem moja…"* (*How beautiful you are, O land of my birth . . .*), a poem that has become one of Slovakia's best-loved national hymns. Written by one of my uncles over a century ago, while he, too, lived far from home, the words suited the moment perfectly.

The next day, June 25, 2002, my wife, Yvonne, and I were aboard the official airplane of the Slovak Republic as it circled the castle-crowned capital city of Bratislava, the flight attendant announcing our descent and landing not in the familiar English but in Slovak: *"Dámy a páni…"* (Ladies and gentlemen . . .). The overnight flight from Chicago had been tedious. Exhausted from three days of receptions, lectures, and the church service, and still dressed in our formal clothes, we had been invited to curl up on the floor of the airplane so we could catch some sleep. Now, we shook ourselves awake and buckled into our seats.

Once the plane touched down, the doors opened onto an unforgettable scene. To one side of the runway stood row upon row of soldiers in dress uniform, gold braids hanging from their epaulets and polished ceremonial swords at the ready. A military band filled the air with stately music. A red carpet was rolled out between the terminal and the plane, and suddenly the chief of protocol was urging us out of the plane: "Please hurry. Never mind your bags. Just go out and stand with the delegation."

Yvonne and I descended the stairs and took our places in the row of waiting dignitaries: the prime minister of Slovakia, the minister of culture, and the prime minister's chief of staff (Plate 4). The band sounded the national anthem as a casket holding Grandfather Hodža's remains and draped with the Slovak flag was carefully lowered from the belly of the plane. The government of Slovakia was redeeming a public promise made at the time of his death by bringing his remains home and thereby publicly recognizing his place in the nation's history.

Six members of the immaculately uniformed honor guard hoisted the casket on their shoulders and carried it regally down the carpeted tarmac toward the terminal. As somber music played, the lone figure of the prime minister walked slowly behind. Then came Yvonne and I, representing the family, and behind us the other dignitaries. Step after focused step we walked until we reached the waiting black limousine. Once the casket, still draped in the flag, was loaded into the limousine, the prime minister turned to greet us with a firm handshake, and in faultless English said, "Welcome to Slovakia." Then the reporters surrounded us, each clamoring for a few words that could be quoted on the evening news or in the next day's newspapers. "How does this make you feel?" they asked. "What is your favorite memory of him?" "Would you stand here so we can get some footage?" "What is his legacy for the modern world?" "Would you step aside for a quick interview?" "Would you sign this book for me?" I, a quiet American professor, suddenly found myself swept up in the glittering and unrelenting flow of an event of state in Slovakia. I mustered all the energy I had to speak the language of my childhood with the throng of reporters. "*Materinská moja reč, aká si mi milá . . .*". (*O Mother Tongue, how dear you are to me . . .*) my poet-uncle had written from his outpost in Budapest a long time ago. I have been given the gift of remembering the language well. It is a key that opens the hearts of Slovaks and makes me deeply welcome in the land I left behind.

Our final destination, the resting place prepared for Grandfather Hodža's remains, was not the bustling capital of Bratislava but Martin, a much smaller city that is about three hours away by car (Map 3, Appendix II). Much of the drama of Slovak history is related to Martin, and it is the home of the Slovak National Cemetery. Brought from Bratislava by limousine, the flag-draped coffin lay in the city's historic Lutheran church for a day. The coffin was flanked by an honor guard of two students, dressed in formal black and white, students from the the nearby Anglo-Slovak Bilingual Gymnasium of Milan Hodža, the public preparatory school that Grandfather Hodža had helped to establish in 1928. All day long a steady stream of people from the area filed by to pay their respects. A few were old enough to have met him in person; most were younger, and to them he could only have been a figure they had heard or read about. All silently waited their turn. When they reached the coffin, some offered flowers and others simply looked and bowed slightly. Young couples brought their children and elders their grandchildren, guiding them to reach out to touch the casket and the flag. It was a day of quiet remembrance in the simple, sun-drenched church.

The next day the church was full for the memorial service, admission by invitation only. The overflow crowd stood outside, listening over loudspeakers. It was a simple ceremony. A few poignant hymns were sung by the choir, "*Aká si mi krásna, Ty rodná zem moja*" among them. A few well-chosen words were offered and a liturgy sung by the much-loved ministers of this historic church. I said a few words of thanks on behalf of the family (Plate 6); the prime minister painted a picture of today's Slovakia as a home to which Grandfather Hodža would be proud to return; and my cousin Jelka, also speaking for the family, concluded with that simple phrase that said everything that was most important: "*Vítaj doma* " (Welcome home).

In the National Cemetery the grave that already held the remains of my grandmother, Irena Hodža, had been opened and a new tombstone erected. The honor guard once again carried the casket, stepping securely between the crowded gravestones and past the throng that had gathered to watch and pay their final respects. Our family stood in the front row, Yvonne and I at the foot of the grave. The national anthem sounded. The honor guard folded the flag and passed it to their captain. Following the time-honored tradition, he handed it to me and saluted (Plate 5). The chief of protocol had alerted me minutes before that this would happen, but I was unprepared for the intensity of the moment and my eyes suddenly teared as I clutched the flag. The bare coffin was lowered into the grave on three thick ropes as the two ministers, father and son, chanted the traditional liturgy. Symbolic handfuls of dirt were thrown into the grave. Moments later the ceremony was over, and a stream of people started to move past us—high government officials, ambassadors of foreign countries, neighbors, journalists, historians, all offering their respects. For some it was undoubtedly a formality, but most, I believe, wanted to be part of something great— part of a moment that stirred their memories, their pride, and their faith in the future. I was the recipient of this outpouring, a gift I will never forget.

The flag had covered Grandfather Hodža's casket from the time his remains were disinterred in Chicago. It was in place during the church service there, while the casket was loaded onto the Slovak government airplane at O'Hare Airport by an honor guard of the U.S. Navy, during the welcoming ceremonies at the airport in Bratislava, on its journey to Martin, in Martin's Lutheran church, and at the final service at the National Cemetery. It came to symbolize not only the final journey of Grandfather Hodža's physical remains to the homeland to whose upliftment he had devoted a lifetime, but also my own return. When a television reporter asked "What was the high point of the ceremony for you?" I unhesitatingly told her, "When I received the flag," and once again I could not hold back my tears. A few days later, while I was doing some shopping in downtown Bratislava, a woman in the crowd came up to me and said, "I saw you on television the other night. It was very beautiful, and you speak such wonderful Slovak. But if I had been in your place, I don't know if I would have cried over the flag. Probably not." Whatever the flag represented for her, for me it meant home—and coming home in honor after a long time away—not only for my grandfather, but for me as well. No wonder I shed a few tears.

With the final closing of the grave and the placing of wreaths and flowers, Grandfather Hodža's exile had ended; he was now home. And I? I would soon return to America, where I had established a family, a professional life, and a deep sense of belonging. But I was changed. It was as if the grave in which I had buried my own past had been opened, and the dead memories had come to life and become part of me again. Those memories drew forth questions to which I needed to find answers—questions about family and nation, poetry and songs, the lives of my parents and their parents, and the whole long bloodline receding into the past. I offer you here the answers I have found—a kind of love story about my Slovakia.

PART I

TWICE INTO EXILE

In Part I, I primarily narrate events that shaped my own life. I start by telling how I came to be born in Paris at the dawn of World War II, and how a year and a half later my family narrowly escaped being carted off to a concentration camp. With the war raging, we managed to reach the United States. After the war we returned to Czechoslovakia, but all too soon were forced to creep back out under the barbed wire of the Iron Curtain. Thereafter, we settled in the United States for good. I tell of struggles and heroism during the war, and of the numbing weight of Communism. And finally, I paint a picture of my own father, whose story I never knew until I traced the source of a handful of photographs in a family album.

CHAPTER 1

Prague, 1935-1938

My parents dearly wanted a child, and when they found out my mother was pregnant, they planned as best they could for its future. My mother could have given birth in Prague, where Grandfather Hodža had settled his family in 1919 and where she and her siblings had grown up. She would have enjoyed the warmth of her parental home and the companionship of friends from her school days, and the medical care she would have received would have been the best. Or she could have given birth in Liptovský Svätý Mikuláš beneath the great Tatra Mountains of Slovakia, home to the Pálkas for centuries (Maps 2, 3, Appendix II). The house my parents had started to build in Mikuláš was nearing completion, and they looked forward to moving in. But neither Prague nor Mikuláš was entered on my birth certificate. In 1939, the year of my birth, the boots of German soldiers resounded through the cobbled streets of Prague, and Mikuláš tensed under the rule of a Slovak government subservient to the Nazis. Because of the threats to my family from these regimes, I was born far away from home, in Paris.

THE POLITICAL EVENTS PRECEDING MY MOTHER'S DEPARTURE were dramatic and complex, far beyond my understanding while I was growing up and my parents were still alive to explain them to me. To develop a coherent perspective on the complex circumstances that forced my mother to give birth to me in exile, I have spent several years poring over contemporary accounts, recent studies by academic historians, and family records. The narrative that follows is based on what I have found. (You will find an overview of Slovak history in Appendix I and a pronunciation guide in Appendix IV.)

Over the years leading up to World War II, Czechoslovakia's political leaders had held no illusions about the danger emanating from Germany. As early as 1924 and 1925 they had negotiated defense treaties with France. Overcoming long-held reservations, in early 1935 Czechoslovakia added a defense treaty with the Soviet Union to its system of international guarantees.[1] Around that time, the Czechoslovak border with Germany began to be studded with underground fortifications bristling with modern weaponry,[2] and as pressure from Germany heightened, long, slender anti-aircraft gun barrels started to be seen in Prague itself, tucked in among the city's ancient domed and gabled roofs.

Thus, the international situation was already tense when Grandfather Hodža was appointed Czechoslovakia's prime minister in November of 1935 and Edvard Beneš assumed the presidency shortly thereafter.[3] One of Hodža's first actions was to strengthen the country's defenses yet further. His new government implemented the expansion of the border defenses, the construction of arms factories, and the improvement of the country's defense communications network.[4]

The domestic situation was equally challenging, largely on account of Czechoslovakia's complex ethnic composition: 4.5 million Czechs, 3.5 million Germans, 2.5 million Slovaks, and smaller numbers of Rusyns, Magyars, and others[5] (Map 2, Appendix II). Almost from the moment of Czechoslovakia's founding in 1918, there had been tension between Czechs and Slovaks. The Czechs were the more affluent, better educated, and more experienced in self-

My grandfather, Dr. Milan Hodža, as prime minister of Czechoslovakia. The portrait was taken in 1938, the year his sixtieth birthday was widely celebrated. Archive of the National Museum in Prague.

government. They tended to look down on the Slovaks who—especially as their own wealth, education, and experience increased—bridled at both real injustices and perceived slights.[6] A powerful movement for Slovak autonomy within Czechoslovakia grew, championed by Andrej Hlinka, a charismatic Catholic priest whose influence became so profound that the party he founded and led was officially renamed Hlinka's Slovak People's Party or HSPP (*Hlinkova slovenská ľudová strana, HSĽS*). Starting in 1923 it was the most powerful Slovak political party. With the exception of a few short periods, it remained in permanent opposition and declined to participate in the long series of multi-party coalitions that governed Czechoslovakia from 1919 to 1939.[7] The Slovak National Party, led by the Lutheran minister and much admired writer and poet Martin Rázus, also espoused an autonomist position but was much smaller and less important than the HSPP.

Grandfather Hodža was the undisputed leader of the second most powerful party in Slovakia, the Agrarian Party. This was a national, not a regional organization, and its Czech and Slovak wings together constituted the most powerful party in the country. Influential in the initial establishment of Czechoslovakia and the holder of a succession of ministerial posts in Prague, Hodža had tried for many years to entice the autonomist parties to join the central government and thus enhance Slovak political influence and contrib-

Funeral of the founding president of Czechoslovakia, Tomáš Garrigue Masaryk, 1937. Prime Minister Hodža (left) and President Beneš (right) are flanked by military officers. Archive of the National Museum in Prague.

ute positively to the building of the state. His slogan was *Všetci Slováci dovedna* (All Slovaks Together), but he had only intermittent success in this endeavor. Once he became the Czechoslovak prime minister—the first-ever Slovak to serve in that position—it was widely expected that he would finally be able to resolve the persistent demands for Slovak autonomy. Hodža had long held an intermediate position on this question, being neither a Prague centralist nor a Slovak autonomist. By the time of his appointment as prime minister his position had shifted considerably in the autonomist direction, but his actions were constrained by political rivalries, by his fear that far-reaching autonomy would lead to the break-up of Czechoslovakia, and by the growing political power of the German population within Czechoslovakia.[8]

Like the Slovaks, the country's second-largest ethnic group, the millions of Germans of the Sudetenland whose families had lived in the borderlands with Germany and Austria for hundreds of years (Map 2) were also raising the banner of autonomy. In the elections of May 1935 the Sudeten German Party (*Sudetendeutsche Partei*, SdP) led by Konrad Henlein not only won the great majority of Sudeten German votes, it also suddenly became the country's largest single party. Publicly the SdP proclaimed loyalty to Czechoslovakia, but Henlein and his party were coming more and more under Hitler's control, transforming themselves into his surreptitious instrument.[9] Increasingly warm relations between the SdP and the more radical, Nazi-sympathizing elements within Hlinka's People's Party exacerbated the situation.[10] Hodža spent endless hours in negotiation, trying to find a resolution that would meet legitimate Sudeten demands but preserve democratic Czechoslovakia intact against forces that threatened to tear it apart. In the space of a year, *The Times of London* carried well over 200 articles in which Grandfather Hodža's efforts figured prominently.[11] These proved to be of no avail. With every conciliatory gesture Hodža made, the Henleinists simply escalated their demands.

IN MARCH OF 1938 CAME THE ANSCHLUSS, Germany's annexation of Austria. Hitler's arrival in Vienna was welcomed by thunderous crowds:[12]

> Before I knew it, I was being swept along in a shouting, hysterical Nazi mob, past the Ring, past the Opera, up the Kärntnerstrasse to the offices of the German "Tourist" Bureau, which, with its immense flower-draped portrait of Hitler, has been a Nazi shrine for months. The faces! I had seen them before at Nüremberg—the fanatical eyes, the gaping mouths, the hysteria. And now they were shouting like Holy Rollers: "*Sieg Heil! Sieg Heil! Sieg Heil! Heil Hitler! Heil Hitler! Heil Hitler! Hang Schuschnigg* [Austria's prime minister]*! Hang Schuschnigg! Hang Schuschnigg! Ein Volk, ein Reich, ein Führer!*" And the police! They were looking on, grinning.

Overnight Czechoslovakia became more vulnerable to invasion. The country's main defenses were concentrated on the border with Germany, while the border with Austria was relatively exposed. Feverish work started immediately to meet the new threat, described vividly by the British war correspondent Sydney Morrell:[13]

> Crossing the border into Austria, I left behind a broad highway of light, running all the way down the frontier towards Bratislava, where Austria, Hungary, and Czechoslovakia meet. But that was no highway for motorists. Under the lights thousands of men were working, digging deep into the earth, building forts, covering them with steel and cement, placing guns of all kinds into position, making a highway of death for the first German army that should attempt to cross that frontier.

The British, who were soon to play a critical role in Czechoslovakia's future, had long held an ambivalent attitude toward the country.[14] British ambassadors in Prague from 1930 on had supported the demands of the Sudeten Germans for autonomy, and many officials in the Foreign Office were at least sympathetic.[15] Following the *Anschluss* the British attitude hardly budged. Within a week a select government committee met to consider possible actions. The foreign secretary, Lord Halifax, prepared a position paper in which various alternatives were outlined, ranging from a "Grand Alliance" (Winston Churchill's evocative phrase) to resist German aggression to the polar opposite, applying increasing pressure on Czechoslovakia to accommodate to German demands before those got even more extreme. Sadly, ". . . no support was given to the idea of protecting Czechoslovakia by the formation of a 'Grand Alliance.' In fact, not one of the cabinet ministers present uttered a single word in defense of Czechoslovakia." [16]

The turmoil in Czechoslovakia now accelerated. On April 24 Henlein openly declared that the SdP embraced Germany's Nazi ideology.[17] In May reports reached the Czechoslovak government that German troops were massing on the border, and a partial mobilization was ordered.[18] In June there were renewed proposals for Slovak autonomy by Hlinka's Slovak People's Party, supported by huge demonstrations in Bratislava. These were followed the next day by equally huge demonstrations staged by Grandfather Hodža's Agrarian Party, which declared itself in favor of parity between the Czech and Slovak regions but opposed to Slovak autonomy.[19] In July the government, under Hodža's leadership, adopted a carefully crafted "statute of nationalities" which would have granted unprecedented administrative responsibilities, but not political and economic autonomy, to four distinct regions: Bohemia, Moravia, Slovakia, and Subcarpathian Rus'. This statute never went into effect. It was blocked by the Sudeten German Party, whose interest was not in reconciliation but in the breakup of Czechoslovakia.[20]

All summer long the SdP staged provocative actions in the border areas. Hodža placed strict controls on the type of response that Czechoslovak police were allowed to make so that they could not be accused of mistreating the Sudeten Germans.[21] No matter. Hitler launched a massive propaganda campaign to persuade European public opinion that the Czechs were the oppressors of the innocent Germans. When an uprising occurred in the border areas, martial law was declared and the army restored order.

It was against this background that in August the British government sent out a mission under the leadership of Lord Walter Runciman to help seek reconciliation between the demands of the Sudeten Germans and the position of the Czechoslovak government.[22] Even though it was clear that British diplomats were strongly inclined to side with the Germans, the arrival of the mission was greeted in Prague with a sense of relief, perhaps because it was seen as a sign of the active engagement of the Western powers with the fate of Czechoslovakia. When the mission arrived on August 2, 1938, "Even the prime minister, Hodža, seized the opportunity, reportedly for the first time since the *Anschluss* in March, to take a weekend break away from the capital."[23] On August 4 *The New York Times* described Runciman's mission and Hodža's role in this way:[24]

> It is easy to imagine the mixed emotions with which Premier Hodza welcomes Lord Runciman as he arrives in Prague.... The position of the British adviser, sent to sit on the lid of Central Europe and keep it from popping, isn't enviable, but it is a sinecure compared to the permanent hot spot occupied by the Czech premier. If there is a less desirable eminence in Europe than Dr. Hodza's, it isn't visible.
>
> ... When to the nagging minorities and the bridling majority inside the country is added the pressure of every capital in Europe; when it is impressed on Dr. Hodza day after day that in his hands hangs the trembling balance of peace and war, it is no wonder that his smile is a bit grim as it meets the determined cheerfulness of the peacemaker from London.
>
> All that Lord Runciman has to learn about Central Europe Premier Hodza knows only too well. If he is the most harrassed of contemporary statesmen, he is by all odds the best fitted to deal with the explosive issue he is trying to solve. Dr. Hodza is a Central European.

He knows his own country to the grass roots. He has lived all his life with the minority question. By background and experience he is a kind of Danubian federation in himself. By temperament and training in the political mélange of old Austria he is flexible and open to compromise. Long before the present crisis he sponsored the most far-sighted and practical plan yet devised to neutralize the racial and political divisions by an economic commonwealth of Danubian nations. If there is any hope for the success of the mission of the English mediator, it is that he meets on the Moldau a man who knows all the questions before they are asked and can supply most of the answers.

However, while Runciman paid formal visits on President Beneš and Prime Minister Hodža, he spent far more time with the Henleinists and with their supporters among the German-Czech aristocracy than he did with the elected leaders of Czechoslovakia. His sense of the basic rightness of the Sudeten Germans' cause grew.[25]

In the midst of the Runciman mission, Andrej Hlinka died and was buried with great emotion and pageantry. Grandfather Hodža had long been Hlinka's political rival and had opposed his demands for Slovak autonomy, but he had great personal respect and affection for Hlinka (see Chapter 25), and delivered one of the eulogies at the funeral on August 21. Unfortunately, the death of Hlinka opened the way among the Slovaks for far more extreme nationalist voices, voices that were at times overtly sympathetic to the Nazis and foreshadowed later events in Czechoslovakia.

THERE WAS NO SUPPORT FOR CZECHOSLOVAKIA from the international community. On September 15, British Prime Minister Neville Chamberlain traveled from London to meet with Hitler in the resort town of Berchtesgaden. Assured by Hitler that the Sudetenland was his last territorial claim, Chamberlain flew back to London. Runciman, who was still in Prague, was recalled for consultations.[26] Within a few days, the British and the French developed a fresh proposal, ostensibly based on satisfying the just demands of the Sudeten Germans:[27] Czechoslovakia should cede directly to Germany all territories with a greater than fifty percent German population, which included most of her elaborately constructed border fortifications. In exchange, the integrity of Czechoslovakia's remaining territory would be guaranteed by Germany, Italy, France, and Britain. However, her existing treaties with France and the Soviet Union would be scrapped. On September 19, the British and French ambassadors in Prague formally demanded of President Beneš that Czechoslovakia accede to this proposal.

Beneš sent an urgent appeal to the Soviet Union for support and called Prime Minister Hodža and his cabinet into session. The president and the ministers, fourteen men altogether, met again the next day, and all day long they waited for a Soviet response. None came. At 7:45 on the evening of September 20, the president handed the two ambassadors a formal diplomatic note—the Czechoslovak government thanked Britain and France for their efforts at mediation but rejected their plan. At 2:00 in the morning, however, the British and French ambassadors returned to the Prague Castle and woke Beneš from his sleep. Their governments demanded that Czechoslovakia accept the plan. Otherwise Germany might well attack. And should such an attack take place, France would refuse to meet its treaty obligations to defend Czechoslovakia. It was an ultimatum. All the next day Beneš, Hodža, and the other ministers deliberated. Just before 5:00 in the afternoon of September 21, they yielded.

As word of the capitulation spread, crowds began to gather at the Prague Castle. By 10:00 that night a large, well-organized group suddenly appeared under the windows of the president's quarters. "Give us weapons," was the shout. They tried to break down the doors. After midnight state police arrived to disperse the crowd. It was, apparently, a Communist attempt to trigger a revolution.[28]

The next day, September 23, huge crowds formed throughout the city. They were seething with anger, not only against the Germans, French, and British, but also against the capitulating government. Both President Beneš and Prime Minister Hodža had come to the agonizing conclusion that yielding to the French and the British would ultimately serve Czechoslovakia better than entering a war alone against overwhelming German military superiority.[29] However, in the minds of most Czechs, Beneš had become completely identified with the Czechoslovak Republic and was immune from major criticism, while Hodža was seen as a controversial figure.[30] The crowd's fury turned on him.

To dampen the threat of a popular uprising, President Beneš acted quickly.[31]

He met briefly with the prime mininster and asked for his resignation. Hodža obliged on the spot and went looking, on Beneš's instructions, for Jan Syrový, the one-eyed army general who had been at the castle since the evening of 21 September. Hodža found him, took his arm, and told him he would have to become the next prime minister. . . . Syrový responded frankly that he did not feel adequately qualified for such a responsible role at the height of the crisis. "Hodža told me," Syrový testified after the war, "that I was a soldier and that when I receive an order I have to obey. . . . "[32]

The following day, September 24, despite its capitulation to Britain and France, the government of Czechoslovakia declared complete mobilization. In less than a week nearly a million and a half trained and equipped men were ready to defend their country against possible German attack.

THIS WAS THE TORRENT OF DRAMATIC PUBLIC EVENTS, seemingly unceasing in their rush to Czechoslovakia's destruction and to war. What about the private lives of the men who were most responsible for making the crucial decisions? Here is a small glimpse into the private side of Grandfather Hodža, recorded by my aunt Vierka Štetková.[33] Aunt Vierka lived with the Hodžas for a number of years while she studied at Charles University in Prague. Later she recorded some of her memories in the form of an autobiographical novel which intersperses accounts of her personal life, dominated by a passionate love affair, with her recollections of the dramatic days of 1938. Her writing, like all oral history, is both vivid and susceptible to error. It is the recollections of a lovestruck young woman, not documentary evidence. Still, it provides a picture that few other sources can.

About Grandfather Hodža in the September days of 1938 she writes:

> He has played the major role in negotiations with the Germans, has put forth superhuman efforts for months. He comes home from the ministry at 2 o'clock in the morning, he doesn't sleep, his clothes are just hanging on him, and all of us tiptoe around afraid to speak in louder tones. . . . If everything turns out badly, they will blame us [Hodža and his supporters]. But they don't know how hard Uncle Milan tried to quiet the Ľudaks [Hlinka's Slovak People's Party] who were consorting with the Henleinists, how much he negotiated with them and with Hlinka personally.

About the full mobilization:

> That 24th of September . . . Uncle Milan's unusual face, excited and comforting, hard and fatherly soft at the same time. . . . His hand resting heavily on my shoulder and his extraordinary voice when he declared, "Vierka, we have mobilized!" The stern military voice on the radio: "Citizens! The President of the Republic of Czechoslovakia and commander-in-chief of the army directs according to paragraph . . . the mobilization of the Czechoslovak armed forces . . . all officers and enlisted men . . . who are forty years of age. . . ." The closing words: "Our battle is just! Long live free Czechoslovakia!" sounded like a Beethoven chorale. As the national anthem was sung, Uncle Milan stood erect like a soldier. . . . His wife, her lips pale, whispered: "O God, our child! Milan, will he have to go as

well?" In the tense silence came Uncle Milan's sternly celebratory: "My son will serve! I am proud of him!" . . . Within minutes of the order to mobilize, the soldiers of the Republic set out with their wooden suitcases, their names painted on the side in white . . . .and with them went our Dišo [the family's nickname for Fedor Hodža, Milan Hodža's only son and my uncle]. The great hymn *A Mighty Fortress Is Our God* sounded. . . .

Then came September 30, 1938, a day that haunted decision makers in the world's governments for decades after and is still a touchstone when leaders are faced with international aggression. The erstwhile guarantors of Czechoslovakia's independence, Great Britain and France, meeting in Munich with the governments of Nazi Germany and Fascist Italy, issued a declaration demanding that Czechoslovakia yield to Germany twenty percent of her territory and over twenty-five percent of her population. In addition, the declaration demanded that territorial claims made by Poland and Hungary, affecting primarily Slovak areas, be settled within three months.[34] The Munich Agreement was negotiated and signed by Britain, France, Italy, and Germany alone. Czechoslovak diplomats were not even in the room; they were simply handed the meeting's outcome in the early hours of the following morning. It was a bitter end to the vision that had created Czechoslovakia almost exactly twenty years earlier. The Czechoslovak government had no choice but to accept.[35]

The British and French leaders were welcomed home as heroes by citizens for whom the memories of the devastating casualties and costs of the Great War of 1914-1918 were still all too raw. Many believed that peace had indeed been preserved by Chamberlain's vigorously pursued policy of appeasement; another war would not come.[36] These popular feelings were understandable, but events would soon prove them tragically misplaced.

In Prague, huge crowds once again gathered in the streets, this time shredding and spitting on copies of the hated declaration and turning against the previously venerated President Beneš. The soldiers who had mobilized so quickly and efficiently, declaring themselves lay down their lives for a cause they held sacred, were ordered home. Uncle Dišo, too, came home. Aunt Vierka reconstructed what he told his father:

Neither one says a word, not a word. Uncle Milan bangs his glass, still half-filled with water, on the glass tabletop and snuffs out his cigarette with his thumb. He blows out smoke, stretches in his armchair, and smoothes out his thinning gray hair, scrutinizing Dišo. "So, Son, begin! Tell me what you saw."

Thank God, he is using a lighthearted tone, just like he uses with me when we walk in the garden, his arm around my shoulders. Dišo looks away. Silently he lets out clouds of smoke as if he had not heard his father's question. There are no traces of nervousness on his face.

"A normal soldier is like a machine, Dad. When you tell him to go forward, he goes, and when you tell him to shoot, he shoots. But this time it was something completely different. . . .The excitement was extraordinary. The men literally went with a song. And if you could have heard the jokes about Hitler and the Germans! . . . The supplies, communications, defenses—all went like clockwork. The people, even the most ordinary, acted without being told to, out of their own conviction and on their own initiative, with an unshakeable willingness to sacrifice their own lives. . . . It was hard to restrain them even for those few days. We had to watch constantly so that in their passion and impatience they wouldn't do something premature. . . .

"And then came that horrible day, Dad . . .

"We sat in some impossibly dirty tavern not far from the border and waited for the decision. The atmosphere was tense to the breaking point, every single one of us felt it. . . . We sat there for hours, drinking and smoking. Never in my life have I smoked as many cigarettes as that night. We sat in the dark in the dense smoke and only the glowing cigarette tips danced from time to time. . . . Then they read the command: retreat and hand over the territory in good order. The colonel almost cried out loud.

"Each lieutenant was to say this to his unit. We were afraid that the men would refuse, that they would revolt. . . . It was bad, Dad. . . . Not so much the curses, the insults, the blaming of everything on whomever came to mind, that wasn't the worst. But to listen to those old men, family men, crying out of helpless fury that they could not fire even a single shot. . . ."

HITLER HAD BULLIED HIS WAY INTO AUSTRIA AND CZECHOSLOVAKIA without firing a single gun. Within months Germany took direct control of Bohemia and Moravia, and Slovakia declared independence. The great Czech industrial complex passed into German hands. Czech and Slovak Jews would soon be hauled off to concentration camps—Terezin near Prague, Auschwitz across the Polish border, Mauthausen in Austria, and others. Hitler was now well positioned to launch his lightning offensive, the *Blitzkrieg,* against Poland and later the Low

Countries and France itself. In every way, the collapse of Czechoslovakia was the prelude to World War II.

This torrent of events, culminating in a national tragedy, forever scarred the lives of Czechoslovakia's leaders. A week after the Munich Declaration, President Beneš resigned and flew to London and from there traveled to the United States. Exhausted, he took some time to recover his health, returning finally to Britain and forming a Czechoslovak government-in-exile. Before the end of the year Grandfather Hodža, likewise exhausted and ill, left the country for medical treatment in Switzerland. He later moved to Paris to initiate political steps intended to assure a strong position for Slovakia in the Czechoslovakia of the future.

Beneš and Hodža had long been political rivals, and their views, both domestic and international, became increasingly divergent. In exile they drifted into a political battle, which Grandfather Hodža ultimately lost. He died in America in 1944, still struggling to find a formula for a new Czechoslovakia in which the old imbalances and inequalities between Czechs and Slovaks would be resolved.

As for the Hodža family, one by one they left Czechoslovakia. My mother was the last to go. Two weeks after she reached Paris, I was born.

CHAPTER 2

Born on the Brink of War

On July 15, 1939, four months after the partitioning of Czechoslovakia and exactly two weeks before I was born, my mother—Irene Pálka née Hodža—sat anxiously in a train compartment, traveling from Bratislava through nearby Vienna and on to Geneva. She was in the bloom of life, twenty-nine years old, happily married, and very, very pregnant. With her were my father's sister, Aunt Ludinka, who was for many years my mother's best companion, and a close family friend and intimate Hodža supporter from Yugoslavia, Janko Bulík. My mother was leaving the new Slovak Republic, which was effectively under Nazi control and had avowedly pro-Nazi elements of its own (see also Chapter 6). Aunt Ludinka and Janko Bulík were going with her for companionship and for at least some degree of protection.

Grandfather Hodža wanted his immediate family out of Nazi-controlled territory so that they could not be held hostage. In April of 1939 Grandmother Hodža obtained a permit from the German Gestapo, which was now running Prague, to visit her ailing husband in Switzerland; her youngest daughter, my Aunt Gláša, went with her. In June, Uncle Dišo was able to do the same. Finally in July it was my mother's turn; she obtained her permit in Slovakia.[1]

These were supposed to be brief visits to a bed-ridden relative, so each member of the family could only carry with them a handful of personal items and enough clothing for a few days' use. Everything else had to be left behind. A small suitcase of clothing for my mother and her soon-to-be-born baby ended up in the Bulík family home in Yugoslavia where it was kept for many years.[2] Exactly how it came to be there is not known. I think that perhaps Janko Bulík, who had traveled as a covert courier for the Slovak anti-Nazi resistance a number of times, decided that it would raise suspicion and had it sent to his own home before he and my mother boarded the train in Bratislava.

In an attempt to ensure that she would have no trouble at the border, my mother was also escorted to the train by a member of the Hlinka Guard, the para-military wing of the ruling Hlinka's Slovak People's Party and one of the

most powerful forces in Slovakia.[3] This young man was a loyal employee of my father's even though he was in the Guard, and he provided perfect cover for my mother—in his company, no one would question her permit. Janko Bulík was on a double mission: to protect my mother as much as he could and to deliver secret documents from home to Grandfather Hodža. For now, my father stayed on in Slovakia.

On the day of my mother's departure from home, the tension ran high. Despite the official travel permit, arrest could come at any moment. Once the train was across the border in Austria, my mother and her companions thought they could relax. In their exhilaration at passing smoothly through Slovak border control, they began voicing anti-Nazi remarks even though they were still in Nazi-controlled territory, assuming that no one would understand their Slovak conversation. Soon, however, a waiter quietly opened the door to their compartment and asked in perfect Czech, *Co si panstvo přeje?* (Ladies and gentlemen, what would you like?) Had he overheard them? Maybe. Would he turn them in? No, he didn't. In Vienna Aunt Ludinka left the group, returning to Bratislava quickly so she could be present as usual in her reserved place at the opera and not arouse suspicion by an unexplained absence.[4] Janko Bulík escorted my mother to Geneva, where Uncle Dišo met them and took her into his care. Bulik then went on to meet with Grandfather Hodža.

GRANDFATHER HODŽA'S MENTAL STATE AND HEALTH had been devastated by the long string of events preceding the resignation of his government and the Munich Declaration that followed quickly after. He stayed on in Czechoslovakia for a few months, meeting secretly with his followers to set in motion some aspects of anti-Nazi resistance and trying to organize the necessary finances.[5] In preparation for his departure, he and his personal secretary spent three days burning many of his papers so they would not fall into the hands of the Nazis.[6] The details of his actual departure have long been obscure. It now appears that in December of 1938, accompanied by a small personal escort, he crossed a remote part of the Slovak-Hungarian border and, by a circuitous route, proceeded to Marseilles, France, and then a short time later to Lausanne, Switzerland.[7] There he checked himself into a clinic for treatment. Grandmother Hodža, along with Aunt Gláša, reached him in April 1939. She later described his state in a letter to one of her sisters: "Milan has recovered pretty well since the time I came to join him. When I first saw him at the train station I was shaken to see how how drawn and emaciated he looked. Now he says that he's feeling much better and he's starting to have some energy for work once again. He says that his nerves were so shattered that for a long time he was completely unable to work."[8]

Further on in this letter, written about three weeks before I was born, Grandmother Hodža sighs like any grandmother would: "Please, dear sisters, take care of my daughter, take my place with her since I can't be there. . . . I was so looking forward to my grandchild, how I would take care of him, and now God only knows when I will even see him." Her prayer was soon to be granted. My mother escaped from Slovakia just a week after this letter was written. The family collected in Paris, except for Grandfather Hodža who was continuing his recuperation in Switzerland. A hospital had been selected for the delivery, the American Hospital in the Parisian suburb of Neuilly-sur-Seine.[9] Despite the tense circumstances, I came into the world on schedule and without complications. I was welcomed into the arms of a family that poured its love and most of its hopes for the future into me, not knowing when, if ever, they would return to the lives they had known at home.

My mother holds me a few weeks after my birth. Author's archive.

My mother and grandmother must often have thought that their lives were now echoing the past, for Michal Miloslav Hodža, Grandfather Hodža's uncle and a towering figure in family and national history (Chapters 18-20), had died in exile. If they could have peered into the future, they would have known that my birth far from home was also a portent of things to come: Grandfather Hodža would die in exile during World War II (Chapter 5); my father, my mother and both of her siblings would die in a second exile during the Cold War (Chapters 12 and 13); and I, the newborn, would know my native land only from brief visits. Only Grandmother Hodža would die at home, but tragically so—incapacitated by a series of strokes and separated by the Iron Curtain from all three of her children; from me, her only grandchild; and from the remains of her husband, left behind in America.[10]

MY MOTHER KEPT A DIARY for the first year and a half of my life. She kept it safe throughout our odyssey from Paris to America, then to Czechoslovakia, and finally back to America. I found it among her papers after she died in 1977, an innocent-looking notebook, small and thin, bound in nondescript tan cloth.[11] It starts this way:

Ján Milan Pálka
narodil sa v American Hospital v Neuilly-sur-Seine pri Paríži dňa
29.VII.1939 o 6.30 hod (v sobotu)
vážil 3.680 g, meral 49 cm

Ján Milan Pálka
was born in the American Hospital in Neuilly-sur-Seine near Paris on
July 29th, 1939, at 6:30 am (on Saturday).
He weighed 3,680 grams [almost 9-½ pounds]
and measured 49 centimeters [19-¼ inches].

With rare exceptions she wrote in the third person, referring to herself as Mama (Mommy), and reveling in detailed descriptions of me and my daily life. Only occasional snippets reveal what she herself was going through while cataclysmic events were swirling all around us—Germany invaded and conquered a succession of countries, World War II was officially declared, people were carted off to concentration camps to suffer and die. France, where we had sought refuge, fell to the Germans. The British evacuated from Dunkirk. It was a turbulent world for a newborn and for the family that did their best to nurture and shield him.

Here are some of my mother's words.

On August 5th, Daddy came to visit him; he got a permit for 14 days. At first he declared that the baby was tiny and wrinkled, but then he came to see us twice a day and the wrinkled one always had to be brought in its crib, and he started to like it, and when he left us on August 15th it was hard for him to say good-bye. Who knows when we will see each other again, with war being declared on September 2nd. Thus far we have no news from him and it is already September 11th. . . .

My mother's diary, at this point and throughout, is totally silent on the question of why my father came for just a brief visit and then, leaving his wife and newborn son, returned to a political environment that was so clearly dangerous. Like my mother, my father traveled on a permit issued by the Hlinka Guard. He obtained permits for trips to Prague and to Paris, giving business as his reason for travel, but this was getting harder and harder to do.[12] The Nazis were tightening the noose, putting in place the policies of the Fatherland not only in the Czech lands that they controlled directly, the Protectorate of Bohemia and Moravia, but also in the nominally independent Slovak Republic. Already the rights of Jews were increasingly being restricted. Soon Jews would be required to wear the hateful yellow stars, and about a year and a half later mass arrests and deportations to concentration camps started.[13]

Until you had proven that you were not a Jew, everyone was under suspicion—everyone including my father. He was required to obtain a certificate confirming his Aryan lineage from the city government of Mikuláš, his home town. The text of the certificate, dated September 7, 1939, reads: "On the basis of birth and marriage certificates submitted to this office it is declared that Ing. Ján Pálka, born on the 6th of April, 1901 [an error—this was the date of his baptism, not of his birth] in Liptovský Sv. Mikuláš, and a citizen here, is of Aryan origin inasmuch as neither he, nor his parents, nor the parents of his parents were Jews.[14]" Presumably, this certificate helped him obtain his travel permits. It did not prevent an order being issued for his arrest later, as we shall see.

> *August 23rd.* Johnny left the hospital for our apartment on the fifth floor of a building on rue Eugène Manuel, Paris XVI, which had been prepared with a crib, baby carriage, scale, and other necessities. Aunt Gláša washed his diapers; Mama fed and changed him; and Grandma got up to take care of him at night, took turns with Mama to bathe him, and cooked. The major housecleaning was done on Sundays when the servant did not get in the way.

This was an all-female household—no father, grandfather, or uncle. A servant was taken for granted by an upper-class European family, even in exile and even when the women of the family scrubbed the floors with their own hands.

A WEEK LATER WE LEFT PARIS AS PART OF THE FIRST WAVE of evacuation from the capital and traveled to Amboise, an ancient city on the Loire some distance southwest of Paris. Another refugee family whose father had also remained in Slovakia joined us.

> *August 30th.* Johnny traveled by car from Paris to Amboise between 4:30 and 9:30 am, first on Grandma's knees, then in the scale's woven basket, then on Mama's knees, and he didn't cry the whole way. Here he is doing very well as his gain in weight shows. He spends all day in the garden, gets bathed in a tub and loves it, smiles, and has his first rattle and a rubber rabbit made in Czechoslovakia. He

is lifting his head energetically and in general is stout as an oak, even though more than half his food is formula. He is very successful with the ladies — besides the old servant Louis he is the only man in the house where there are six women. He has a very loud voice, and since his crib looks like a cage, he has received the nickname "Lion of Bohemia" from the landlady.

The day after we reached Amboise, civilian evacuations from London began.[15] The following day Hitler invaded Poland with a massive, highly mechanized force of fifty-four divisions supported by devastating air power. Units of the army of the puppet Slovak Republic participated in this invasion. The Polish army was large and fought valiantly, but its largely horse-mounted cavalry was no match for Hitler's tanks and warplanes. Britain and France declared war against Germany on September 2, 1939, though they did not immediately come to Poland's defense. The United States, in contrast, declared its neutrality. A British Expeditionary Force of 161,000 men plus equipment was transported across the English Channel to the Continent. The Soviet Union invaded Poland on September 17, sealing its fate. Warsaw fell on September 28.

With the advent of open war, our situation changed. Hitler went from victory to victory, and the territory he controlled in Europe grew rapidly. My father was still in Slovakia, and any further visits from him would be problematic at best. France remained a relatively safe area—there was no bombing or shooting—but the army was mobilizing, and refugees from other countries were beginning to consider what they might do, where their next refuge might be when a shooting war erupted here. For my mother, caring for a two-month-old baby and with her husband behind Nazi lines, this must have been paralyzing. Grandfather Hodža finally left the sanatorium in Switzerland where he had been recuperating and relocated to Paris. From there he came to see us.

September 29th. For his two-month birthday Johnny received a visit from his grandfather, whom he found extremely interesting. He stared at him intently, and it seems that his glasses impressed him the most even though he sees glasses aplenty on his mother, grandmother, and aunt. Grampa is anxious about him, especially when he strains to lift his head or when we carry him up and down the stairs, which are slick wood with no carpets and where it is often dark because the windows are covered with blue paper for defense purposes. He never wants us to let Johnny cry, he's always sending one of us out to see whether he's not crying. However, we don't want to spoil him too much so sometimes we let him yell.

On this very day, September 29, 1939, Germany and the Soviet Union divided up Poland. The stresses on the family must have been immense, but most of my mother's diary relates the minutiae of caring for a baby. Perhaps this was a welcome relief. However, every mention of my absent father brings the desperation to the surface.

October 13th. Today Grandma finished knitting Johnny's first pants. They are of blue wool, with matching knee socks. There was universal applause and great delight because he looked so cute, like a doll. He liked himself in the mirror, just staring at himself and grinning from ear to ear. He now has pink cheeks and dimples on his elbows and knees, he loves to exercise, and always smiles while he is doing it. Even his eyes smile, and he winks one of them flirtatiously.

We finally received a letter from Daddy which made us very glad. The first letter after so many weeks. Mama joked all day long, cried out like an animal, has already written him one letter and is getting ready to write another to a different address. If only more letters would come!

His letters were sparse, partly due to war conditions and censorship by the Slovak Republic, partly just because he rarely wrote. My mother sometimes went for months with no news from her husband. In her diary she continued to remain silent as to why he chose to remain exposed to immediate danger in Slovakia, the homeland that seemed increasingly far away.

November 11th. We finally baptized Johnny. Pastor Šimovec, the mission pastor of the Lutheran Church, came with godfather Dišo, there was a celebratory lunch and, after lunch, the baptism. Since the baptism was on the day of St. Martin, and our servant is a great devotee of St. Martin who is buried in nearby Tours, we gave the child the name Martin as his third name [the other two were Ján after my father and Milan after my grandfather]. He behaved beautifully during the baptism, he watched the pastor and kept his hands folded, just after the sacrament he gave a deep sigh as if he were glad it was all over. . . . The servant gave him a medallion portraying St. Martin and tied it to his crib with a blue ribbon. May St. Martin and God protect him! . . . The poor child, he was even baptized without his daddy, without his grandpa, without his other grandma, his godmother, and the rest of his family.

At the baptism I was dressed in a white, beautifully embroidered gown that had been made for my father's baptism and that my mother had carried with her on her escape.

November 19th. We took Johnny to have his first photograph taken. He was very upset at the studio, he started to wail as soon as we got there and didn't stop until he was in his carriage half a kilometer away. We barely calmed him down enough for the photographer to take four pictures. Two are OK, at least Daddy will see what he looks like.

THE SHOCKS OF WAR SPREAD FURTHER in Europe. The Soviet Union invaded Finland on November 30. The Finns battled fiercely, stopping the Soviet advance and counterattacking effectively. My father finally left Slovakia.

December 9th. Glory be, we found out that Daddy is in Belgrade now and will soon come here. Thank God, now our child won't be growing up without his father. In her joy Mommy couldn't decide whether to laugh or to cry and it seems that she did both at the same time. Just let him come soon!

December 20th. Grandma found Johnny's first tooth. This great event occurred while Mommy was on her first trip to Paris. She went to meet Daddy and also to see a seamstress. But she came home without Daddy.

December 22nd. When there was no news, Mommy sent a telegram. Half an hour later a long letter arrived from Daddy explaining that he had been waiting for Uncle Dišo for some important discussions. So there was huge disapppointment and disgust with the way the men organized things. Mommy declared that she was going to call her boy not Johnny but Martin, so he would be wiser when he grows up.

December 24th. Our Christmas was strange and sad, not even Grandpa [Grandfather Hodža] came from London. Our boy got an ivory ring with silver bells, a white rabbit and Mickey Mouse from his godfather, Uncle Dišo. There was no Christmas tree, just a creche, and it didn't even seem like Christmas. But maybe that's better, we weren't quite so sad because it did not remind us of our lost home.

January 15th. Today brought great hopes, but I don't dare to rejoice yet so that something won't go wrong once again. Dišo met with Daddy and said that Daddy is determined to come after us by February 15th. Dear God, give him back to me and don't let Johnny grow up without his father!

On the day of this entry, January 15, 1940, the 1st Czechoslovak Infantry Division was formed in France.[16] This division comprised 11,000 men, approximately half of them Slovak and half Czech, most of whom had been living in France even before the war. It was commanded by the Slovak general Rudolf Viest, later one of the two commanders of the Slovak National Uprising against the Nazis (Chapter 6). Around 1,000 Czech and Slovak pilots had escaped from their homeland since the break-up of Czechoslovakia, mostly across the Slovak-Polish border, and made their way to France. They joined the French air force, representing nearly twenty-five percent of the strength of its fighter wings. On January 30 the Slovak Republic and Nazi Germany signed an economic agreement that gave Germany direct control over Slovak defense industries, steel mills, anything needed for the German war effort. February 15 came and went, and my father still stayed away, despite the increasing danger from both the Slovak authorities and the ever-present Germans. Finland was unable to continue the fight against the Soviet Union and capitulated on March 13.

> *April 8th.* It seems like Daddy will really come now. I'm going to Paris to meet him again, but I don't dare to be happy until I finally see him. After so many disappointments and so much waiting, I'm hardly breathing for fear that something may still go wrong.

Germany invaded Norway and Denmark on April 9, 1940. Denmark did not resist. Norway, with Allied help, held out for a few months. France still seemed safe, and my mother took the train to Paris, staying with Uncle Dišo.

> *April 13th.* Daddy really came! Dišo and I waited for him furiously from early morning until almost midnight because his train from Belgrade was delayed by 13 hours. But finally we really do have him!

The family was now together, but its situation was precarious. The newspapers were full of stories about German advances. The French army was moving quickly to man its border defenses. The tension in Paris was acute.

CHAPTER 3

Eluding the Gestapo

My mother quickly returned from Paris to Amboise because we would have to move further away from the capital. Stories about German intentions were worrisome, and a family with a baby could not respond to changing events very quickly, so being significantly further from the French capital seemed advisable. On April 17, 1940, just four days after my parents' joyous reunion, we gathered up all our carefully packed belongings and boarded the train for Nantes, and from there to the little resort town of La Baule on the Atlantic coast of Brittany—around the corner, so to speak, from the English Channel. My father stayed on in Paris.

La Baule was a small resort town set on one of the most beautiful bays in Europe. The bay's five-mile-long sandy beach was mostly fringed by dunes, a setting inviting endless play in the water and drawing tourists since the nineteenth century.[1] At the time of our arrival it was still rather remote. Though road access existed, the rail link through Nantes provided the main connection to the rest of France.

There was much to do to get established in a new place, and no chance for my mother to rejoin her husband in Paris. Then one evening, just about a week after our move and with no warning, my father suddenly arrived.

April 22nd. Johnny, of course, was already asleep. However, around 10 o'clock he started to make himself heard. So, I thought, "Come, Daddy, get acquainted with your son." I worried that Johnny would wail again since right now he is so afraid of unknown people and he'd be sleepy on top of it. But no, he took a liking to Daddy right away, he wasn't scared at all, and in two days' time they were already the best of friends. Dear God, what a relief! After so many lonely months of waiting, I could finally watch my husband and my son playing together. I felt that now nothing could harm us any more.

My father did not stay long. In a few days, taking my mother with him, he hurried back to Paris to get his official papers in order and to try to gain a picture of the overall war situation and our options. He had been traveling on a Yugoslav passport that identified him not as Jan Pálka of Liptovský Svätý Mikuláš (Czechoslovakia), but as Janko Pavković of Novi Sad (Yugoslavia). This had been arranged in Belgrade by Janko Bulík. At the Yugoslav embassy my mother and I were added to this passport. Now we would no longer be the Pálka family but the Pavković family. All of us traveled under this assumed identity for nearly a year and a half, until we set out on the final leg of our circuitous journey to the United States. Like my mother's diary, the passport survived all of our travels and is now stored in our safe deposit box, both a personal treasure and a source of valuable information.

At the beginning of May, Grandfather Hodža left Paris for London for the last time, part of a flood of officials and others who were leaving the continent for the relative safety of Britain. My mother, accompanied by Uncle Dišo, returned

Title page of Yugoslav passport that for a year and a half provided my family a false identity and protection against the Nazis. Issued through the help of Janko Bulík (Chapter 30). Author's archive.

to La Baule, while my father stayed on to take part in political discussions. The Yugoslav passport shows that he had a permit to stay in Paris until May 31.

EXCEPT FOR THE LIGHTNING CONQUEST OF POLAND, during much of 1939 and the early part of 1940 Hitler had bided his time. Now, however, the German advance was swift and unrelenting.[2] In the early morning of May 10, 1940, two days after my mother returned to La Baule, the invasion of Holland, Belgium, Luxemburg, and France began. Dutch resistance was fleeting. On May 13, the Dutch Queen Wilhelmina and the whole government sailed for safety to England, and on the afternoon of the next day the general who had been left in charge surrendered the country. At the same time German troops crossed into Belgium. During the two weeks that fighting continued there, the Germans raced on along the coast of the English Channel and threatened to cut off the retreating Allied troops. The bulk of the great evacuation from the Belgian coastal town of Dunkirk to England took place in the nine days between May 26 and June 3. In this evacuation, 198,000 British troops were rescued, as well as an additional 140,000 others, mainly French. Masses of equipment were left behind. Belgium surrendered on May 27. In less than three weeks, while my mother and I were in La Baule and my father mostly in Paris, the Germans had driven the Allies out of a huge swath of Europe and taken more than a million prisoners.

My mother had returned to La Baule with Uncle Dišo, but he stayed only a day before going back to Paris, so she was once again left with neither her brother nor her husband. My father finally joined the exodus from Paris on May 17, bringing with him yet another Slovak family, the Paulinys, who would be with us for many months. Our little beach house in La Baule now housed fourteen people, including small children as well as adults. They strained for every bit of news about the furious German advance and wondered what their own fate would be. Many other Slovak refugees congregated here, offering fragments of news. Uncle Dišo was expected—he had even sent his things—but he never arrived, and we had no idea where he was. There were reports that he had gone back to Bratislava[3].

After a brief pause Hitler focused his attention on the conquest of France. On June 5 the drive south began. Soon the final evacuation of Paris was ordered. People left in droves, taking whatever necessities and most precious belongings they could. The roads were clogged with cars, trucks, buses, taxis, bicycles, farm carts—anything that moved on wheels. Towns and villages in the countryside overflowed with refugees. Every so often the planes of the Luftwaffe dropped their lethal loads of bombs in attacks on the retreating French troops, leaving villages in ruins amidst plumes of black smoke.[4] The Germans entered Paris on June 14, 1940.

With the continuing frightening news about the war, many of the refugees in La Baule started to move on, using whatever transport they could arrange, even buying decrepit horse-drawn carts. We could not leave because the Pauliny family, who had become our principal companions in exile, expected a baby any day. The war, which had thus far been rather distant, was suddenly on our doorstep. There were dogfights in the skies, the sounds of artillery fire, orders to retreat to bomb shelters that we could not follow because our house had no basement. Though La Baule itself was not attacked, bombs sometimes fell on nearby towns and shook the house. The bodies of dead English soldiers washed up on the beach. On June 15, the day after the Germans entered Paris, the Pauliny baby was born.[5]

Less than a week later, on June 21, the first German soldiers arrived in La Baule. At first there were only four in an open motorcar, but soon they were arriving by the truckload. Some went on; some stayed. They took up residence in the hotels and cottages, mainly ones that were unoccupied. We had soldiers in the cottage to the left of us, the cottage to the right, and also across the street.[6]

The French-German armistice was signed on June 22. Mussolini's Italy had also joined in the attack, and the French-Italian armistice was signed on June 24. The terms of the armistice called for France to be divided into two approximately equal regions. Occupied France, in the north and west, was ruled from Paris directly by the German commander. Free France, with its capital in Vichy in central France, was ruled by a government that, while French, was weak and included a number of Nazi sympathizers. Brittany, where La Baule was situated, was deep in occupied France. The line between them was heavily guarded.

We were trapped in Occupied France, and remained so for over seven months, not knowing whether the authorities might notice who we were and immediately have us arrested, then shipped off to concentration camp.

In this setting, on July 29, 1940, I celebrated my first birthday:

Johnny had a cake with a candle but he could only look at it, he couldn't manage to blow it out. Now that he is a year old, we can boast about all the things he can do and say. He can stand nicely on his own and can take a few steps from Mommy to Daddy and back. We do this mainly at the beach on the hard sand where nothing can happen to him. When asked, he can raise his hand and wave. Sometimes this looks like a fascist salute and soldiers from military trucks often respond by saying, "Heil!" He can clap loudly if we tell him "*tăp, tăp.*" He is starting to understand quite a lot of what we say to him, and if he's in the right mood, he will even do it, for example bring something. He knows how to say *mama* [mommy], *tata* [daddy], *bába* [doll] and *papu*. By *papu* he means *papuča* [slipper] or shoe. He absolutely loves to be surrounded by piles of footwear that he can dig through. He can play this way forever.

The rest of my mother's diary is filled with enchanting descriptions of my playing on the beach, tracing hoofprints left by the horses of German soldiers, splashing in a big hole dug in the sand which had filled up with water, playing hide-and-seek with a stone or with my mother's handkerchief that she tucked into her bathing suit, being carried on my father's shoulders. There is an hour-by-hour description of our daily schedule, additional words that I learned to say, my progress in walking, my fascination with the warplanes that swooped low over the beach. Nothing more is said about the war, only about me. The last entry, dated October 15, 1940, takes another five full pages to describe a typical day, and at the end all the precautions they had to take to protect the clothing, shoes, and furniture from my burgeoning energies. Even the little bathing tub had to be placed out of my reach, for I loved to bang it on the bathroom floor.

WE STAYED IN LA BAULE UNTIL JANUARY 1941. There were many interludes when my parents' joyful attention was focused on me, but the reality was harsh and nearly culminated in our arrest and deportation to a German concentration camp. Here is how my mother described this incident in an essay many years later:[7]

> We had been trapped by the advance of the German troops in La Baule, a summer resort town on the Atlantic coast of France. We saw streams of refugees from Belgium and northeastern France passing through our little town in their cars, with bullet-riddled mattresses strapped to the top for protection; we heard horror stories of refugees machine-gunned on the road by low-flying German planes; we saw the evacuation of the British troops; we saw brand-new bombers and fighter planes abandoned for the Nazis to find on the local airfield. All this discouraged us from trying to get to Bordeaux [further south on the Atlantic coast] where everybody was going to board a ship for England. It was too great a risk for a group including four little children, the oldest five years old and the youngest only an infant.
>
> For several months we waited and watched for an opportunity to escape into free France. Summer passed, and fall, and Christmas, until we finally dared to travel to Paris to prepare a way for the whole

group to cross the heavily guarded line between occupied France and free France. There were ten of us: my mother [Grandmother Hodža], my sister [Aunt Gláša], a friend of ours [Mr. Pauliny] with his wife and three children, my husband, my baby son, and myself.

I went to Paris to arrange our escape. When I returned to La Baule to tell my family and friends that everything was ready, I found a scene of utter desolation in our rented house. The Nazi Gestapo had paid us a visit that day and searched the house. They ordered us to report to the nearest large city, Nantes, within 48 hours, each with a small suitcase. It could mean only one thing—concentration camp.

Anything was better than that. We decided to try to slip through Nantes to Paris before the time allotted to us ran out. Mr. Pauliny went to Nantes at once to plead for an extension of our deadline, to gain some time for our preparations. The women had accomplished wonders in a day: they shipped our trunks to Paris, they sorted everything, they gave some things away, they stored others, they took care of the myriad things involved in moving a large family from its home. And all that with the children constantly underfoot.

By the time I arrived from Paris, all that had to be done was to pack our smaller luggage and prepare all the baskets and bundles we had to carry with us for the children. We worked until late at night, and at six in the morning, in complete darkness, we plodded to the station. We had decided to get away at once, without waiting for Mr. Pauliny's return. There was little hope that our request for an extension would be granted. In fact, the Gestapo might decide to arrest him on the spot. We had to trust that his ingenuity would help him find us either at the station in Nantes or in Paris.

The trip to Nantes was a nightmare. We barely managed to get on the train. There was no light, no porters. We managed by flinging our bags aboard pell-mell and scrambling after them as the train was already moving.

Arriving in Nantes before noon, we found that we had to wait for five hours for our train to Paris. It would have been folly to linger at the station and attract the attention of the police. We had to find a place where we could spend the time in comparative safety. Piling into a coach, we started the rounds of the local hotels. They were all crowded, but we finally managed to find a room. We sat in it huddled together, scarcely daring to breathe and expecting the police to come pounding at the door any minute. Mercifully, the children slept. Feeding bottles, diapers, blankets, shoes, clothing and food were strewn all over the furniture and spilled onto the floor of the little room.

By the grace of God, we were not disturbed. As we were boarding the night train to Paris Mr. Pauliny suddenly appeared. He had returned home only to find us gone, and he had made the trip to Nantes on a borrowed bicycle. You cannot imagine how happy we all were. His children clung to him, his wife wept for joy as we fought our way into the crowded train. We dared to breathe again as the train pulled out of the station. We were exhausted, disheveled, grimy, but filled with pride and joy. We had outwitted the Gestapo and escaped the nightmare of a Nazi concentration camp.

IN PARIS WE OBTAINED THE HELP OF THE FRENCH RESISTANCE. Our guide across the line from occupied France into free France was a local baker who had joined the Resistance early on and was familiar with the terrain. He took us stealthily in the middle of the night, just our family of three.[8] Grandmother Hodža and Aunt Gláša made their way separately.

Now our goal was to get out of Europe. On March 16, 1941, our Yugoslav passport was extended for two months at the Yugoslav embassy in Vichy, the capital of free France. What we would do next was uncertain. My father had originally thought of taking us to Yugoslavia where he was well connected. However, Germany conquered Yugoslavia between April 6 and 17, closing off this possibility. As the Pavković family we obtained another two-month passport extension on May 17 while staying in Marseilles on the Mediterranean coast. A few days later we secured an immigration visa for Panama. From Marseilles we journeyed to Pau, a small town in western France close to the Pyrenees, and on June 7 obtained a visa to transit Spain. On June 19 we were back in Marseilles and obtained a Portuguese visa. On July 15 the French authorities in Pau gave us an exit permit for Spain and Portugal, and on July 22 the authorities in Vichy authorized us to carry dollars across the border. Finally, on July 28, after five months of anxious searching for a way out, we took a bus across the Pyrenees and into Spain.

Franco's Spain was sympathetic to Nazi Germany, but our Yugoslav passport and our painstakingly obtained visas served us well and we had no difficulty. On July 29, my second birthday, we were in Madrid, and the next day, July 30, 1941, we crossed into Portugal and relative safety.

Lisbon was the last open port in Europe, and thousands of refugees gathered there seeking passage to South America, Central America, Mexico, Canada, and the United States.[9] The situation was tense. In the time since my father had joined our family for good on May 17, 1940, Germany had waged its ferocious bombing war on Britain; war was raging in North Africa; Greece as well as Yugoslavia surrendered to Germany, and Romania, Bulgaria, and Hungary all joined the Nazi cause; some counterattacks by the Allies had begun; and Germany launched its great attack on the Soviet Union. On August 20, following our arrival in Lisbon, the siege of Stalingrad began. On September 3 the gas chambers at Auschwitz started to operate. On September 11 we departed Lisbon for the United States.

Reaching the United States was no simple matter. When we arrived in Lisbon, we had a visa only for Panama, and U.S. visas were not readily granted. At this point, the Czechoslovak government-in-exile in London, which had generally been rather non-communicative because of the conflict between President Beneš and Grandfather Hodža, helped us, and we were able to travel once again under our own names and using Czechoslovak passports. Once visas had been obtained, my father had to find us passage. Fortune was again kind to us. We were able to book passage on what was apparently the last commercial flight from Lisbon to New York, aboard Pan Am's Dixie Clipper.

At the time, the clippers were the state-of-the-art in aviation.[10] With four engines, two decks, a dining room, a lounge, and comfortable sleeping, they pioneered transoceanic passenger service, first across the Pacific and then across the Atlantic. Special terminals were built for them, since they landed on water, not on runways. The Boeing Company built only fourteen clippers, each of which was given its own name and number, and during the war all of them were commandeered by the military. None of these remarkable planes exist any more, but they have a following of aficionados who know the exact fate of every single one, and much of this information is available on the internet. This is how I discovered that the Dixie Clipper (No. 18605), our plane, had made the very first scheduled transatlantic flight on June 28, 1939, just a month before I was born, and later carried President Roosevelt to his conference with Churchill and DeGaulle at Casablanca.

Stored in my memory is an image: my mother is holding me on her lap while we are seated along one wall of the airplane and are looking across the aisle at someone seated opposite us. Airplane passenger seats, of course, are normally one behind the other facing forward, not backed up against the walls and facing sideways. For many years I didn't know what to think of my image, and my mother was no help; she told me that the Dixie Clipper's seats were in the usual arrangement. On the internet, however, I have been able to find the seating plan of the Dixie Clipper.[11] While the seats in the passenger cabin were indeed arranged as usual, the seats in the lounge were placed along the walls so that passengers could face each other as they relaxed with their drinks. So, my image may be a true one after all! If it is, it is my earliest conscious memory, for I was only a few weeks past my second birthday as we flew from war-ravaged Europe to safety in America.

CHAPTER 4

Immigrants in a New Land

On September 12, 1941, the Dixie Clipper, No. 18605, landed in New York City at its specially-built home, the Marine Air Terminal of La Guardia Airport, then known as New York Municipal Airport. Years later, when we lived in New York, our apartment was just a mile or two from La Guardia, and we sometimes strolled close to it on a Sunday afternoon family walk. Inevitably my father would point to the Marine Air Terminal, across the bay from the more recently built main terminal, and remind me that it had been our first point of entry into the United States. It is now an official historical landmark, commemorating a glamorous era in American aviation history.

Following our joyful arrival in New York came a period of difficult adjustment. My father spoke Hungarian, German, and French fluently in addition to Slovak, but he knew hardly a word of English. He hired a tutor for a crash course in conversational English so that he could start looking for work.[1] He also bought a car, a wine-red Pontiac sedan that I remember vividly, and ultimately drove the whole breadth of America to the West Coast and back, looking for a job in which he could use his professional expertise in leather tanning and the manufacture of leather goods, which had been the Pálka family business for generations. Even though it was wartime and workers were in high demand, he could find nothing. With no money coming in, the financial reserves of the family were dwindling rapidly. My parents faced a bleak situation.

As they were trying to gain a foothold in America, the Germans swept into the U.S.S.R. and, on December 7, 1941, the Japanese bombed Pearl Harbor. The next day the United States and Great Britain declared war on Japan, and four days after that Hitler declared war on the United States. The American military immediately entered a period of massive expansion, and industrial production was overwhelmingly committed to the war effort.

In the midst of personal misfortune and a drastic world situation, my family had a great source of joy—me! Here is how Aunt Glása describes me in a letter dated April 28, 1942, to Uncle Dišo, who was in London:[2]

Johnny is growing both in height and in girth. He entertains us no end and also makes us mad. This applies especially to Grandma, because he insists on "helping" her in the garden, and you know what such a helper can get up to. He's made friends with a neighbor boy, so he's always at his house and comes home so dirty that he yells from a long distance, "Glánka, come wash me!" And you should see him in the car! His father has taught him where all the levers and pedals are, and he could play in that car all day long.

After almost a year of living with a distant relative of Grandmother Hodža's in Poughkeepsie, New York, we moved to Chicago. We were able to rent an apartment in a duplex house owned by another Slovak, Emil Langsfeld. The Langsfelds were a notable family from Sučany, the home town of both of my Hodža grandparents[3]. Uncle Emil had emigrated to the United States many years earlier, made his living as a house painter, and gradually acquired a couple of houses that he fixed up and rented. He and his wife had the lower apartment in our duplex, and we lived upstairs.

SETTING UP A HOUSEHOLD IN CHICAGO, in the American heartland, was a novel experience for my parents. My mother wrote about it to Uncle Dišo in her amazingly good English on June 16, 1943, a month before my fourth birthday:[4]

Our people here have been wonderful to us. They gave or lent us quite a lot of things for our household, invented all sorts of amusements, invited us quite often to their houses, and lately gave us a so-called housewarming party. I don't know whether you know this custom. You don't invite your friends to your new house, but the friends organize everything, invite themselves, bring everything with them, cook and serve everything and bring you a present besides. Very good, isn't it? We had here between thirty to forty people, and there are still some who want to come from another part of the city.

My mother's letter to Uncle Dišo also glowed with delight and pride in me:

Your nephew is developing into a little rascal. Lately he is spending all the time at our neighbors'. They are elderly people with sons in the army; they have a litle garden with a swing and let him use all possible tools he can't have at home. He is always "repairing" things, working in their victory garden, making mud cakes, washing the uncle's socks, etc. We have to drag him away from there with promises or by force every evening after we come home from work. He's always awfully dirty, but happy. But I will have to do something about it, because they speak a horrible dialect and I don't want them to spoil his language. Everybody admires how beautifully he speaks, and I am very proud of it, too. We are looking for a nursery school chiefly to let him come together with other children and to learn English before he goes to school.

We joined a Slovak Lutheran church, not in Chicago but all the way across the city in Whiting, Indiana. This entailed a long drive through most of Chicago and through the industrial city of Gary, Indiana, with its many smokestacks belching fumes and topped by flames, all of which I found fascinating. Whiting was, and still is, a major Slovak settlement, and my parents particularly liked the pastor there, Rev. Ján Bradáč (Chapters 5 and 15). He conducted services in the way they were used to at home, in Slovak, of course, and singing almost all of the liturgy rather than reciting it. He was also a leader in the wider Slovak community and very sympathetic to Grandfather Hodža.

DESPITE THE CHEERY TONE OF MY MOTHER'S LETTER, life was hard. There was no money to spare. My mother got a job as a file clerk in an insurance company. As a prime minister's daughter with a doctorate of law, she must have felt odd working in an entry-level office position alongside high school girls, but she took it all in stride. My father finally found work as a manual laborer in a leather tannery. After some weeks he moved to the assembly line at F & B Manufacturing, a maker of electrical components for cars and airplanes.[5] At first he did quality control work, later installation of finished components. He shared this job with a new friend, Uncle Miško Múdry, a Slovak who also helped to organize the many lectures Grandfather Hodža gave after his arrival in the United States in the fall of 1942.[6] In the intense Chicago summer, when a temperature of ninety-five degrees Fahrenheit and humidity of ninety-five percent were not uncommon, the long workday was exhausting.

Every year we had a wonderful Christmas tree lit by traditional candles, not electric lights, but the number of presents depended on the meager bank balance. During the summer, our family managed to take some vacations in nearby Wisconsin. Most of these activities we shared with the Múdrys. At home, the radio became the center of many family activities. It was a classic Zenith console that stood on the floor. On its face was a large and conspicuous silver knob used to select between local broadcasts and various shortwave bands, and when I turned it a new set of colored metal plates embossed with the names of world cities would appear behind the big front glass. We listened to war news every evening, and my father challenged me to try to identify all the various languages that hissed and crackled as I turned the tuning knob. On Sunday afternoons he would tune in to a station that broadcast Hungarian Gypsy music and stretch out on the living room couch to listen. Within minutes he'd fall asleep from exhaustion.

When we'd arrived in Chicago, my parents had been optimistic. A year and a half later, financial and political pressures had taken a heavy toll on my family. My father was not much of a correspondent, but he unburdened himself in a long letter, four hand-written pages filled with tiny handwriting, written on February 27, 1944, to a dear friend, Vladimír Žuffa:[7]

> Miško and I put our noses to the grindstone at least 10 hours a day, often longer, 11-12 hours, and we earn $50 to $100 a week. Our wives earn around $25 weekly. Our son usually goes to the neighbors, who really like him. Maminka [Grandmother Hodža] cleans, washes, cooks, does the shopping, sews and crochets. We come home exhausted for dinner, and I regularly fall asleep while listening to the news between 9 and 10 in the evening. In the morning we start all over again. This goes on day after day. No changes. We don't go anywhere at all, except the women go to the movies once or twice a month . . . . The so-called society here is totally fragmented both politically and religiously [Lutherans and Catholics], and with all the doings surrounding Dad [Grandfather Hodža] and Miško [Múdry], the circle of friends is none too great. Hats off to some of them, though, who are strong and fearless. . . . I thought that I would be able to establish myself financially here and provide both for my family and for other important things, but it's all gone the other way—my pockets are empty, and I have what I earn each week. If I don't work, I don't earn and I have nothing. . . . I haven't even had time to learn English because the whole neighborhood is Slovak: my employer, the shoemaker, the merchants, our landlord, the neighbors, everybody. Attending night school is out of the question given our physical exhaustion. . . . We have had absolutely no news from home for ages, so I would be very grateful if you wrote us anything you learn. You know that every tidbit is a relief for us from this tedium and constant chasing after a living. . . . I'm enclosing a picture of our Johnny. At least you'll see what is our, and my, only joy in life. . . .

No wonder I never—either as a child or as an adult, and no matter what the external circumstances might have been—felt the least uncertainty about my parents' profound love for me.

CHAPTER 5

Milan Hodža in America

In late 1941, war was raging not only throughout Europe, but also the Middle East and North Africa. German troops were at the gates of Leningrad and Moscow. The gas chambers at Auschwitz were activated. The United States was still officially neutral, but Roosevelt and Churchill had proclaimed the Atlantic Charter, and convoys of ships were transporting millions of tons of equipment and supplies from America across the Atlantic to Britain and other allies.[1] German U-boats were on the prowl; by the end of the war they were to sink over three and a half thousand Allied ships.[2] Passenger liners were not entirely immune to attack either, though only a handful were actually sunk.

It was in this setting that Milan Hodža set sail from England for America, landing in New York on November 1, 1941. Since his departure from Czechoslovakia in December of 1938, he had spent three difficult years trying to recover his health and waging an ultimately futile battle with Edvard Beneš, primarily over broadening and strengthening Slovak representation in the London-based Czechoslovak government-in-exile and over Slovakia's place in a future, reunited Czechoslovakia.[3] Blocked in his political efforts, virtually excluded from the government, and seriously ill, he decided on one last push, this time in America.

WHAT EXACTLY DID HODŽA STAND FOR, and why did he encounter such fierce opposition from Beneš? We can highlight the conflict under three headings:

Slovak autonomy. Over the years, Hodža had come more and more to oppose the Prague-centered perspective of Beneš and most Czech political leaders (Chapters 1 and 27). His views had moved quite close to those that had been held by Andrej Hlinka, his long-time friend but political rival, including a Slovak parliament that would legislate in all areas that did not primarily concern Czechoslovakia as a whole, a Slovak judiciary, and Slovak as the official language of Slovakia. He wanted a formal commitment that Czechoslovakia would move in this direction upon the war's conclusion. Beneš would have none of this. He remained loyal to the notion of a single Czechoslovak ethnicity rather than a union of separate Czech and Slovak nations, and he considered Slovaks to be

Grandfather Hodža with our family shortly after his arrival in the United States in november 1941. From left to right: Grandmother Hodža holding me, Grandfather Hodža, my mother, and my father. Author's archive.

traitors who had enabled the Munich debacle. He argued that no revision of the formal Czech-Slovak relationship could be undertaken, or promises made, by the government-in-exile; changes would have to wait until the country was once again united. Hodža had little faith in such an unsecured future.

Federation in Central Europe. Hodža had long been a leading proponent of the idea that the relatively small nations of Central Europe, from Poland and the Baltic states in the north all the way to Greece in the south, should band together—initially economically but eventually also politically—in order to stand up to both German and Soviet expansionism. (This idea is now often viewed as one of the important predecessors of the concept of the European Union, see Chapter 27.) Slovakia would remain an essential component of Czechoslovakia, and Czechoslovakia itself would find her greatest security within such a federation.[4] Beneš, in contrast, continued to see Czechoslovakia's security primarily in terms of alliances with the great powers and increasingly so with the Soviet Union.

Soviet influence. A long-time anti-Communist, Hodža was extremely wary of the intentions of the Soviet Union. He would try to convince U. S. officials that allowing post-war Europe to be divided into spheres of influence, one of them falling to the Soviets, would be disastrous. Beneš moved in the opposite direction. He saw the Soviet Union as probably Czechoslovakia's most important ally. He developed closer and closer ties with the Soviets, enjoying a warm personal reception from Stalin during a series of visits to Moscow—before the war in 1935, during the war in 1943, and on his way home to Czechoslovakia as soon as the war had ended in1945. While he rejected the totalitarian aspects of the Soviet regime, he greatly admired its social and economic goals, and his plans for the reconstruction of post-war Czechoslovakia included a Soviet-style nationalization of major segments of the economy. Evidently, he also trusted Stalin and his promises about the future.[5]

These were huge differences on matters of policy. In addition there were deepening personal animosities between Hodža and Beneš, and especially a number of Beneš's supporters. The outcome was political warfare, often dirty, first in Britain and later in the United States.

IN THE U.S., HODŽA PLANNED TO PROPAGATE HIS PRINCIPLES—a substantial degree of Slovak autonomy in the Czechoslovakia of the future, and a federated Central Europe able to withstand both German and Soviet pressures—focusing his efforts on representatives of the American government and on the major Slovak-American organizations.[6] He set to work immediately after his arrival on American soil.

On December 7, 1941, *The New York Times* published a lengthy interview with Hodža in which he elaborated his views concerning Central Europe.[7] That very day, Japan bombed Pearl Harbor. On December 8 the United States declared war on Japan. On December 11 Hitler declared war on the United States. The German-dominated Slovak Republic followed suit the following day, thus becoming America's declared enemy. The wider American public had followed Central European affairs to some extent, especially the turmoil surrounding Munich and the break-up of Czechoslovakia, but now interest in the future of this region suddenly became the domain of just a handful of specialists in the government and in academia.

Nevertheless, Hodža had an audience.[8] On December 4, just before Pearl Harbor, he met with an official of the Office of the Coordinator of Information, the immediate predecessor of the wartime Office of Strategic Services (OSS). Right after Pearl Harbor, on December 9, he met with Adolph A. Berle, a prominent member of President Roosevelt's famed "Brain Trust" and the wartime Undersecretary of State for Latin American Affairs. To their face-to-face discussion, Hodža brought a written memorandum in which he summarized the history of Czech-Slovak relations, criticized the centralism prevailing in Czechoslovakia, and argued for the right of Slovaks to autonomy within the broader structures of the Czechoslovak Republic. He concluded with a scathing critique of the Slovak puppet government in Bratislava and asserted vehemently that it did not reflect the true wishes of the Slovak people.

Hodža was to have private conversations with American officials every few months and to author several memoranda on major political isues. He most emphatically warned about Soviet intentions in Europe in a memorandum sent to the U. S. State Department in the winter of 1944. This analysis, entitled *Europe at the Crossroads*, set forth clearly the probable disastrous consequences of dividing Europe into spheres of influence between the West and the Soviet Union, and argued once again for a strong, federalized Central Europe. Unfortunately, Hodža's words went unheeded and as a result Communism held sway in Central Europe for four decades.[9]

Hodža's approach to the Slovak immigrant community was implemented through existing clubs and associations. Most of these organizations were local, but there were also two major umbrella groups: the Slovak League of America for the Catholics, and the Slovak National Assembly, formally non-denominational but in fact primarily Lutheran. Hodža engaged with both of them, but they provided him with serious challenges. From the moment that Slovakia declared its independence on March 14, 1939, the leaders of the Slovak League had supported the new Slovak Republic. They saw its establishment as the culmination of a struggle for Slovak nationhood that had begun centuries earlier during Magyar rule (Appendix I and Part II). They viewed Hodža as far too much of a Czechoslovakist. The Slovak National Assembly, in contrast, was a strong defender of Czechoslovak unity and statehood, and saw the breakup of the country as a national tragedy precipitated at least in part by the uncompromising demands of Hlinka's Slovak People's Party. The personal loyalties of the leadership were divided, but a strong faction supported Beneš, not Hodža, because it placed primary importance on maintaining Czechoslovak unity in the struggle against Germany and saw Hodža as too much of an autonomist.

Thus, when he arrived in the United States, Hodža faced a daunting challenge in his efforts to rally American Slovaks to his views.[10] However, he was undeterred. He wrote extensively in the immigrant press. At the invitation of the various organizations, he undertook a series of speaking tours to major Slovak centers around the country, including Detroit and Chicago, and drew extraordinary crowds—often 500 to a 1000 people came to hear him, instead of the relative handful that came to most political meetings. Everywhere he went he argued the same basic points: autonomy for Slovakia but firmly within the framework of a united Czechoslovakia, and the importance of regional cooperation in Central Europe as a bulwark against both German and Soviet expansionism. He converted many people to his side, and won a number of significant organizational endorsements. Even the Slovak League sided with him, at least temporarily, especially now that the Slovak Republic had declared war on the United States.

WITH THE ADVENT OF WAR, THE GOVERNMENT of the United States decided to consolidate and greatly expand its intelligence gathering capabilities. In 1942, the old Office of the Coordinator of Information, as well as several military agencies, were replaced by the Office of Strategic Services (OSS), the first real spy agency the U.S. ever had. Included in its purview were the activities of the scores of organizations established by the nation's many immigrant groups. (It was estimated that at this time fully one third of the American population were first or second generation immigrants.) With the Slovak Republic at war with the U.S., Slovak organizations, their leaders, and Milan Hodža were squarely in the sights of the OSS, and especially its Foreign Nationalities Branch. They did not much like what they saw.[11]

First and foremost, the United States wanted to see a united, not a fractured, front against Hitler, and in this quest it had recently cast its lot with Beneš by officially recognizing his government-in-exile. The Slovaks of America, however, were divided. For two years the Slovak League had been an active supporter of the Slovak Republic, an enemy nation. Later, for some time, it supported Hodža. The leadership of the Slovak National Assembly was almost exactly evenly divided between supporters of Beneš and supporters of Hodža. Hodža's declared goal was to unite Slovak-Americans behind a single vision of the future, but given the political realities of the time this could not be done without a struggle. It is perhaps not surprising, therefore, that much as U. S. officials valued Hodža's insight into the forces at play in Central Europe, they gradually came to regard him—in the words of the Slovak scholar Roman Ličko—as an "unwelcome guest." Nonetheless, during the war years Hodža appears to have been the only Slovak to present the Slovak case in person to members of President Roosevelt's administration.

The OSS also had good insight into the dirty tactics that were being used against Hodža by Beneš and particularly by his two principal representatives in the United States, the ambassador of the Czechoslovak government-in-exile, and the chief of the Czechoslovak Information Agency.[12] These included feeding distorted information both to the OSS and FBI and to the immigrant and the American press, culminating in articles that were so libellous that Hodža initiated court proceedings to clear his name. The smear campaign started even before Hodža reached the U.S., and it continued after his death. A decade later, my mother still could not speak about those many attacks without bitterness showing in her usually calm and thoughtful voice.

IN ADDITION TO THE POLITICAL BATTLES he was fighting, Hodža faced a health crisis.[13] Uncle Miško Múdry, who acted as his personal secretary as well as tour organizer during much of his time in America, described him this way:[14]

> Shortly after his arrival in America, in November of 1941, several of us met with him in Pittsburgh. . . . However solid his physical stature might have been, following all those difficult pre-Munich years and his trying exile, Hodža looked tired, dejected, and exhausted.

Very shortly following his arrival in America, Hodža had two back-to-back cases of pneumonia. At that time there were no antibiotics available, so he was cared for at warm-weather spas where the infections were basically allowed just to run their course. He was then sixty-three years old and had been ailing for some time, so the pneumonia left him in a terribly weakened state. As my mother wrote in her letter to Uncle Dišo (Chapter 4):

> We got rather a scare about father's illness. Like usual, we didn't know how serious it was until the worst was over, but to have had pneumonia twice at his age is no joke. He is much better now, but he will have to stay in Florida for another month at least.

As soon he had the strength, he re-entered the political fray, but illness dogged him.

By 1943 the tide of war was turning. The German offensive against the Soviets was turned back, the war in North Africa swung in favor of the Allies, and Allied forces landed in Italy, which soon surrendered. Despite this encouraging news, however, life for my family continued to be bittersweet. My parents were barely eking out a living in Chicago. Meanwhile, Grandfather Hodža regained enough strength for a series of fiery presentations of his vision for Czechoslovakia that again drew large and enthusiastic audiences. But, as Miško Múdry writes, his health was increasingly precarious.[15]

> Even after he recovered [from his initial bouts with pneumonia] his health remained undermined. I was very often with him, I traveled with him. After his speeches in Detroit and in Chicago, he asked me to take him to some unused room where he changed his clothes because his shirt was totally soaked through. He carried spare clothing with him. And when I saw that he was eating only purees and milk, and when he confided in me that he had digestive problems, I suddenly feared that his illness was far more serious than any of us had believed.

HIS BUSY SCHEDULE WAS INTERRUPTED BY RETREATS for recuperation. In the winter of 1943-44, my grandmother and I went to see him in Clearwater, Florida, where he was convalescing. In the springtime, when his physical state had improved somewhat, he came to see us in Chicago. My mother wrote a brief reminiscence of this visit:[16]

> In the anti-Nazi resistance, my father was called "the old man" by both his followers and his opponents. I often thought, this name doesn't fit him in the least. Only during his last visit in Chicago, in the spring of 1944, when we were walking together as we always had, but this time just around our modest apartment, it occurred to me, maybe they are right. I don't know why, whether it was because his step was not as firm as it had been or because his hand rested more heavily on my shoulder, but the thought suddenly passed through my mind that perhaps he really is an old man. But I never thought that this walk might be the last one, that I would never see him alive again.

The telegram came from Clearwater on June 28, 1944: Grandfather Hodža had died shortly before midnight while being operated for advanced colon cancer.

His body was brought by train to Chicago. There was no local Slovak cemetery, so it was prepared for burial in the grand, old Bohemian National Cemetery. The funeral was arranged by the funeral home of John Židek and

Milan Hodža's funeral at Trinity Lutheran Church in Chicago, July 3, 1944. Left to right: my mother, grandmother, and father. Author's archive.

Son, whose founder was an admirer of Grandfather Hodža and had even made a special trip to meet with Hodža when he first arrived in America. Fifty-eight years later, in June of 2002, the grandson of John Židek, Lad (Ladislav) Židek, presided over the ceremonies in Chicago that initiated the final transfer of Grandfather Hodža's remains to the National Cemetery in Slovakia. [17]

On that day in 1944, a long procession of black limousines rolled past our house and picked up Grandmother Hodža, my parents, and Aunt Gláša. I had to stay behind because I was ill, but I remember watching out of the front window of the living room. The open convertibles, with their back seats filled with flowers, remain the most vivid in my memory. As I came to know later, in part from Lad Židek who was a boy at the time, the funeral was an extraordinary event, unlike any seen in the Slovak immigrant community before or since. The church was alive with flowers and, literally, overflowing with people. According to *The New York Times*, "thousands of Slovaks attended the funeral service as a tribute to Dr. Hodža." Grandmother Hodža, my parents, the Múdrys, and crowds of other Slovaks came in black, shocked at Grandfather Hodža's sudden death and mourning the loss of a man who, right up to his very end, stood for the best in Slovakia.

Jan Masaryk, the highly respected son of Czechoslovakia's first president and the foreign minister of the Czechoslovak government-in-exile, was then on his way from Washington to London but abruptly changed his plans and came to Chicago to participate in the memorial services. Masaryk was a firm supporter of President Beneš and a blunt-spoken political opponent of Grandfather Hodža, but his tributes to my grandfather were direct and moving,[19] The text of Masaryk's eulogy at Grandfather Hodža's funeral was printed in a Czech newspaper, *Denní hlasatel* (*The Daily Herald*) in Chicago[20]:

> Hodža was the most influential political figure of the past half century in Slovakia. His name will remain one of the most important in Slovakia's history. Even though there were frequently differences of opinion between Hodža and his colleagues, fundamentally Hodža had the same plan as all of us: a strong, independent Czechoslovakia in which Czechs and Slovaks will live together as brothers, where the mistakes of the pre-war era will not be repeated, where there will be no masters and servants, where there will be social justice and everyone will have the opportunity to work and live decently. I know that Milan Hodža agreed with this vision because I discussed it with him several times.

> Hodža left us prematurely, unexpectedly, and exceedingly tragically. For a while he will rest in the free and democratic soil of America.

Then we will take him home, and we will always remember him as a great son of his nation. In the name of my government, as well as in my own, I express to Hodža's family my deepest condolences. The life of us exiles is never particularly happy. Mrs. Hodža's is especially sad. May God give her the strength to live to see, with her children and grandson, her return home, where everyone—I know it well—will welcome her with open arms.

Good bye, Milan, rest in peace.

Many leading newspapers, including *The Times of London*[21] and *The New York Times,*[22] published detailed obituaries recounting Hodža's long political career, as did virtually every Slovak, Czechoslovak, and Czech publication in America, whether it supported him or opposed him. Accounts of the funeral itself were widely published in the immigrant press, along with evaluations of his life's work presented from the viewpoint of each individual newspaper. One of the most interesting appeared in *Slovenská obrana* (*Slovak Defender*) published in Scranton, Pennsylvania, and perhaps the most influential of the publications advocating complete Slovak independence. It begins with these words:[23]

[Dr. Hodža] came from a famous Slovak family. The Hodžas were tough Slovaks, rebels and fighters. And Dr. Milan Hodža, even though he over time occasionally deviated from the traditions and spirit of his ancestors, was also a Slovak.

He served his nation best during the dark days of the Magyar regime (Appendix I and Part II) as a fearless defender of his nation and an enterprising and untiring worker in his nation's interests. He was always a practical realist and also an opportunist. He tried to elevate his nation from the heavy poverty which was the source of its spiritual slavery. And for his accomplishments in this field, his nation will be forever grateful to him.

The obituary goes on to recount and criticize his efforts on behalf of a united Czechoslovakia and concludes with the following evaluation:

To the question whether the late Dr. Hodža was a faithful Slovak [some Slovak nationalists denied him a Slovak identity because he was such a staunch defender of Czechoslovakia] we can answer, with some reservations, that he was. And we can affirmatively answer another question, whether he served his nation well. But he wandered far as a politician and statesman of European stature, far beyond the boundaries of his narrower homeland with which he identified himself through his ancestry, but which was too small for his political vision and for his personal ambitions. If he had devoted his extraordinary capabilities exclusively to the interests of this homeland, he would have become a great historical figure not only for his nation but for the whole world.

When we weigh the entire public life of the departed, as it really was, with all its virtues and faults, we can say: a great man and great Slovak has died. All honor to his memory.

In the end, the leaders of both of the factions opposing Grandfather Hodža—the unwavering Czechoslovakists with a centralist vision and the equally unwavering Slovak separatists—eloquently acknowledged and honored his lifelong efforts and accomplishments. Despite this acclaim, unfortunately, and even after his death, public polemics continued to rage between his devoted followers and his personal and political enemies. The strident tone and the harsh arguments moved my mother to publish an article entitled "In Defense of My Father."[24] This was a hard time for the family, and it left a bitter taste for many years.

As Jan Masaryk had said, it was fully expected that, as soon as the country was liberated, Grandfather Hodža's remains would be transferred to Czecho-slovakia. For this reason his body was not actually buried but was held in the Židek funeral home in a special sealed casket. But the end of the war came and went, and the Czechoslovak government seemed to forget Masaryk's promise and declined to give permission for the transfer.[25] When the Communists came to power in 1948, it became clear that a transfer would not take place and so, four years after his funeral, Grandfather Hodža was finally physically buried. In 1951 the Association of Czechoslovak Exiles (*Sdruženie československých exulantov*) erected a monument over Grandfather Hodža's grave in the Bohemian National Cemetery (Plates 7 and 8, Appendix VI). During the ceremony, Dr. Jozef Lettrich, widely regarded as the most distinguished of Hodža's followers (Chapter 6), and like us a refugee from Communism, gave the principal oration.

In 1990, soon after Czechoslovakia shook off the Soviet yoke and while it was still united, Jan Masaryk and Milan Hodža were simultaneously awarded the country's highest honor, the Order of Thomas Garrigue Masaryk (First Class), by then-president Václav Havel.[26] Then in 2002, the government of newly-independent Slovakia finally brought Hodža home in the extraordinary ceremony of state in which Yvonne and I participated (Prologue). More than fifty years after his death, as Masaryk had promised would happen, the nation welcomed Hodža home.

CHAPTER 6

Slovakia Rises and Heroes Come Forth

Ten weeks after Grandfather Hodža's sudden death and funeral, our Zenith radio brought a brief report on Slovakia, announcing a rebellion that has since come to be known as the Slovak National Uprising (*Slovenské národné povstanie, SNP*). For Americans this was a mere footnote to the war, but for Slovaks it was a momentous national event, the outcome of processes set in motion years earlier.

After the drama of 1938—the Runciman Mission, the Anglo-French Ultimatum, the resignation of Grandfather Hodža's cabinet, the signing of the Munich Declaration, and the resignation of President Beneš (Chapter 1)—two further events determined Slovakia's path during World War II. The first, in late 1938, was the recognition of Slovak autonomy within Czechoslovakia; the second, in early 1939, was the declaration of Slovakia's total independence.[1] Now, in 1944, Slovaks rose up against their own government which, despite its pride in the fact that it was the first-ever independent Slovak state, was a *de facto* puppet of Hitler's Germany.[2]

AUTONOMY WAS THE OUTCOME of internal discord that had festered within Czechoslovakia almost since the country's founding in 1918 (Chapter 1). A week after Munich, after years of political jousting and with Czechoslovakia facing a continuing German threat, Hlinka's Slovak People's Party (HSPP), the Agrarian Party whose Slovak wing had long been led by Grandfather Hodža, and all other Slovak parties with the exception of the Communists and the Social Democrats signed an agreement supporting proposals for Slovak autonomy that the HSPP had advanced earlier.[3] Autonomy was formally implemented by action of the Czechoslovak parliament in late November. All of a sudden, Czechoslovakia became administratively asymmetric, with a national government in Prague that managed the affairs of the entire state and also the affairs of the Czech lands of Bohemia and Moravia, and an autonomous regional government in Bratislava that managed the affairs of the Slovak portion of the country.

Independence came not long after, in the spring of 1939. On March 13 Hitler called Jozef Tiso, the leader of the HSPP and the first prime minister of autonomous Slovakia, to Berlin and demanded that Slovakia declare its full independence. Tiso refused, on the grounds that only the Slovak parliament could take such a step. The parliament acted promptly; on March 14, 1939, Slovakia declared its independence and Czechoslovakia ceased to exist. On March 15 Hitler pronounced Bohemia and Moravia to be a protectorate of Germany, and on March 16 Germans troops occupied Prague. Hitler's plan to destroy Czechoslovakia was complete, with hardly a shot having been fired.[4]

THE SLOVAK REPUBLIC WAS NOW A SOVEREIGN STATE and would be so until Czechoslovakia was re-established following the defeat of Germany at the end of World War II. The proponents of a united Czechoslovakia despaired, but many Slovaks had long dreamed of autonomy, if not independence, and for them this was a heady time. The new state could claim some real accomplishments: important new educational institutions were established, the Slovak Academy of Sciences was founded, the arts flourished, and the economy did as well, although it was subservient to Germany.[5] Most important, for the first time in history Slovakia ruled itself.

Unfortunately, the new state was also tragically flawed: It quickly adopted a totalitarian structure, powerful factions of its leadership were blatantly pro-Nazi, and it legislated reprehensible anti-Jewish policies. In all important respects it was a puppet of Germany, even though the strong nationalist sentiments of its leadership and its staunchly Catholic worldview sometimes led to an unwillingness to follow German orders. Religion was written explicitly into the Slovak Republic's constitution, which attributed the state's authority to God, not to the consent of the governed.[6]

The HSPP quickly re-structured the party system to give itself unrestricted power. The Communists and the Social Democrats were banned, while the Agrarians and all other parties including a Fascist one merged with the HSPP. Only two small national parties—the German and the Hungarian—were permitted to remain alongside the HSPP. This set the political stage for the totalitarian state that was soon to evolve.[7] The Hlinka Guard, a paramilitary (trained but unarmed) organizaton that had older roots within the HSPP, was formally established and modeled itself after the Nazi *Sturmabteilung* (SA) or Brownshirts. The Office of Propaganda, headed by Alexander Mach, one of the most pro-Nazi of the Slovak leaders, placed government commissars in the offices of all the daily newspapers and soon almost completely eliminated the free press. "Elections" were held in December, 1938, but only a single, government-selected list of candidates was permitted.

Within this monolithic formal structure there existed a long-running power struggle. The moderate wing of the HSPP was headed by Jozef Tiso, like Hlinka a Catholic priest who saw his religion and state as intimately intertwined.[6] Prominent in the party for many years, Tiso was elected the prime minister of autonomous Slovakia and later president of the independent Slovak Republic. The principal leaders of the radical wing of the party were Vojtech Tuka and Alexander Mach. As early as 1923, Tuka had been the founder of the *Rodobrana*, the paramilitary precursor to the Hlinka Guard. In 1929 he was imprisoned by the Czechoslovak government for treasonous collaboration with Hungary; he was released in 1937. In the Slovak Republic he was first prime minister and later foreign minister. Mach headed the Office of Propaganda as well as the Hlinka Guard; he later became interior minister. Tuka and Mach were the most blatantly pro-Nazi and anti-Jewish Slovak figures. They struggled with Tiso for party leadership; Tiso ultimately won.

Though a moderate compared with Tuka and Mach, Tiso, too, had a chillingly totalitarian vision for Slovakia, as these words show:[8]

> The party must be the organizer of the whole of public life and it must hold this function forever. The party gives the state a parliament and government in the name of the nation. The party is the nation and the nation is the party. The nation speaks through the party. The party thinks in place of the nation.

Totalitarianism was proclaimed to be superior to democracy. In the words of Jozef Kirschbaum, general secretary of the HSPP:[9]

> ... the values of democracy are discredited, the authoritarian principle now shows the way. If we sincerely want to build a totalitarian party, which would be the bearer of political power and representative of a united nation, we must follow where Germany has gone, but without the intention to imitate it.

IN THIS WAY, POLITICAL FREEDOM as we usually understand it was taken away from the whole of Slovak society. However, Slovakia's Jewish citizens suffered incomparably more. Anti-Semitism had long been widespread in the country, and prominent in the philosophy of the HSPP.[10] When the party came into power, government-sanctioned exploitation of Jewish businesses started. In 1939 legislation was adopted that initiated the formal process of *aryanization*, the forced transfer of Jewish properties to "Aryan" individuals or directly to the government.[11] In these transactions, the financial compensation to the Jewish owners was minimal. The Slovaks who came into ownership of these Jewish businesses were often not qualified to run them, so the state ultimately had to step in and take over in an effort to minimize the economic consequences of so many failures. The homes of Jews were confiscated and sold, as were synagogues. Their contents—furniture, artworks, books—met the same fate.

At the same time, laws progressively restricting everything in Jewish life were enacted. The culmination of this process was the so-called Jewish Codex of 1942. This infamous decree permitted Jews to be employed only with official approval; excluded them from all secondary schools and all higher education; prohibited them from attending public social, cultural, and sporting events; and established a morning and evening curfew. Jews were forbidden to marry non-Jews. They could not assemble or travel. They were required to identify themelves by wearing a yellow Star of David. Many were interned in labor camps.[12]

The tens of thousands of Jews whose livelihood had been taken away, and who had no rights, became a social burden. The "solution" was to ship them to German camps, which by that time had become extermination camps. During six months in 1942 approximately 58,000 people, about two-thirds of the Jewish population of Slovakia at the time, were deported to these camps, and the Slovak government paid Germany for the privilege.[13] The ultimate horrific irony was that the funds came from the proceeds of the aryanization process—Jews paid for their own extermination.[14]

When my mother left Slovakia in July of 1939, the policies that culminated in these monstrosities were already starting to be enacted. However, at this time the government was still in the hands of the moderate wing of the HSPP who proceeded relatively slowly. The government's anti-democratic, anti-Semitic, and pro-Nazi thrust accelerated markedly during 1940-42 when, with direct support from Hitler, the radical wing headed by Vojtech Tuka and Alexander Mach gained its greatest influence.

BUT TROUBLE FOR THE SLOVAK REPUBLIC WAS BREWING. Immediatelty following Munich, anti-Nazi resistance groups had started to form, both in the Czech lands and in Slovakia. Before he left, President Beneš himself organized a group loyal to him who would serve as his contacts with his homeland. Similarly, Grandfather Hodža met with a handful of his most trusted followers who would start to build a network capable of taking action against the Nazis and be his link to home, not only in Slovakia but in Prague as well.[15] His chief representative, Ján Lichner, later described the situation in this way:[16]

> I visited Dr. Hodža in early December of 1938. We discussed the situation in Slovakia and in the world. We shared the view that Hitler's actions would certainly result in war, and that our further efforts

must be directed to the battle against Fascism and Hitlerism, and coordinated with forces that were already working and fighting toward this goal. For the first time Hodža confided in me that he had decided to go into exile, specifically to Switzerland, and he asked me to stay at home and start to organize a domestic resistance . . . . On the 18th of December, I said good-bye to Dr. Hodža for the last time, and on this occasion we again clarified our joint actions in the future. He abroad and I at home.

Many insurgent groups organized, at first largely independently of each other.[17] A key aspect of their work was to carry information—the mood of the populace, the movements of the Germans, the status of the economy and the food supply, the names of people who could reliably be recruited into the insurgency, and so forth—from home to the leadership in Paris and London, and to convey messages from the leadership in the other direction. They also helped many escape to the West or to Russia, to join military units preparing to fight alongside the major allies.

The evolution of the resistance in Slovakia was remarkable. Within two years the country was riddled with resistors—men and women in all sectors of society: career political figures, military commanders, judges, bank officials, government officials at many levels, police officers, lawyers, businessmen, church leaders, peasants. In retrospect it seems astonishing that such an immense movement could have been organized under the nose of the often pro-Hitler government and in the presence of many German troops and officials, but it was. Of course, there were failures along the way. At times the information networks were penetrated by German agents. In 1940 Hodža's lieutenant, Ján Lichner, was forced to flee, escaping arrest only by hours.[18] Members of the underground were captured and tortured. Overall, however, the resistance grew astonishingly, from small, scattered beginnings to a truly national movement.

There were two main political streams behind this increasingly coordinated action. The democratic stream was led primarily by men who had been closely associated with Grandfather Hodža. Ján Ursíny and Jozef Lettrich had been his personal protégés and had held significant positions in the Agrarian Party, Matej Josko was a newspaper editor.[19] The Communist stream was led by Karol Šmidke (a long-time party activist), Gustav Husák (an attorney), and Laco Novomeský (a well-known poet). It was influenced by Klement Gottwald, a Czech living in Moscow and working with Stalin's regime. Gottwald ultimately led the coup that installed the Communist dictatorship in Czechoslovakia in 1948.[20]

The two groups had profoundly different long-term goals. The democrats worked for the reestablishment of a free, independent, and united Czechoslovakia but with the true parity between Czechs and Slovaks that had been lacking previously— basically the Hodža position.The Communists initially envisioned a country that would be affiliated with the Soviet Union or even become a Soviet republic. However, this vision was actually rejected by Stalin, and Czech and Slovak Communists embraced the restoration of Czechoslovakia.[21] In addition, the Slovak Communists were, for the most part, committed to their movement in an idealistic way. This opened the way to a close collaboration between the two streams, and in December 1943, they signed the so-called Christmas Agreement. The agreement put in place an underground Slovak National Council (*Slovenská národná rada*, SNR), which was to assume full governmental powers within Slovakia at the proper moment, and in which the Democrats and the Communists were represented in exactly equal numbers. In the agreement, the Communists accepted the democrats' vision of the future—a united Czechoslovakia with true Czech-Slovak parity.

THE GOAL OF THE SLOVAK NATIONAL COUNCIL was nothing less than to organize an armed Slovak National Uprising that would both topple the pro-Nazi Slovak Republic and drive the Germans out of Slovakia.[22] To accomplish this, it would be necessary to enlist the armed forces of the Slovak Republic in anti-state activities. The key figure in this effort was Lt. Col. Ján Golian, who recruited many other high-ranking military leaders to put their units at the disposal of the National Council. Golian developed a strategic plan for the military aspects of the uprising that, for full success, depended on timely support from Soviet forces that were massed across the Slovak border in Ukraine. The Soviets were needed because the Slovak forces lacked air support, heavy artillery, and tanks.[23]

Throughout the long preparations for the uprising, the democratic leaders maintained contact with London and were dismayed at the growing friction between Beneš and Hodža. Even though they were long-time followers of Grandfather Hodža, they finally threw their lot with Beneš, both because they believed that in fighting for the restoration of Czechoslovakia a united front was vital and because material support could come only from the official government-in-exile. The democrats undertook a risky, clandestine flight to London in order to hold personal consultations with the president. More than once they felt disappointed, and even insulted, by the way they, and Slovaks in general, were treated by the Beneš group.[24] Meanwhile, it was up to the Communist members of the Slovak National Council to ensure the timely participation of Soviet forces, and to this end they sent a delegation to Moscow.[25]

In parallel with the systematic underground effort of the Slovak National Council, scattered groups of armed partisans—many Slovak, but some also from the Soviet Union, France, and other countries—were running their own covert operations across the country.[26] In 1943 they intensified their guerilla actions, blowing up bridges, destroying railroad tracks, and killing not only Germans but also Slovaks whom they suspected of collaborating with the Germans. These partisans were a mix of true patriots, violent criminals, and Soviet fighters who took their orders only from the Soviet leadership. The Slovak National Council was unable to control them, and their actions had precisely the effect the Council feared most—intervention by the German military well before the preparations for an armed uprising had been completed.

In response to increasingly frequent partisan actions, the Germans invaded. On August 29, 1944, the Slovak minister of defense in a radio broadcast asked the people to welcome and support them. This forced the hand of the leaders of the uprising. On the same day Col. Golian broadcast a prearranged, coded message to his military leaders, setting the uprising in motion. Two days later, on September 1, broadcasting from its provisional capital in the town of Banská Bystrica in Central Slovakia (Map 3, Appendix II), the Slovak National Council publicly proclaimed itself the only organization entitled to speak in the name of the Slovak nation and announced the renewal of a united Czechoslovakia. It was now open rebellion.

AT ITS PEAK, THE SLOVAK NATIONAL UPRISING included 60,000 regular troops of the Slovak Republic, an estimated 18,000 partisans, and untold numbers of civilians.[27] The Germans sent in six army divisions. The two sides had about the same number of soldiers, but the Germans had far more battlefield experience and far better equipment and training. It was a battle the Slovaks could not win. There were other problems as well. Because of the precipitous actions of the partisans, the uprising had to be launched prematurely. Certain aspects of its organization failed. The promised Soviet military aid never arrived. The delegation from the Slovak National Council that went to the Soviet Union to negotiate the details of that aid was even held for some time under house arrest.[28] The Czechoslovak government-in-exile provided no meaningful assistance, and potential assistance from the three Western Allies was blocked by the Soviets. As a result, a few months after the fighting began, the Germans gained the upper hand. The partisans and deserting Slovak soldiers retreated to the mountains of Central Slovakia, where they held out for nearly a half year and maintained harrassing actions. Total casualties on the two sides exceeded 10,000.

While the military victory belonged to the Germans, it cost them dearly. They could ill afford the diversion of so many troops at this time. The Allies were now on the offensive. Italy had been invaded and had joined the Allies, and Allied troops were sweeping in from the beaches of Normandy. More importantly, the uprising represented a clear turning point in Slovak history, away from the totalitarian and often pro-Nazi philosophy of the Slovak Republic and toward a boldly declared commitment to democracy and a united Czechoslovakia. However, the major role played by the Communists foreshadowed events to come.

THE WIDESPREAD PARTICIPATION in the Slovak National Uprising and in anti-Nazi resistance in general, both in Slovakia and among Slovaks in exile, brought into being many heroes. Thousands of people—from all walks of life, across religious boundaries, of differing political persuasions—collectively risked their lives for a noble cause. Let me tell you about one of them, Jozef Bučko, the father of my cousin Jelka.

Jozef and Lýdia Bučko on their honeymoon in Venice, 1936. In 2002, Aunt Lydia's daughter, my cousin Jelka, helped welcome Grandfather Hodža home in her father Jozef's church, the Lutheran church in Martin. Original in Bučko family archive.

Bučko was born in 1907 into a poor farming family.[29] He studied theology, and in 1933 he became a much-loved assistant pastor in the Lutheran church in Martin, the very church in which the final funeral services for Grandfather Hodža were held three-quarters of a century later. Bučko left for a few years to serve in another town, Vrbové, and in 1936 married Lýdia (Lydka) Pivko, one of Grandmother Hodža's nieces (Family tree 2, Appendix V). The couple returned to Martin for good in 1939, the year of my birth. Their children, my cousins Milan and Jelka, were born in 1941 and 1942. This is the same Jelka who welcomed Grandfather Hodža home at the ceremonies in her father's church in Martin sixty years later (Prologue).

Bučko wrote frequently and fearlessly, both in church publications and in the secular press. On the day of Christmas Eve 1941, he wrote a long editorial for *Národnie noviny* (National News), the only remaining newspaper not strictly censored by the government. It was titled *Verím* (I Believe), and during a time when the Slovak government was squarely on the side of Nazi Germany, he publicly took as his theme Winston Churchill's famous V-for-victory sign:[30]

> In almost all cities, even in the villages, we see the letter "V." We see it on the streets, the shop windows, in movie theaters and in private homes. Walls and windows are covered with it. All of Europe, and perhaps the whole world, has chosen it as its symbol. It represents hope and strength. It is an expression of faith (*viera*), not just of victory. . . .
>
> I believe in the victory of faith in God, even if all our churches burn to ashes and faithlessness sweeps the world. I believe that justice cannot fall, that injustice cannot triumph, even if all humans abandon justice and glorify injustice. I believe that hatred will not undermine love, and good will not succumb to evil, because man will not prevail over God. Herod with all his power, fame, ability to oppress, murder, deprive individuals and nations of freedom, torture, and all his great successes will fall, even if he has the support of supplies, armies, enthusiasm, and devilish cunning. Christ will triumph with his love, forgiveness, mercy, and good, even if He sometimes has to save Himself by escaping to Egypt or retreating to the catacombs or mountain hideouts or the silence of the grave.
>
> These holidays are the voice of faith, and thus of victory and life, and good, and truth, and justice.

He railed against the treatment of Jews by the supposedly Christian Slovak Republic, and against the way the press had been taken over by the state:[31]

The secular press is losing its moral foundation and denying the principles of Christianity. When political newspapers, and many church publications as well, whip up hatred to the highest pitch, laugh at people's suffering, sate themselves with shed blood, then the press of the Lutheran Church must proclaim that the laws of humaneness must never be trod underfoot.

His views and his various actions were followed by the secret police, and at one point Bučko was jailed. When he was released, he wrote:[32]

Dear God, give me the strength to resist.... No matter what pressure, no matter what imprisonment, I cannot in the smallest way depart from Christ's principles, teaching which is my life's vocation.

Several underground political groups formed in Martin beginning in the autumn of 1943, and Bučko was involved in the very first one as an organizer and source of spiritual support and guidance. Initially, he kept his activity secret even from his wife. In time, however, the work of these organizations became apparent to all. Within twenty-four hours of the entry of German troops into Slovakia on August 29, 1944, 5000 men in the region of Martin took up arms. The German advance proved to be unrelenting, however, and a month later Martin fell. Just before the Germans took control of the town, Bučko fled across the mountains to the center of the Slovak National Uprising, Banská Bystrica. Here he volunteered with the organized army and served as a chaplain and as an orderly in the military hospital.

After the uprising was crushed and the remaining fighters fled to the mountains, Bučko hid his wife and two tiny children in a remote village. He was arrested by the Gestapo on November 2, 1944. As a member of the organized resistance, he was prepared for this eventuality and carried false identification papers. He had shaved off his beard and dressed in disguise. Thus, he could have presented himself as someone completely different. But no. When the interrogating German officer asked him, "What is your name?" he answered honestly, "I am Jozef Bučko, the Lutheran pastor of Martin." We have these words from an eyewitness who reported the event, another Lutheran pastor:[33] "I stood next to him as if frozen, because I expected that he would give his false name. I, too, had a forged identity card with me in the name of Ján Zachar, woodcutter from Brezno. When Jozef gave his true name the officer, unexpectedly civil, said, 'Pastor, you are on my list. The Slovaks are looking for you, and I cannot let you go home. You must stay here.'" The witness asked Bučko as soon as he could, "Why did you give your name?" And Bučko replied, "Ivan, when I was standing before that Gestapo officer I couldn't lie, so I told him my name openly, come what may!"

THE NIGHT AFTER BUČKO WAS ARRESTED, he was allowed to sleep in the parish house of the local Lutheran church. He could have tried to escape, but he had given his word to return to captivity and he did so without hesitation. He managed to scribble a brief note to his wife, Aunt Lydka:[34]

Dear Lydka,

I have been arrested. I am going to Bystrica for interrogation. I'm writing only briefly. Please forgive me, don't be angry at my leaving. I hope that I will return. If not, take care of our children, raise them to be good Christians. These last days I have been much on edge. Love and kisses. Give my best to everyone at home.

Jozef

My Aunt Vierka, herself a fervent member of the resistance and the uprising, saw Bučko under guard in the streets of Banská Bystrica. Shocked, she, too, pressed him for the details of his arrest, and heard from his own lips that he could not lie, no matter what.[35] He was transferred to Bratislava and from there shipped with about 250 other prisoners—Slovaks, Russian partisans, Jews, and even ethnically German citizens of Bratislava, seven truckloads altogether—to the concentraton camp at Mauthausen in nearby Austria. Along the way allied airplanes strafed the convoy. A hundred prisoners were killed or heavily wounded, but Bučko saved himself by hiding under a burning truck. Of the original 250 prisoners, only 162 reached Mauthausen, crowded with its thousands of emaciated living dead.

It is almost impossible for a modern sensibility to cope with the reality of Mauthausen.[36]

Unlike many other concentration camps, intended for all categories of prisoners, Mauthausen was mostly used for extermination through labour of the *intelligentsia*, who were educated people and members of the higher social classes in countries subjugated by the Nazi regime during World War II. . . .

The camp served the needs of the German war machine and also carried out exterminations through labour. When the inmates were totally exhausted after having worked in the quarries for 12 hours a day, or if they were too ill or too weak to work, they were then transferred to the Revier (*Krankenrevier*, sick barrack) or other places for extermination.

Although not the only concentration camp where the German authorities implemented their extermination through labour

(*Vernichtung durch Arbeit*), Mauthausen-Gusen was one of the most brutal and severe. . . .

The rock-quarry in Mauthausen was at the base of the infamous "Stairs of Death." Prisoners were forced to carry roughly-hewn blocks—often weighing as much as 50 kilograms (110 lb)—up the 186 stairs, one behind the other. . . . The SS guards would often force prisoners—exhausted from hours of hard labour without sufficient food and water—to race up the stairs carrying blocks of stone. Those who survived the ordeal would often be placed in a line-up at the edge of a cliff known as "The Parachute Wall" (German: *Fallschirmspringerwand*). At gun-point each prisoner would have the option to be shot or to push the prisoner in front of them off of the cliff. . . .

After the war, the few Slovaks who survived Mauthausen uniformly testified to Bučko's unwavering courage and spiritual strength, which served to support and inspire them all.[37] The Slovak prisoners were assigned to a work crew whose task was to clean up the nearby bombed-out village of Amstätten. They labored even at night, slept on straw, were constantly wet, inadequately fed, and plagued with lice. Bučko contracted dysentery and an inflammation in his left hand.

As the Allied front approached, the prisoners were transferred to the concentration camp at Ebensee near Salzburg, perhaps even worse than Mauthausen. Ebensee held about 18,000 prisoners, and hundreds died daily from hunger and exhaustion.[38]

The crematorium was unable to keep pace with the deaths. Naked bodies were stacked outside the barrack blocks and the crematorium itself. In the closing weeks of the war [when Bučko was there], the death rate exceeded 350 a day. To reduce congestion, a ditch was dug outside the camp, and bodies were flung into the quicklime. On a single day in April, 1945, a record eighty bodies were removed from block 23 alone; in this pile, feet were seen to be twitching. . . .

Every morning at three, Bučko's work detail was awakened, given three cups of wretched coffee substitute, walked to the train station, and transported forty kilometers to their work spot on the railroad. During the long day of heavy labor breaking up rocks, they subsisted on a lunch of soup made from potato peelings (the German SS got the potatoes). At six in the evening they were transported back to Ebensee, fed a broth made of horse bones and a small serving of bread made of bran and sawdust. Then they were allowed four to six hours of sleep before the next exhausting day started.

On the third day after his arrival at Ebensee, Bučko was admitted to the hospital and treated. The infection had spread into his arm, however, and his condition deteriorated. Here, from a fellow prisoner, is an account of what happened next:[39]

> On the 5th of May the Americans finally liberated us. As they inspected the camp and the crematoria, these battle-hardened Americans declared that this was truly a camp of death, that it was unimaginably bestial. They could not stomach this torture chamber of the Nazi regime and had it burned to the ground. . . .

> Alas, not all of us lived to see liberation. Among those who on the very day of liberation gave up the noble soul of a martyr was the Lutheran pastor Jozef Bučko, well known to all of us as a resistance fighter and the soul of the revolutionary movement of Martin. I slept in one bed with him even in Mauthausen, we supported and encouraged each other all this time.

> On May 5th I brought him the good news of liberation and the arrival of the Americans. I begged him to hold out another 24 hours until we could get some medication and effective medical help. He lived to see liberation but not to return home. He died the same day of exhaustion, even though Czech doctors tried to save him. Twelve hours after the subjugation of the German murderers at Ebensee, he breathed his last, with a prayer for a better future for Slovakia and Czechoslovakia on his lips.

Memorial plaque honoring Jozef Bučko, placed in the compound of the Lutheran church in Martin. Photo author.

CHAPTER 7

The Dream Is Shattered

My father smoked for most of his life. Cigarettes. But every so often, on a special occasion, he would light up a cigar and take at least a few puffs. In a glass-fronted cabinet in the living room of our apartment in Chicago was a large cigar that remained untouched for several years, saved for that most special of occasions, the end of World War II. On Tuesday, May 8, 1945, while the streets of London spilled over with a million revelers singing, dancing, and drinking, and Times Square in New York was so jammed that the crowd could hardly move, my father cut the cigar in half and lit the first portion. This was V-E Day, Victory in Europe, the day of Germany's unconditional surrender to the Allied powers. On August 15, V-J Day, Victory in Japan, he smoked the other half. Less than a month later he boarded a ship to England, the first leg of his journey back to Czechoslovakia.

Life in Chicago had been hard for the whole family, but it was especially so for my father. What weighed on him, even more than the grueling physical labor and the limitations imposed by his rudimentary English, was his heartache for Slovakia. He wanted nothing more than to return to his native place once again, to rebuild his business, to settle back into the tightly knit society in which he had grown up, to wander in the hills and mountains, to make a fire in the woods and roast bacon over the flames and bake potatoes in the ashes and sing. So, as soon as he possibly could, he headed for home.

Knowing that our home town of Liptovský Mikuláš (Map 3, Appendix II) had been badly damaged while the front between the retreating Germans and the advancing Russians moved back and forth across it for a month, and knowing that we might not even have a place to live, my father set out on his own to prepare the way for the rest of us. When he reached England, he found that transportation in Europe was so badly disrupted that he had to wait for a whole month before he could finally set out for Czechoslovakia.

The war had devastated much of the country and its economic base,[1] and Mikuláš had certainly not been spared. Fortunately, the building of my father's leather factory was functional, and some stores of raw materials had been preserved, so production could be restarted fairly quickly. Our house had been hit by machine gun fire but was intact, though you can see some of the bullet holes even today. Once he had set in motion what needed to be done in Mikuláš, my father returned to the United States.

AS MY FATHER SET OUT ON HIS JOURNEY HOME to Czechoslovakia, I started an adventure of my own—kindergarten. For the first time I had to get along in an English-language environment. Having reached the mature age of six, I could walk home by myself from the school, which was just two or three blocks away. The route lay through the alley behind our house where trash was deposited for pick-up—a treasure trove for me! Much to the family's dismay, I brought home many items that had called out to me to fix them. Discarded radios were my special prize. The dining room table became my temporary workbench. The radios under my repair were joined by switches, transformers, and other valuable items that my father and Uncle Miško Múdry had brought home to me, rejects from the factory's assembly line. As an adult scientist, I always enjoyed building simple apparatus for my experiments. Perhaps this is where it all started, on the dining room table in Chicago.

During the second half of 1946, after two years of evading the Nazis in France and four years of eking out a living in Chicago, our family finally organized to return home. At the age of seven I would, for the first time, experience the home my parents loved so dearly. They started to describe for me what this might be like. We would have our own house, I was told. I would have my own room and not just a cot in my parents' bedroom. There would be a huge yard and lots of cousins to play with, and the air would be cool and clean. We would spend our summers in the mountains. In short, a paradise.

Before we left Chicago there was a small going-away party in our apartment. Uncle Miško brought his new pride and joy, a recording machine. This was a bulky affair with a turntable that firmly held blank plastic discs, bright red, while it turned them under a heavy arm fitted with a cutting needle. You would talk into a microphone, and the machine would make a 78 rpm record lasting about three minutes on each side. I have five of these records, so I know that I was the star of the party, the bold interviewer. This is how it went:

"Speaking into the microphone are Uncle Langsfeld and little Johnny Palka. So, Uncle Emil, how was your vacation?"

"Our vacation? Well, let me tell you what sort of animal we saw, that had legs on its back and a tail on its snout!"

"I know. It was a fish."

"You don't believe me? It wasn't a fish, it was on dry land."

"Then I don't know. I've never heard of such an animal."

"It was a bear lying on its back, with its legs sticking up in the air! And this was way out west, in Yellowstone Park.'

"I know, Yellowstone National Park. I read about it in a newspaper or magazine. There was a bear, and he was standing there with a cup, and people were giving him things, somehow he managed to stop everyone who was going by . . . . "

I discoursed about my expectations of my home-to-be, recited poetry, and sang songs in both Slovak and English. My Slovak was simple but flawless, my English was fluent but heavily accented.

What would a boy of seven sing, without forewarning or preparation, for his Slovak family and friends in the middle of Chicago, and for the cousins he would soon meet at home? I initially sang a couple of church songs in English, but my voice was tremulous. Then Uncle Dišo asked, "Don't you know some Slovak songs? Some livelier ones?"

"Only *Hej, Slováci* and *Nad Tatrou sa blýska*," I replied, these being the most frequently sung Slovak patriotic song and the national anthem. "Mama taught me others, but I've forgotten them."

"So sing *Hej, Slováci*."

And out poured a full-throated rendition, loud, on pitch, rhythmic, full of life:

Hej, Slováci, ešte naša slovenská rec žije,
dokial' naše verné srdce za náš národ bije:
žije, žije duch slovenský, bude žiť na veky,
hrom a peklo! márne vaše proti nám sú vzteky.

O Slovaks, our Slovak language still lives,
while our faithful heart for our nation still beats:
it lives, it lives that Slovak spirit, and will live forever,
thunder and hell! vain is your fury against us.

There was no doubt about which song had captured my boyish heart!

AFTER ALL THE FAREWELLS, we took a train to New York, where we stayed for a few days in Aunt Gláša's tiny apartment. During the war years, she had attended nursing school at St. Catherine's University in Rochester, Minnesota, and I well remember driving from Chicago to see her graduate in her resplendent robes. Now she was working as a nurse in a big New York City hospital and had decided to remain in America.

Then came our transatlantic voyage on the S.S. America, the largest passenger liner ever built in the United States and just recently released from service as a troop ship. The December crossing was rough, and I was seasick. We stopped briefly in Southampton, England, disembarked in the French port of Cherbourg, and went on from there by train. What should have been an overnight journey from Paris to Prague took a day and a half. The train was dirty and cold, the food was awful, and I was sick. When we finally reached Prague, we were met by my father's youngest brother, Uncle Dušan, who took us home to his apartment, where I promptly went to bed, snuggled in under the thickest, lightest, whitest quilts you can imagine. It was Christmas 1946.

After a few days in Prague we hurried home to Slovakia (Maps 2 and 3). Since our house in Mikuláš was still being repaired, we stayed for some time with Aunt Ludinka in her apartment in Bratislava. Before fully settling in, we went to meet other members of the family as well. What I remember best is the country villa in Benice. Benice is a small village (today's population is around 300) with a recorded history dating back to the thirteenth century. Grandmother Hodža came from a well-to-do farming family of that region, and her youngest sister, Aunt Mária—the mother of Jozef Bučko's wife, Aunt Lydka—owned a modest-sized agricultural operation, which she ran from the villa with an iron will. Hogs, sheep, cattle, and chickens were slaughtered there; sausages made; hams cured; and all manner of country delicacies prepared that were prized far and wide.[2] For years, children from our family had come to visit Aunt Mária for a taste of the country life.

The day we traveled to Benice, the snow was heavy and our car made slow headway. By the time we arrived, it was nightfall. Oil lamps had been set out at the gate to mark the way for us in the dark.[3] The house, hundreds of years old with masonry walls two feet thick and covered with whitewashed plaster, was festive. There were lights and Christmas decorations everywhere, and the heavy old table was covered with a crisp, white tablecloth and laden with generous helpings of Aunt Mária's fabled food. The room I slept in had a huge tile stove in the corner, and the bed, like the one in Prague, was covered with downy quilts. This was a far cry from our narrow, second-floor apartment in Chicago, with its thin, wallpapered walls, its noisy radiators, and a couple of blankets for the night! It was even a far cry from the images I had conjured up back in Chicago. This was like a fairy-tale dream.

Once we returned to Bratislava, it was time for me to start school, and this I found difficult. I didn't know any of the other children. I was unfamiliar with classroom etiquette, like standing up when the teacher came in. My classmates were all writing cursive, whereas in my school in Chicago, the teachers had taught us only how to block print. There was another challenge: The Bratislava students were using old-style quill pens with split metal nibs that needed to be dipped in an inkwell, and all I knew how to use was a pencil. Night after night I sat at a little desk in the big study in Aunt Ludinka's apartment while my mother patiently helped me to catch up. My handwriting was terrible and stayed that way for years. I was very glad when the school year was over.

By that time our house in Mikuláš had been fixed up, and we could move in. I did get a small room of my own. I could spread out the toys we had brought from America, especially the electric train set whose tracks could be arranged in various ways and the locomotive made to speed up, slow down, stop, or reverse by means of a knob on the transformer. I started to make friends with boys who came over to play, whether with my toys or in the huge, grassy backyard with trees at the back and bushes along the side fence. And in the summer, we did indeed go up to the mountains.

THE TATRA MOUNTAINS that form part of the border between Slovakia and Poland are compact, but also tall and extremely rugged. A small chain of resort towns and spas catering to the wealthy of Hungary had been built at intermediate elevations starting in the nineteenth century,[4] and in the 1920s Grandfather and Grandmother Hodža had bought a picturesque house on a sizeable piece of property on the outskirts of one of them, Tatranská Lomnica. This became the summer retreat for the entire extended family. The adults came and went as they had time, but the younger generations spent most of the warm months there, often bringing their friends. There could be as many as twenty people of all ages gathered for a week, and Grandmother Hodža presided over the entire assemblage. You can ask anyone in any branch of my family for a favorite memory, and a story about Lomnica is guaranteed to come forth, often involving Grandfather Hodža, who used to come for brief periods from Prague.

I spent much of the summer of 1947 in Lomnica with three cousins just slightly younger than I: Aunt Ludinka's son, Karol, and Aunt Lydka's two children, Milan and Jelka. The miniature teepee we had brought from America was set up on the lawn, and the four of us took turns wearing the colorful Native American feather headdress that trailed all the way down to the ground. Then there were the cap pistols, genuine toy Colt revolvers with long barrels and bullet chambers that you could turn. I was the proud owner of all these treasures, much envied by the others! We improvised bows and arrows out of local materials. Back in the woods, it was more serious. Remnants of World War II were still to be found, including machine gun barrels and grenades. Needless to say, we had strict orders not to touch them.

Happy days for the Lomnica counsins, summer 1947 or 1948. From right to left: Karol Pavlů, son of Aunt Ludinka (my father's sister) and of the attorney and resistance member, Dr. Karol Pavlů; Milan Bučko, son of Lýdia Bučko and Jozef Bučko; and I. Author's archive.

When there was a lull in our great battles, we held foot races and played other games. In town we could go to the tennis courts that had been my mother's favorites when she was a teenager, or to a swimming pool, or for an ice cream treat. In the evenings there might be a bonfire, especially if my father was there. Once the ash pile was big enough, potatoes wrapped in wet newspaper were buried in it to bake. A slab of bacon was sliced into thick pieces, and each piece deeply incised from the free edge. A forked stick, each of its two prongs sharpened with a pocket knife, was pushed in through the skin, so the slice, now a row of stubby fingers of meat and fat, could be held securely over the fire. The fat dripped into the flames, and soon the fingers fanned out around the forked stick. Bacon fried in a pan never tasted like this! Thickly sliced bread could be toasted, held over the fire by a similar forked stick, then flavored with bacon drippings. As we nibbled on these delicacies, we sang folk songs endlessly. This was the gay times of the 1920s and 1930s on a small scale, the paradise my parents had promised me.

Back home in Mikuláš, I attended second grade in the Lutheran school, the same school that my father had attended when he was a boy. It was just a few blocks away from our house so I could easily walk there, either with him or with a neighbor boy, my best friend, Ivan Rázus. School hours were from 8:00 a.m. until noon and from 2:00 to 4:00 in the afternoon. During the long lunch break, everyone went home for the main meal of the day. After school was playtime, then a substantial tea whose main feature was toasted bread rubbed with garlic and goose fat. This kept even active boys filled until dinner around 8:00. Between tea and dinner was time for homework, and soon after dinner came bed.

During the winter, which is very cold in Mikuláš, I had my first experience with winter sports. We made a skating rink in the front yard, a rectangle edged with compacted snow and flooded with water to make a lovely frozen surface. We could skate most any afternoon. There was skiing as well. I had a pair of long, wooden skis with cable bindings and bottoms that had to be coated with a hard, dark wax smelling like the trees of the evergreen forest. Almost every winter day I would gulp my lunch as quickly as I was allowed, put on my skis, and stride the length of the backyard, out the rear gate, over the railway tracks, and on to the great hill just beyond the edge of town. I would zigzag up through the woods for a bit, cross over to the open slope, and glide straight down. If there was time, I'd do it again. Then I hurried back for the afternoon session of school.

And so the days passed. My parents were happy. They spent time fixing up the house, making plans for planting a garden, entertaining family and friends from whom they had been separated for so long. My father was immersed in rebuilding his business, a factory that made a variety of leather goods, particularly elegant items like briefcases and ladies handbags. This was the continuation of the family business that had started many generations earlier as a leather tannery. I went with him a few times to see what he was doing, and was amazed at the huge machines, the clanging and rasping noises, and the variety of useful and beautiful leather objects that emerged.

CLOUDS, HOWEVER, WERE GATHERING. The Democratic Party, formed during the heady days of the Slovak National Uprising, had swept the elections of 1946 in Slovakia with an unprecedented sixty-two percent of the vote, but the Communist Party had done well in the Czech lands; in the coalition government it had taken over a number of crucial ministries, including the Ministry of the Interior with its police powers. Through street demonstrations, political maneuvering, and effective threats the Communists took control of one ministry after another, until by February of 1948 they had gained *de facto* control of the government. They called it the "Victorious February," *Víťazný február.*[5]

The consequences for democracy in Czechoslovakia were all too apparent. Almost immediately, voices of dissent were silenced and politically motivated arrests began to take place. Despite his long history of trust in the Soviet Union, President Beneš resigned. Frail and disconsolate, he died a few months later. Under threat of persecution, several of the principal leaders of the Democratic

Party escaped across the border to the West. Others elected to stay behind and were imprisoned by the Communists for many years.[6] All were close friends of our family. And we, like they, were vulnerable to the heavy hand of the Communist state.

On April 6, 1948, not even a year after our return to Mikuláš and barely three months after the Communist coup, four unknown men knocked on the door of our house and asked to be let in. One of them later came outside where I was playing and asked me to show him how to start our car. I did it, proud to show that I knew how. I had no idea, of course, that these men were from the secret police and had come to search the house for suspicious materials and to confiscate the car. Two days later, my father was arrested and taken away to prison in Bratislava.

For weeks there was no news of him. Then came the first postcard, dated May 8, 1948. It was addressed and written to me, though it seems to have been meant mainly for my mother. My father wrote:

Dear Pikulík [that is what he called me when I was little],

Maybe I will be home soon. I just have to wait for a man who said various things about me that he has to explain, but he won't be here until Wednesday. I really want to be home so we can play together again.

Your Daddy

Then on May 15 he wrote,

I thought that the man who said all those things about me would be here last week, but he still hasn't come. Nobody has come to see me, not the lawyer, not Mama, not Aunt Ludinka. I hope that someone will come to visit me this week.

What he didn't know, of course, was that both my mother and his sister, Aunt Ludinka, had tried frantically to see him, and had been refused.

Isolated in prison, wrongly accused, held by a system of which justice could not be expected, my father must have found it a frightening and numbing experience. Fortunately, on July 3, three months after his arrest, he was released. After this our life was never the same, even though in the summer of 1948 we again went to Lomnica and in the fall I returned to school. Unbeknownst to me, my parents were now looking for a way of leaving Czechoslovakia again, a way to go into a final exile.

CHAPTER 8

Under the Barbed Wire

First my parents tried to leave the country legally. They applied for passports, for exit permits, for American visas. They took the paintings off the walls and, together with other precious possessions, had them packed in crates. They made endless trips to Bratislava and to Prague, sat forever in shabby government offices. But everything moved very slowly, and nothing was certain.

With the Communists firmly in power, no response from the democratic West, new arrests every day, confiscations of property all around us, and no progress on obtaining passports and exit permits, our situation was precarious. Then came whispered word that my father was to be arrested again. There was no more waiting for documents. We had to leave as quickly as possible; we had to try to escape under the barbed wire as many had done already.

Once my father came back from prison to Mikuláš, he was a watched man. Trying to find an escape route, which would have to be through far-off Bratislava, was particularly hazardous. Most critically, escape required finding a guide who would take us across the border and not betray us. This could only be done by word of mouth, and the more people who knew of our intent, the greater the danger of betrayal. It also required collecting a large amount of money to pay the guide. I do not know how much we were charged, but I can make a guess. A Catholic nun who was part of an underground network helping priests to cross the border, and who escaped herself about a year after we did, told her story grippingly in the book, *The Deliverance of Sister Cecilia*.[1] She paid 15,000 crowns per person, then about three months' salary for an average Slovak. With my father's prominent position and affluence, we undoubtedly paid more. Accumulating perhaps a year's salary or more in cash without arousing suspicion, especially since my father was being watched, must have been daunting and nerve-wracking. It was later estimated that about one third of the population in Communist countries served as informers, so caution would have been essential even if my father had not so obviously been under close observation.

My health provided a bit of a cover for my mother. As a child, I was prone to chest infections and went through several bouts of pneumonia in Chicago. This was at a time when antibiotics were not yet available, and pneumonia could be life threatening. Tuberculosis, another dangerous and basically untreatable condition, was also suspected. This proved to be a stroke of good fortune because, without arousing suspicion in Mikuláš, my mother could take me to Bratislava every few weeks to see a doctor for my continuing cough, and use the occasion to make arrangements for our escape. Of course, I knew nothing whatever about these machinations. We did indeed go to see doctors and have TB tests done. When pricked with needles carrying the test material, the skin on my arm swelled up and itched, which worried both the doctors and my parents. Only in my late teens did I outgrow this false-positive reaction.

FINALLY THE CRITICAL DAY CAME. This is how I remember it, with some filling in by members of my family who shared in the experience. It was springtime, and the weather was unpleasant. We took the drafty, noisy train from Mikuláš to Bratislava yet again, and went as usual to Aunt Ludinka's apartment. But that evening we also visited Aunt Lydka's sister, Aunt Marieta. With the curtains carefully closed, my mother set to repacking our luggage, making sure that each suitcase held some clothing for each member of the family. Marieta's husband, Uncle Otko, was to take them to the train station and ship them to Brno (Map 2, Appendix II), from where they would be forwarded to a prearranged address in Austria. It must have been a sad reminder of the first time my mother escaped from Slovakia, when her carefully packed suitcase, with clothes for herself and her unborn child, could not accompany her and ended up far away in Yugoslavia with the family of Janko Bulík.

A little later, still in the early evening, we put on our coats and took a bus to Petržalka. Today Petržalka is a massive suburban development with huge apartment buildings and shopping centers that dominate the skyline, but then it was still a large but sleepy village across the main bridge over the Danube. There was a park along the river, as well as many small houses, cottages, and scattered orchards. We got on the dimly lit, crowded bus, trying to look like any of the other families returning home after working in Bratislava during the day. That meant just a briefcase for my father and a purse for my mother. Into these my parents packed whatever we had that was small and valuable: watches, jewelry, a couple of cameras, gold coins, cash. Later, selling these items would have to sustain us because no one would be able to work. We wore extra clothing since we could not carry suitcases or packs of any sort.

In Petržalka we got off the bus in the dark and went to a cottage, a prearranged place to wait. "Soon we will be like Indians," my mother explained to me quietly. "We'll go out into the woods and over the fields as quietly as possible, so that no one will see us. There will be no talking, not even whispering. You watch the grown-ups. That way you'll know what to do. Guides will show us the way." I had read many stories about Indians, so this suited me just fine. In fact, for a boy of ten it was exciting.

After some time a guide arrived and silently led us out into the nearby woods. We were joined by a few other people, brought by another guide. The moon was bright, nearly full, and high in the sky—good for making our way without flashlights, but good, too, for being seen by others. It was dangerously light for crossing the border. Our group, about eight in number, stopped and sat, huddled against the tree trunks, and watched the sky. No one spoke. It was chilly, for it was only March and spring comes late to the heart of Central Europe. The branches of the trees were outlined sharply against the sky. Then, slowly, wisps of clouds began to blur the outline of the moon, and a mist gathered low to the ground. The time passed excruciatingly slowly, the mist grew thicker and thicker, and still we waited. The dimmer the moonlight and the thicker the mist, the safer would be our crossing.

It must have been well after midnight when the signal to move was finally given. We followed the two guides to the edge of the woods, and there we saw an expanse of open space ahead of us. This was the no-man's-land: a wide swath stripped of all vegetation, plowed, and split down the middle by a barbed wire fence. Every few hundred feet there was a tall watchtower, manned by soldiers and equipped with searchlights and machine guns. We would have to cross this open and heavily guarded space undetected.

By now the mist was heavy enough that the nearest tower was barely visible, and another member of our group some twenty feet from me disappeared almost completely from my sight. This was good. Even if one of us were spotted, the others would have a chance to scatter. The low visibility brought its own dangers, however, because only the guides knew where we were going. It was vital that, while out of sight of each other, we stay connected. The guides, one at the front and the other at the back, stretched a long cord between them, and each of us held on to it tightly as we proceeded.

The searchlights scanned the ground, round and round. We ran while our patch of ground was in shadow, struggling to keep our footing over the big clods of plowed earth. As soon as the beam swung in our direction, we dropped to the ground. Once, twice, over and over, the beams circled. We were always at risk that the path of the beam would be readjusted and we would be spotted. Even to a ten-year-old boy playing Indian, this felt real and scary.

Suddenly, we came to the fence, and one of the guides forced two of the barbed wires apart so we could crawl between them. On the other side, the naked, plowed-up stretch of no-man's-land was just as wide and just as dangerous, and we continued our deadly dance with the sweeping searchlights. Finally we reached the shelter of forest again, this time in Austria. We waited until the whole party had made it across. Then we walked on to a cottage that was part of the escape route. My mother put me to bed under a thick quilt, and I slept soundly until the morning.

Our escape was not yet over. The region of Austria adjacent to the Czechoslovak border was under the control of the Russians, and we could still be arrested any moment. Vienna was not far away—too far to walk, but not long by car or bus. After the war, Vienna had been divided into sectors, each occupied by one of the victorious Allied powers: the United States, Britain, France, and the Soviet Union. Our escape had been well organized, and someone was available to drive our family into Vienna, where we boarded a city bus that crossed from one sector into another. At the crossing, the bus would be stopped and inspected by the border patrol. We carried forged papers, identification cards that showed us to be an Austrian family living in the Russian sector but working in the American sector. My father's Viennese German was flawless, because in his youth he had studied in Vienna. He would do whatever talking was necessary. My orders were not to say a word under any circumstances. I couldn't talk to my mother, who sat next to me. I couldn't read anything, for the language in my book would give us away. We couldn't even hold hands for fear that any sign of emotion might attract attention. So, I looked intently out the window of the bus and put my attention on the cars in the streets, trying to figure out their makes as I had enjoyed doing in Chicago. When the inspector came, he paused to look at me but didn't say anything. Once we were in the American sector, I finally spotted some familiar American cars!

The same day we took a train from Vienna, embedded in the Russian zone of Austria, to Innsbruck, in the French zone. Many refugees from Communism were caught while trying to leave the Russian zone, but once again forged papers served us well. We arrived safely in this beautiful, old city in the valley of the Inn River amidst the Tyrolean Alps. A turn-of-the-century cable railway, whose base station was right in the city, took us to our lodgings in a mountain inn called the Alpengasthof Gramarthof, near the resort village of Hungerburg. I remember it well. The thick steel cable ran between the rails and pulled one car up from the city on the single set of tracks while the other car descended from the upper station in Hungerburg. Right in the middle, the track divided into two so the cars could pass each other. The inn, expanded and modernized, still exists and is easily found on the internet;[2] in fact, our daughter Tanya and her family were recently able to visit there. When I started writing this book, Hungerburg was still reached by the old cable railway. In December 2007 a new rail line was opened along a different route. It is an architectural marvel of fluid shapes, almost as much an attraction to tourists as are the stunning mountain scenery and the endless opportunities for outdoor activities.[3] We remained at the Alpengasthof Grammarthof for most of the nine months it took to obtain visas for returning to the United States.

The United Nations Refugee and Repatriation Agency (UNRRA) operated a camp in Innsbruck, providing shelter and food for the many refugees moving about the city who had made their way from nations behind the newly-established Iron Curtain. There was a flourishing black market, where the refugees sold valuables for the cash they needed to survive. It was a dark and chaotic time, and perhaps the authorities looked the other way. Every so often, two or three of the men in our party would take the cable railway from our refuge in Hungerburg, down the steep mountainside into Innsbruck. They would hide another item from our own stash of valuables in a briefcase or a pocket, sell it on the black market, and bring back cash that would pay the lodging and board for the next period of time. As to the suitcases that my mother had so carefully repacked just before we walked to the bus headed for Petržalka, never to return again—did they ever reach us, or did we have to buy fresh clothing? I don't know.

AT THE GRAMARTHOF THE ATMOSPHERE was quite jolly. The sleeping quarters were upstairs. The downstairs dining room was always filled with cigarette smoke, and the wooden benches and chairs around the tables were rarely empty. The adults sat for hours playing cards, mostly a popular game called *Preferans* that's played with large and ornate European cards, much more elegant than the decks we use in America. Later, we took the cards with us to America. On weekends it would become quite festive. Families came from all around, the women in bright costumes with embroidered skirts and blouses with puffy sleeves, and men in traditional *Lederhosen*, leather shorts greasy from years of use and sporting a wide flap in front. They were held up by fancy, embroidered suspenders and decorated with shiny metal buttons. The outfit was completed by a white shirt and a green felt hat sporting feathers. If it was chilly, the visitors might come wearing a Loden coat, the traditional design of green felt that really keeps the wind out. They danced to lively accordion music, slapping their hands, thighs and kicked-up heels in complicated rhythms in the *Schuhplattler*, the "shoe-slapper."

Alpengasthof Gramarthof, above Innsbruck, our refuge for most of nine months after our escape from Czechoslovakia in 1949. Author's archive.

It must have been a challenge for my parents and the other adults to keep a ten-year-old boy occupied every day. They invented many things. Some days we braided thin, smooth twigs together, formed them into Native American-style headbands, and then went into the woods looking for suitable feathers. One of the men in our party made me a "radio," a small wooden cabinet, nicely joined together and with a sloping front panel. He showed me how to make a silky smooth finish on the wood by scraping the surface with shards of broken glass. No matter that there was nothing inside, it was still a radio.

My mother taught me to play Battleships, a game that occupied us for long periods. It required nothing more than a couple of pieces of paper and pencils, even though these days you can buy a plastic version for a small bundle of money. We played indoors and out, in all kinds of weather. This was not new for my mother. Even in the back of the diary she kept after I was born in Paris she drew the two ten-by-ten grids of a game of Battleships, but they are blank. I wonder what interrupted her game then.

During the summer, as the weather turned balmy, we spent more and more time outside. The Tyrolean Alps are beautiful and walking paths are everywhere, so we spent a lot of time in the woods. Often we collected bright and delicious chanterelles that grew there abundantly. Mushroom hunting is a favorite pastime in Central Europe, and several edible species are known and loved by nearly everyone. I can still taste those chanterelles, lightly pan fried in butter!

Austrians are great walkers. All the more popular excursion sites sold brightly embossed metal medallions, badges that represented mountain achievements, for hikers to nail on their walking sticks. I had a small collection myself. This is still a custom. Our daughter Tanya and her family spent three years in northern Italy in the late 1990s. When they visited Austria, they bought a walking stick and a few medallions.

My parents were extraordinarily good at keeping the danger we were in from my awareness. I don't remember any great sense of fear during our escape under the barbed wire or any public jubilation once we were safe. I remember mostly fun from our stay in Austria and excitement at the prospect of returning to America. In hindsight, I realize that disaster threatened at every turn. The guides had to be found and paid, not a simple task when there were many eyes watching us, ready to report anything suspicious to the police. These guides were mostly mercenaries playing a dangerous but lucrative game, and we would have to trust them not to betray us. The border crossing went well for us, but other families trying to escape by the same route a few days before and a few days after us were caught and turned back. Who knows what happened to them.

During our time in Austria, we lived by illegal means—selling smuggled goods on the illegal black market. We could have been arrested at any time. We also could have run out of items to sell and thus out of money on which to live. We hoped to get back to America, but our paperwork was partly lost and partly mixed up, and with immigration quotas now in place, there was no guarantee that we would ever be admitted. Despite all this, both my parents maintained a cheerful front with me, never revealing what was weighing on them. Looking back, I see that this was truly a gift!

These are childhood memories, and I have often wondered how accurate they are. For our life in Austria, I have photographs to confirm what my mind conjures up, but for the central event, slipping under the barbed wire, I had nothing—until June of 2006.

Living in Bratislava is Uncle Zdeno Jurenka, whose grandmother was the sister of my grandmother Darina Pálka, née Jurenka (Family tree 3, Appendix V). Zdeno is about ten years older than I, long retired from his job as a bank accountant, and acutely interested in family history. One day I went to see him to glean as much about Grandmother Pálka's family as I could. As the conversation meandered, we rather incidentally got on the topic of our escape, and then the bombshell dropped. He was there with us!

At the time he was a young man of twenty. His older brother, Ivo, whom I remember well from Austria, was escaping with us and, in fact, had been the main organizer. He lived in Bratislava and thus was much better able to find guides, contact them, and negotiate all the details than my mother, who came only periodically from far-off Mikuláš. He and Zdeno made the trip to Petržalka, met us there, waited with us in the woods, crawled up to the barbed wire. At that point Ivo went on with us, and Zdeno turned back.

I had never, ever imagined that I would meet someone who was a participant in that fateful night. After recovering somewhat from my amazement, I probed for details, trying to check my own memories against his. We agreed on everything except one point—where our whole group gathered. I remembered meeting up in the woods, but Zdeno explained that we met in the village in a safe house to which everyone could be given directions. This was important, as it was nighttime and finding each other in the woods would have been difficult at best. From there we all went together.

So, I have told you a true story, engraved in two independent memories for over sixty years.

CHAPTER 9

Living and Dying in the Communist Nightmare

My parents and I were safe now in the democratic West, but most of the rest of our family stayed behind in Communist Czechoslovakia. My parents had urged Grandmother Hodža to escape with us, but she refused—she was afraid that at her age she would not be able to run over the rough clods of the no man's land and crawl under the barbed wire, and thus would place us in unnecessary danger. After we were outside the country, my parents managed to arrange a separate escape for her, but she decided firmly that she would only leave Czechoslovakia legally. Confident that this would be possible, she applied repeatedly for a passport and an exit permit, but each time her request was turned down. The new "workers' paradise" refused to let an elderly widow join her family. In the meantime, the Iron Curtain grew ever tighter, and an illegal escape became unthinkable. My grandmother was now stranded in a cruel system while all of her children, her only grandchild, and her husband's remains were unreachably far away.

Grandmother Hodža had lived with us in Mikuláš. At the time of our departure, our house had been rented to friends, and she continued to have a room of her own there. Within a short time, however, the house was confiscated, and for the next several years she lived with other family friends in Mikuláš.[1] In 1957, after suffering two strokes, she moved to Martin to be with to be with two of her nieces, my aunts Vierka and Zorka (Family tree 2, Appendix V), who had spent many summers in Lomnica and had also lived with the Hodžas while studying in Prague. They took care of her until she died in 1961. She was buried in the Slovak National Cemetery in Martin in a ceremony at which the secret police were said to outnumber the grieving family. Stories about her funeral circulate to the present day. On a visit in 2012, we heard additional details from a young man who had himself heard them from eye witnesses. Apparently, the Communist government tried to keep the news of my grandmother's death and funeral secret for fear that it would arouse memories of the freedom represented by inter-war Czechoslovakia. However, word got out anyway, and the funeral proved to be the largest the cemetery had yet known. And yes, the secret police were recognized as being a large part of the crowd.

EVEN BEFORE THE COMMUNISTS GAINED FULL CONTROL of the government on February 25, 1948, they had launched a coordinated attack on the Democratic Party and on its leaders.[2] As early as September 1947, Czechoslovak State Security (*Štátna bezpečnost, ŠtB*), an organ of the Ministry of the Interior which was already in Communist hands, claimed to discover evidence of widespread crimes against the state. More than 700 people were arrested. Leaders of the Democratic Party that had swept the elections of 1946 were indicted. Among them were the wartime democratic leaders of the Slovak National Council and the Slovak National Uprising: Jozef Lettrich, now chairman of the Democratic Party; Ján Ursíny, now deputy prime minister of Czechoslovakia; and Matej Josko, now Slovak commissioner for finance. Others included my Uncle Dišo, Fedor Hodža, now general secretary of the Democratic Party. Formal charges were filed against Uncle Dišo; one of Ursíny's office staff was arrested, and others were fired; Josko was physically asssaulted. All of this happened in rapid succession, and shortly thereafter Ursíny was coerced into resigning his position as deputy prime minister. The entire democratic leadership was in personal danger.

Jan Masaryk, who had spoken so eloquently at Grandfather Hodža's funeral in Chicago, had been foreign minister in the Czechoslovak government-in-exile headed by President Beneš; he was now the foreign minister of post-war Czechoslovakia. On March 10, 1948, barely two weeks after the Communist coup, he was found dead, sprawled on the pavement beneath the bathroom window of his apartment in the Prague Castle, dressed only in mismatched pajamas. Suddenly, this widely respected voice for democracy and for strong ties to the West was gone. Did he commit suicide, as the Communist government immediately claimed, or was he murdered? Most scholars believe that he was murdered, either by Czechoslovak or by Soviet agents, but no unambiguous evidence has ever been provided.[3]

After their 1948 coup the Communists held unrestricted power, and they used it to the full. As many as 28,000 state employees were thrown out of their positions, accused of being reactionary agitators. A quarter of the university students, about 7,000, were expelled. Arrests began, with charges fabricated for convenience. Lettrich, Josko, and Fedor Hodža escaped across the border to the West. Ursíny, who decided to stay, was arrested and, in a show trial of the "anti-state conspiracy" that had suppposedly been uncovered the previous September, was sentenced to seven years in prison. My father was arrested in

April. One of the several charges brought against him was that he must have known about the impending flight of Lettrich and Hodža, who was his wife's brother, and had failed in his duty to alert the authorities.

THE WORLD MY PARENTS AND I HAD LEFT BEHIND was bizarre and dangerous not only for opponents of the regime, but for Communist leaders as well.[4] Starting in April 1950, two years after the Communists took power, the leaders who had implemented the Communist coup in Czechoslovakia were themselves subjected to unrelenting persecution. The first assault was against the three Communist members of the wartime Slovak National Council, Karol Šmidke, Ladislav Novomeský, and Gustav Husák.[5] In 1950 these three, who had been ardent Communists for decades, were accused of being "bourgeois nationalists" and were expelled from the Communist Party. Šmidke was sidelined into a minor position and died in December 1952. Husák and Novomeský were arrested, interrogated, and tortured. The trial dragged on for three years. In 1954 both were found guilty of espionage, sabotage, and treason. Husák, who had resisted heroically throughout the trial, was sentenced to life imprisonment; Novomeský received a sentence of ten years.

The prosecution of Šmidke, Novomeský, and Husák was initially conducted not by the national government but within the structure of the all-powerful Communist Party. The orchestrator of the prosecution was Rudolf Slánský, the party's general secretary. His position in the party made Slánský the second most powerful man in Czechoslovakia after the president, Klement Gottwald. Slánský and Gottwald vied with each other for demonstrating their loyalty to Stalin, as well as for personal power. In an ironic twist of fate, in November 1951, the arch-prosecutor Slánský and thirteen others were arrested and themselves charged with anti-state conspiracy. It was the most notorious and celebrated show trial of the entire Communist period in Czechoslovakia. Tortured repeatedly, all fourteen confessed to every one of the detailed, but entirely fabricated, charges brought against them. In court they read aloud the texts that had been prepared for them by the prosecutors. Ultimately, three of them were given life sentences; eleven, including Slánský, were hung.

In the later 1950s, many of the convicted and jailed Communist leaders of the wartime naational uprising were freed. Over the years they, and ultimately even some of the democrats, were rehabilitated—their innocence was declared by formal court action.

Trials like this affected our family directly. Aunt Zorka's fiancée, Miloš Frkáň (Uncle Milo), had fought in the Slovak National Uprising with one its most charismatic leaders, Viliam Žingor.[6] Uncle Milo had been in charge of obtaining supplies for Žingor's group, which required feeling out who among the villagers might be willing to provide food and other materials in secret; he also took part in some disruptive actions—destroying bridges, railway lines, and so forth. After the war Žingor, initially a committed Communist, recognized the utterly despotic nature of the regime he saw operating all around him and turned against it, taking to the hills once again. Ultimately, he was captured, tried, and hung. Uncle Milo, too, was arrested and convicted for failing to report to the authorities his former commander and now personal friend, Žingor. He was sentenced to four and a half years, which he served in various prisons, including the worst of them all, the uranium mines at Jáchymov. He and Aunt Zorka were married after his release. During the liberal period of the Prague Spring in 1968, Uncle Milo was finally officially rehabilitated.

EVEN THE MOST MINOR PRIVATE ACTIVITIES outside the state system were forbidden. For instance, the farm women who used to sell spare produce in Mikuláš were no longer allowed to do so. More than once Grandmother Hodža wrote to Aunt Lýdia asking for simple food supplies from Benice to supplement what she was able to buy, because supplies in the state stores were insufficient.

Private property was no longer sacrosanct. The Communists established stringent rules regarding accommodations, prescribing how many square meters each person would be allowed in any living quarters. If there was too much space per person, renters were assigned by the state, and the owner had no voice in the matter. Suddenly, a person could find they were sharing the bathroom with someone unknown, someone who was potentially a police informer. The only way to avoid such a situation was for extended families to crowd together tightly enough that total strangers could not be forced in. Once someone was assigned, that person had rights of residency. Aunt Zorka's family, for example, was assigned a laborer who worked in the newly-developed tank factory in Martin. Subsequently, he married, and he and his wife had two children. This family of four then occupied the main part of the house, including the kitchen and bathroom. The two parents (Aunt Zorka and Uncle Milo), their young daughter, and Aunt Zorka's mother were left with just two rooms, a toilet, and a hotplate—and it was their house!

Often the property was taken away altogether. Many families were impacted by the so-called Action-B (*Akcia-B*), a policy by which the properties of bourgeois city-dwellers were confiscated and the former owners shipped to outlying villages where they were assigned to any ramshackle dwellings that might be available. Generally there was no employment in the villages for these urban exiles, so they had to commute to the closest town for whatever work they had been assigned. Educational opportunities for their children were minimal.

This is precisely what happened to Aunt Ludinka. Her husband, a lawyer who had been active in the Uprising, had died of a liver ailment immediately after the war, so she was a single mother. The small apartment building where my parents and I had stayed when we first arrived in Bratislava after the war was her property. It was confiscated almost immediately after the Communist coup, but she and her son, Karol, were allowed to stay in one of the apartments. Then came Action-B. In 1952, when Karol was around eleven years old, they were told to leave Bratislava and relocate to the village of Il'anovo near Mikuláš. They arrived in Il'anovo in the bitter cold of winter with the few suitcases they could carry, and they remained there for three years. Then in 1955, after the deaths of Stalin and Gottwald, the political situation eased a little, and Aunt Ludinka and Karol were allowed to return to Bratislava. Aunt Mária's family farm in Benice was likewise confiscated and the family relocated.

Ostensibly, Action-B was meant to remove class-based differences in opportunity. In reality it was a mechanism for suppressing the influence of anyone who might challenge the thought-hegemony of the state.

RAISING CHILDREN UNDER COMMUNIST RULE represented a wrenching dilemma for democratically-minded parents, as my family well remembers. If a child was allowed to hear the truth about the Communist regime discussed in the home, there was always the danger that they would inadvertently carry the discussion to their school and thereby place the entire family in danger of retribution. The parents would be in danger of interrogation, loss of jobs, and potentially imprisonment. The child's own future would be jeopardized— they might be expelled from school or prohibited from any advanced education. On the other hand, if the parents kept silent about the reality of the world around them, their children would have no way of knowing anything that was not filtered through the ideology of the Communist Party; their children would be, effectively, brainwashed. Of course, political resistance did take place, and independent thinking was not altogether lost, but the pressure for obedience was huge and oppressive.

The Communist regime often used educational opportunities for children as a lever to gain the cooperation of their parents. Most parents saw education as the key to establishing the best possible future for their children, and the Communists used this perception to support their own agendas. One of the Communists' major national programs was the abolition of private farming and its replacement by huge collective farms. The children of parents who did not wish to turn over their farmland to the local collective were barred from attending even elementary school. As a result, most parents relented.

At higher educational levels, there were other factors at play. Admission to universities and professional schools was neither automatic nor by open competition. Rather, available spaces were first filled by students from "proletarian" families, and the children of educated parents were slotted into whatever spaces might be left over—unless a suitable bribe were offered to the right minion of the bureaucracy.

UNDER COMMUNISM THE ART OF BRIBERY reached a high level of refinement throughout the society. Medical treatment, living quarters, school admission, travel—all were regulated by an enormous and unwieldy bureaucracy that was staffed by people for whom their work was a mind-numbing routine and who could be bribed. Aunt Ludinka made a number of trips abroad to visit her brothers, Uncle Miško in England and my father in the United States. She even came to our daughter Rachel's wedding and to stay with my father after my mother died. Virtually all of these trips were against the regulations. Aunt Ludinka, however, cultivated the official who could grant her a travel permit, regularly supplying him with bottles of liquor that she smuggled into Czechoslovakia on her return from each trip to the West. With a bottle of whiskey for an exit permit, she was always able to go again.

Dishonesty was embedded in the Communist regime from top to bottom, and at the core of that dishonesty was the pretense that the Communist Party represented and defended the welfare of the ordinary citizen. The opposite was true. Party members sent their children to the best schools; they traveled abroad; they lived in luxury. Not only did the party hold all power in the state, but its higher echelons constituted a privileged class that lived in extravagant luxury while ordinary citizens often had to stand in line for meager supplies of food and even toilet paper.

THE COMMUNIST PARTY RULED THE COUNTRY. It was the only party, so its members were regularly "elected" to office with ninety-nine percent of the votes cast. The managers who ran the huge collective enterprises that replaced private businesses and farms were its appointees. Advancement in one's profession required party membership. The party held all political and judicial power in its hands.

As powerful and as feared as the Communist Party was the quasi-independent State Security (*Štátna bezpečnosť,* ŠtB)[11]. Officially an agency of the Department of the Interior, the ŠtB was a political police that at times seemed to set its own agenda. The targets of its scrutiny came from all classes of society: professionals, manual workers, intellectuals, and, importantly, even members of the Communist Party. The ŠtB had the ability to ruin the lives of not only ordinary people but also the highest party functionaries. It operated all over the country, from the center of power and intrigue in Prague to remote Slovak villages. It recruited as informers people in all walks of life, including some of the highest functionaries of both the Catholic and the Lutheran church. Torture of those arrested was commonplace. Forced, usually totally fabricated confessions were used to incriminate yet more victims. My father was jailed upon the accusation of a victim of just such a process. The goal was to break the prisoner psychologically and thus turn him into an instrument of the state. Few survived imprisonment with their personalities intact.

Of course, some fine work was undertaken during the Communist era. The folk dance ensembles *Lúčnica* and *SĽUK* were formed then, and continue to preserve folk culture and thrill audiences today. Numerous works of scholarship that remain valuable were produced. Czechoslovakia's first national park, located in the Tatra Mountains (*Tatranský narodný park,* TANAP), was established under the Communists. There were excellent artists, physicians, mountain climbers, scholars, engineers, musicians. Theater and opera flourished. Teachers taught their students math and science, music and literature. People fell in love, married (though in offices, not in churches), and raised their children with as much devotion as before. And yet, the party was everywhere and was the key to every major decision. Life went on, but anyone who crossed the limits set by the party had to beware.

So, despite some features of normalcy, the Communist era was, in most respects and for most people, a nightmare. There was loss of personal property; loss of control over one's own dwelling; loss of civil liberties; loss of the freedom to travel except to other Communist countries; loss of access to information except that approved by the government and the party; a completely controlled press; control of the entire operation of the government from Moscow; the prevalence of dishonesty and bribery; the control exercised by the only political party, the Communist Party; the pervasive presence and virtually unlimited power of a political police force, the ŠtB; and the constant doublespeak that twisted facts and common sense to fit whatever happened to be the goals of the party at any given moment. This is why the Communist regime erected the Iron Curtain, and why so many men and women, including our family, risked bullets and electrocution to escape across it.

CHAPTER 10

" . . . So He Won't Forget . . ."

Finally, in December of 1949, the nightmarish world of Communist Czecho-slovakia and the months of uncertainty in Austria were behind us. We were now passengers on the Holland-America liner S. S. Veendam, steaming from Southampton, England, to New York City. The passage was calm, and we enjoyed walking the decks, climbing up and down the many sets of stairs, eating in the dining room, playing the inevitable games of Battleships. It grew misty as we finally approached New York, but everyone was eager, and we crowded onto the foredeck. Whoever had binoculars got them out. And then, like so many immigrants before and after us, we saw it—the first faint, mist-shrouded glimpse of the Statue of Liberty rising above the gray waters of the harbor. Cheers went up. We steamed on, and more of the statue was revealed. An impatient milling-about started, not ceasing until we passed her, docked, and formed lines for the first of many formalities. Finally, we were able to take our suitcases and step, single-file, down the steep gangplank, onto the dock, and into the arms of Aunt Gláša.

We now started our new life in New York, politically free but economically struggling. Our apartment was a modest, rent-controlled unit on the fourth floor of a brick-faced, six-story building that occupied an entire block in Jackson Heights. It was much like all the other buildings that occupied block after block in this part of the Borough of Queens, an area in which many immigrants from Central Europe had found a new home. Our apartment consisted of a living room, a bedroom, a tiny bathroom lined with black and white tiles, a kitchen with barely room for two, and an eating area just big enough for a small table and my bed. As I got older this became my room, and the table was moved into the entryway.

My parents furnished this space with whatever they could afford at the city's many auction houses. Some of these auction items were quite nice, and in our home today you will still find a bronze standing lamp and an ornately framed oval mirror from that time. The apartment was also graced with a treasure. When we were leaving Czechoslovakia, we had packed eleven wooden crates of belongings that were initially meant to be taken with us legally, but in the end had to be smuggled out by rail. Of these eleven crates, the fate of ten remains unknown. Only one actually reached us. In that one crate, however, were my parents' most cherished possessions—a collection of oil paintings and watercolors. They were displayed on the walls of our tiny apartment in Jackson Heights, reminders of a world that would never be again. Most of them depicted rural scenes from my father's beloved region, County Liptov and the Tatra Mountains. The paintings pictured in Appendix VI were among them: farmers in billowing white shirts and their wives in long skirts and kerchiefs tied around their heads tending the fields; a pair of snorting horses, steam rising from their nostrils, pulling a sleigh with a couple heavily wrapped in their dark coats and cloaks, she in her kerchief and he in the huge, broad-brimmed hat worn by the villagers of the region; a beautiful village girl, a shawl over her shoulders and a kerchief over her head. In New York, they were constant reminders of our Slovak homeland. Now they hang on the walls of our house in the far northwest of the United States. To me, they speak as eloquently of my parents, now dead for over thirty years, as they do of the life they once imagined for me in the Liptov my father loved so much.

IN NEW YORK, MY MOTHER WORKED at Radio Free Europe (RFE), a broadcast network that beamed news and other programs to the many East and Central European countries that had been swallowed up by the Soviet Union following World War II[1]. The Manhattan offices resounded with Polish, Czech, Slovak, Hungarian, Lithuanian, Latvian, and numerous other languages. All the broadcasts were controlled by the U.S. government, so the scripts had to be translated from their original languages into English. My mother did such translation, and her boss was Uncle Miško Múdry, our dear friend from Chicago days, who was an editor in the Slovak section. My father tried his hand as an export-import broker, negotiating deals between suppliers of raw or partly processed materials and manufacturers who needed them, taking advantage of his multiple business contacts from past years and various parts of the world. He shared a one-room office near the New York Public Library on 45th Street in Manhattan with a Czech colleague. However, his commissions barely covered the rent for the office and in not too many years he retired and devoted his time to stamp collecting. It was my mother's job as a translator and later a librarian at Radio Free Europe that kept us afloat financially.

The Jackson Heights apartment buildings were all cut from the same mold. You could walk on the flat roof and hang your laundry there, but no one ever did any more. You washed and dried your laundry in coin-operated machines in the basement. The basement was also prominently marked with yellow-and-black signs as a bomb shelter, a reflection of the tensions of the Cold War. You collected your garbage in paper grocery bags, which you stuffed into a chute that dropped into the huge incinerator in the basement. Its smoke joined the black smoke from all the coal furnaces in the neighborhood, the soot gathering on the windowsills and gradually smudging the furniture and the floors. The A & P supermarket, tiny by today's standards, was a few blocks away. My father and I shopped there on Saturday and brought our purchases home, like everyone else did, in a fold-up aluminum cart. These carts held up to four grocery bags, but with our limited means ours was never full. My mother cooked the meals, my father and I washed and dried the dishes every day. I learned to be frugal. We even tore the paper napkins in half before placing them on the cheap, formica-topped table. We dined properly but reduced the cost in whatever ways we could.

My school, Public School 69, was also a few blocks away, in the opposite direction from the A & P. I went there for four-and-a-half years, from the middle of fourth grade until I graduated from eighth grade. It was an ordinary neighborhood school that served me well enough. I was a good student and graduated second in my class, with assorted certificates for outstanding work. I memorized poems that I can still recite, and learned how to use woodworking and metalworking tools, skills that serve me to the present day. Much to my mother's dismay, there was no sports program, and I never mustered the courage to join in the impromptu games that took place in the schoolyard after classes were over. Most of all, the teachers could not give special attention to yet another shy immigrant boy, whether or not he studied well.

My parents were now confronted with the classic immigrant dilemma: how to raise their son so that America would be a true home to him and at the same time to nurture the roots from which he came. There is no simple solution to this dilemma. Some families deliberately suppress their traditions and language, believing that this is the way to integrate into their new society. Others hold on to selected aspects of their original culture while living a largely American life. Still others live in immigrant communities so that the old ways live on, not only in the family but also in a wider network. There is a spectrum of options, and these may be selected consciously or imposed by circumstances.

My parents sought a middle road for me even while they themselves remained mostly in Slovak society. They wanted me to be a dual citizen, at least from a cultural point of view—to flower in America but keep my Slovak roots intact. When I was around eleven years old and in fourth or fifth grade, I made a birthday card for my mother that she kept carefully for all of her life

(Plate 9, Appendix VI). On the cover I wrote "Happy Birthday" in English and placed a photograph of her taken in front of our Jackson Heights apartment building. Inside I wrote *Štastlivé narodzeniny* in Slovak and placed a family photograph from our stay in Austria. On the back I used crayons to draw the flag of Czechoslovakia above and the American flag below. Truly a picture of what my parents were hoping for! But it took a conscious effort to nurture the feeling that the card expresses.

We tried as best we could to keep connected with the family in Czechoslovakia, especially Grandmother Hodža. We wrote to her, but all the letters were read by the Communist censors and therefore could contain only the most innocent family chit-chat. On account of his political activities, Uncle Dišo could not be referred to by name; he became "Muninka." We sent packages of supplies every few months, because there were serious shortages of food and clothing everywhere behind the Iron Curtain. Only used items were permitted. Clothes that I had outgrown went primarily to Aunt Ludinka's son, my cousin Karol. Other items were distributed among the family. I well remember preparing these packages, folding the clothes into cardboard boxes that were exactly the maximum allowable size, wrapping the boxes in heavy paper, sealing them carefully with brown paper tape moistened with a sponge, and finally tying them with twine. After the customs declarations were filled out and attached with twisted wires, we carried the packages to our local post office for mailing. It took about two months for them to reach Czechoslovakia.

Language was pivotal in my upbringing. At home we spoke only Slovak. But I was going to school in English, and home conversation was all that kept my Slovak alive. I did not read much in the language, and writing to Grandmother Hodža was a dreaded chore to a twelve-year-old. From my mid-twenties on, after I left home, I spoke Slovak only when I called my parents on the telephone and during occasional visits. I should have forgotten much of it, and certainly should have started to speak it with an American accent. But I had internalized the language of my home, and my Slovak has retained its purity, even though to modern ears it sounds a little old-fashioned and my vocabulary is based primarily on what a schoolboy once talked about with his parents.

MOST OF OUR FRIENDS WERE SLOVAKS. Our apartment might have been small, but it saw many a gathering of Slovak exiles lasting late into the night. At the time I saw these people simply as friends who had come together for a birthday or holiday, or because someone was visiting from far away. I now realize, however, that most of them had made significant marks on Slovak public life, and many of them were leaders of the Slovak National Uprising and the Democratic Party. [2]

Miško Múdry and his wife, Jarmilka, whom we first met in Chicago, remained very close friends. They lived not too far away and visited us often. As editor of the Czechoslovak desk of Radio Free Europe,[3] every so often Uncle Miško would invite me down to the RFE offices in Manattan, sit me down in a studio, and conduct an interview with me. "Today we are speaking with Janko Pálka," he would start. "He is going to school here in the United States, and we have brought him to the studio because he is the grandson of Milan Hodža. So, Johnny, tell us about . . ." And so the interview would go on.

There were others too, plus, of course, family members: often Aunt Gláša and her close friend Ria Michal, and, on rare and greatly welcomed occasions, Uncle Dišo who for many years lived and worked in Paris. Uncle Dišo was always the star attraction—handsome, athletic, sophisticated, utterly charming, and a great chef. His culinary specialty was *steak tartare*: raw ground beef prepared from the finest and leanest cuts, raw eggs, raw onions very finely chopped, salt, and lots of black pepper. Nowadays people would hesitate to eat such a dish for fear of infection, but to us it was a great delicacy. (While on a family visit to Slovakia in 2012, we had a chance to savor *steak tartare* again. The ingredients were brought to our restaurant table and I had the honor of mixing them thoroughly and in the proper proportions!) Whenever Uncle Dišo came, the apartment filled with guests and the atmosphere became electric.

A social gathering was also a time for singing. I doubt if there were ever more than half a dozen adults at our home without talk turning into song. One song would follow another from the huge repertoire of Slovak folk music that was long ago adopted by urbanites as part of the movement for national liberation. There were courtship songs and drinking songs, songs about battling the Turks, children's lullabies, and many others—all in a steady stream. No instruments, just voices. My mother was the main resource for the words to all the verses, but after every prompt, her voice was drowned out by the more energetic singers. I learned many of these songs, committing them to memory and also writing them down in my ill-formed hand. Many of the song sheets still survive in my childhood files. The songs survive too, and when a group starts to sing in Slovakia today, I can join in almost like a local, to my great joy and everyone else's delight. Singing is truly the way to the Slovak heart.

SUCH A STRONG FOCUS ON OUR HOME COUNTRY did not meet with the approval of the whole family, however. Aunt Gláša had made different choices in her life, opting for maximum integration into American life. She did not return with us following World War II but stayed in New York, pursuing a career in nursing at the Rockefeller University Hospital. Reminiscing about old times in Czechoslovakia felt like a burden to her, something that kept us, her family,

The three Hodža siblings celebrating Christmas in our apartment in New York. 1950s. Left to right: My mother; Fedor Hodža, Uncle Dišo; and Aglaia Hodža, Aunt Gláša. Author's archive.

from making our way successfully in our new country. For music she and her friend Ria turned to jazz and swing, and for food to steak and salad. I remember overhearing more than one heated argument about my upbringing, usually late at night when I was supposed to be asleep, "Where is America and the American way of life in the way you are raising Johnny?" they asked. "How will he ever feel at home here if you never let go of the old country?"

To provide a bit of a counterbalance, Gláša and Ria would periodically invite me to their apartment in Manhattan, feed me American food, and talk about things American. I would make my way home to Jackson Heights by subway long after nightfall, excited to have been treated like an adult guest. I remember these evenings fondly and well, but in truth what created a home for me in America was not these well-intentioned but sporadic efforts on their part, but rather the education I received later.

For Christmas when I was fifteen years old, Uncle Dišo gave me a large, cloth-bound picture book. It was a collection of photographs of Slovakia by Karel Plicka, the dean of Czechoslovak photographers. Plicka was a Czech, but he fell in love with Slovakia's countryside and mountains, architecture and people, and spent a lifetime photographing them. One of his most famous books is called simply *Slovakia*.[4] Its first picture is of the the ruins of the ancient fortress of Devín, on the Danube near the capital city of Bratislava, its battlements jutting defiantly upwards from rocky pinnacles. The last is a little boy in traditional dress, cradling a toy wooden horse on his lap and gazing at it intently. In between you find mountains, churches, people of all ages in traditional dress, countryscapes, cityscapes, each one glowing with light, as masterful photographs do, and revealing Plicka's love for what he saw. Uncle Dišo wrote an inscription in this book: "To Johnny, so he won't forget."

I have not forgotten.

CHAPTER 11

Separating from the Past

The Pálka family had been strong members of the Lutheran Church in Slovakia for many generations, and many Hodžas had been Lutheran ministers. Whatever might have been my parents' personal beliefs—they never talked about them—they supported my continuing the family tradition by making sure that I received a Lutheran religious education in our new country.

For this reason I went not only to Sunday school but also to Wednesday afternoon catechism classes. Then, when I was in eighth grade and thus approaching both graduation and confirmation, my mother unexpectedly broached the subject of religious education in a different way. It was a bright, sunny morning and we were casually walking to our church, about a mile from our Jackson Heights apartment. Suddenly she turned to me. "Your father and I have been thinking about where you should go to high school," she said. "Pastor Leininger would like you to go to a Lutheran school, and he said he would recommend you for a scholarship." She paused. "But we don't think this is a good idea. We would rather not have you influenced too much at an early age."

The good pastor persisted and even suggested that I might go on to seminary.[1] However, I was an independent-minded student and soon became so critical of church dogma that seminary would have been the last among my choices. Indeed, once I left home I ceased to be a practicing Lutheran. One thread to my Slovak past was broken. If my parents were disappointed, they never let me know.

AS FOR MY ACADEMIC FUTURE, I could have taken advantage of one of New York City's several outstanding public high schools to which admission was competitive.[2] These schools have served as gateways to higher education and professional life for generations of gifted students of all backgrounds and financial situations. My path was to be different, however, and it was my Slovak heritage that opened the door.

My mother had come to know Dr. Ruža Stuerm of the Masaryk Institute of New York. The primary mission of this organization, named after the founding president of Czechoslovakia, was to place immigrant Czechoslovak students in American schools. From Dr. Stuerm she learned that Cherry Lawn School, a small private school in Connecticut, had earlier given a scholarship to a Czech student who was just graduating. This student had so impressed her teachers that the school was specifically looking for another student from Czechoslovakia. Cherry Lawn offered me a full scholarship for tuition, room, and board. My only expenses would be for spending money, insurance, and books. With some trepidation my parents agreed, and so in 1953, at the age of fourteen, I took my first big step away from their cozy apartment filled with Slovak art and music and language and society.

The intellectual and cultural atmosphere at Cherry Lawn was electric.[3] The school's director, Dr. Christina Staël von Holstein Bogoslovsky, was a Swedish countess who taught us European history and opened her house to us for evening music history classes. Her husband, Dr. Boris Bogoslovsky, was a Russian physicist who had been a member of the short-lived Kerensky government that first toppled the tsarist regime before giving way to the Bolsheviks. He originally taught physics at Cherry Lawn, but while I was there he headed the translation service at the United Nations.

During the school year, I came home only every six weeks and then only for a few days at a time. During the summers I worked at a day camp run by the school on its lovely rural campus, so I was living at home less and less. The year after I started at Cherry Lawn, I was naturalized as an American citizen. My horizons were expanding, and my academic aspirations soaring. As I followed my own interests, things Slovak slipped further and further from my mind.

AFTER HIGH SCHOOL CAME SWARTHMORE COLLEGE, considered to be one of the best colleges in the United States.[4] I was able to attend because I won a highly competitive and coveted National Merit Scholarship. Like Cherry Lawn School, Swarthmore College, founded by Quakers in 1860, was built on a philosophy that we students could feel a hundred years later, and that permeates the college up to the present day. Its chief attributes are striving for the very best, most challenging education, combined with a constant attention to ethical questions and a deep appreciation of the humanities. Among the college's earliest proponents were pacifists, abolitionists, and defenders of women's rights.

The academic expectations were extremely high, and the workload sometimes staggering. As students we took pride in the rumor that, in comparison, Harvard was a party school. The Honors Program was modeled on the Oxford system of tutorials, and final examinations for Honors students were administered not by Swarthmore faculty but by leading outside experts.

Family portrait in taken in New York when I was graduating from high school in 1956. Author's archive.

It was at Swarthmore that I found my professional calling, biology, and I met my future wife, Yvonne.

AS SOON AS YVONNE AND I GRADUATED in 1960, and prompted by a challenge from one of our Swarthmore professors, we were off for a year of study and adventure in India. We were supported primarily by a fellowship I won from the National Science Foundation. India—the proverbial land of enchantment and also the land of utter poverty, the home of an ancient culture and also the home of a booming hi-tech industry, the model of nonviolent political action under Gandhi and also the stage for centuries of war. When we traveled to this fabled destination in 1960, we were fresh out of a sheltered American college existence, barely into our twenties, in a relationship with each other that was only exploratory, and, basically, both on our own for the first time. When we returned to America a year later, we were married, and life was never the same again.

We traveled to India the long way, aboard the MV Hellenic Splendor, a freighter offering cheap passage. She steamed out of New York on July 2, 1960, fully a month after her scheduled departure. She carried twelve passengers: a Pakistani doctor and his wife who were returning home after many years in the U.S.A.; an American family with two young sons on their way to a Fulbright teaching assignment in Dacca (the capital of what was then East Pakistan and is now Bangladesh); a mother and her daughter eager to join the father who was working as a geologist for USAID in Pakistan; an American missionary heading to the Sudan; an Indian filmmaker on his way home to Mumbai (then known as Bombay) with equipment that would be admitted into the country only if suitable bribes were offered; and the two of us.

One of our ports of call to load and unload freight was Port Said, at the mouth of the Suez Canal. Among the cities of the Middle East, Port Said is undistinguished, and yet its significance in my life is great—this is where Yvonne and I got engaged. We spent a long time hunting and bargaining for a ring in the shops and stalls of that bustling market town, and finally settled on a ring with a lovely and sizeable stone, alexanderite, in a modest gold setting. On Yvonne's finger it became the first announcement of our great step. A few days later, steaming through the Red Sea, we were treated to a surprise party complete with streamers, balloons (where they came from, I have no idea), and a cake. The Mumbai filmmaker took a few precious photographs and sacrificed one of his essential bribes—a bottle of champagne! Everyone sang a song whose words were composed by the missionary, a woman with a generous and romantic heart who also could not resist a jab at the dull and heavy food we had been eating onboard our ship:

'Twas on the Hellenic,
The dolphins were playing.
While boiled beef sat heavy,
They went for a walk.

They said, "Twas star-gazing,"
But ain't it amazing
The stars that glowed brightest
Were those in her eyes.

Port Said was quite hot,
The merchants persistent,
But that did not stop him—
The ring was obtained!

The mission accomplished,
We all join rejoicing,
And sing our best wishes
To John and Yvonne!

Just three months later, on October 29, 1960, when we were living in Delhi, we took our second great step—marriage. We had discovered the Quaker International Centre, not far from our one-room apartment and reached by walking or bicycling over a beautiful forested ridge. Meeting for worship was held there every Sunday morning, attended by a handful of Americans and

Our wedding at the Quaker International Centre, Delhi, India,
October 29, 1960. Author's archive.

by Indians who held the Quaker way in high esteem. The Centre became our
spiritual home, and its directors, Bradford and Marion Smith,[5] agreed to coun-
sel us and to have our wedding there. We had little money but enough to buy
two simple rose gold wedding rings and an embroidered silk sari for Yvonne.
Traditional Indian wedding saris are red silk ornamented with gold threads,
but we held to Western custom and chose white with gold for Yvonne's. The
invitations were plain white paper folded over, with a pair of peacocks drawn
on the outside and the brief text lettered on the inside, every one lovingly
handmade by Yvonne.

At 2:00 in the afternoon on the designated Saturday, a small group gathered
in the Quaker Centre to be our witnesses. A Quaker wedding is utter simplicity.
After a brief introduction everyone goes into silence, and when the couple feel
the right moment has come, they stand and exchange the traditional vows.
These vows are brief, direct, and powerful, and to this day not only do I remember them, but I can rarely say or read them without tears coming to my eyes.

In the presence of God and these, our friends,
I take thee, Yvonne, to be my wife,
promising, with Divine assistance,
to be unto thee a loving and faithful husband
so long as we both shall live.

Yvonne hand-lettered the wedding certificate that now hangs in our bedroom, black India ink on white paper that has yellowed over a time that has now passed fifty years.

We had no family at our wedding, and we hadn't known any of the witnesses for more than two months. There was no bridal shower, no rehearsal dinner, no grooms or bridesmaids, no one to give away the bride, no wedding presents, and no honeymoon. At Wenger's on Connaught Circus, the vast, circular shopping heart of imperial New Delhi (the shop is still there), we had bought a small wedding cake, which we cut in traditional style at the reception. After the reception we went out for dinner at the Volga Restaurant, also on the great Connaught Circus (and also still there). Then we went home, married for so long as we both should live.

Our time in India was filled with life-changing events and adventures, and it would take a book of its own to recount them all (Plates 10 and 11, Appendix VI): months of trekking on pilgrimage and trade routes in the Himalayas; visiting a score of India's great temples, mosques, and Gandhian institutions; volunteering in village medical clinics; spending time with spiritual teachers; encountering for the first time the Indian music that we have come to love so deeply; and simply experiencing daily life in the amazingly crowded markets and buses and trains, where the concept of personal space is nonexistent. We felt, underlying it all, the pulse of an ancient culture, intact for thousands of years, and we were drawn by its spiritual and devotional quality. For a time we stepped away from our own cultures, not just the Swiss roots of Yvonne's family and the Slovak roots of mine, but also from the American experience that had formed us both for most of our young lives.

AFTER OUR RETURN TO AMERICA came four years at UCLA, where we both earned Ph.D.s in the neurosciences. Then, as quickly as we could, we went back to India with the support of the Fulbright Program. It was 1965, and Yvonne was pregnant. A month after our arrival our first daughter, Rachel Sushila, was born in a Lutheran mission hospital in the tiny village of Thukivakkum, on the outskirts of the railway town of Renigunta, which is itself a few miles from the pilgrimage town of Tirupati in South India. Tirupati is the home of Sri Venkateswara University, which is a fine if provincial institution. This was where I taught neuroscience. Yvonne mostly stayed at home, tending to Rachel and making sure the monkeys didn't abscond with our fruit. With a new baby we couldn't go on quite as many adventures as we had during our first year, but there were still trips and outings possible for a young couple with a baby in a pack. Sometimes we rode our bikes to villages around Tirupati, where a white baby was always a source of great excitement (Plate 12). During university holidays we traveled by bus around South India. We spent Christmas in the state of Kerala, with its large Christian population and red stars everywhere proclaiming its Communist government. Around the corner from the guest house where we stayed in Cochin was a temple in which an all-night performance of Kathakali dance was in full swing. When we entered the temple courtyard we were immediately seated on the stage, just feet from the fully costumed and masked dancers and the deafening drums to which Rachel, peacefully sleeping on the floor, paid no attention whatsoever. We loved India once again.

When we once again returned to America, we took university jobs in Houston, Texas. I taught physiology at Rice University, and Yvonne did research in reproductive endocrinology at the Baylor University Medical School. Our second daughter, Tanya Elizabeth, was born. After three years we moved to Seattle, our dream city, and settled there for the next thirty-two years. I taught and conducted research at the University of Washington, specializing in neuroscience (Plate 13, Appendix VI). Yvonne, who held various positions over the years, taught for twenty-three years at Antioch University.

The United States was very good to me. I attended Cherry Lawn School on a scholarship provided by the school itself. I was able to attend Swarthmore College because I won a National Merit Scholarship. A fellowship from the National Science Foundation made our first year in India possible. My Ph.D. training was largely supported by NASA. When we returned to India, I taught under the Fulbright Program. We spent the year 1975-76 in Cambridge, England, where I conducted research as a Guggenheim Fellow, and in 1983 I returned to India to teach once again as a Fulbright Fellow. My neuroscience research was supported briefly by the U.S. Air Force Office of Scientific Research, and then for thirty years by both the National Institutes of Health and the National Science Foundation. At every step of my academic career I benefited from the generosity of my new country.

Cherry Lawn School, Swarthmore College, India, marriage, graduate school, back to India, a baby, onward to tenure-track university careers, another baby—no trace of Slovakia here! Seattle is very far from New York, so once we settled there we saw my parents and touched my Slovak roots only very rarely. Apart from occasional telephone calls, I stopped using the language; in Seattle I knew no Slovaks with whom I could speak. I was true to my upbringing and to Uncle Dišo's wish for me—I did not forget my original homeland. However, I also did not give it much active attention.

CHAPTER 12

Reconnecting

While still in my twenties I had had the urge, from time to time, to visit Czechoslovakia. My parents, however, would not hear of it. They knew of other young men who had gone back home and promptly been drafted into the Czechoslovak army on the grounds that they had never renounced their citizenship and thus were subject to the country's universal military service. Later, when I was older, married, and had children, and it was presumably safe to go, I did apply for a visa, but it was denied in both Washington and Prague without explanation. In 1975-76, however, while we were spending an academic sabbatical year in England, I applied to the Czechoslovak embassy in London, and visas for our whole family came by return mail. So, Yvonne, Rachel (age 11), Tanya (age 9), and I set out to visit what should have been the land of my birth and, most of all, to meet my extended family. It would be the first direct family contact in twenty-seven years.

In May 1976 Uncle Dušan met us at the airport in Prague, as he had met us at the train station in December 1946. And just as he had done thirty years earlier, he took us home to his apartment. There we were quickly reminded of what Communist rule meant in everyday life.

Exposed to the regime's minimal allotments of living space per person (Chapter 9), Uncle Dušan and his wife shared their apartment with their older son and his family. Like housing, employment was at the government's discretion. Uncle Dušan's wife was born the daughter of a wealthy banker, but now worked as a custodian in a hospital, scrubbing floors and taking out the trash. Dušan himself had been trained as a lawyer, and at the time of the Communist coup in 1948 was working in a government office. In 1951 he was dismissed from this position and assigned to work as a laborer in a state-owned enterprise for repairing refrigerators. He was a slight man, however, and heavy manual labor was more than he could physically manage. In 1954 the regime relented, and he was able to do what he really loved—write popular dance music and songs (Plate 14, Appendix VI).[1,2] Communism professed an ideology of eradicating class differences, but its practices were arbitrary, cruel, inefficient, and, as history showed, unsustainable.

*The family villa in Lomnica, 1976. It was in a desolate state
even at this time. After the fall of Communism it was sold
to a private investor who razed it to the ground and built a
modern guesthouse in its place. Author's archive.*

After visiting for a few days, we took the train from Prague to Bratislava,
where we stayed with Aunt Ludinka, her son Karol (my closest cousin and one of
the foursome who had played together in Lomnica), and his wife, Darina. Then
another train took us to Martin, into the arms of more family (Family tree 2, Appendix V): Aunt Lýdia (Lydka), the widow of Jozef Bučko (Chapter 6), and her two
children—the other two Lomnica cousins, Jelka and Milan, now likewise married
and with children of their own; Aunt Vierka, legendary in the family for her long-
distance hiking tours and for her outspoken opposition to the Slovak Republic
during World War II; her sister, Aunt Zorka, my father's favorite from Lomnica
days, married to a resistance fighter, Uncle Milo (Chapter 9); and Aunt Lydka's
brother, Uncle Igor, and his wife Aunt Magda who to this day (despite now being
a widow) showers all of us with the delicious mushrooms she has gathered in
the woods and dried in her tiny apartment. We were taken to visit to my father's
hometown of Mikuláš and the house my family had lived in after the war and
from which the secret police had led my father away to prison. We saw the grave
of Michal Miloslav Hodža, Grandfather Hodža's uncle and also a heroic figure in
Slovak history (Chapters 18-20), and a statue in his honor in front of the Lutheran
church of Mikuláš. We took a hiking trip into the Tatra Mountains, walking in
places my parents had loved (Plate 15). And then there was the surprise gift to
Rachel and Tanya of elaborate folk costumes, hand-stitched especially for them[3]
(Plate 16). In short, we were enfolded by generations of my family, welcomed
with open arms, let go with tears. It was a trip like no other trip.

Visiting family in 1976. Back row: Aund Ludinka, Yvonne, Ludinka's son Karol, his wife Darina. Front row: Tanya, Rachel. Author's archive.

It was clear to me that the heavy weight of Communism, in place for nearly thirty years since February of 1948, impacted everything and everyone. Even we visitors felt it every day. In public we could not, under any circumstances, talk about anything even remotely touching on politics. All public spaces were assumed to be riddled with hidden microphones, and any passing stranger could be an informer. A report from an informer could mean interrogation and potentially prison. Political conversations were held at home, behind closed windows and curtains, and in quiet tones. The streets of Prague and Bratislava were half empty, and the people were shabbily dressed. The building facades were gray and peeling. The autos were tinny, and all were of domestic or Soviet make. Only a handful of government newspapers and magazines were available. The transmitters of the Voice of America and Radio Free Europe were regularly jammed, but many people took the risk of trying to listen to them anyway. At the border, all luggage was searched and Western publications confiscated. If you took the train across the border in either direction, you could expect a long wait while armed guards searched every compartment and under the carriages, looking for people crossing illegally. It was dismal and oppressive and, while our time with the family had been heartwarming and exhilarating, we breathed a sigh of relief when our British Airways flight took off from Prague and headed back to London.

THE TIES TO HOME AND FAMILY that had been reforged during our brief visit to Czechoslovakia were soon to be strengthened in an unexpected way. Shortly after our return from our sabbatical year in England and from our visit to Czechoslovakia, my parents made a huge personal decision. The next year, in the spring of 1977, they would move from the New York apartment they had lived in since 1950 and join us in Seattle. With great excitement they told all their friends and wrote back to Czechoslovakia. We found a lovely, ground-level apartment for them in a park-like setting by the shore of Lake Washington, and helped them set out their furniture and hang their beloved Slovak paintings. We saw them every day during Seattle's wonderful spring, sharing meals and walks and delighting in Rachel's and Tanya's activities. They went with us to Rachel's graduation from eighth grade. And then, early the next morning, just three months after their arrival in Seattle, my father telephoned: *Mama Ti v noci zomrela* ("Your mother died last night.")

Taking only Rachel with me, I raced over to the aparment where we found my father both shattered and remarkably composed. My mother had been treated for congestive heart failure for several years. There was no warning sign that it had gotten worse, but during the night she had gotten very weak and died quietly in her sleep. She was still lying in bed, propped up on her pillow, when Rachel and I arrived.

Letters of condolence came from far and wide, full of shock and grief, as well as sympathy for my father who, especially because he was legally blind, was now primarily in my care. It was my first real encounter with death (Plate 17). When we placed her urn in the soil of Seattle's Lakeview cemetery and covered it with the simple marble slab that held her name, I could hardly believe that this small metal box held all that remained of the mother who had given me birth, who had endured so much hardship and given so much

My parents' gravestone in Lakeview Cemetery, Seattle.
Author's archive.

joy, who had been full of vitality all the years I had known her, who had never stopped aspiring for the best for me, who had made certain that I would never forget my homeland. Suddenly her entire life on this earth was reduced to a few handfuls of ash in a place she hardly knew.

MY MOTHER'S ENGLISH HAD BEEN IMPECCABLE for many years, but she was a perfectionist and, while I was going to Cherry Lawn School, she signed up for an after-work language class at Columbia University, riding the subway for over an hour to get home long after nightfall.

She saved all her assignments, just as they came back with the teacher's comments. After her death, I found these essays among her papers. They speak of life back home, of her memories and experiences, and of her wishes for the future. One of them is entitled "A Letter to My Son." Though it was written when I first went to Cherry Lawn at the age of fourteen, I did not read it until I was forty-two years old. It is one of my greatest treasures:[4]

A Letter to My Son

My Dear Boy,

There are things that I want to say to you now that you have become familiar with your new school. I did not speak of them while you were home because they might have made our parting more difficult.

While your father and I are very happy that you are at a fine school and that you live with many friends your own age, we cannot help missing you very much. Moreover, we feel that your going away marks the end of the first chapter of your young life, and that you will no longer be as completely ours as you have been in your childhood. It is the natural course of nature: when a fledgling is grown, the mother bird pushes him out of the nest. He has to learn to use his wings and learn to take care of himself. Not that we love you less, you know that, but you are now out of the nest.

You know, my son, that your father and I have always tried to do our best by you. I believe that it has been more difficult for us than for most parents because of the circumstances under which we had to live. Nevertheless, we have managed to give you a fairly secure and happy childhood. You don't remember all the changes, travels, anxieties, and dangers you have lived through with your family. You cannot remember how your father carried you in his arms and baby food for you on his back on our way across the heavily guarded line between occupied France and free France back in 1940. You cannot remember that you flew across the ocean at the age of a little over two years. I am sure you have already forgotten how you traveled back to Europe aboard ship and how you cried from cold as we arrived at the station in Prague in the cruel winter of 1947. You did not know that the Communists were taking your father to prison when you saw him leave the house one day with four gentlemen. You felt only a childish sense of adventure when we escaped from Czechoslovakia after the Communist coup. You played Indian: you crept cautiously behind the leader of the group, you fell flat when he did, you ran when he ran. You lived with us the life of a refugee in Austria. You must have lost the feeling other children have that your parents were omnipotent and that they always knew what to do, for you have sometimes seen them helpless, but I hope that you did not lose the feeling that they were watching over you and protecting you from every unpleasantness. For we never let you know that we were worried or anxious or afraid.

When we finally found a haven here in the country that is now our home, there were still difficulties, this time, thank God, only the everyday cares that all other people have. We tried to give you everything you needed to become self-reliant, independent, strong in mind and body. We encouraged you to engage in sports, we tried to make you see why it was important that you should be a good student and prepare for making a place for yourself in this country. We made you catch up with your religious education that had been somewhat neglected. You have been confirmed in the faith of your fathers, you have graduated from grammar school, and you have won a scholarship at a fine school. It is now up to you, my son, to study hard, to prepare yourself for a career, and to become a man your family can be proud of. You have your parents' best wishes, their love, their support, but you are on your own. You are a bird that has been pushed out of the nest. It has been a wrench for your mother, a wordless regret, a hidden sorrow mixed with pride in you and with the pleasure of seeing you get a good start in life.

This is what I did not tell you while you were at home, my son. Remember that your parents' blessing will follow you always.

Your loving mother.

October 30, 1953

CHAPTER 13

Discovering My Father

In his last years, after my mother died and I knew him better than before, my father was a small man. He was hunched over and moved slowly. His legs were spindly, and his hands were knobby with arthritis. He was legally blind.

I talked with him every day because, more than anything else, that was what he wanted. Often I would go through the nearby park to his house, on my bicycle or running. As we sat and I read the letters that had arrived or wrote the letters he no longer could, he would sometimes talk. He wanted to know the latest tidbits about our children or what our immediate plans were. And often he would say, "I dreamed again last night. I always dream about things from long ago." How I wish that I had kept a record of those dreams!

One winter evening he was at our house for a holiday dinner, and he made magic. We had a black upright piano on which our daughter Rachel had taken lessons, but it wasn't used much any more. While the meal was being cooked, my father sat down at that piano. We all gathered round and watched in wonder as his gnarled fingers started to move over the keys he couldn't see and his feet found the pedals. Suddenly there were waltzes and tangos from his youth, with the rhythms firm and the melodies vibrant. He was not a trained musician and hadn't touched a piano in forty years, but that night he made it sing. We all cried. He never played again.

My father was not always small and stooped. His American naturalization papers from the 1950s say that he was six feet tall. My mother was fond of saying that when they were young, he would strap an accordion on his back and carry it up and down the mountain trails all day long, so they could have music wherever they stopped. She knew my father as a strong, bold, capable, and handsome man who loved life and loved his country. Our family's second exile broke his spirit and made him shrivel physically. He may have been bent, arthritic, and nearly blind at the end, but I like to think of him as he was for most of his life—a man full of life.

My father was born in Mikuláš in 1901. He took over the family leather-working business from his father in the early 1930s and married my mother in 1935; they were deeply in love. Then came World War II and exile, after the war a brief moment of sunshine at home, then the Cold War and a second exile, business failure, increasing blindness, and finally lung cancer. He died in Seattle in 1981. It is a bleak picture in its outlines, but hidden within it is great richness that I have uncovered only bit by bit. Let me start to fill in the picture and tell you about a man who had a great heart, loved his native place, and risked his life for a cause he believed in.

Leatherworking was the economic foundation of Mikuláš, and a dozen or more factories sprouted in locations where there was a convenient supply of good water. The owners became wealthy, but the work was hard. Sons worked with their fathers to learn the trade, and each generation aspired to a higher level of formal education than the one before. Thus, after elementary school in Mikuláš, my father started gymnasium in Kecskemét in today's Hungary. However, he showed his Slovak patriotism and as a result, like many other outspoken Slovak students, he was expelled, not just from the school in Kecskemét but from all schools in Hungary (for the pressures of the policy of *Magyarization*, see Appendix I, as well as Part II starting with Chapter 17, *The Rise of Nationalism*). At the time he was only fourteen. He finished secondary school in Vienna, attended technical school in Prague, and finished his education in Lyon where he earned a master's degree in tanning chemistry. Thus, in his youth he studied in five languages: Slovak, Hungarian, German, Czech, and French. When he was home, he worked as an apprentice in Grandfather Pálka's factory.

The Mikuláš of my father's young adulthood was a vibrant place. The leather business brought not only wealth but also connections with the wider world. The town teemed with sport and theatrical clubs, some 140 of them organized by a population of just a few thousand.[1] Playwrights, poets, and novelists were born and worked there. Painters loved the countryside and the villages, and village crafts were proudly displayed in the town's big houses.[2] Slovak culture was as important as business in the lives of the professional class.

In this yeasty atmosphere my father was a well-known character. He rode a motorcycle, oftentimes with a group of painters whose names are still prominent in Slovak art history: Janko Alexy, Zolo Palugyay, and Miloš Bazovský. He became something of a patron of Ján Hála, a Czech painter who fell in love with Slovakia and settled in the village of Važec, just a few kilometers from Mikuláš, living and painting there until he died in 1959. Hála wrote and illustrated countless articles about his beloved Važec that appeared in national publications. He wrote in Czech but also in immaculate Slovak, and presented

My father as a youth in Mikuláš, c. 1916. Author's archive.

the traditional culture of Slovakia perhaps more compellingly than any other artist of his generation. Važec burned to the ground in 1931, and Hála wrote and illustrated a nationally published eulogy for the village that comes straight from the heart.[3]

> The finger of God or the hand of the Devil smote the village. In six hours it turned to ashes. I stare and stare, and I cannot believe my eyes; I cannot believe that the rubble, the cinders, the solitary chimneys, the charred thresholds are my village under the Tatras. The heart quakes and tears come to the eyes. . . . It is the end of the fairy tale of Važec.

One of his last books is called *Pod Tatrami* (*Below the Tatras*).[4] It begins:

> If I were a poet, I would sit day after day on the fresh earth behind our village, and every day I would write a poem celebrating the beauty of the Tatras. In the morning I would watch their pink outline, as it emerges from the mist like some noble vision. And an hour later I would admire a different picture, no less beautiful. . . .

The book closes 184 pages later with another eulogy to his village:

> It was a delight to walk here in Važec, to paint here, to look at the Tatras and laugh at the passing of youthful years. Today, it is the graveyard of dreams, each burned out chimney like a cross. The source of my delight died here, my joy is buried here. I walk in this cemetery and do not know, do not know where to bury my sorrow and my grief. I must place it in my heart. There is no place here for me to bury it.

More than half of the paintings that were so dear to my parents in their second exile and that hang in our house today are by Hála. On the wall of my study hang pencil sketches Hála made of my father and of Uncle Dišo in 1927 when they went on a joint excursion to Zakopané, a tourist center on the Polish side of the Tatra Mountains. My father took me to Hála's studio when I was a boy, and I well remember marveling at the light streaming in and at the many paintings hanging on the walls. We visited the rebuilt Važec and Hála's studio, now a museum, in 1992. One of the older attendants told us, "Oh, I remember the Pálka brothers. They would come roaring into Važec on their motorcycles, and we would be sure to bring our prettiest girls to dance with them!" Važec was an intimate part of the land my father so dearly loved, and Hála the painter and my father's friend was an intimate part of Važec and indeed of Slovakia.

Pálka brothers on their motorcycles. On the left my father and an unknown young woman, on the right his brother Michal (Uncle Miško) and sister, Aunt Ludinka. Late 1920s. Author's archive.

Soňa Kovačevičová-Žuffová, one of Slovakia's leading ethnographers, grew up in Mikuláš next door to the Pálka family and remembers my father well:[5]

> In Mikuláš there was an unwritten law that the factories would sound their whistles one after the other. The housewives could tell by the tone of each whistle when their husbands were leaving the factory, and they started serving the soup so that it would be hot on the table when the man of the house walked in. While waiting for our father, who came from Palúdzka [a nearby village, now a suburb of Mikuláš] we would walk back and forth in front of the house. But the Pálkas usually arrived first, the young men with their father in the lead. And with this, the discipline of my home evaporated. The eldest son, Janko [my father] lifted me in his arms, set me on his shoulders, and carried me off to their house. All that was lacking was marching music, because the youngest brother, Dušan [the future composer of much-loved dance music] was still away at school. . . . They gave me a chair at the huge table that was set out in a wooden cottage in the backyard, built in the style of village cottages. My nose hardly reached over the table. . . . When I was worn out with excitement and the huge meal, they finally carried me home.

Life was gay for the Pálkas and their friends.

FOR ALL THE YEARS I CAN REMEMBER, my father talked wistfully about an organization called the *cecha*. It had gathered every Wednesday evening, without fail, and had been a focal point of his life as a young man. My mother and others teased him mercilessly about the *cecha*, but he never gave up mentioning it, and everyone understood that it represented a treasured part of the life he had left behind and could never recapture.

In 2005, with the persistent help of my best friend from childhood, Ivan Rázus, I found the archive of my father's *cecha*, everything from the charter to a full set of annual reports[6]. It had been founded in 1921 by a group of the town's intelligentsia and modeled after the craft guilds of old. Its goal, however, was very different from that of a guild. Article 1 of the Charter of the *Poctivá cecha literárna* (The Honorable Literary Cecha) stated that "The Literary Cecha is an association of men at Trnovský's Tavern in Vrbica, established for their musical education and self-advancement." Further, fines for transgressions against the rules of the *cecha* were to be paid in flagons of wine. So, was it a male singing and drinking club? But Article 8 specified that a meeting was to be recognized as official only if a lecture were given and a discussion held. "The intention of this Article is to ensure that the *cecha* will not degenerate into a simple drinking society." And indeed, the records show that the lecture topics ranged from accounts of the members' travels, to aspects of history and economics, to technical presentations on the manufacture of leather and paper.

Several years later I encountered a vivid account of the *cecha* from the pen of one of its founders and officers, the writer Ivan Stodola.[7] Stodola's account confirmed what my father had always said—the *cecha* met every Wednesday evening after dinner. Now, however, I began to have a sense of the spirit of these gatherings:[7]

> The *cecha* modeled its articles of incorporation on the articles of the leatherworkers' guild written in 1750, and accordingly established as its members masters, journeymen, and mischievous apprentices. . . . The *cecha* had certain official expenses. If a master's wife bore a son, a budding apprentice, the *cecha* gifted him a gold ducat; if a girl, she received a roll of linen for her dowry.

> The meetings of the *cecha* opened with the singing of its hymn. . . . It had several most noble verses, the last of which closed with the words, "And when the shepherd sounds his horn, every member must head for home." You see, in the olden days, in Mikuláš and nearby villages they sounded the horn at intervals throughout the night, and the watchman made his rounds carrying a halbred.

> Following the old articles, in our *cecha* we shared wine on the occasion of name days [each day of the year has a name, usually that of a saint, associated with it; even now, especially men but also women are honored on their name days], baptisms, and weddings. When a journeyman married, he was accepted as a master, but only under the condition that he say some wise words—this was his *majsterstück* [lit. masterpiece; for the significance of the masterpiece in traditional guilds, see Chapter 16]. For the privilege of his new status he paid with wine.

The participants included many of the Mikuláš elite—doctors, lawyers, businessmen, writers—though certainly not all. Grandfather Pálka, for example, was not a member, but his passing was noted in a moving obituary in the annual report for 1935 (Chapter 23).

The annual reports are full of anecdotes about the members, all written in mock serious style. My father's name appears frequently. For example, in 1929 it was noted, "Ján Pálka keeps going to Važec. This will not help him become a master, so he should change his ways." And in the report for 1935 we find that "on June 12th Ján Pálka organized a celebration bidding farewell to his

My father learns the leather trade in his father's factory, 1920s. Author's archive.

bachelorhood, a life step that entitled him to move from the status of journeyman to that of master. The celebration lasted nearly twenty four hours." And so on and so forth. Usually funny, sometimes a bit crude, these reports always showed a genuine concern for the welfare of the members.

The men of the *cecha* were devoted to their group and gloried in its meetings and many annual festivities. By 1938, however, the shadow of impending war had fallen even on the *cecha*. The report of the presiding officer of the *cecha*, the *Cechmajster*, starts this way:

> Reviewing previous reports, both my own and those of my outstanding predecessors, it was satisfying to see that the life of the *Cecha* flowed smoothly and that larger events did not muddy it. This cannot be said of the year just past. All the storms that passed through Europe, and that violently struck our young country, were reflected also in the life of the *Cecha*. We could see it in our discussions, lectures, and conversations, as well as in the reduced number of official meetings. . . . We know the reason very well. It was the mobilization of our country starting on September 25th, 1938, during which the *Cecha* did not meet. Thank God that the storms have

passed, and that our country, albeit badly injured and diminished in size, continues nevertheless. . . .

When Czechoslovakia was partitioned in 1939, the *cecha* was discontinued. After the war this organization, which had provided a lively, humane, stimulating, and caring community to scores of the leading men of Mikuláš for eighteen years, was revived briefly. Finally, under the stresses of Communism, it dissolved with hardly a trace.

As THE ELDEST SON OF ONE OF THE MOST RESPECTED businessmen of Mikuláš, my father grew up and moved in circles of privilege. His wedding to the future prime minister's eldest daughter on June 21, 1935, was a grand occasion. The garden of Grandfather Hodža's large house in Prague overflowed with flowers and with guests in formal attire. My mother's dowry included not only silver but also an immense set of white china edged in gold, and etched stemware of the thinnest, most delicate glass I have ever seen. The family hid it all during the war; our daughter Tanya has it now. The bride and groom looked like movie stars, and they honeymooned at Lake Bled in Yugoslavia. They moved into a large apartment in the house of the Krivoss family in Mikuláš, bought a substantial piece of property from the Lutheran church, and started to build a house.

These were tumultuous times, however, and the Pálka family was not protected. Grandfather Pálka's leather tanning business, battered by a succession of economic downturns and finally by the worldwide depression that started in

My parents' wedding portrait, 1935. Author's archive.

1929, had gone into bankruptcy in 1932.[8] The bank repossessed both the factory building and the family home. My grandparents moved to Bratislava, where my grandfather died not long after my parents' wedding. My grandmother suffered with cancer for several years before she died in 1942, in the midst of war.

My father was able to buy back from the bank a portion of the family business, and he turned it in a new direction—no longer tanning leather, but manufacturing leather products. These included industrial articles, such as the huge belts used to drive machinery in factories and leather bushings for the axles of automobiles, as well as leather belts for military uniforms, briefcases, and ladies' fine handbags. Within a few years he employed over 150 men. In 1936 he entered into a partnership with the Žuffa family, forming a company that expanded beyond the manufacture of leather goods. A new factory building was constructed in the nearby village of Palúdzka, and employment exceeded 200. After the dissolution of Czechoslovakia following the Munich Agreement, however, all military orders were cancelled, and work at the new factory nearly came to a halt.

AFTER CZECHOSLOVAKIA WAS TORN APART by Hitler, my father sent my pregnant mother into exile, but he himself stayed behind for almost a year before escaping (Chapter 2). What might have seemed so important to him that he would leave his family for most of a year at a time when a shooting war was ever more likely? I only found the answer many years after my parents' death. While I was rereading some of the papers in their files, I came across a copy of a letter written by my father on March 9, 1960, and addressed to someone who had asked him about his wartime activities:[9]

> I stayed behind after Irene's departure in July 1939, for these reasons: to sell what I could and to get the largest possible amount in foreign currency out of the country; to establish connections with Prague and put in place liaisons and an information route Prague-Belgrade-Paris; and to make possible the escape of people who were in danger of imprisonment in Slovakia or in German concentration camps.

> Before my definitive escape I made three trips to Belgrade during which I was able to carry out sizeable sums. This money I sent, via a French courier faithful to us, to my late father-in-law [i.e. Milan Hodža], and he used it, among others things, to support various other people. This was, of course, in addition to expenses for the late Dr. Bulík, on whose behalf I borrowed 400,000 dinars when he returned from prison in Budapest and found his law office in ruins. These di-

nars I returned in America in dollars. In Belgrade I also contributed significantly to the support and activities of Vladimir Žuffa [a very close friend to whose memoirs we shall turn momentarily], activities that are well known to you. Here I would also add that Janko Lichner let me know that his situation was getting precarious but that he couldn't leave because he couldn't provide for his family. He escaped a few days after receiving 100,000 crowns from me. . . .

In addition to Lichner and Vladimír Žuffa, I helped Volko, a student in Mikuláš who later served us as a courier between Belgrade, Budapest, and Košice [the major metropolis of Eastern Slovakia]. The majority of Bulík's travels also went through me. . . .

Thus while we were in France, my father was selling or otherwise encumbering his business in secret to obtain funds for the support of anti-Nazi activities both in Slovakia and in Yugoslavia. He was carrying foreign currency across Nazi-controlled territory. He was recruiting couriers who would carry information and documents all the way from Prague, across Slovakia and Hungary, into Yugoslavia and thence to Paris, and would bring messages from the leadership-in-exile back to the areas controlled by Hitler. At every point on this journey these couriers risked their lives—just as my father did to make such work possible.

I was able to track down independent records of my father's activity in Slovakia on the eve of World War II with at least some success. The city archives of Mikuláš hold a confidential exchange of letters between the headquarters of the Slovak National Security Agency in Bratislava and police headquarters in Mikuláš.[10] The most telling letters, responding to sometimes naïve queries from Bratislava, are dated May 27 and 31, 1940. The Mikuláš police report that Ján Pálka left Mikuláš on February 9, 1940, has not returned, and his present whereabouts cannot be ascertained. He is of Slovak nationality, a Lutheran, and the son-in-law of former Prime Minister Dr. Milan Hodža. With regard to his trustworthiness, he is of dubious character, which can be seen from his departure and also because he is well known as a "Czechoslovakist." His wife Irene, née Hodža, has also most probably left the country because it has not been possible to discover her whereabouts. This all demonstrates that with respect to his loyalty to the Slovak nation, he is completely untrustworthy. As regards his morals, he is upstanding. (At least he was given credit for that!)

What prompted my father finally to leave Slovakia and leave behind the information service that he had so painstakingly built up? Here is his own account, part two of his letter of 1960:

I would summarize the reasons for my ultimate escape from Slovakia as follows: first of all the entire family, including Irene and the boy [that's me!], were already in exile, so that my personal safety in Slovakia was very tenuous. In addition, as Hodža's son-in-law, I was *persona non grata* for the Slovak authorities. This was made worse because, among other things, as president of the Mountaineering Club I refused to lead the club in Hlinka's spirit; I refused any sort of support for the Hlinka Guard, which at that time was virtually treason; I did not fire any Czech employees; etc. In January 1940, the situation had worsened to the point that I was designated for Il'ava [the most infamous of the Slovak prisons and the embarkation point for German concentration camps]. That I was not arrested, I owe only to the timely warning given me by the late Ľudo Méhéš, mayor of Mikuláš, who one day at 6 a.m. woke me up with the warning that I should not stay because the next night they were to take me away to Il'ava. This was the decision of the party and the Hlinka Guard, which he knew about in his role as mayor. The same day I left via Budapest for Belgrade from where, as you remember, I successfully reached France on a Yugoslav passport. [This is the passport secured with the help of Janko Bulík that served all of us so well in France, Spain, and Portugal (photo p. 37).]

ONE OF THE FAMILY TREASURES that have come down to me is a photograph album kept by my mother. Near the beginning, sandwiched between baby pictures of me taken in France, are two pages with five photographs labeled just "Kovačica, 3-3-40." For years after being given the album, I wondered about those photographs. They show my father a few weeks before he joined our family on April 13, 1940, in the company of striking people, several in some sort of folk dress. There is an old man with a wonderful, long, bushy moustache and a cylindrical hat of curly black sheepskin. There is a stout, older woman in a long skirt and a blouse with puffy sleeves, her head covered by a kerchief. Other men are in city clothes, even though most of the pictures were taken in front of a village house. And a boy of about ten is standing in front, dressed in an army uniform and holding a pistol proudly across his chest. Everyone is obviously celebrating, but celebrating what? Who are they? What is the significance of Kovačica? And most especially, why was my father there, rather than with us in France?

In 2003 I was given a book entitled *Skok do neznáma* (*Leap into the Unknown*).[11] Not realizing how important it would be to me, I put the book on the shelf

Kovačica, Easter 1940. One of the photographs that led me to uncover my father's role in the anti-Nazi resistance. Front row, left to right: Júda Bulíková, mother of Janko Bulík; Jano Bulík, son of Janko Bulík, age 10; Fero Bulík, father of Janko Bulík. Back row, left to right: Dr. Jozef Rudinský, Catholic priest, writer, and supporter of Milan Hodža; Janko Bulík; Vladimír Žuffa; my father; Jozef Struhárik, doctor in Kovačica and brother of Ján Struhárik, Bulík's deputy in Belgrade. Identifications courtesy of Jano Bulík, Pozdišovce. Author's archive.

without reading it and quite forgot about it until I traveled back to Slovakia a year later. I decided to take *Leap into the Unknown* along to read on the airplane. Settling into my seat, I took out the book and started to browse. Within minutes I saw them—three of the five mysterious photographs from Kovačica! Besides the photographs, the book contained some thirty pages of text which described my father's activities in Yugoslavia and fleshed out the information provided in the letter I have quoted above.

Leap into the Unknown proved to be the edited diary of Vladimir Žuffa, the dear friend to whom my father had written his plaintive letter from Chicago (Chapter 4) and a scion of the Žuffa family with whom my father had formed his business partnership in 1936. Žuffa left his home at 5:00 a.m. on February 8, 1940, leaving his family behind. For a year he had been active in the anti-Nazi underground, personally smuggling documents back and forth between Slovakia and the Czech lands that were controlled directly by the Germans. Secreted in his little car during his flight from his homeland were documents that he was to deliver in Belgrade. Along the way a ferocious snowstorm forced him to turn back and, ultimately, to abandon his car. He stuffed the secret documents under his clothes and traveled on by train. On his way out of Hungary, he was arrested by a border guard, but he managed to bribe his way to freedom. On February 12 he reached Belgrade. There he was able to deliver the papers to the pivotal figure in Slovak resistance efforts in Yugoslavia, Dr. Ján Bulík, the same Janko Bulík who had escorted my mother as she left fascist Slovakia in 1939, just before giving birth to me in Paris.

In Belgrade, Žuffa was dismayed to discover that the resistance in Yugoslavia was fragmented. There was military resistance and civilian resistance, Czech resistance and Slovak resistance. The deepening political and personal antagonism between President Beneš and Grandfather Hodža was mirrored in what should have been a united effort against the Nazis. One of the consequences of this fragmentation was that no funds were made available by the Beneš-led Czechoslovak government-in-exile to Slovaks working in Yugoslavia. Following his third and final trip to Yugoslavia my father, with his business expertise and connections, stepped into this breach and provided connections for business transactions whose profits would be funneled into resistance activity. In wartime, however, business deals are chancy at best, and most Slovaks who escaped had done so with no money of their own. Immediate funding was needed. Bulík had been using his personal resources to support these men and their work, but his funds were running out. He himself had been arrested by the Gestapo and held in prison in Hungary. When he was released and returned to Belgrade, he found that his law office had been ransacked and that reestablishing a livelihood would take time, if indeed it would be possible at all. My father introduced Bulík to a business associate, Dr. Adolph Weismann, who was originally from Prague. When he heard about Bulik's situation, Dr. Weismann pulled 100,000 dinars out of his desk drawer and handed the cash to my father, who passed the bundle to Bulík. No questions, no promissory note—just a handshake sealed the transaction. Over time Dr. Weismann provided more funds, a total of 400,000 dinars, and established a branch in his company to support the business transactions my father was negotiating for the financial benefit of the resistance.

How much was 400,000 dinars worth? Tucked into my mother's diary is a letter from Žuffa to my father dated July 17, 1940, in Belgrade. He expresses his fervent wish that we are all well and describes in detail how the various business openings that my father had set up have all come to nothing. Attached is a detailed accounting of funds that my father had given him for his personal use. For example, he took a taxi ride for 15 dinars, sent telegrams for 50-100, purchased office supplies for 331, paid rent of 1,150 (he considered his apartment to be very expensive), took a train to a town at a medium distance for 130 dinars round trip. So, in terms of purchasing power, a dollar today would seem to correspond to some 5 to10 dinars in 1940, so that 400,000 dinars was worth as much as $80,000. No receipt. Just a handshake.

A year and a half later, when my father and mother and I were in Lisbon trying to get to America, our money was running out. By sheer chance, my father met Dr. Weismann on the street.[12] Weismann's family, Jewish, had been killed in Belgrade, and he was now passing through Lisbon on his way to Cuba with his brother and his family. Following a conversation about the travails of exile, he handed my father, in cash, 2,000 U.S. dollars, then a very large sum, to help us out. Again, there was just a handshake. It was many years before my father was able to repay these extraordinary loans. I remember overhearing telephone conversations in New York that started with "Herr Weismann?" never knowing what a guardian angel was on the other end of the line.

Using his own funds, plus the loans from Dr. Weismann which he would later have to repay, my father sent significant sums to Grandfather Hodža to support his political activities in Paris, as well as providing directly for the livelihood of Vladimir Žuffa, for the continued work of Janko Bulík, and (through Bulík) for the support of a number of resistance workers.[13] Before his departure from Slovakia, my father had also given crucial support to Ján Lichner. All of these other men were heroes. Žuffa came close to losing his life as a courier for the spy service that my father had, among many others, helped to establish.[14] Cut off from Western Europe, he made his way through the Middle East and around Africa to England. Because of his advanced training in pharmacy, he was appointed coordinator of the Red Cross in Slovakia and worked in the post-war ministry of health. When the Communists came into power, Žuffa was persecuted. He died a dispirited pauper. Janko Lichner risked his life in the resistance, represented Slovaks in the Czech-dominated government-in-exile in London, and held important posts in the immediate post-war Czechoslovak government. He was sentenced by the Communists to seventeen years imprisonment and served ten before being released. And Janko Bulík? I'll tell you about him in Chapter 30.

And now the photographs. At Eastertime of 1940 my father, Žuffa, and several friends traveled with Bulík to the village of Kovačica, the ancestral home of the Bulík family, to celebrate the holiday with Bulík's parents (Kovačica was one of a number of ethnically Slovak communities in Yugoslavia. For their origin, see Appendix III.) They went together to celebrate Easter in the village church. This is what Žuffa records in *Skok do neznáma*:[15]

According to the custom in Kovačica and, I believe, among all Slovak Lutherans in Yugoslavia, the Lord's Supper (communion) is not served on Good Friday. However, at the request of Janko Pálka our beloved pastor there, the Rev. Janiš, gladly obliged us. In Slovakia, you see, communion on Good Friday is the most glorious of the whole year. At least in spirit we wanted to be in Bratislava, in Mikuláš, in La Baule, where our loved ones were now gathered by the altar. In this way we wanted to be connected to them at least for this little while.

After the regular service in church, we moved to the front pew. Janko Pálka, two from the Bulík family. . . , Dušan Čaplovič and I. It was the most moving Good Friday of my life. Almost all of the local people stayed to be witnesses to the communion we were to receive. And Rev. Janiš offered us communion not only with the brotherly love of a minister, but also as a man who understood us completely, in the most dignified and moving way possible. In his homily he acknowledged the voluntary sacrifices for nation, mankind, and the message of Jesus made by faithful exiles who, although not forced in any way, followed the voice of their conscience and their heart. They left behind their families, wives, children, and beloved native land to give themselves in service to a higher calling, knowing that they would never return home until they could see their nation free and independent once again.

While in Kovačica, my father learned of the work of the local Lutheran orphanage. He was touched by the care that it provided to so many children, and by its financial need. All available resources had been used to construct a new building, but this was still mainly an empty shell with no furnishings. As accounts of the history of the orphanage testify, my father acted generously[15]:

Recently the orphanage received a gift from Ing. Ján Pálka on the occasion of receiving communion while he came as a refugee in Kovačica, 10,000 dinars for the furnishing of a bedroom with 14 beds. This room was named after his newborn son, Johnny.

He may have been far away and occupied with important political doings, but my father did not forget me!

On April 13, 1940, some two months after his arrival in Belgrade, my father finally took the train to Paris to join his family (Chapter 2). Janko Bulík traveled with him, carrying documents for Grandfather Hodža and for the government-in-exile. They would never see each other again.

EARLY IN HIS LIFE, MY FATHER LIVED IN PRIVILEGE. His family was wealthy, and he was the outgoing eldest son whom everyone loved. A few years ago I made a point of interviewing people in Slovakia who had known him personally, asking for their recollections. The tone of their responses was always the same—wistful, as if remembering both a man and a time that had been deeply good but were now lost. Aunt Zorka knew him especially from the long family summers in Lomnica, and remembered him as her favorite grown-up. She was a sickly child and somewhat shy, but with him she could be his "princess," someone who felt treasured. Uncle Zdeno Jurenka, too, remembered him as a man who was particularly gentle, kind, and lighthearted. Aunt Olga Osuská, now retired from her position as one of Slovakia's first ophthalmologists, recalled vividly how, when she was a young girl, he had surprised her one day with the gift of a bicycle for which she had long yearned. And I have already told you how Aunt Soňa Kovačevičová remembers her gallant and playful neighbor.

Unpretentious, gentle, kind, generous, lighthearted, easy and fun to be with—that was my father in his youth. In his middle years he showed his strength: he rebuilt the family business, he acted heroically during the war. Then came arrest, release, and a second exile. Collectively, they broke his spirit. Nevertheless, my father was to the very end of his life unpretentious, gentle, and kind.

PART II
BIRTHING A NATION

Part II is about the more distant past. I tell about my ancestors from the age of the great craft guilds, many of them engaged in tasks that have long since faded out of existence. I tell about rising from poverty to wealth. Most of all, however, I focus on building a nation—on conceiving and defending the idea that Slovaks have a distinctive identity, strongly linked to language, and that it is right to struggle against deliberate attempts to destroy that identity. This struggle began while Slovaks lived in the Kingdom of Hungary, and saw its resolution in the building of new states, first Czechoslovakia and later today's independent Slovakia. In the framework of this grand national story, I tell the stories of three visionaries—my great-granduncle Michal Miloslav Hodža, and my two grandfathers, Milan Hodža and Ján Pálka—whose lives embodied national and social ideals that still resonate today.

CHAPTER 14

The Deepest Roots
of My Mother's Family

Most people of Slovak descent living in the United States and Canada conceive of their homeland as being rich in tradition, often village-based, but very poor, a land which their ancestors left because of economic hardship, lack of opportunity, and sometimes political or ethnic oppression. This is indeed a true picture. It is the main reason why there was a massive migration of Slovaks to the United States at the turn of the nineteenth and twentieth centuries, and why at least a third of the families of today's Slovakia have relatives in America.

However, Slovakia, like all societies, is complex, and other family stories are equally true. My own ancestors, both on my mother's and on my father's side, were able to rise above the prevailing poverty, confront the oppression, and devote themselves to the flowering of the Slovak national ideal. Sometimes this was at great personal cost; at least ten members of my family up to and including my parents' generation died on foreign soil, a number of them in forced exile.

MY MOTHER DID HER BEST to keep these family stories alive for me. When I was in my early thirties and trying to understand something about my own life, I wrote to her asking her about the circumstances of my birth. Here is how she responded to my questions:

> My dear son,
>
> You have asked for the details of your birth. I will gladly describe them to you, for they are as vivid in my memory as if they had happened only last week. However, I can't do this without first explaining the events that led to your being born as an exile. Being an exile is quite in the Hodža tradition. . . .
>
> The first of your forebears to die in exile was Michal Miloslav Hodža, your mother's grand-uncle (1811-1870), the hundredth anniversary

of whose death was celebrated even by the Communist regime. Even it recognizes his contributions to the establishment of the Slovak literary language and to the Slovak nation in general. He was a pastor in Mikuláš. You probably don't remember that we showed you his grave, where in 1922 a grateful Czechoslovak Republic brought his remains from exile. . . .

Unfortunately, I wanted to know mainly about myself, and I did not pursue the stories my mother was longing to tell me. When the search for family legacy finally became urgent for me, both of my parents had been dead for twenty years and the stories they could have told me were gone forever. I realized that what I had left were only disconnected glimpses of a receding past.

Despite this loss, I became determined to learn the whole chronicle, to reach back in time as far as I could, and to develop an understanding of who my people were, how they had lived, and what they had contributed. This entailed assimilating the history of Slovakia itself—from the arrival of Slav tribes in the region of Central Europe by around 500 C.E.; through the thousand years of incorporation within the Kingdom of Hungary (1000-1918), including the period of maximum Ottoman control (1526-1683); the Slovak National Awakening of the mid-nineteenth century; the long Slovak struggle against Magyarization, the ever-intensifying pressure for ethnic assimilation exerted by Hungary's ruling Magyars, that peaked during the time of the Austro-Hungarian Empire, 1867-1918; and the exhilarating but often turbulent era of Czechoslovakia (1918-1992). I re-tell this long story briefly in Appendix I. Into the framework of the national story I was able to place the documented family story, which starts around 1700, shortly after the Ottoman Turks retreated from most of the territory of the Kingdom of Hungary.

I gradually realized that my ancestors lived out their lives in a society in which they were a double minority: Slovaks in a Hungarian state dominated by increasingly chauvinistic Magyars (for the relationship between ethnic Magyars and the Hungarian state, see Appendix I), and Lutherans among a majority of Catholics. This minority status even affected my own research. The violent side of the Counter-Reformation included not only intimidation and persecution of Protestants such as Lutherans, but also the destruction of their birth, baptismal, marriage, and death records. These are precisely the records that form the bedrock of genealogical research. Sometimes Lutheran families went to the local Catholic church to record baptisms and marriages, but for a hundred years these normally meticulous chronicles were interrupted. Slovak culture gives a great deal of attention to genealogy, so much so that the Slovak National Library has a Division of Genealogy supported by a professional research staff.

Usually, however, even these experts cannot reconstruct the family trees of Slovak Lutherans much prior to the beginning of the eighteenth century. These family trees, including mine, were chopped off and their roots lost.

Reestablished church records, coupled with records of guild memberships, occasional censuses, and other documents, have allowed expert genealogists to trace Lutheran families with some regularity to the early 1700s. From their work, I have assembled a picture of the way the roots of my family are embedded in the very soil of Slovakia. My narrative begins with the lineages of all eight of my great-grandparents, set in the environment of the Habsburg Empire and later the Austro-Hungarian Empire.

Great-grandfather Ondrej Hodža, Lutheran pastor

For centuries, the Kingdom of Hungary was divided into counties, each headed by an administrator responsible ultimately to the king. While the details changed over time, during Austria-Hungary, when my great-grandparents lived, the counties numbered seventy-one[1]. Thirteen of them, forming an arc along the kingdom's mountainous northern frontier, were inhabited primarily by Slovaks. They were often known collectively as Upper Hungary or *Felvidék*, but this designation gave them no special status and they were basically indistingushable from the other counties of Hungary. The story of the Hodžas takes place primarily in County Turiec, starting in the small village of Rakša in the hills a few miles away from Martin and later moving to the town of Sučany.

The name Hodža is unusual in Slovakia. Here is a legend about how it arose.[2] In 1683 the Turks were defeated at Vienna and fell into retreat, but they held many captives from the areas that they had previously controlled or through which their armies had passed. Among the captives was a group of Slovaks, and among these was one named Ďurčansky from a family of minor gentry. This Ďurčansky was an eloquent speaker and, as a good Lutheran, knew his Bible. He often quoted from scripture to encourage and uplift his fellow prisoners, and the Turks, seeing this, started to call him *hodža*, which means "teacher" in Turkish. After twelve years he managed to free himself from Turkish captivity and make his way back to his home town of Ďurčiná in County Trenčín, only to find that his relatives had pronounced him dead and had appropriated his portion of the family property, including his manor. The family, and indeed the whole region, had reverted to Catholicism. So, now being landless and in a religiously hostile setting, he moved to tiny Rakša in neighboring County Turiec, which was predominantly Lutheran. He renounced his title, renounced the family name of Ďurčansky, and took the title his Turkish captors had given him, *hodža*, as his new surname, Hodža. To make a living he became a miller.

It sounds like nothing more than a romantic legend. However, records do indeed show Slovak gentry by the name of Ďurčansky, who gained their title in 1587 for service to the king, living in Ďurčiná, and mention a Ďurčansky in Rakša in 1709[3]. Furthermore, the first recorded reference to the name Hodža anywhere in Slovakia is in Rakša, starting in 1714. From these records it seems likely that some time in the late 1600s or very early 1700s, the first Hodža settled in Rakša and bought or built the upper of two water-driven grain mills, the main buildings of which are still seen in the village today. So, legend or no, the story is consistent with available research.

From 1746 on, the Hodža genealogy is rather complete. Sons inherited the mill and stayed on in Rakša, most often marrying the daughters of local families. After a few generations there was a second mill. The upper mill was owned by Ján Hodža, a Slovak patriot who married Mária Hrianka from nearby Mošovce; his brother Juraj built the lower mill.

The village of Rakša, whose recorded history goes back to 1277,[4] had been owned by the Magyar noble family Raksány for many years. Rakša's peasants were the serfs of the lord, owing him labor and a sizeable share of their crop for the privilege of farming his lands. They were beholden to him for every event of their meager lives. Without their lord's permission, most peasants could neither marry nor move, and education for their children was out of the question. Ján Hodža was different in this respect. Even though he needed to remain in the good graces of Lord Raksány, Hodža was a free man, operating his own business. He had a sophistication beyond that of most villagers—he was, for instance, an excellent chess player—and he saw to it that his children were very well educated indeed. Most importantly, at a time when national identity was rarely in the consciousness of village people, Hodža transmitted to his children a strong sense of being Slovak.

Ján and Mária sent three of their sons to be educated, and all three opted for theology. Michal (1811-1870) completed his studies in Vienna, and Ondrej (1819-1888) in Halle (Germany); both became Lutheran ministers. Juraj (1824-1879) ultimately became a lawyer (Family tree 5, Appendix V). All three were active in the nineteenth century movement for Slovak emancipation from Magyar oppression. Michal (who adopted the middle name of Miloslav) became the Lutheran pastor of Mikuláš and achieved an unforgettable place in Slovak history. Michal's younger brother, Ondrej Hodža, was my great-grandfather. He served as the Lutheran pastor in Sučany, a small town near Martin, and he too was an outspoken Slovak patriot. The younger of his two sons was Grandfather Milan Hodža (Family tree 1).

The Hodža family home, birthplace of Michal Miloslav and his brothers, still stands in Rakša, maintained as a museum in his honor.[5] On the slope above it is a channel, bringing water from the surrounding hills. The branch of this channel that once powered the mill cavorts alongside the house, though the water-wheel, driveshaft, huge wooden gears, and flat grindstones of the mill itself are long gone. The museum is now a place of pilgrimage on one of Slovakia's beautiful byways. Ondrej's home and the birthplace of his children was the parish house just off the main square in Sučany. You can see it there today. On a stretch of green between the parish house and the church is a statue honoring Milan Hodža.

Great-grandmother Klementína Plech, pastor's daughter, pastor's wife

During the darkest period of Magyarization, from the time of the Austro-Hungarian Compromise in 1867 until World War I, the small stratum of stubborn Slovak nationalists most often found their centers of education, debate, and mutual support in private homes, and especially in the parish houses of small-town clergy.[6] Such was the parish house of Ján Plech, the Lutheran pastor of Liptovský Sv. Peter, not far from Mikuláš. Ján had two daughters, Emília and Klementína, who grew up in this atmosphere and absorbed it thoroughly.

In 1858 Emília married Ondrej Hodža, fully as ardent a Slovak patriot as was her own father[7] (Family trees 1 and 5). She bore him a daughter, Mária, and a son, Ján. Then, tragically, she died after only six years of marriage, leaving Ondrej to care for the two young children. Two years after Emília's death Ondrej remarried, taking her younger sister Klementína as his wife, a common arrangement in those days of frequent deaths, especially in childbirth. The new couple were childless for 19 years. Then, on February 1, 1878, their house was filled with joy, for it saw the birth of a baby boy, soon to be christened Milan. Klementína was thirty-six, Ondrej was nearly sixty. Milan Hodža was my grandfather.

A side root: The Ursínys of Rakša, farmers

Across the stream from Rakša was the village of Nedozor where the Ursíny family of farmers and occasional leather tanners settled. Over time the two villages merged under the name of Rakša. The Ursínys came from County Orava in the eighteenth century and, being hardworking and prudent, were able to buy land and add to it bit by bit until they had substantial holdings, some of which are in family hands even today.[8] The Ursíny and Hodža families were close, and several intermarriages occurred over the generations, starting with Mária, the sister of Michal Miloslav and Ondrej, who married Ján Ursíny.

Out of the Ursíny-Hodža lineage came a man we have already met, the Ján Ursíny of the twentieth century: devoted follower of Milan Hodža, hero of the

Slovak resistance and National Uprising, and victim of the twisted Communist quest for power. He had married Anna Hodža, and his admiration for Grandfather Hodža was so great that he named his firstborn son Milan. To make sure that the Hodža name would be preserved in Rakša, he legally changed young Milan's surname from Ursíny to Ursíny-Hodža, and a few years later dropped Ursíny altogether so that another Milan Hodža appeared.[9]

I am proud that I was able to know this Milan Hodža of Rakša personally. He grew up during the hard times of World War II while his father was often away and in constant danger. Milan remained unbowed under Communism despite the persecution and imprisonment to which his father was subjected. Much later, he became a regional organizer of *Verejnosť proti násiliu, VPN* (Public Against Violence), one of the organizations that precipitated the fall of Communist rule in Czechoslovakia in 1989. A shining representative of the dedication of both sides of his family—the Ursínys and the Hodžas—to democracy, decency, and political engagement, he died suddenly in 2009 while serving on his local electoral commission.

Great-grandfather Andrej Pivko, *šafraník* and *olejkár*

The Hodža name has a recent history. In contrast, Grandmother Hodža's maiden name, Pivko, is known on the territory of Slovakia from at least the year 1250.[10] Some Pivkos were landowners who obtained their properties, and occasionally titles as minor nobility, as rewards for distinguished service to the king. Over time, two distantly related branches were established in County Turiec, one in Sučany and the other in Benice.

Great-grandfather Andrej Pivko (Family tree 1) originally belonged to the Pivkos of Benice. He made his living primarily as a trader in saffron and medicinal oils—he was a *šafraník* (saffron trader) and *olejkár* (trader in oils). This seemingly exotic business was one of the traditional occupations of County Turiec. It is mentioned in chronicles dating at least as far back as the sixteenth century, and archeological evidence indicates that it was practiced as early as the thirteenth century.[11] A distinguished Hungarian anthropologist wrote in 1949[12] that "A few old *olejkárs* are still to be found in Czecho-Slovakia today in the county of Turiec." For at least 500 years, then, and perhaps for 800, Slovak men carried backpacks or drove horse carts loaded with herbs and oils which they sold for use in the medicine and dentistry of the times. Though they were basically uneducated, some of these men spoke five languages and traveled throughout much of Europe—from France in the west, through Sweden, Holland, Switzerland, Poland, Latvia, Lithuania and all the way to Turkey. Their greatest market, however, was in Russia, even into faraway Siberia.

Russia was the territory in which Great-grandfather Pivko made his fortune.[13] He was orphaned at an early age. When he was only twelve years old, he started as an apprentice to a distant relative who was an *olejkár* and *šafraník* and who took young Andrej on his first journey, the long walk from Sučany to Russia. Over time Andrej became independent, and traded not only in saffron and oils but in general household goods as well. By the nineteenth century, household goods had surpassed oils and saffron as the principal business of these wandering traders. He took advantage of a supply house in Warsaw owned by two brothers from County Turiec by name of Orságh. Andrej bought goods from the Orságh store and hired several men to distribute them by cart and backpack all over Russia. For twenty years he made frequent journeys to Russia, meeting his distributors, resupplying them, and settling accounts.

Great-grandmother Zuzana Majtáň, keeper of the homestead

When he was twenty-seven and had become modestly wealthy, Andrej Pivko's aunt arranged a marriage for him.[14] The bride, whom he had never seen before the wedding day, was nineteen-year-old Zuzana Majtáň, the daughter of a well-to-do farming family in Sučany. The profits from Andrej's trading in Russia were combined with those from the successful farming operation of the Majtáňs, and the family prospered.

During Andrej's long absences, the care of the large household, as well as the running of the farm, fell to Zuzana, who was a no-nonsense manager and strict disciplinarian. And the household was large indeed, for nine children were born to Andrej and Zuzana. Four died in infancy. Zuzana poured her heart into raising their only remaining son, Pal'o, but he carried a hereditary muscular dystrophy. From the age of nine he could no longer walk. Death came at the age of fifteen. The grieving Zuzana focused her enormous energies entirely on increasing the family fortune for the benefit of the four daughters who lived to adulthood.

Ondrej Hodža described Andrej Pivko as "the best friend and collaborator we could have in the church and in our national activities.[15]" Andrej's national feeling carried over to his and Zuzana's daughters. The Pivko sisters, as well as their husbands and their children, dedicated their lives to the national cause (Family tree 2). Irena Pivko married Milan Hodža and supported his many activities. Mária Pivko married Cyril Pivko of the Benice branch of the Pivko family, who was a prominent member of Grandfather Hodža's Agrarian Party and represented the party in the Czechoslovak Senate. Mária herself stayed at home and ran the farm in Benice with force and determination, as her mother had done in Sučany. She is the Aunt Mária whose house in Benice stands out so vividly in my memories of our return to Czechoslovakia following World War II (Chapter 7). Their daughter Lýdia married Pastor Jozef Bučko, the martyr of the Slovak National Uprising (Chapter 6). Anna Pivko married Pastor Ján Milan Štetka, a signer of the declaration that proclaimed the intention of Slovaks to join Czechs to form Czechoslovakia in 1918. Štetka was also the author of an important account of forced Magyarization that played a significant role in the peace conference in Paris that ended World War I. His daughters are my aunts Vierka and Zorka (Chapters 9 and 12). [16] Only Paulína stayed out of political engagement; she lived a quiet life as the wife of a pharmacist.

Four Pivko sisters, photographed in the 1950s. Front row, left to right: Anna, married to Ján Milan Štetka; Irena, married to Milan Hodža. Back row, left to right: Mária, married to Cyril Pivko; Paulína, married to Pavel Gazdík. Author's archive.

The roots of my mother's family were literally close to the soil of Turiec—peasants, millers, traders in spices and oils, and the wives who bore the children and kept the homes. The Lutheran clergy in the family tended not only to the spiritual lives of their flocks, but also to their place in society. In nationally embattled times, they embraced the sense of their own Slovakness and transmitted it to their congregations and to their own children.

CHAPTER 15

The Deepest Roots
of My Father's Family

The main economic bases of the Slovak counties of the Kingdom of Hungary were agriculture, mining and smelting, and crafts.[1] Many of the miners were Germans, brought in specifically for their technical expertise. Most Slovaks, apart from some minor nobility and a small stratum of clerics and other intelligentsia, were peasants and craftsmen. These social and economic realities are reflected in the lives of all the branches of my family. The earliest Hodžas, stemming from minor nobility, were millers; the Pivkos were peasants and traders. The Pálka side of my family started as craftsmen.

For hundreds of years, the lives of craftsmen were ruled by craft guilds. Guilds originated in Europe in the twelfth century and in Slovakia in the year 1307.[2] They did not fully fade out until well into the nineteenth century. Each local guild was run by a guild master elected by all the members of the rank of master, and the Pálka name appears repeatedly on the list of guildmasters of the Leatherworkers Guild. A guild operated under local or even royal charter and had many powers. It regulated the number of masters in a region, the supply of raw materials, and the production, prices, and sale of finished products. Effectively, a guild held a monopoly on its craft in its own region. It also regulated the personal behavior of its members—for example, cursing was forbidden and attendance at church required, with cash penalties for transgressions[3].

Great-Grandfather Janko Pálka, entrepreneur in leather

County Liptov, bordering on County Turiec, is the place my father loved so dearly and for which he yearned so deeply during all his years in exile. The ancestral home of the Pálkas is the village of Vrbica, dating at least to the ninth century and believed to be one of the original Slav settlements in County Liptov.[4] Long an independent village, Vrbica was incorporated into the bustling town of Mikuláš only in 1923.

The oldest known written record of a member of the Pálka family in County Liptov dates from 1703.[5] Though most of the inhabitants of Vrbica were peasant farmers, this Michal Pálka was one of the landless poor and made his living working with leather, like virtually all Pálkas right down to my own father. We know about Michal because he was a member of the Leatherworkers Guild, whose records show that in 1703 he completed his apprenticeship and was declared a journeyman. Records preserved in the Catholic church of Mikuláš show that he married Dorota Mikulca with whom he had several children, both boys and girls. The boys went on to become leatherworkers like their father. For want of earlier records, I think of Michal as the founder of the Pálka lineage.

During the nineteenth and twentieth centuries, most of the Pálkas of Vrbica, and later of adjacent Mikuláš, were still leather workers. During this period, however, they were known for their financial success, their devotion to the Slovak national cause, and their religious faith and support of the Lutheran church. How did a poor and landless family, barely getting by in a lowly craft, achieve such status and recognition?

Some clues come from the records of the Leatherworkers Guild. For over 150 years, from the early 1700s until the dissolution of the guilds by imperial decree in 1860, the Pálka name appears regularly among the officers of the guild, including the highest, the guildmaster or *Cechmajster*. Evidently, these men were not only successful in their craft, they were also highly respected by their peers. They laid the foundation for the success of later generations.

A turning point in family fortunes came in the late eighteenth and early nineteenth centuries, during the lifetime of Ondrej Pálka the elder (1780-1848), my great-great-grandfather (Family tree 3, Appendix V). Ondrej decided to diversify his leather business by adding an apparently unrelated component—trading in tobacco. It was a shrewd move. He drove his wagon, loaded with tanned hides, to markets in many of the major towns of Hungary and brought back raw hides to supplement the supply available locally in Mikuláš. On the same journeys he also bought, transported, and sold tobacco. From the combined profits, he was able to buy the property next door to his own. Now he had space to store hides and especially the large quantities of bark from which tanning solutions were prepared. His business prospered, and as profits accumulated, he bought additional properties.

Ondrej enjoyed very high esteem in the community. A notable teacher and chronicler of the times wrote of Ondrej and his family:[6]

> God helped him, so to speak, in front of our very eyes. . . . God's blessings upon them were evident from their hard work as tanners

and traders in tobacco, the acquisition of properties, and the cleaving to religious piety. . . .

In addition to working hard in his own shop and business, Ondrej served as guildmaster for almost three decades, from 1809 until his death in 1848, with only minor interruptions. He was also a functionary in the municipal government of Vrbica and a generous supporter of the local Lutheran church. Even half a century after his death he was described as " . . .the first among us, teaching morality by his example."[6]

Ondrej the elder, who lived to see the rise of the Slovak National Awakening in the middle of the nineteenth century (see Chapters 17-22), died of hepatitis in 1848, the year that revolution swept the Slovak counties of Hungary as well as most of the rest of Europe. In 1800 his eldest son, Ondrej the younger, had started a family chronicle. This is how he described his father's death and funeral:[7]

> On the 22nd of June, at two o'clock in the afternoon, our beloved father, Ondrej Pálka, died and passed on to eternity. He had weakened since March, but only for the last two weeks did he lie in his bed quietly, groan sometimes, and sleep much; thus he came quietly and peacefully to the end. His body, from which the soul had departed, was taken to the body of God the next day at 7 o'clock in the evening. . . . It was accompanied by an uncountably large procession of people, led by pastor Ján Lehocký from Trnovec because our own Pastor Hodža was in Prague at the time [Michal Miloslav Hodža].

Ondrej the elder's second son, Ján, known to everyone as Janko, was my great-grandfather. His best-known descendant was my grandfather, also named Ján Pálka (Chapter 23 and Family tree 3). This is the branch of the family into which I was born in Paris a century later. Great-grandfather Janko's young life, was formed during the tumultuous years of Michal Miloslav Hodža's functioning in Mikuláš (Chapters 18-20). His career as a successful entrepreneur in leather continued until his death in 1904 (Chapter 23).

Great-grandmother Zuzana Bella, furrier's daughter, actress, poet

Great-grandfather Janko Pálka married Zuzana Bella, a vivacious and gifted amateur actress, during the heady days of the Slovak National Awakening.

The roots of the Bellas were in the little town of Kráľova Lehota, some miles up the river from Mikuláš. Here, around the end of the thirteenth century, Slovak royal servants keeping watch over the king's hunting domains in the remote reaches of County Liptov founded a village at the confluence of the rivers White Váh and Black Váh (*Biely Váh* and *Čierny Váh*). In 1361 King Ludevít I officially gifted this village and extensive properties to several of these servants in recognition of their loyalty and the services they had performed for him during his hunting expeditions.[8]

Reflecting this history, through the years Kráľova Lehota was distinguished by the presence of an unusually large number of Slovak landed gentry. Serving these nobles were peasants, among them the family Bella. In the late 1700s the peasant Andrej Bella married Júlia Kmotrík, who, on February 13, 1810, bore him a son, Jozef.[9] Young Jozef was a gifted child. He completed his elementary school education in Kráľova Lehota, but he had higher ambitions. Instead of remaining a peasant farmer like his father and his ancestors for many generations, he apprenticed himself to a master furrier in the nearby village of Hybe. He progressed to the rank of journeyman and set off to perfect his craft in places as distant as Miskolc in the far eastern reaches of today's Hungary. Studies completed, he became a master and moved to Mikuláš where he established himself as an independent furrier. His shop prospered, and he became one of the town's prominent citizens, eventually serving as the notary and as mayor. He supported Michal Miloslav Hodža in his efforts on behalf of Slovaks and against persecution at the hands of Magyars and their allies, was imprisoned during the revolution of 1848, and later carried a petition for Slovak rights from Liptov to the emperor himself. As his life neared its end, his furrier's business gradually faded and ultimately failed.

When he was twenty, this furrier-born-of-a-peasant had married Mária Lang. The couple had seven children, among them Zuzana Bella, my great-grandmother (Family trees 3 and 4). It was a remarkable family, every one of them contributing to the Slovak national cause (Chapter 22). After she married and stopped performing in the theater, Zuzana's artistic side emerged primarily in poetry. She lived a long, family-centered life, dying only in 1932 at the age of eighty-eight (Chapter 23).

Great-grandfather Samuel Jurenka, scion of peasants and *pytlikárs*

In 1901 Grandfather Ján Pálka married Darina Jurenka. Her parents, my great-grandparents, were Samuel Jurenka and Judita Poláček of District Myjava near the Moravian border (Family tree 3; Map 3, Appendix II). Like Turiec and Liptov, Myjava was a center of Slovak national consciousness and of resistance to Magyarization. The Jurenkas were related to Milan Rastislav Štefánik, one of the most influential leaders of the movement to form Czechoslovakia (Chapter 26), whose parents were Pavol Štefánik and Albertína Jurenka.[10] The Poláčeks were related by marriage to Jozef Miloslav Hurban, one of the three greatest leaders of the Slovak National Awakening[11] (Chapter 19).

The Jurenka family were farmers for generations. Over time they acquired extensive properties and ultimately were able to hire others to do most of the back-breaking work in the fields. It was no longer necessary for the sons to remain on the land. They were also prominent in the rise of a specialized craft, the making of sleeve-like woollen bags that collected and sifted the freshly-ground flour in traditional flour mills.[12] Such a bag was called a *pytel*, its maker was the *pytlikár*, and his guild was the *pytlikársky cech*. Once he had made a supply of *pytels*, the *pytlikár* would set out, usually on foot, to sell them to the many small mills that were scattered throughout the Habsburg Empire and later the Austro-Hungarian Empire. Many *pytlikár* families became rich. Ultimately, however, improved mills were invented in Europe, introduced on a large scale in the American Midwest, and then found their way back to Europe;[13] they made woollen *pytels* obsolete. When the crash came, in the latter part of the nineteenth century, Myjava fell into a deep economic recession, and *pytlikárs* had to find a different way of making a living[14]. In search of new opportunities, many emigrated to the United States. Rev. Ján Bradáč, whose church we faithfully attended in Chicago, was among those emigrants.[15]

Matej Jurenka (1784-1848) helped to establish the *pytlikársky cech* in Myjava in 1833, and was its *Cechmajster* from 1837 until his death.[16] His son Samuel the elder (1819-1883) was a businessman who increased the family's wealth, served as the mayor of the town of Myjava, and held important lay positions in the Lutheran church. His son, Samuel the younger (1854-1930), was my great-grandfather (Family tree 3).

This younger Samuel had an entrepreneurial streak. Looking to the future, he studied business in Vienna before setting out on his own. One of his earliest ventures might be surprising to modern sensibilities. In those days the mail was not always a government-operated enterprise, as we take for granted today. Rather, independent businesses, contracting with the government, hired men to go from house to house in wagons, collecting and distributing letters and parcels. Young Samuel developed one of the first such mail businesses in Myjava. In 1883 his license was taken away by the Hungarian government on the grounds of suspicion of Slovak national activity and "failure to agree with the modern intelligentsia."[17]

Later, after diverse and considerable business successes, as well as leadership in civic activities such as the establishment of a book club, Samuel took what proved to be his greatest step—he played a major role in establishing the *Myjavská banka*, Myjava Bank.[18] The Myjava Bank grew out of the efforts of *pylikárs* to help their community during economic hard times. Initially, in 1868, they formed the *Spolek pytlikársky*, an association for wine and liquor sales independent of the established Jewish taverns and, more importantly, for providing loans at modest rates of interest. In the hands of moneylenders, interest on loans had climbed to thirty percent and even fifty percent, and relief from usury was badly needed. The *Spolek,* with great-grandfather Samuel as one of its officers, stepped into the breach and offered its members low-interest loans. Over time, the activities of the *Spolek* expanded to establishing grain reserves that could be loaned out to members much as money was loaned out.

Starting in 1892, the *Spolek* was replaced by a full-fledged bank, the *Myjavská banka*. The prime initiator and co-founder of the *Myjavská banka* was great-grandfather Samuel, who also served as its director until 1924, more than thirty years. At the time of its founding, it was only the sixth bank in all of the Slovak-inhabited counties of Upper Hungary to be owned by Slovaks and designed to serve a Slovak clientele.[19] All the hundreds of other banks operating in the Slovak counties were owned by Magyars, Germans, or Jews, and they catered to larger business interests. Most Slovaks were farmers or owned small businesses, and if these larger banks lent to them at all, it was at exorbitant interest rates. The Myjava Bank maintained the interest on loans at five to six percent, and despite this low rate successfully provided all basic banking services to the poor Slovak rural population of the region.

In this way, the Myjava Bank served as a significant social resource and also supported the Slovak national cause. In 1942, to celebrate the fiftieth anniversary of its founding, the bank published a small book describing its history and evaluated its own impact in this way:[20]

> The Myjava Bank, right in the first years of its functioning, became a benefactor of the whole region, because by providing low-interest loans it freed the deeply indebted people from the influence of foreign capital and especially from the hands of small money-lenders of whom there was an abundance everywhere, and in this way saved many from financial ruin.

Over the decades the bank experienced a complex history. After 1947 Communists nationalized all banks and imposed a series of mergers. The Myjava Bank finally became just a branch of the Slovak Tatra Bank headquartered in Bratislava.

Great-grandmother Judita Poláček, daughter of sheep-drivers

It is said[21] that when the Myjava Bank was founded, or when it experienced financial difficulties under great-grandfather Samuel Jurenka's directorship, the rich dowry that great-grandmother Judita Poláček (1852-1947) had brought to their marriage in 1876 provided significant assistance. The story of how the wealth of the Poláček family grew is remarkable.

Like virtually all of my other ancestors, the Poláčeks started in poverty in a lowly profession. The first written records that are reliably linked to great-grandmother Poláček's family come from the guilds and show that they were butchers.[22] The Butchers Guild of the town of Brezová in District Myjava became independent of the regional guild in 1708. This required organization, drafting of articles, permission from the parent guild, and approval by county or royal officials. The Poláčeks were part of this legal process, and their names appear regularly in the records of the new guild. They maintained the family profession as butchers for many generations and also expanded their work in an interesting way.

In those days, the raising of cattle, sheep, and swine was a very big business in widespread regions of southeastern Europe centered in today's Romania and the Balkans. Far more livestock was raised than could be consumed locally. On the other hand, there was a shortage of meat in Germany, France, and other areas of western Europe. Enterprising men, such as three Poláček brothers named Ján, Martin, and Juraj, bought sheep in Romania or the Balkans, drove them across the Hungarian lowlands, and sold them for a good profit in Germany and France. The entire journey was made on foot. The way was long and arduous, and they had to graze their animals as they went, which often meant poaching on lands owned by assorted nobility. This was a decidedly dangerous proposition, especially when their herds got mixed up with local ones and they were discovered by the lords' shepherds! Still, over the years no lives were lost and no jail sentences incurred.

For men who were skilled, strong, and brave, driving sheep was exceedingly good business. According to a family story, for many years the brothers kept all the money they made in bags at home. Once banks were established, however, they deposited their cash in the various cities through which they passed. In 1870, so the story goes, brother Martin stopped at the Reiffeisen Bank in Brno (in Moravia), walked up to the teller, and asked to deposit 40,000 pieces of gold. The teller, looking up at the huge, ascetic-looking man with his giant walking stick and 40,000 gold pieces in his hands, became very nervous, and ran off after the director of the bank. The director started to inquire as to the source of all that money, expecting that it had been stolen or at least found. To get to the bottom of the matter, he asked if he might send a letter of inquiry to Martin's home town of Brezová. It took a few days to get a response because the telegraph line only went part way, and the letter had to go by messenger from the last station. The return letter from the town council of Brezová said, "Yes, Martin Poláček is a citizen of our town, and he certainly may have 40,000 gold pieces with him. What is more, if one of the other sheep traders is with him, they could just buy your bank!" Records of this affair, including the original telegram, are preserved in the archives of the National Savings Bank in Brno.

The lucrative sheep herding business came to a close after railways were built in the late nineteenth and early twentieth centuries. Despite their wealth, the Poláčeks were unpretentious and devout. In addition to driving sheep, they coaxed a bountiful harvest from the rocky soil of Brezová and supported worthy causes. Over time, the family abandoned its butchering, sheep driving, and farming origins and moved into a variety of professional fields.

In 1930, Samuel Jurenka committed suicide, apparently distraught over bank matters.[23] Great-grandmother Judita continued to live on the family property in Myjava until her death in 1947. Annual visits by her children, grandchildren, and the wider family, including my parents and Uncle Zdeno Jurenka (Chapter 8), were obligatory and festive occasions. I never met her—there was no family gathering in 1947—but her life overlapped my own. In a way, she was my link back to the days of the craft guilds and the *pytlikárs*, the days before the railroad when travel was on foot or horseback, wagon or carriage, the days when entreprising men delivered the mail to remote regions and when a Slovak could get rich driving sheep from Romania to Vienna.

Peasants, millers, *šafraníks* and pastors, leatherworkers, furriers, *pytlikárs* and butchers—these were my ancestors. They were neither serfs nor nobles, but enterprising and frugal members of a small, emerging middle class. They found ways to work themselves out of pervasive poverty and to advance in the world. They were able to seize the few and precious educational opportunities, cultivate a sense of Slovak identity, realize the importance of language, and provide leadership for emancipation within the Habsburg Empire and its successor state, the Austro-Hungarian Empire. It was primarily those in the middle class—craftsmen, free peasants, and minor entrepreneurs—whose sons (and later daughters) provided the intellectual leadership, the political power, and the financial resources for birthing a nation.

CHAPTER 16

Ondrej Pálka—"The Father of Our People in Mikuláš"

Leather was the life work of Pálkas for at least two and a half centuries, from some time before 1703, the year Michal Pálka completed his apprenticeship and graduated to the position of a journeyman in the Leatherworkers Guild of Mikuláš, until 1949, when my father was jailed and his factory was confiscated by the Communist government of Czechoslovakia.[1] At the beginning of this period, Turkish hegemony over southeastern Europe was just beginning to wane, and the Austrian Habsburgs ruled over a resurgent Hungary (Appendices I and II). There was no politically-defined Slovakia yet, only Hungarian counties inhabited primarily by Slovaks. By the time the period was over, the Kingdom of Hungary had achieved parity with Austria in a carefully balanced Austro-Hungarian Empire, this empire in turn had dissolved in the ashes of World War I, and newly-formed Czechoslovakia had passed through the traumatic events of World War II and into a Communist dictatorship. One of the final products my father's factory made while he still owned it was a shiny, black, leather briefcase that he brought home for me. After that the factory belonged to a faceless state. It existed until very recently, manufacturing leather articles of much the same sort that my father introduced into its inventory and selling them on the European market.[1]

CONVERTING RAW HIDES INTO LEATHER—soft and supple, tough and durable, sometimes split, often dyed—is an ancient craft. In addition to footwear, clothing, and furniture, leather once had major industrial uses as well, including drive belts, sometimes hundreds of feet long, to move the complex machinery of the industrial revolution; bushings to hold spinning axles in place, and others.

The modern process of turning raw hides into workable leather is highly automated and speedy. Traditionally, however, it was labor-intensive and very slow.[2] Even at the end of the nineteenth century, it could take months.[3] The first step was soaking them so as to facilitate later scraping. The soaking required hefting whole, heavy hides in and out of large vats or wooden barrels, using long poles to lower the hides into the soaking solution and, at the proper time, to fish them out again and move them to the next vat. Once the soaking was complete, the craftsman would lay the hide across a trestle, grasp a dull, two-handled knife in both hands, and meticulously, stroke by stroke, scrape the hair off the outer surface of the hide and whatever fat and muscle remained off its inner surface, without cutting into the hide itself (see photo, p. 121). This was demanding work that required both physical power and mental focus.

Later, a hide would be tanned so it would maintain its strength. Tanning required soaking the hide once again, this time in a series of solutions made out of the bark of the spruce trees that grew abundantly in the surrounding hills. The master tanner had to buy the bark and store it, so it would be ready for use when needed. He also had to have access to clean water, to make the various solutions and especially to rinse the hides to stop the chemical reactions before they did any damage. A stream formed the boundary between Vrbica and Mikuláš, and whenever possible, the masters tried to secure plots of land along this stream to set up their homes and shops, so they could use its water whenever they needed it. As the stream proceeded past the shops, it turned black with their effluents.

Finally, the craftsman would dry the tanned hide to just the right stage and laboriously work oil into it to make it waterproof and supple. Once a raw hide had been transformed in this way, the leather was either cut and stitched into simple footwear or sold to other craftsmen to be made into more complex articles.

The water of the stream (reputed to be particularly good for the tanning process), the proximity of spruce trees and their bark, and the abundance of cattle and sheep grazing in the fields and meadows all combined to make it possible for leatherworking to develop into a prominent craft in Vrbica and Mikuláš.

AN ASPIRING YOUNG CRAFTSMAN like Michal started by apprenticing to a master. (The charter of the Leatherworkers Guild of Mikuláš had been granted in 1508.[3]) He was obligated to the master for a period of three years. In return, the master taught him the craft and provided a very modest stipend and lodging. The master, and whatever journeymen and apprentices he might have, all lodged and ate together like an extended family. The master's wife was kept busy providing meals to several hard-working, hungry men.[4] Once the apprentice had learned the necessary skills, the guildmaster wrote out a formal certificate to that effect, which also recommended that other masters take the erstwhile apprentice, now a journeyman, into their shops.[5]

Just promoted, the new journeyman continued his education for another three years, journeying from one master to another to learn as much as he could. Finally he prepared a masterpiece (*Meisterstück* in German) that demonstrated his skills. Michal the journeyman would have presented a superbly prepared hide, uniformly thick, strong, and glowing with oil, to the masters of the guild as the piece required for his promotion to the rank of master. Upon its successful presentation to the guild, he was certified as an independent master. This was a grand and extravagant occasion at which the new master was expected to provide a lavish feast for his new colleagues, as well as various fees payable to the guild.[6]

> Then it was time for the great feast, the *oldomáš*. This included a roast pig and goose, as well as mulled wine, *hriate*, prepared in each home according to the family's secret recipe. After being pronounced a master, the ex-journeyman was entitled to drink from his very own glass. . . The Leatherworkers Guild was considered to be the cream of the guild world. For drinking to the *Meisterstück*, there suddenly appeared at the table not only *hriate*, but also flagons of fine Hungarian wine.

It might take a new master several years to make full payment to his moneylender for the expenses.

Mikuláš was home to at least thirty guilds, and leatherworking itself was subdivided into several specialties, notably tanners, shoemakers, bootmakers, saddlemakers, and furriers. The guilds provided advancement and security for generations of craftsmen, but they were also extremely restrictive and were finally abolished by imperial decree in 1860. Many of their practices survived for some time, particularly in the Hungarian region of the monarchy, but ultimately they were replaced by other, more entrepreneurial forms of craft organization. Private businesses started springing up. Their owners hired employees for help, rather than relying on apprentices or journeymen. The new businesses were referred to as *manufactories*, from the Latin *manus*, meaning hand, and *facere*, meaning to make—thus, a place where things are made by hand. (Only later did the term "manufacture" come to signify mechanized mass production.) As the number of employees in a firm grew, production could be streamlined, the total amount of business substantially increased, and greater profits accumulated.

ONDREJ PÁLKA THE ELDER (1780-1848), who was introduced in Chapter 15 (Family tree 3), lived and worked entirely in the era of the guilds and was guildmaster of the Leatherworkers Guild for many years. Like all guildmasters of the times, he would have had journeymen and apprentices in his shop, his wife would have fed everyone at shared meals, and he would have been responsible for the discipline of his guild members.

Upon his death, his son Ondrej the younger (1800-1877), according to custom, took over the workshop and also the tobacco trading business.[7] He was elected to the position of guildmaster that his father had held for so long. As a master he, too, trained journeymen and apprentices, his house was home to the apprentices, and his wife Zuzana mananged the home and the meals. It was during his lifetime, however, that the guilds were abolished by law and ceased to be a dominant force in practice. Being an enterprising man, Ondrej the younger established his own leatherworking manufactory. We have some data for this business:[8] In each of the years 1857-59 he employed three or four assistants and processed a total of 3200 to 4500 hides, or an average of about ten per day. There were several other tanneries in Mikuláš as well, so the total demand might have approached 100 hides per day. Even though cattle were an important part of the still primarily agricultural economy of County Liptov, the region could not possibly supply this number of hides, and Ondrej brought his from the whole of Slovakia, and also from distant Vienna and Budapest. He also sold far and wide, south to the cities of the Hungarian plain, north to Poland, and west to Vienna and beyond.

The railway did not reach Mikuláš until 1872, so the transport of all materials, whether the raw hides, the finished leather, the raw materials needed for processing, or the tobacco that Ondrej also traded, was by heavy, horse-drawn wagons or by rafts.[9] In those days transport in the region was hard and dangerous work. The wagons, drawn by teams of four to eight horses and equipped with only rudimentary brakes, had to negotiate steep slopes on the ancient dirt roads and could easily careen out of control. The rafts, poled by skilled raftsmen, had to negotiate rapids in the river, and every so often a raft and its crew were lost. At this time in the history of Hungary there were neither railroads to carry raw materials and finished hides, nor machines to assist in the hard labor of tanning or working leather. Various kinds of businesses were being established all over the kingdom, but the Industrial Revolution had not yet arrived.

Ondrej the younger became even more prosperous than his father. Like his father, he invested in real estate, buying several properties on which he constructed tanning workshops, stables, barns, and ultimately a two-story house. But Ondrej the younger went even further. In 1851 with his brother Samuel, and again in 1854 with two other partners who had also prospered in the leather trade, he did something that earlier would have been unthinkable in County Liptov—he bought substantial pieces of rural property from members of the Pongrác family, the noblemen who had far the largest land holdings in the county and who were the hereditary owners of Mikuláš itself. This transaction was a sign of the vast social changes taking place everywhere in Europe, changes that were marked by the string of revolutions that had occurred in 1848 (Chapters 17 and 19). It was equally a tribute to the high regard in which Ondrej was held by all levels of the society of County Liptov. In 1860, when he was 60 years old, he passed on his business to his two sons.

IN THE BOX LABELED "PÁLKA" in the archives of the Museum of Janko Kráľ in Mikuláš is a handwritten family chronicle started by Ondrej the younger, according to the custom among leading families of the time. Its opening passages are clearly retrospective, for the first entry, dated October 6, 1800, records his own birth:

> On the 6th of October I was born and christened as Ondrej Pálka in the church of Vrbica and St. Mikuláš.

The entries describe births, baptisms, marriages, deaths, and major business ventures, as well as calamities such as floods, fires, and cholera epidemics. They are succinct, factual, and not in the least introspective—the writer does not reveal himself, he records only what he considers to be the most important events in the history of the family.

Despite its reserve, the chronicle offers some insights into the life of this devoted family man and engaged citizen. Here, for example, is his description of how he came to be married:

> *September 11th, 1825.* Through the will of God, I started to change my state into the married state, which happened in the following way. We young people decided to organize a ball in the hall of the royal inn of Vrbica, which was announced for Sunday. At the ball I communicated and discussed my decision to enter into the state of marriage with the honorable Miss Zuzana Scholtz, and she neither accepted nor denied me, explaining that she needed to consult her father and her grandmother. On September 13th I went to visit her father, and on September 14th I indeed gained Miss Zuzana Scholtz for my future wife. This happened at 12 o'clock. Then I left for the market in Tokay to buy tobacco, and returned from my journey in 10 days.

Courtship and prospective marriage were not allowed to interfere with business! The wedding followed in a month. The minister, Jíří Scholtz, was also the bride's father. The day was beautiful. There was a mid-day banquet for sixty guests, and in the evening a dance. Almost exactly a year later the couple's first child, a boy, was christened Ondrej after his father and grandfather (Plates 18, 19).

Over the years, Ondrej the younger held various municipal and county offices. He participated in the establishment of a cooperative savings bank in Vrbica, one of the first in Slovakia. Like his father, he was a generous supporter of the Lutheran church—he donated the building in which the Lutheran girls' school could be housed (the same school that I attended many years later), made substantial contributions to a foundation for the support of Lutheran schools, and so forth. Together with Jozef Bella, great-grandmother Pálka's father, Ondrej served as supervisor of the several local Lutheran schools. Partly as a staunch supporter of Michal Miloslav Hodža, he was engaged in the Slovak national awakening in may ways (Chapters 17-20).

Ondrej was highly respected and honored in his own lifetime.[10]

> He "wove himself a wreath of glory" in our nation, especially with his support of national literary undertakings, for wherever in Slovakia funds were being collected, there his name is always found. There was no Slovak book that he did not buy.

For this reason, one of Slovakia's greatest poets, Andrej Sládkovič, called him the "father of our people in Mikuláš."

ONDREJ THE YOUNGER'S BUSINESS of turning raw hides into beautiful, supple leather went through three additional generations of family ownership, though not with such remarkable success.[11] During this time, steam-driven machinery was introduced, and the nature of the products evolved somewhat. The last owner, Igor, was drafted into the Austro-Hungarian army in 1914, at the beginning of World War I. In his absence Igor's wife ran the business, but shortages of both raw materials and labor required her to curtail production. Finally, at the end of the war, the factory closed. Igor had deserted from the Austro-Hungarian army and joined the Czechoslovak Legions in Russia (Chapter 26), returning home in 1920. He did not attempt to restart production. Rather, he became an executive in the firm of Lacko-Pálka in which my Grandfather Pálka and later my father was a partner. Later, like so many nationally-minded, middle-class Slovaks, Igor suffered under the Communist regime. He died in 1957.

Igor's death marked the end of the 150-year lineage of leatherworkers founded by Ondrej Pálka the elder in his workshop on the banks of the little stream separating Vrbica from Mikuláš. The other significant lineage of Pálkas stemmed from Ondrej the elder's second son, Ján. That is my own lineage—I am its fifth Ján.

CHAPTER 17

The Rise of Nationalism

Andrej Sládkovič, one of the greatest poets of the Slovak National Awakening[1], called Ondrej Pálka "the father of our people in Mikuláš." *Our people.* The very phrase conveys a sense of connectedness and distinctiveness, and almost a familial bond. Of course, by *our*, Sládkovič meant *Slovak,* the Slovak people, who were different from the Magyars who effectively ruled Hungary, and different from the Germans who were the dominant cultural force in the whole of Central Europe—different, in short, from all other national groups even though they were close to other Slavs, especially the Czechs.

A hundred years earlier, Ondrej would have given money and bought Slovak-language publications without attaching any political meaning to the act, and Sládkovič would have hailed him for his good works but would probably never have thought of referring to him in a national context. Europe was long divided into empires, kingdoms, principalities—units with hereditary rulers at their head. The rulers raised armies to battle with each other, or formed alliances by marriage, and the nobility often jousted with them for political power, but none of this was done primarily in the context of nationhood. The vast majority of ordinary people, of course, were mainly concerned about surviving from day to day and not being conscripted into the army for the noble's or the king's next battles. They may have cared about religion, but not about nationhood.

WHILE THE EMERGING IDEAS OF NATIONHOOD and rights not just for the noble, but also for the common man, had a complex history in Europe,[2] it was in the still-forming United States that they first took a concrete political form. The Declaration of Independence, adopted on July 4, 1776, opens with these words:

> When in the course of human events it becomes necessary for one people to dissolve the political bands that have united them with another. . .

And the second paragraph continues:

> We hold these truths to be self-evident, that all men are created equal, that they are endowed by their Creator with certain unalien-

able Rights, that among these are Life, Liberty, and the pursuit of Happiness. That to secure these rights, Governments are instituted among Men, deriving their just powers from the consent of the governed. . . .

This great document, therefore, contains two key concepts. The first gives to "a people" the right to make choices about political allegiance. It does not define what "a people" is, but it certainly implies a strong bond among its members. I take this to be the essence of the idea of nation and nationalism. Scholars have long struggled with definitions of nationalism, including the question of whether national aspirations necessarily include the establishment of an independent nation-state[3]. As we shall see later, Slovaks gradually moved from struggling for primarily cultural and linguistic recognition and rights within the Kingdom of Hungary, to leaving Hungary and choosing a new political union with the Czechs, to embracing the concept of a fully independent Slovakia. This evolution took place over more than two centuries, and only recently did Slovaks finally "dissolve the political bands that have united them with another."[4]

Primarily during the nineteenth century national feelings, often increasingly focused on the political unity and independence of an ethnically defined nation, quickly spread throughout Europe. Regrettably, not all nations that evolved a keen sense of distinctive identity also embraced the second key concept of the Declaration of Independence, that the governed are ultimately superior to those who rule—in other words, a democracy. We need only recall Nazi Germany in this regard: shouting blatantly nationalist slogans like *Deutschland über Alles* (Germany above all), Germans of the time gave unlimited allegiance to their single *Führer*. The wartime Slovak Republic, among others, echoed the German example. Despite the words of America's founding fathers, nationalism and democracy proved to be only sometime companions.

Still, nationalism became the greatest political force of the nineteenth century,[5] and it retains its power to the present day. I recognize it in my own life. For example, while I was attending elementary school in New York City, students in the seventh and eighth grade were still required to memorize poems. We were given assignments from the classics of English and American literature, and on the dreaded day we had to stand up at our desks and recite stanzas aloud. It was terrifying. Nonetheless, I learned poems in this manner that I can still recite today, more than fifty years later, with great enjoyment.

One that I found on my own and committed to memory is a famous passage from Sir Walter Scott's romantic ballad *The Lay of the Last Minstrel*. It starts like this:

Breathes there a man with soul so dead
Who never to himself hath said:
"This is my own, my native land"?
Whose heart hath ne'er within him burned
As home his footsteps he hath turned,
From wandering on a foreign strand?

When I was fourteen years old, something within me responded in a visceral way to this poem about homeland, especially these first lines. That's why I memorized them then, and why I still remember them today.

At about the same age, I went several times to a YMCA summer camp, which was situated in wooded, hilly country a few hours to the west of New York City and provided a chance for the sons of poor families to experience nature, live in rustic cabins, and learn traditional sports and crafts that were long gone from the concrete environment of the city. Our mornings started with the bugle call of "Reveille," long ago adopted from the French military,[6] and ended with the somber notes of "Taps," dating back to the American Civil War.[7] In the morning we gathered at the flagpole, set on a modest hilltop, to watch the raising of the flag; at sunset three campers lowered the flag, folded it with precision, and placed it in its designated spot. Like Scott's poem, the bugle calls and the ritual raising and lowering of the flag penetrated deep into my psyche, sometimes bringing unexplained tears.

The poem was about love of home and country. It didn't matter that the poem was about Scotland, that I learned it in America, and that my parents' hearts were in Slovakia. It also didn't matter that I had no special previous attachment to the American flag, that the bugle calls were completely new to me, and that I had only been back in America for three or four years. What was most powerful was the sense of having "my own, my native land."

IN MY ADULTHOOD I BEGAN TO HAVE EXPERIENCES that brought a more specific allegiance to Slovakia to my awareness. While Czechoslovakia was still a single country, I often had a particular sort of exchange when the conversation turned to the question of national origin:

"Oh, so you weren't born in America. Where are you from?"

"Czechoslovakia."

"That's wonderful. Do you speak Czech?"

Speaking Czech was taken to be synonymous with being Czechoslovakian, and the possibility of a distinct Slovak language and identity was not even considered. To my well-meaning companions, the true soil of my roots was invisible.

After the Velvet Divorce of 1993, when Slovakia and the Czech Republic became separate states, the conversational refrain changed slightly:

"Where are you from?"

"Slovakia."

"Oh, I just love Prague!"

Invisible again! And here's another version: I've just had a long conversation with someone about my homeland and my family, and someone else walks up. I am introduced: "Joe, this is Johnny. He was just telling me about his family roots in Slovenia." The geographical area into which my origins can disappear and become invisible just increased by a few thousand square miles!

I FIND THAT JUST AS I CRINGE when someone makes a mistake about my nation of origin, I glow with delight when someone compliments me on my ability to speak Slovak despite my having grown up in America. Speaking Slovak seems to make me more a Slovak, even in my own eyes. Why does all of this matter so much to me? Why not simply be an American with a slightly exotic background? Why, in earlier years, did it matter so much to my parents that I should learn and retain a pure form of the Slovak language and that I should not forget my homeland?

Many thinkers have explored the link between language, national identity, and a person's individual sense of identity. For Central Europeans, Slovaks among them, perhaps the most influential was the German philosopher Johann Gottfried von Herder in the eighteenth century. Herder's contemplations on this topic helped to provide the philosophical underpinnings for the emerging nationalist movement, particularly the form it took in Central Europe. His ideas, both on language and on the nature of nations, profoundly influenced a whole generation of Slovak nationalists, including Michal Miloslav Hodža.[8]

Herder wrote in 1784:

> Has a people anything dearer than the speech of its fathers? In its speech resides its whole thought-domain, its tradition, history, religion, and basis of life, all its heart and soul. To deprive a people of its speech is to deprive it of its one eternal good. . . . As God tolerates all the different languages of the world, so also should a ruler not only tolerate but honor the various languages of his peoples. . . . The best culture of a people cannot be expressed through a foreign language; it thrives on the soil of a nation most beautifully, and, I may say, it thrives only by means of the nation's inherited and inheritable dialect. With language is created the heart of a people; and is it not a high concern, amongst so many peoples—Hungarians,

Slavs, Rumanians, etc.—to plant seeds of well-being for the far future and in the way that is dearest and most appropriate to them?

So, Herder saw language as the soul of a nation, deserving of the highest honor and respect, and the hearts of Slovak and other national leaders responded immediately to this view.

In addition to articulating the importance of language to the nation,[9] Herder also had a theory of what constitutes a nation, and his ideas on this became widely influential among Central European intellectuals. In his view, national identity rested in large part on the combined influence of physical environment, history, and "national character," a concept he elaborated at length. He attributed a very progressive character to Slavs, whom he saw as the future leaders of Europe. I like to imagine a Slovak student, exposed throughout his life to a system in which the Magyar language ruled, the Slovak language was suppressed, and Slovaks themselves were despised, hearing Herder's words while studying in Germany, the heartland of Central European culture. It's no wonder that the leaders of what became known as the Slovak National Awakening of the mid-nineteenth century returned home from their studies inspired by Herder's words!

CONSIDER THE MILIEU IN WHICH RISING SLOVAK NATIONALISM expressed itself, the Habsburg Empire. This empire, in which the Pálkas and my other ancestors labored, was an amazingly complex creation, unlike any other realm in Europe. Stitched together over centuries by marriage, conquest, and election, the Habsburg Empire held within its borders a stunning variety of lands and peoples. Oszkár Jászi, a leading Magyar statesman and scholar who spent his last years as a professor at American universities, wrote of it in 1929:[10]

> In this vast empire, which concentrated more than fifty-one million inhabitants in an area of two hundred and sixty thousand square miles, were almost ten nations and twenty more or less divergent nationalities in political or moral bonds.... In this vast empire there was going on, during more than four hundred years, an effort to keep together this variegated mosaic of nations and people and to build up a kind of universal state, a "supranational" monarchy, and to fill it with the feeling of a common solidarity.

> This experiment, which the greatest state of the European continent (leaving out of account Russia and the powers with colonies outside Europe) undertook with colossal military, economic, and moral forces through almost sixteen generations, was one of the greatest and most interesting attempts in world-history. Had this experiment

been successful, it would have meant more from a certain point of view than all other efforts of state-building ever recorded. For, if the Habsburgs had really been able to unite those ten nations through a supranational consciousness into an entirely free and spontaneous cooperation, the empire of the Habsburgs would have surpassed the narrow limits of the nation state and would have proved to the world that it is possible to replace the consciousness of national unity by a consciousness of a state community.

This great experiment in state-building, which lasted from 1526 until 1918, ultimately failed. The nations of the monarchy were not united "into an entirely free and spontaneous cooperation." Rather, these many nations clashed as the more powerful among them sought to dominate the weaker ones. The Magyars and the Czechs strove to keep their national identities from being swallowed up by the Germans of the Viennese court. The Slovaks, Serbs, Croats, and others struggled to keep from being assimilated into the Magyars. These conflicts were led by the intelligentsia; the poor peasants still labored in a largely feudal system.

OVER TIME, THE CULTURAL INFLUENCE of the German-speaking Habsburg court throughout the monarchy became enormous.[11] Vienna was the center to which the nobles gravitated. The great Hungarian lords owned ornate mansions in Vienna, attended Viennese concerts and the opera, and enjoyed the city's dizzying social whirl. The Hungarian Diet—the great assemblage of the kingdom's highest ranking and wealthiest nobles, as well as the highest ranking officers of the Catholic Church—continued to meet primarily in Bratislava[12] until the revolution of 1848. It was easy to take a coach the short distance from Vienna to Bratislava when the nobles were needed there, and from Bratislava back to Vienna as soon as their duties allowed. Indeed, the highest strata of the Hungarian nobility, ethnically almost entirely Magyar, became thoroughly Germanized, to the point of forgetting their mother tongue. It was proposed at the Diet of 1811 that Magyar become the official laguage of the Kingdom of Hungary, replacing the German that had been mandated earlier by Emperor Joseph II. The proposal was voted down, verbatim records show,[13] because "there would be no one among the nobles who could speak Magyar."

But in this age of rising nationalism, the dominance of Vienna, seemingly a triumph for Habsburg statecraft, actually set the stage for a convulsive reaction. In Hungary the charge was led by Count István Széchenyi, one of the kingdom's highest nobles.[14] In some ways he was no different than the other magnates—his Magyar was so bad that he wrote even his private diary in German. But in 1825 Széchenyi launched an era of reform by a sensationally symbolic action: He addressed the upper chamber of the Diet in his broken Magyar rather than his polished German. He wanted Magyar to be the language of administration and commerce, restoring to the Magyars the elevated sense of nationhood that many of their leaders had gradually lost. He linked this sense of nationhood to a liberal social agenda: He supported rights for the serfs, particularly the right to own land; he advocated the abolition of the nobility's freedom from paying taxes; and he called for an end to the guilds that restricted entry into the craft professions. It was through Széchenyi's efforts that the first permanent bridge connecting Buda to Pest across the Danube was built. On his insistence, it was a toll bridge and everyone, commoner and noble alike, paid the fee. Democratic ideals were on the rise and, in Hungary, were given their earliest voice by a member of the highest nobility.

Over time a charismatic new Magyar leader, Lajos Kossuth, took up the cause of social and economic reform. Like Széchenyi, he advocated a liberal political agenda and greatly increased rights for the lower classes. At the same time, however, he etched himself forever in the memory of Slovaks as an implacable enemy. Among the causes for which Kossuth fought was the imposition of the Magyar language on all public functions—in education at every level, in all communication and record-keeping in government offices, and in the courts. The Slovak language, and with it Slovak identity, was to be swallowed by the Magyar. Kossuth went further. When the was editor of the influential newspaper *Pesti Hírlap*, he wrote:[15] " Wherever we look in Hungary, there is no entity that would constitute a Slovak nationality/nation." It is no wonder that this man, a hero to the Magyars, was anathema to Slovaks.[16]

WITHIN THE HIGHLY STRATIFIED, MULTIETHNIC, POLYGLOT Habsburg Empire, ruled autocratically from ethnically German Vienna, the awakening sense of nationhood soon erupted into a multi-way struggle and later armed revolution. Both Czech and Magyar patriots fought against German domination. The rising tide of Magyar nationalism, acccompanied by systematic efforts to magyarize Hungary's substantial ethnic minorities, called forth a powerful upsurge of Slovak consciousness and activism,[17] the Slovak National Awakening.[18] Many members of my family were prominent among the Slovak leaders. The foremost among them was Michal Miloslav Hodža (Chapters 18-20), but Hodža's father Ján, the miller of Rakša (Chapters 14, 19, and 24); brothers Ondrej (Chapters 14, 24, and 25) and Juraj (Chapter 24); and daughter Marína (Chapter 21) all played significant roles. On my father's side, Ondrej Pálka (Chapter 16), Jozef Bella (Chapters 15, 19, and 22), Janko Pálka (Chapter 23) and others likewise lent their support, both moral and financial, to the Slovak Awakening.

CHAPTER 18

Michal Miloslav Hodža
and the Slovak Language

When I was a boy in Chicago, I absorbed from my parents not only the Slovak language (Chapters 4 and 7), but also three great hymns: the Slovak national anthem, *Nad Tatrou sa blýska* (*Lightning Strikes over the Tatras*); a great Lutheran hymn, *Kto za pravdu horí* (*He Who Burns for the Truth*); and most of all *Hej, Slováci* (*O, Slovaks*), probably the most often sung of all Slovak patriotic hymns. Now, many decades later, I recognize in *Hej, Slováci* not only a much-loved song about Slovakia, but also a reflection of the link between language and nation that Herder so forcefully articulated:

> *Hej, Slováci, ešte naša slovenská reč žije,*
> *dokial' naše verné srdce za náš národ bije:*

> O Slovaks, our Slovak language still lives,
> As long as our loyal heart for our nation still beats:

This link has been a recurring theme in Slovak history, and no song expresses it better than *Hej, Slováci*. Recently I was amazed to discover, however, that *Hej, Slováci* is not purely a Slovak song. In fact, its history is astonishingly international. I started to uncover it after I saw *Hej, Slováci* reprinted in *Slovo*, the magazine of the gymnastic and cultural organization Czech and Slovak Sokol of Minnesota,[1] but with the text written not in Slovak but in Czech; its title was *Hej, Slované*, meaning *O, Slavs*. Puzzled about why a Slovak song I had known since childhood should be printed in Czech and not even refer specifically to Slovaks, I started to investigate.

At first I thought I might just be seeing an indication of the mixed Czech and Slovak membership of Sokol. However, the score and text published in *Slovo* were drawn from a collection of songs published in Chicago in the 1930s for children attending Czech-language schools in America.[2] So, at least in America, Czechs considered *Hej, Slované* to be their own.

A search into the life of the author of *Hej, Slováci,* a contemporary and friend of Michal Miloslav Hodža, not only solved the puzzle but also gave me new insight into language, nation, song, and the whole ethos of Romantic nationalism within which my great Hodža forebear had lived and worked. In particular, it helped to illumine the long, interwoven relatonship of Slovaks with their Czech neighbors. Here is the story.

IN THE FALL OF 1834 SAMUEL TOMÁŠIK, a Lutheran minister from County Gemer in the Slovak lands, stopped in Prague while on his way to Germany to complete his theological studies, a common practice for Slovak Lutherans at the time. For this young man, Prague was an almost mythical center of Slav culture, far grander than anything he might experience at home. He was looking forward to savoring an environment in which his Slav brethren, the Czechs, held their heads high and spoke in their own language.[3] To his great dismay, what he heard spoken in Prague was not the Czech language he admired so much, but German. In the Prague of that day, German was the language spoken in government offices, in the courts, on the streets, in the cafes, at the university. To have seen a play in the National Theater performed in Czech, Tomášik would have had to go on a Sunday afternoon or on a holiday. At all other times, German was the language of the theater as well.

Although at that very time Czech intellectuals were generating a renaissance of their native language, many Czechs had become thoroughly Germanized. As Tomášik recorded in his diary for Sunday, November 2, 1834:[4]

> My mind was dejected and my heart angry. Will mother Prague, the center of the Western Slav world, be lost to us? If we lose her, we Slovaks too are lost! And then I thought of my dear homeland in Slovakia, and asked whether my nation, which draws its spiritual inspiration from Prague and the Czech lands and which remembers Prague with joy in its heart, whether that nation too will in time disappear, drowned in a foreign sea. No, that must not, cannot happen. Sunk in such thoughts, I walked quickly from the theater to the inn where I was staying, and along the way I remembered the old Polish song that begins „*Jeszcze Polska nie zginela, poki my zijemy.*" (Poland has not yet perished, as long as we live.) While I rehearsed the melody in my mind, as if from my heart, from the depths of my soul, appeared the verses, "*Hej, Slováci, ešte naša slovenská reč žije.*" (O Slovaks, our Slovak language still lives.) I stepped into my room, lit the lamp, and immediately wrote down three verses in my diary with a pencil. . . . From my initial enthusiasm [at being in Prague] I had

fallen into doubt, but finally my doubt was conquered by faith and by hope for a better future for my beloved Slovak nation.

Tomášik was just twenty-one years old at the time.

The song spread quickly among the youth. Tomášik himself translated it into Czech, then modified the words to refer to all Slavs, not just Slovaks, under the title *Hej, Slované* (O, Slavs). [5] Besides Slovak and Czech, it was soon sung in Polish, Russian, Slovenian, Serbian, Croatian, Bosnian, Macedonian, and Bulgarian. Its rapid spread was partly due to the Sokol movement, which adopted *Hej, Slované* as its own anthem. During World War I, Slav soldiers drafted into opposing armies sang it to each other across the battle lines. After World War II, it became the national anthem of Yugoslavia. With the breakup of Yugoslavia in 1991, it remained the national anthem of Serbia and Montenegro. Only in 2006, after Serbia and Montenegro separated, did its life as a national anthem come to an end. What an odyssey for a song written by an agitated Slovak twenty-one year old on a brief visit to Prague back in 1834!

To the present day, every Slovak child learns *Hej, Slováci*. It is the song I sang for Uncle Dišo in 1946, when I was seven and my parents and I were finally leaving Chicago for our home. It was adopted by the nationalists of the World War II Slovak Republic almost as a replacement national anthem. They used *Hej, Slováci* to cheer for independence from the Czechs, forgetting that it was composed in Prague because its patriotic Slovak author lamented not hearing Czech spoken there and that, after writing the song, he almost immediately translated it into Czech.

As HERDER HAD SO CLEARLY UNDERSTOOD, using one's own language and the sense of belonging to a treasured nation are inextricably linked. Tomášik sang about this in *Hej, Slováci*. But Tomášik was also a firm believer in the fundamental unity of all Slav peoples, and particularly the Slovaks and Czechs, and for this reason he wrote many of his works first in Czech and only then in Slovak, as he described in the foreword to a retrospective collection of his poems and songs. [6]

> Inasmuch as my poems were, from the year 1834 until about the year 1854, written and published in the Czechoslovak language [by this he meant Czech with some Slovakizing elements added] and only later rendered into Slovak, I present them here [in their original versions] as they can be found in various magazines and annuals. I do this in the hope that this will not be taken amiss by either one side or the other, indeed that by doing this I will contribute something to brotherly relations between Czechs and Slovaks in the field of literature. For the academically educated Slovak, Czech is and will

always be a necessity, and the Czech will be well served by a closer familiarity with literary Slovak.

In his vision of Slav unity and the importance to Slovaks of the Czech language, Tomášik was in close alignment with the two most influential Slovak scholars of the age, Ján Kollár (1793-1852) and Pavol Jozef Šafárik (1795-1861), both of whom had an idealized view of the greatness and fundamental unity of all the Slav nations, and also ardently defended the use of Czech as the literary language of Slovaks.[7] At first their advocacy of Czech gained many supporters. Later, however, the tide turned and the use of a freshly codified literary Slovak became a key element in the Slovak National Awakening.

It was a difficult and complex process to develop a widely acceptable written form of a language as rich in dialects as is Slovak. Further, because language was perceived as being integrally linked to nationhood, every twist and turn in the language debates had immediate political implications.

FROM MORAVIA IN THE WEST TO UKRAINE IN THE EAST, Slovaks spoke their own language. Yet, a villager from the west, where the language blended into Czech, could hardly understand a villager from the east, where both the intonation and the vocabulary blended into Polish.[8] The Bible was only available in the classic Czech translation of 1613, the so-called *Kralice* Bible (contemporaneous with the King James translation of 1611). There was no Slovak-language Bible. In fact, there was no generally accepted Slovak written language, as defined by a book of grammar and a dictionary. Men of letters generally wrote in Latin, German, or Czech, even though they spoke their regional Slovak at home.

In the late 1700s, Catholic priests in the western Slovak counties started to develop a literature for teaching their parishioners in the language of the home.[9] Their efforts coalesced around the work of Father Anton Bernolák, a dedicated and prolific scholar, who in 1787 published a treatise on Slovak grammar and, thereafter, another on spelling. For the rest of his life, he worked on an immense project: the *Slowár slowenski česko-laťinsko-ňemecko-uherski* (the *Slovak-Czech-Latin-German-Hungarian Dictionary*). The work comprised six volumes with over 1,000 pages and some 31,000 entries. It was published posthumously, starting in 1825, the same year that Count Széchenyi dared to address the Diet in Magyar rather than German—a reflection of the growing importance of language to all of the peoples of the Kingdom of Hungary.

The Slovak literary language formulated by Bernolák came to be known as *bernoláčtina*. It was a heroic effort, but *bernoláčtina* never gained general acceptance. Only a few writers of distinction adopted the language. The Lutherans refused to support it, clinging to the classical language (*bibličtina*) of the Czech Bible as their literary language. Kollár and Šafárik argued that creating a Slovak literary language separate from the Czech was a misguided effort to begin with, and that the future of Slovaks lay rather in strengthening their historical connections with the Czechs.

However, under the influence of rising national feeling among the Magyar aristocracy and intelligentsia, the pressures on Slovaks and other minorities to assimilate were growing. Every time the Hungarian Diet met, it passed new laws increasing the impact of Magyarization. Many among the young Slovak intelligentsia were worried about the very survival of the Slovak nation within Hungary and sought ways to assert Slovak identity. Codifying a Slovak literary language that could gain the widespread acceptance that had eluded *bernoláčtina* became a major element in their program. While a number of writers, priests, pastors, and other intellectuals were involved, three made the greatest impact on this decisive movement for national awakening: Ľudovít Štúr, Jozef Miloslav Hurban, and Michal Miloslav Hodža. Štúr, acknowledged as the dominant personality, was born in 1815 in Uhrovec (County Turiec), the son of a teacher and organist at the local Lutheran church. Hurban was born in 1817 in Beckov (County Trenčín), the son of a Lutheran minister. And Michal Miloslav Hodža, born in 1811, we already know as the second son of Ján Hodža, the humble miller of Rakša.

The upper mill in Rakša saw the birth of eight children, six of whom survived to adulthood (Family tree 5, Appendix V).[10] Michal was the second, my great-grandfather Ondrej was the third. Quite early on, Michal was recognized as an exceptionally gifted student, and his teachers suggested that he be sent to better schools than Rakša could provide. His father concurred, and young Michal started leaving home to obtain a first rate education, first to nearby Mošovce (Ján Kollár's home town) to complete elementary school, then to Banská Bystrica[11] and the Magyar-dominated town of Rožňava for gymnasium.

Michal came to Rožňava at the age of fifteen primarily to perfect his Magyar language, but what he encountered was Magyar chauvinism.[12] Almost all of the professors were Magyar gentry, and they did not hesitate to express their distaste for Slovak culture. Any student caught speaking Slovak was forced to wear a sign around his neck signifying his transgression, and as further punishment, he had to memorize a large number of Magyar verses and recite them aloud. He was whipped for every error. Magyar students did not hesitate to spy on the Slovaks in their dormitories and report them if they heard Slovak being spoken. Some students were cowed by this treatment, but not Hodža. He clung stubbornly to his Slovak identity, and thus was an inspiration to his younger Slovak friends, including Samuel Tomášik and several others who later also became prominent in the Slovak National Awakening.

Michal ultimately moved to the Lutheran Lyceum in Bratislava where he first met Ľudovít Štúr and Jozef Hurban.[13] He was drawn to the school's Department of Czechoslovak Language and Literature, unique in the Kingdom of Hungary, but even more to the students' Czechoslovak Society, which he immediately joined. The goal of the society was to provide a forum for the students to practice their language skills and to present their own literary works, which Hodža did with a passion that first gained him his reputation as perhaps the greatest orator of the Štúr generation.[14] Following the inspiration of Kollár and Šafárik, the students focused on Czech as their literary medium, and on the unity of the great Slav nations as their central vision.

The Lutheran Lyceum in Bratislava was a hotbed of student activism. Student societies were popular at the time, and the Czechoslovak Society was far from the only one. Many of these groups took on an increasingly political focus, to the growing discomfiture of the government. In 1837 students of the Magyar Society at the Lyceum started to agitate in support of demands being made by several Magyar members of the Hungarian Diet for the abolition of serfdom. Slovak students, yearning for Slovak enlightenment, joined in the agitation of Magyar students who were yearning for social justice. The government would not tolerate such overt political action and closed down all student societies in the Kingdom of Hungary.

With their accustomed forum for discussion and planning suddenly abolished, the most politically oriented Slovak students resorted to forming a secret society, Vzájomnosť (Reciprocity), modeled after a similar secret society in Poland.[15] It was in place within a few months. Hodža and Hurban, both of whom had by now graduated from the Lyceum, were quickly enlisted among the members; Štúr was abroad studying.

Despite its small size (only fifteen members) and its short existence, Vzájomnosť undertook an ambitious program. Among other constructive actions, it organized teachers for mutual support in deflecting Magyarization efforts in the schools; collected funds to support a Slavic Institute in Bratislava; collected reports of the repression of Slovaks, especially in the countryside where it would otherwise go unnoticed; and initiated efforts to start a Slovak national magazine or newspaper.

In 1840 a secret Slav organization in Vienna, linked to a similar organization in Poland, was uncovered by the imperial authorities. Štúr learned of this in Prague and immediately upon his return home asked Hodža to warn the members of Vzájomnosť to destroy any materials that might link them to the Viennese group. This threat of discovery effectively meant the end of Vzájomnosť.

IN THE VERY YEAR OF THE FOUNDING OF *VZÁJOMNOSŤ*, 1837, Michal Hodža was un-expectedly called to become the Lutheran pastor of Mikuláš. The congregation there had recently lost its senior pastor, and initially invited none other than Ján Kollár himself to take over the post. Kollár declined, citing as his principal reasons advanced age and obligations in Pest, and in his stead recommended Hodža, then twenty-six years old and not even fully ordained. Hodža confessed that he was not certain about accepting a pastorate, inasmuch as he was also considering an academic career. After contemplation, however, he accepted the offer from Mikuláš. He was ordained in Bratislava and immediately thereafter assumed his new position.

The congregation in Mikuláš was excited—Hodža was arriving with recom-mendations so high that the usual formal interview had been waived. Ondrej Pálka the younger, in his usual terse style, recorded the day in the family chronicle:[16]

> *27 August.* Mr. Michal Hodža was inducted as the senior minister of the Lutheran Church of Vrbica and St. Mikuláš. . . .

When Hodža first mounted the steps of the stone pulpit and looked out over the one-and-a-half thousand people assembled there, and called out in the mighty voice that was needed to reach all of them in the days before mi-crophones and loudspeakers, he made his devotion to his nation clear in the first words he spoke:[17]

> I hold you and my nation dear. . . . I offer you my love with all my heart, my dear fellow Slovaks, sharing a single mother tongue, belonging to a single nation.

Later in this same inaugural sermon, as if anticipating a difficult road ahead, he also proclaimed:[18]

> If the world, happiness, and good will should worsen above me, if they should turn away from me and turn their full power against me, I will, according to the advice of the Apostle Paul, gather my strength from my inner being. From all the storms of reality, I will turn into my inner world; I will take refuge in my heart, in that . . . deepest safety.

Though he had a national vision, M. M. Hodža was no politician. He was a man who searched inwardly, who had already embarked upon a journey into the world of the spirit. Nonetheless, by this time he had made two major de-cisions that committed him to life in the public realm. Rather than the quiet cultivation of an inner life, he had undertaken to serve a huge, 6,000-member parish with over a dozen outlying churches under its wing.[19] At the same time, even while his life as a minister placed him squarely in the public eye, through *Vzájomnosť* he had decided to serve his nation in secret, under threat of discovery and imprisonment, if not worse.

His life was suddenly very full: preparing thoughtful sermons for every Sunday, comforting people in need, administering the enormous congregation of Mikuláš, assuming significant roles in the wider Lutheran church organization, fulfilling his pledge to *Vzájomnosť*, and engaging in virtually every significant Slovak national undertaking of the time. The years went by in a heady whirlwind, a mix of glorious successes and threats for the future.

IN 1841 THE LEADERSHIP OF THE LUTHERAN CHURCH was nearing the end of the long process of preparing a new hymnal. The revered *Cithara sanctorum* (Lyre of the Saints) compiled by Juraj Tranovský (Chapters 20 and 28) had served Slovak Lutherans since 1635 and gone through well over a hundred printings and editions. But over these two centuries, social and political circumstances had changed, and the theological perspective of the Lutheran church had to some degree evolved. It was time for a new collection of hymns, hymns reflecting contemporary conditions. The young pastor of Mikuláš was asked to join the editorial board and to act as its secretary.[20] When the hymnal was published in 1842, forty-three of his own hymns, written over the period of a decade, were selected for inclusion. In the eyes of many, Hodža's hymns were among the most moving. A second edition of the new hymnal did not appear until 1995. Lutherans in Slovak congregations everywhere sing from it, and Hodža's poetic voice is still heard today (see Chapter 30).

During the time he was working on the hymnal, a remarkable thing happened to the young pastor. One Sunday morning, so the story goes,[21] as he was opening the doors of the church, a gust of wind suddenly wrapped his long, black robes around the slender frame of a young woman who was just leaving the church. She was Kornélia Kellner, the daughter of the German physician of Mikuláš. It was the first direct encounter between the two, and the starting point of a life of companionship, mutual support, and deep love.[22] They were married not long after, on February 27, 1842. The ceremony took place at 7:00 in the evening, an unusual hour, especially in the dark days of winter in the time before electric lights. The explanation[23] gives us a glimpse of Hodža's busy life: That day he conducted two funerals and went immediately from the second to his own wedding. Even during the wedding ceremony, a wake following one of the funerals was being held just four houses away. On average, he conducted a funeral at least once every two days.

AN INTELLECTUAL TREND THAT HAD BEEN ACCELERATING for a number of years now took hold of the Slovak intelligentsia, including Štúr, Hurban, and Hodža, the great "Slovak Three"—to regard Slovaks as a nation of their own, not as a component of a broader Czechoslovak nation in the way Kollár, Šafárik, and many Czech scholars had conceived. Since nationhood and language were felt to be so deeply intertwined, this changed perspective quickly led to the most decisive step in the Slovak National Awakening—the formulation of a universally adopted literary Slovak language.[24]

This was a complex process. Štúr, Hurban, and Hodža and the others who flocked to the cause did not always agree with one another even on seemingly simple matters of spelling.[25] They also faced an enormous external challenge. In order to gather support for the new literary Slovak, they wanted to avoid alienating Kollár and Šafárik, their Czech colleagues, the many Catholics who supported the previously developed *bernoláčtina*, and the Lutherans who wanted to hold on to *bibličtina*.

One of their most effective steps was the establishment of an all-Slovak literary and publishing society. It would publish only in the new literary Slovak language. The first meeting of the new literary society was held in 1844, in Hodža's parish house in Mikuláš. Its declared mission was to galvanize Slovaks for their own cultural and social development and to do so specifically on the basis of the new literary Slovak language. As the minutes of the first meeting declare, "The field of its activities is the whole spiritual life of the nation. Ways and means include everything allowed by the country's laws."[26]

The prospective members came on foot and horseback, cart and carriage, from all over the Slovak counties—pastors, priests, teachers, craftsmen, minor nobility, students, perhaps fifty in all—a modest number, perhaps, but more than the organizers had dared hope for. They sat in the front room of Hodža's parish house, with Štúr presiding, and talked. What should they call this brave new effort? They decided on *Tatrín*, a name echoing the majestic Tatra Mountains. Who should be the officers? The roster is rich with the names of my family: Hodža was elected president, while Štúr and Hurban became members of the steering committee. The post of treasurer came to be shared by Ondrej Pálka the younger and Jozef Bella. My great-grandfather Ondrej Hodža was a founding member, as were Ján Plech, the father of Ondrej's wife Klementína (Chapter 14), and the youngest of the Hodža brothers, Juraj (Chapter 24). And another familiar name appears on the list of members—Samuel Tomášik, also a graduate of the Bratislava Lyceum and a member of *Vzájomnosť*, whose *Hej, Slované* was now inspiring patriots among all the Slavs of the Kingdom of Hungary.

Only four annual meetings of Tatrín were held, all under Hodža's leadership. The first three were held in his own Lutheran parish house, the fourth in the parish house of the Catholic Jozef Urbanovský. By this time Hodža had worked out a spelling designed to be in close alignment with the Czech, and thus also acceptable to the bernolákists, who were led at the time by the linguist Martin Hattala. This became known as the Hodža-Hattala Reform and, especially with Hattala's more scholarly presentations in subsequent years, became the standard accepted by Catholics as well as Lutherans.[27] With minor revisions, it is used to the present day.

Tatrín published a book of Slovak grammar by Štúr, and soon thereafter three volumes by Hodža. A dozen young men, mostly students, were provided stipends to support their work, both literary and artistic. School curricula in the new literary Slovak were drafted. A campaign against alcoholism, the greatest plague of the villages, was launched.[28]

In 1848, with revolution swirling all around, the government stepped in and closed Tatrín forever.

IN AN IMPORTANT SENSE, SLOVAKIA WAS CREATED during the national awakening of the mid- nineteenth century, of which Tatrín was a powerful manifestation. Finally, Slovak was established as the literary, not just the spoken, language of the whole Slovak people. The greatest national songs were written then.[29] Fresh poetry and drama captured the spirit of ordinary people. For the first time, there were serious discussions about the political future of the Slovak homeland. The first declarations of independence were proclaimed. A small cluster of counties in the north of Hungary, inhabited largely by an impoverished Slovak population, started to feel itself a nation.

The awakening was inspired and led by a small group of educated patriots, mostly young and numbering perhaps only fifty to a hundred. Chief among them were Štúr, Hurban, and Hodža—the "Slovak Three." Each was a distinct personality, had his own strengths and limitations, and found a personal way of combining his public and his private life. Perhaps the most complex of the three was M. M. Hodža. Even my mother, who talked about Grandfather Milan Hodža frequently, described Michal Miloslav not as a person whom she understood intimately, but by a list of his accomplishments.

These chapters contain what I have been able to piece together about this monumental but enigmatic figure in Slovak history, a man who accomplished much for his nation, endured years of persecution and poverty, led an intense inner life, and, like Grandfather Milan Hodža a generation later, died in exile.

CHAPTER 19

Michal Miloslav Hodža in the Midst of Revolution

In 1848 revolution swept Europe.[1] Hungry peasants, disenfranchised nobles, and liberal intellectuals all rose up against the established monarchies and clamored for greater rights. There were riots and battles in the streets of Paris. In February the French monarchy was toppled and the French Second Republic installed. Uprisings followed in much of the rest of Europe—Berlin, Milan, and Venice erupted, and even in Denmark the monarchy lost much of its traditional power.

The Habsburg Empire was especially hard hit. On March 12 there were massive anti-Habsburg demonstrations in Vienna. On March 14 the Hungarian Diet, meeting in Bratislava, put in place the March Laws—a revolutionary program terminating feudalism, giving serfs ownership of land they had worked for generations, abolishing many of the privileges of the nobility, and granting equal rights under the law to all residents of the kingdom. The next day, March 15, is celebrated by Hungarians even today as the day the Magyars launched their greatest revolution for national liberation.[2] Led by students, tens of thousands in Pest demonstrated. On March 23 Hungary declared itself a constitutional monarchy, independent of Vienna except through the person of the king. Vienna accepted.

During the feverish months of April and May, nationalities throughout the Kingdom of Hungary rose to formulate their own demands for independence. The Croatians met in Zagreb to demand rights like those just achieved by Hungary. The Serbs, the Saxon Germans of Transylvania, and the Romanians all gathered to formulate their own aspirations and demands. Here is how Grandfather Hodža described this ferment almost a century later:[3]

> . . . All these non-Magyar groups presented their demands to the Magyars and personally to the leader of the anti-Habsburg Magyar revolution, Louis Kossuth.

It was at this critical moment that the Magyars, and Kossuth in particular, committed the greatest political blunder which a nation and its leaders can commit. They refused to recognize any ethnic rights for the non-Magyars. They set out not only to rule but to dominate and Magyarize those minorities which, in the aggregate, actually constituted a majority of old Hungary. Kossuth, on the occasion of receiving a special delegation from the Serbs, uttered the notorious declaration: "The sword will decide between us!"

THE SLOVAKS GATHERED IN MIKULÁŠ to formulate their demands.[4] First came a gathering on March 28, just days after the proclamation of the March Laws, at which a small group of Slovak leaders including Michal Miloslav Hodža explained to masses of ordinary people the great changes that were taking place.[5]

> Crowds of several thousand welcomed with inexpressible joy the announcement that the worst restrictions of the feudal order had been removed and that taxation would now apply to all classes. Hodža emotionally recalled that the courtyard of the county seat echoed with cries of "*Sláva*," [Glory! in Slovak], for the first time in centuries.

Then on May 10, 1848, in Hodža's parish house, in the same room in which Tatrín had been founded with great elation and with Hodža once again presiding, one of the foundational documents of Slovak history was written and signed. The principal authors were Hodža, Štúr, and Hurban. Called *Žiadosti slovenského národa* (Petition of the Slovak Nation) and addressed to the emperor in Vienna, the Hungarian Diet, and leading state authorities, this document laid out the most coherent political program yet formulated by the burgeoning Slovak national movement. Notably, rather than being a call for secession or independence, it was a program for dignity and rights within the Kingdom of Hungary, not only for Slovaks but for all nations living within that kingdom. Its fourteen points begin this way:[6]

> I. The Slovak nation in its Hungarian homeland, after a sleep of nine hundred years as the primordial nation of this land, feels this holy land to be its motherland. It is the source and cradle of tales about the ancient glories of the nation's ancestors, and the stage on which its fathers heroically shed their blood for the Hungarian crown. The crown until recently acted as merely a stepmother, treating the [Slovak nation] cruelly and holding her language and nationality in the chains of insult and shame. . . . For all these rea-

sons, as the primordial nation and once the only owner of this holy land, we call, under the flag of this age of equality, for the equality and brotherhood of all the nations of Hungary. . . .

Therefore we ask:

II. For the establishment—on the principle of equality among all the nations living under the crown of Hungary—of a single parliament of brotherly nations in which each nation shall be represented as a nation. Each member of this parliament shall be bound to represent his nation in its own language, and to know the languages of all the other nations represented in the parliament.

The petition further called for such elements of governance as: the right to vote for all inhabitants reaching the age of twenty; freedom of the press and freedom of assembly; regional parliaments to look after the well-being of each nation; the definition of territories occupied by Slovaks; the use of the Slovak language in all Slovak regional offices and courts; the establishment of Slovak national schools up to and including a national university, with the medium of instruction being Slovak; the teaching of Slovak in Magyar schools and the teaching of Magyar in Slovak schools; and the elimination of all domination by one nation over other nations in the Kingdom of Hungary.

These were extremely progressive and egalitarian demands, formulated by a handful of brave members of the tiny Slovak intelligentsia.[7] They stood in direct opposition to the view now sweeping the Magyar leadership: that Hungary was a Magyar state, that all other nationalities were not only subservient but fundamentally inferior to it, and that only Magyar was acceptable as an official language in Hungary. The revolution's greatest Magyar leader, Lajos Kossuth, embodied this view and proclaimed it more than once:[8]

In Hungary everything—land, laws, history—is exclusively Magyar. Slovaks, Romanians, Serbs, Rusyns are only "peoples," they are not nations. In Hungary only Magyars have the right and the duty to be a nation.

The Hungarian government's response to the Slovak demands was immediate: on the day after the petition was proclaimed, martial law was declared and orders were issued for the arrest of Hurban, followed a few days later by similar orders for Štúr and then Hodža. Upper Hungary was flooded with posters describing the three men and offering a reward for information leading to their arrest.

*Arrest placard in Magyar, German, and Slovak for Hurban,
Hodža (Magyar spelling), and Štúr distributed throughout the
Slovak counties of Hungary immediately after the Petition of the
Slovak Nation was submitted in 1848. For each man a physical
description is given: size and build, face, nose, eyes, hair and age.
Courtesy of the Slovak National Library, Martin.*

The three took shelter with friends, moving secretly from house to house
and field to field. They managed to flee across the border into Moravia (see
Chapter 24). Once out of Hungarian reach, they traveled to Prague to attend
a long-planned international congress of Slavs, the greatest yet held.[9] Poles,
Russians, and of course Czechs were represented, as were Moravians, Slovenes,
Croats, Serbs, Ukrainians, Lithuanians, and many others. The Slovak delegation
was particularly strong and influential. Students in their hundreds participated.
The opening ceremonies on the sun-lit first day of the congress, June 2, 1848,
were held at the great Týn cathedral that draws such crowds to the heart of
ancient Prague today, whence the colorful procession, waving national flags,
marched to the nearby locale where the proceedings would be held under
the leadership of František Palacký, one of the most prominent leaders of the
Czech national renaissance (who himself had studied at the Lutheran Lyceum
in Bratislava). The status of Slovaks was high on the agenda. Štúr, Hurban, and

Hodža all spoke eloquently, each from his own perspective, addressing the status of Slav nationalities, but especially of Slovaks, within Hungary. All three were greeted with the greatest enthusiasm. Hodža's speech, one of the politically most moderate, was nonetheless judged to be one of the most moving:[10]

> The sonorous yet soft voice of Hodža, the fiery light in his eyes, and the modest nature of his gestures all contributed to the effectiveness of his speech. Only the equally deep and deeply felt presentation of Šafárik could compare with it.

In its proceedings, the congress considered various recommendations on how political freedom for Slovaks might be implemented, including a union of Slovaks, Czechs, and Moravians or a separate Slovak political entity within the broader framework of either Hungary or Austria. However, as the congress was meeting, in Prague nationalist passions were surging. Suddenly, like other capitals before it, the city erupted into an armed anti-Habsburg uprising. Flames leapt in the streets. On June 12, 1848, the congress came to an abrupt halt. Austrian troops moved swiftly and unrelentingly to put down the uprising, but they could not stop the momentum for revolution.

WITHIN THE KINGDOM OF HUNGARY, the rise of nationalism had given rise to a complex internal struggle. The Magyars now revolted against the emperor in Vienna. The Croats revolted against the Magyars and supported the emperor with substantial forces. The Slovaks likewise revolted against the Magyars. The Slovak leaders saw in the emperor protection against Magyar oppression, and for this reason they aligned themselves with Vienna, despite the fact that the Magyar social agenda was far more progressive.

Hurban, Štúr, and Hodža found themselves leading a revolutionary movement that would soon include armed conflict.[11] Each played a distinct role in seeking financial support, arms, and men for armed insurrection.[12] In September, they met in Vienna and formed the Slovak National Council which was to lead an armed revolution.

The Slovak National Council assembled a small armed force led by Czech officers who had been enlisted in Prague. When they had 500 volunteers, they moved to a staging area in Moravia, where they were joined by another 500 men from Prague and Brno, the Moravian capital. On September 18, 1848, this force, tiny compared with the armies of the emperor or of the rebelling Magyars, crossed the border from Moravia into Upper Hungary. The next day, September 19, in his home district of Myjava, Hurban presided over a large public gathering at which independence from the Magyar-controlled government in Pest was declared, the first-ever Slovak proclamation of independence. More men volunteered to join the Slovak forces. Local officials who were Magyars or Magyar-sympathizers began to be replaced by national-minded Slovaks. The home of Ján Poláček (one of the Poláček brothers who drove flocks from the Balkans to Vienna, Chapter 15) and Dorota Jurkovič served as the headquarters of the Myjava volunteers and their officers.[13] Hurban had married Anna Jurkovič, Dorota's niece, so he often stayed at this house, from which arms and supplies were also distributed.

Hodža was in Prague, openly calling for rebellion against the Hungarian government.[14] An arrest warrant was issued for him in Hungarian territory, placing his family in Mikuláš in danger. Kornélia took their four-year-old son Cyril and set out across the mountains to Poland and thence to Prague to join her husband.[15] She left their younger daughters and nanny with friends and relatives in Vrbica; when danger threatened, they were smuggled to a mill in the nearby village of Smrečany, and when discovery was again imminent, transferred once more.

Hodža was with the first volunteers who crossed from Moravia into District Myjava. He was at the victories of the first few days and also at the first defeat. In that battle fourteen Slovaks were killed, twelve captured, and nine wounded—serious losses for the small Slovak force. These battlefield realities weighed heavily on Hodža's introspective nature. On the evening of the same day, he left for Vienna abruptly and without explanation.[16]

Despite his deep disquiet about the realities of military life, Hodža's insight was keen—he was the first to sound the alarm that, rather than supporting the Slovak volunteers, the imperial armies were standing aside or even shooting at them. The volunteers could not possibly stand up to a regular army: they were not trained, and many were not even armed. Indeed, military action had not actually been anticipated. There had been rhetoric about war, but the role of the volunteers had been conceived primarily as a catalyst for masses of Slovaks to join the insurrection of other nationalities against the Magyars. The Slovak volunteers could accomplish nothing in isolation. Within two days they were dispersed, and Štúr and Hurban followed Hodža to Vienna.

After this initial failure the Slovak volunteers regrouped, and were far more successful in subsequent military actions against the Magyars. Their operations were conducted in coordination with the imperial armies, as had originally been anticipated, and also with the substantial Croat forces who also represented the emperor.[17] Hodža participated in these activities, dividing civilian leadership responsibilities with Hurban and Štúr. The Magyar leader, Kossuth, declared all three men traitors against Hungary and issued further warrants for their arrest.

EVEN AS THE IMPERIAL TROOPS and the Slovak volunteers enjoyed some important successes, the control of Upper Hungary was patchy. Magyar troops were sent to County Liptov, long known as a center of Slovak national feeling and activity. There they arrested eight of the region's most prominent Slovak leaders, a number of whom had signed the Petition of the Slovak Nation in 1848. Among those taken were my ancestors Ondrej Pálka the younger and Jozef Bella, the same two friends who had served as treasurers of Tatrín.[18]

The prisoners were to be held not in Mikuláš but in Debrecen, a town in the eastern Hungarian lowlands that served as the capital of the Hungarian rebels. It was a long way to Debrecen, and the prisoners were taken there in a convoy of horse-drawn army wagons. Ondrej Pálka was among the oldest and was ailing; he was released after the wagons and their military escort reached the eastern city of Košice, several days' distance from Mikuláš.

The remainder of the party proceeded in stages, reaching Debrecen after three weeks. There the Slovaks were interned in the town's moldering old prison. Within five weeks, they were all placed in solitary confinement where they had no opportunity to speak to anyone or to exercise. The cells were too dark for reading, even in the middle of the day. Their allotment of food was a quarter of a loaf of bread per day. Finally they appealed to the wife of Lajos Kossuth, who arranged for them to be placed once again in a joint cell.

On the walls of that cell Jozef Bella boldly wrote these ironic words of protest, referring to the new constitution adopted by the Hungarian rebels:[19]

> Freedom in prison, Equality on paper,
> Brotherhood on the tongue, but poison, fury in the heart,
> May God protect all nations
> From such Brotherhood, Equality, and Freedom!!!

These details about their life come from Jozef Bella's memoirs, which are now lost but were reported by his son Ján, the brother of Great-grandmother Zuzana Pálka née Bella. When Ján wrote in 1897, he had at his disposal not only his father's memoirs but also his hymnal. This slender volume, on which Michal Miloslav Hodža had worked so hard, had been pressed into Jozef Bella's hands by a well-wisher from Hybe. Hybe, along the dirt road east of Mikuláš, was the town in which the young Jozef had apprenticed as a furrier. The hymnal was offered to him as a source of comfort and prayers on his uncertain journey. He also used it as sort of a journal, writing notes and poems in the margins. Many of the passages are laments for home or cries to God for mercy and sustenance; others record his experiences with more than a little bitterness:[20]

> Fenuš from County Šariš, a teacher and local judge in Tolčemeš, died. He asked for a priest to give him confession, but they refused.

So without confession and mainly of hunger and cold, he died in this underground prison. . . .

WHILE BELLA AND HIS COMPANIONS REMAINED IN PRISON, on the battlefield the advantage swung in favor of the Magyars.[21] At one point they fielded as many as 150,000 men led by several brilliant field commanders. Vienna erupted again, and the seat of the Habsburg government was moved to Olomouc (Olmütz) in Moravia. There, Emperor Ferdinand V abdicated and was replaced by Franz Jozef I, only eighteen years old. On April 14, 1849, the Hungarian Diet, meeting in the great Calvinist church of Debrecen, declared that the Habsburgs were now deposed as rulers of Hungary. Kossuth was named the leader of the new Hungarian government.

While the outcome of the war was still uncertain, the Slovak leadership took a bold step: For the first time, it proposed political autonomy for Slovakia directly under the imperial crown.[22] A delegation including Hurban, Hodža, and Štúr went to Olomouc in March 1849 to present this request to the new emperor. The emperor and his advisers acknowledged that Slovaks needed protection against forced Magyarization, but the court was unwilling to take any concrete steps that would help the Slovak cause.

Suddenly, the revolution took an unexpected turn. With the Magyars claiming more and more victories and Habsburg rule in serious danger, the tsar of Russia stepped in with military aid to the emperor. As Russian troops approached Debrecen, the rebels shifted their capital back to Pest, taking their Slovak prisoners with them. Now imperial troops were on the offensive from the west, while the Russians swept in from the east. Pest was attacked, and the Magyar rebels fled in the direction of the Lower Lands (Appendix III). They released all but two of their Slovak prisoners; these two were taken on the rebels' flight to their new and last rebel capital, Szeged. The Magyar fighters now faced overwhelmingly superior forces. On August 11, 1849, Artúr Görgey, the most brilliant of the Magyar commanders, capitulated to the Russians at Világos, a village in County Arad in what is now far western Romania. The remaining two prisoners from Mikuláš made their way home from Szeged.

THE SLOVAK LEADERS REQUESTED FORMAL PERMISSION from the imperial court to recruit additional volunteers and to organize against the common enemy, the still-rebelling Magyars. Instead, they were allowed only to go to home and urge their people to be loyal to the emperor. Slovak youth who were physically capable were encouraged to join the military, but only under direct imperial leadership, not in separate Slovak units. Even though the Slovak volunteers were on the winning side, they continued to be viewed with suspicion.

M. M. Hodža returned to Mikuláš in triumph, greeted by masses of people.[23] Fourteen Magyars whose assignment was to arrest him were caught by a local guard unit organized to protect Slovak interests. Hodža recruited hundreds of Slovak volunteers in Mikuláš and its surroundings before greater tasks called him to Vienna. Slovak leaders were told that the Habsburg government was now considering their request for the creation of a separate Slovak homeland responsible directly to Vienna, and that petitions requesting such a change would be viewed favorably. Many such petitions were sent. The petitions asked as well that Slovak be established as the official language in schools, government offices, and municipalities, and that all persons who had risen against the emperor—that is, the Magyars—be removed from public office. The petition of County Liptov was carried to Vienna by Jozef Bella.[24] None of these requests were ever granted.

BY THE END OF NOVEMBER 1849, little more than a year after the first Slovak volunteeers had crossed into District Myjava, the volunteer units were officially disbanded and the revolution was over. Hungary had lost its fight with the imperial armies. The emperor and his prime minister, Alexander Bach, immediately imposed extremely tight rule throughout the country, exercising power not only through the army and the police, but also through a secret service that thoroughly penetrated all of Hungarian society. The imperial court held all effective political power in its own hands; it was the era of neo-absolutism.

The Slovak leaders returned, at least in part, to their personal concerns and families. Štúr, under constant police surveillance, went home to his birthplace of Uhrovec to care for his ailing parents, and soon thereftter moved to Modra, a small town near Bratislava where his brother Karol had just died and the seven orphaned children needed suppport. He died a few years later, at the age of 41, of a bizarre, self-inflicted wound incurred accidentally while hunting in the hills. Hurban, likewise, was placed under police surveillance and forbidden to engage in any political activity. He served his congregation in Hlboké, renewed his study of theology, and wrote extensively. He survived the neo-absolutist period and continued to be active in church administration, public affairs, and literature for many years. Of the great "Slovak Three," Hurban was the only one to live out a long and productive life.[25] M.M. Hodža's tragic story forms the following chapter.[26]

CHAPTER 20

Michal Miloslav Hodža— Poet-Prophet

Hodža first arrived in Mikuláš in 1837 to great acclaim. However, his outspoken advocacy of Slovak national identity and political rights, beginning with his inaugural sermon, almost immediately won him sustained persecution by both Magyars and *magyarones*. *Magyarones* were Slovaks who threw their allegiance with the Magyars but went beyond simple assimilation, often outdoing the Magyars themselves in their condescension to all things Slovak and in their unbending opposition to Slovak aspirations. The Magyars and *magyarones* were small in number, especially within the overwhelmingly Slovak Lutheran congregation, but their positions in society and in the hierarchy of the Lutheran church made them powerful. During his first decade in Mikuláš—while he was secretly active in *Vzájomnost'*, working on the Lutheran hymnal, collaborating with Štúr and Hurban to develop a Slovak literary language that would finally take hold among all Slovaks, helping to found and lead Tatrín, coauthoring the Petition of the Slovak Nation, and playing a significant role in the revolution, to say nothing of marrying, establishing a family, and conscientiously leading a 6,000-member congregation—Hodža was under constant personal attack.[1]

THE MAJORITY OF THESE ATTACKS CAME FROM WITHIN Hodža's own Lutheran church. Even his chaplain was his enemy.[2] This man had been the chaplain of the church for a number of years, and had himself applied for the position of pastor which he felt was his by right of seniority. He resented Hodža's appointment and within a year of his arrival lodged a formal compaint to the church council, accusing Hodža of failing to carry out the responsibilities that had been defined for him by the council. His complaint was supported by an influential *magyarone*, the director of church schools,[3] but it was not upheld. This first attack on Hodža came while he was in a particularly delicate position, being both new to Mikuláš and active in the secret society *Vzájomnost'*.

In 1842, the year the new Lutheran hymnal was published, Hodža undertook one of his several deputations to the emperor in Vienna.[4] The Slovak delegation had four members, with Hodža designated as the chief speaker on account of his eloquence and self-assurance in elevated social circles. They presented a petition that carried many signatures and focused on a long series of complaints and requests. Among them, the Slovak Lutheran intelligentsia pointed to many attacks on its leadership from the side of Magyars and *magyarones*, and to the prohibition of the use of literary Slovak (at this time still *bibličtina*) in schools where it was forcibly being replaced with Hungarian.

Hodža and his colleagues had high hopes that their petition would result in the redress of their grievances, for one of the emperor's highest function-aries, Count Kolowrat, had declared:[5] *"Die Deputation soll nur kommen, sie wird schon gut empfangen werden. Denn es ist höchste Zeit, dass die Slowaken einkommen."* ("The deputation should just come, it will be well received. It is high time that the Slovaks came.") They were received by the emperor, who had encouraging words for them. However, no changes in Magyar practices resulted.

While traveling, Hodža wrote almost every day to his beloved Kornélia, and several of his letters have been preserved. In one of them he penned this prescient sentence:[5] "I believe and feel that through you God means to replace everything that the world takes away from me, or that I deserve but am never given." It was almost as if he were awaiting an oppressive fate.

In this same year an extensive complaint, alleging a whole series of mis-behaviors, was filed against Hodža. The complaint's author was the church inspector of Mikuláš, a *magyarone* and one of Hodža's implacable enemies. He was the presiding officer of the church council and thus its highest lay func-tionary, and also a nobleman and one of the highest officials of County Liptov. Thus, he posed a double threat—both through the church and through his civil position. The council asked for a statement from Hodža, who responded in thirteen pages of close, point-by-point argument, written in Latin. After some time he was exonerated. The church inspector was unrelenting. In 1844, the year that Tatrín was founded and Hodža became its president, the inspector took his complaint to a higher authority, the council of the Western District of the Lutheran church, which had jurisdiction over the church in Mikuláš. The following year Hodža was once again exonerated.

In the same year of 1844 the Hungarian government, as part of its policy of Magyarization, directed that all church records be written in Magyar. This included the registry of births and baptisms, the only family record most people had. Even while the church inspector's complaint with the church council was still in process, the director of schools filed a new complaint with the govern-ment alleging that Hodža was keeping records in Slovak. A commission came to investigate and found that Hodža was keeping records both in Slovak and in Magyar. He was exonerated once again.

Next, Hodža's antagonists charged him with inappropriate alterations of the liturgy. He received an admonition to make no changes without the explicit approval of the council of the Western District of the church but was otherwise yet again exonerated.

As revolution broke out in 1848, the Hungarian government issued an arrest warrant for Hodža, Hurban, and Štúr. On this basis the bishop, Hodža's immediate superior in the church hierarchy, suspended him from his position as the minister of the church of Vrbica and Mikuláš. This suspension was later lifted and, as we have heard, Hodža returned from the revolution a hero. His enemies, however, pressed for his permanent suspension as soon as they found an excuse.

From the moment he arrived in Mikuláš until the end of the revolution, M. M. Hodža led almost a double life: He played a leading role in every aspect of the Slovak National Awakening at exactly the same time he was forced to fend off one personal attack after another. After the revolution, he retreated from national life and devoted himself primarily to church affairs. These were dominated by Magyar efforts to gain control over the powerful Slovak element in the Lutheran church and the struggles of Slovaks to retain their autonomy. The church was the battlefield, but the prize was the nation.

In July of 1860 Hodža once again traveled to Vienna as a member of a delegation to the emperor. He was the chief spokesman, making the case to the emperor that he should support the independence of the Slovak Lutheran Church against Magyar efforts to dominate it. The emperor responded with some encouraging words. However, in an ironic twist of fate, it was precisely while Hodža was pleading the Slovak case in Vienna that his enemies finally succeeded in having his meager church salary stopped. For the next year and a half, Hodža's family with its five children was largely dependent on food, clothing, and household items provided quietly by supportive parishioners. Even without a salary, however, Hodža continued in his position as the senior pastor of the church of Vrbica and Mikuláš, and his passionate defense of the Slovak cause never wavered.

In 1862 Hodža, despite his increasingly precarious position, published several sharp critiques of the newly-installed Lutheran bishop, Ľudovít Geduly, a *magyarone* who aggressively pressed a Magyarization agenda within the church.[7] Indeed, Hodža (Plate 20, Appendix VI) refused to acknowledge Geduly as his bishop, and a number of the pastors of Liptov supported him in this position. Geduly immediately went on the attack and demanded that Hodža be suspended from his pastorate. In a massively flawed proceeding (for example, the group that investigated Geduly's complaints was actually under his direct jurisdiction), the suspension was enacted.[8] However, Hodža's followers succeeded in having their decision reversed, and Hodža himself continued to write in support of the patent and against unification. Frustrated at lower levels, his enemies went to the emperor. The emperor sent an investigator to Mikuláš who quickly fell under the influence of Hodža's enemies. For three intimidating months, he collected evidence against Hodža before returning to Vienna to submit his report.

Not satisfied, two of the *magyarone* gentry physically attacked Hodža and one of his faithful supporters, the teacher Ján Drahotín Makovický, injuring them both seriously. At this there was a huge protest, led by Hodža's eldest daughter, Marína, who was arrested. Hodža himself filed a complaint with the local imperial military, eighty-three pages in length, in impeccable German. It was something of an autobiography, in which he described his life's work and demonstrated his loyalty to the emperor. Indeed, Hodža's attackers were convicted and jailed. Hodža traveled once again to Vienna, where he received assurances from the emperor that the damaging and one-sided report of the imperial investigator would be ignored. Finding reason for cheer, he wrote an optimistic letter to his wife. However, Hodža's suspension from his position was still in place.

THE EMPEROR WAS UNDER ENORMOUS POLITICAL PRESSURE. He had lost important wars with Prussia and Italy. The imperial treasury was increasingly dependent on contributions from Hungary, and the influence of Magyars on the emperor's actions grew correspondingly. Ultimately, the emperor yielded to unrelenting Magyar pressure and let Hodža's suspension from office stand.[9] Hodža received the news in his parish house, while he was having breakfast with his family between the two services on Easter Sunday, March 24, 1866. When he returned to the church, he stood in front of the altar and read the formal letter of notification. The congregation froze, and Hodža started to sing, in a voice permeated with grief and pain, the last two verses of the hymn, "Sun of Justice," "*Slunce spravedlnosti*" known to Slovak Lutherans ever since the *Cithara sanctorum:*[10]

> This life is constant struggle, battle,
> pains and sorrows along the way,
> Help me, Savior, the good fight to wage,
> hold to my faith, and with Paul declare:
> "I fought the good fight until my very end,
> and kept my faith, my conscience clear,
> And finally the crown of immortality
> the Lord in his mercy will give to me."

While he sang the church was deathly still; when he finished, many in the assembly wept.

The Lutherans of Mikuláš tried one more time to keep Hodža in their midst, but in the end he gave up. Now that he would have no income at all, he traveled once again to Vienna, this time with a petition to the emperor for a pension. The petition was granted under the condition that he would forever abstain from both political and religious activity. Hodža accepted the condition and waited. When no funds came for almost a year, he made new plans: He would send his wife and four children to wherever he could find shelter for them, and he himself would pick up the mendicant's staff and go wandering, hoping to find a place to settle in some corner of the Czech lands. Finally, Hodža sent yet another petition to the emperor. This time his cause was taken up by his antagonist of many years, the overseer of County Liptov, Martin Szentiványi, on condition that he leave not only Mikuláš but the entire Western District of the Lutheran church. Hodža left, then, for Tešín, an ancient town in the borderlands between Moravia and Poland and the birthplace of his great predecessor in Mikuláš, Juraj Tranovský, the author of the *Cithara sanctorum*.

IN THE COMPANY OF HIS TWO OLDEST DAUGHTERS, Hodža traveled to Tešín in September 1867, and was taken in by a local friend. Later, his wife joined him, having stopped on the way to be with their first grandchild, just born. The family lived quietly on Hodža's modest imperial pension and even managed to pay off some of the debts they had accumulated over the years of meager salary and generous financial support to others. Immersing himself in writing a monumental poetical work, *Vieroslavín*, Hodža remained true to his promise not to engage in political or church activity.

In the fall of 1869, a painful, undiagnosed illness set in. The doctors could do nothing. His wife cared for him as best she could. The end came on March 26, 1870, one day before Easter Sunday.

The funeral was held on Monday. It was a miserable, wet, snowy day, but 2,000 mourners came to the mortuary and 3,000 to the church. The services were conducted in Polish and German, Tešín's principal languages, and Hodža's hymns, many of which had been included in the Polish hymnal, were sung. Hodža's only son came from Bratislava. The German pastor conducting the service admonished him:[11]

> You, the only son of Hodža! Your father left you no riches . . . but never fear, for he left you a beautiful inheritance, a good, unsullied name. Never forget that this name is like a tender flower. . . . Tend and protect this flower, and never forget that your father was

Hodža, a true son of Slovakia, a distinguished servant of God, and a patient Christian!

He repeated these words to each of the daughters.

A memorial service was held in Hodža's church in Mikuláš, but the church council pointedly failed even to mention Hodža's death in its proceedings. The council of the Western District was similarly silent. Not until the 100th anniversary of M. M. Hodža's birth, in 1911, were there major celebrations in his honor in Mikuláš. After the establishment of Czechoslovakia, the recently constructed gymnasium was renamed in honor of Michal Miloslav Hodža, the name which it still bears.

In 1922 the Lutherans of Mikuláš undertook, with the support of Slovakia's most important cultural organization, *Matica Slovenská*, and the agreement of the family, to bring the remains of their beloved Michal Miloslav Hodža from Tešín back to the city he had served so long and so nobly.[12] A sizeable delegation of citizens made the journey to Tešín. The remains were exhumed and placed in a new casket. Services were held in the city's old church. Then a procession formed around the funeral carriage that held the casket and wound its way through the city, stopping from time to time for speeches and celebrations. At one of these stops Milan Hodža, then the Czechoslovak minister of education, spoke about his uncle, little imagining that death in exile and a delayed funeral at home would one day be his own fate as well.

Procession accompanying the remains of Michal Miloslav Hodža when they were brought home from Tešín to Liptovský Mikuláš in 1922. Archive of the Museum of Janko Kráľ, Liptovský Mikuláš.

In Mikuláš, an honor guard and a huge procession accompanied the casket from the railway station, along Hodža Street, through the city square and on to the Lutheran church. The casket stood before the altar for a full week. On Sunday, April 2, 1922, the church was filled to the last seat and the square likewise was crowded. Two of Hodža's daughters, both widows, were present. His hymns were sung, and eulogies were delivered. A procession moved from the church to the Lutheran orphanage, where a monument had been prepared: the cross from the monument in Tešín atop a new foundation. The grave was blessed, again hymns were sung, and speeches followed. The military band sounded national hymns, the guns fired a salute. Finally *Hej, Slováci* issued in celebration from the whole throng. The casket was lowered into the grave, and the crowd quietly dispersed, only to gather once again in the evening for more speeches and songs, all in memory of a great Slovak spirit.

The year 1938 was the twentieth anniversary of the birth of the Republic of Czechoslovakia. It was also the year of the most intense Nazi pressure and of the Munich Declaration, but despite the grave international situation, celebrations were held. In Mikuláš a new plaque was added to the wall of the Gymnasium of M. M. Hodža; you can see it on the cover of this book. It reads:

> Michal Miloslav Hodža, whose name this institution carries, writer and national awakener, was born in the year 1811 in Rakša, and died in the year 1870 in exile in Tešín. He is buried in Liptovský Svätý Mikuláš, where he worked.

> On the 20th anniversary of the Czechoslovak Republic, from its grateful students.

Plaque in Hodža's honor on the gymnasium in Liptovský Mikuláš that has carried his name since 1919. The plaque was placed in 1938, on the occasion of the twentieth anniversary of the founding of Czechoslovakia. Photo author.

Flanking the main door of the Lutheran church today are two larger-than-life, sandstone statues of heroes of the church (Plates 21, 22). On the left is Juraj Tranovský, author of the *Cithara sanctorum*, born in Tešín and died in Mikuláš. On the right is Michal Miloslav Hodža, worked in Mikuláš and died in Tešín.

The statues, which were erected only in 1950, early in the Communist era, have an interesting history. One of a group of noted painters associated with Mikuláš during the middle of the twentieth century, and a good friend of my father's, was Janko Alexy. Not only did Alexy gain national recognition as an artist, but he invested immense energy in conserving historical landmarks, most notably the castle of Bratislava, and in finding vivid, public ways to commemorate Slovak history. After much struggle with the Communist bureaucracy, he succeeded in having the two statues prepared and installed in this place of honor.[13]

On the pedestals are engraved words evoking the lives of Tranovský and Hodža. On one face of Hodža's pedestal is the epitaph he wrote for himself:

> *Narodil sa, trpel pod uhorským panstvom,*
> *umrel, utrápený ľudu svojho manstvom.*

> He was born, suffered under Hungarian rule;
> he died, griefstricken at his people's enslavement.

HODŽA WAS AN EXTRAORDINARILY COMPLEX MAN. He was committed to his people, and he played a major role in sweeping political events. It seems to me, however, that Hodža was not primarily a political being, adroit at maneuvering within the political sphere. Rather, he was a prophet, driven by an inner vision, a vision in which the Christian faith and the Slovak people played equally powerful and constantly intertwining roles.

In this journal entry from June 13, 1855, a few years before the battles over the Protestant patent, Hodža made clear that his spiritual sustenance came not from his analytical study of the scriptures or from his political fervor but from the Slovak people he served and from their simple faith:[14]

> How far had I wandered from my home, drifted away from the religious life. Dear God, I was like a devil walking over parched lands and fields, and when I came to the service of the Gospels—to which only the mercy, the person of the Savior and his love brought me—what an emptiness, dryness and wasteland I found. And from that time to this, how my life has moistened, having been so dry. The life of Christ is strong. And through whom did it work on me? It lives in the hearts of our people. . . . Christ's pains are the bloody tears of the soul of the pious Slovak. . . .

The life of our people supports my life and the lives of my companions, those who are worthy of it and attend to it. From the people, the feeling of prayer and piety enters my heart. In my heart's otherwise overwhelming weakness, this is its strength. Just as I was born in a house of faith, born of parents most pious, so the love and mercy of Christ let me take birth in the life of the Slovak people. This life birthed me forth—so that in the truth of truths, I am the son of the Slovak people, the Slovak-Christian people.

M. M. Hodža was a brilliant scholar and propagator of ideas. He wrote systematic theses on the importance of the Slovak language and on its linguistic structure, and point-by-point critiques to answer the arguments of those who held opposing views. He could engage in intellectual jousting with any scholar. Ultimately, however, he was not interested in ideas merely as intellectual constructs. He wanted truth. Truth as he experienced it might be evoked by what he read, but he saw it ultimately as a gift of the spirit that came from within himself. Here is another passage from his journal:[15]

Whatever I read, I forget, because I never exercised my memory or my attention.... And when I read books, no matter how excellent, it seems to me as if I know more than the author, have read more than he has written.... At the same time, when I read a book, whether excellent or miserable, it is as if I have never known anything and everything is new, as if I had never completed my education. And finally, nevertheless, this way or that way, what I read I forget, and I know only that which the spirit has shown me, that which has become clear to me, which has come to me through the lightning flash of the Son of God.

With the passage of years, Hodža's reliance on the inner voice became ever greater. He wrote extensively in his journal, composed epic poems, delivered weekly sermons. In his sermons he always dealt with universal questions—faith, good, evil, love, death, family, and nation.[16] He had no simplistic, ready answers. Rather, he wrestled with these vast concepts, and, increasingly, revealed his inner struggles to his parishioners. His sermons are difficult to read, and they must have been even more difficult to follow while sitting in the simple wooden pews in the cavernous church of Mikuláš.

Especially in his later years, Hodža cast his struggles and musings in increasingly complex language.[17] He used many words and expressions that had, even in his day, faded from common use. He collected words like some people collected folk songs or tales. As he went from place to place, he listened to ordinary people speaking in the most local of dialects, noted down their words, and made them his own. And when all else failed, he invented his own words.[18]

Where before the revolution Hodža had written primarily linguistic and political tracts, his last compositions are three epic poems portraying the glories of Slavdom: *Matora*, *Slavomiersky* and *Vieroslavín*.[19] They are massive works. *Vieroslavín* has some 8,000 lines of pulsing, rhythmic, rhyming verse. During this most difficult period of his life, following the failure of the revolution and facing personal attack, poverty, and the death of five of his children, Hodža had a vision, a vision of a glorious future in which all Slavdom, rich in heart, spirit, and Christian faith, would triumph, and Slovaks would finally live in freedom. Faith and freedom would come together. He held on to this vision even though his own life had brought him not triumph and freedom but persecution and exile.

So this was Hodža, the second son of the miller of Rakša. In the words of Jur Janoška, a great later pastor of Hodža's Lutheran church of Mikuláš,[20] he was a

> . . . deep thinker, rousing and captivating preacher-orator, poet-prophet rising to the heights of the psalmist-prophets who were lifted up by the spirit of God Himself; unbreakable fighter for truth; unconquered hero of the faith; sufferer, exile, martyr according to the teaching and example of Christ.

CHAPTER 21

Marína Hodža—Patriot-Feminist

During the 1860s, a brief period following the revolution when Magyarization efforts were slightly relaxed and several important Slovak cultural institutions were founded,[1] a young woman appeared on the national scene with verve, energy, and boundless passion for the future of her people—Marína Hodža, Michal Miloslav's eldest daughter.[2]

Marína acquired an education that was unusual for a Slovak girl during this period of history. She learned to both speak and write German and Magyar, and also studied French and Russian. She traveled, not only in the nearby Slovak counties but also to Vienna and Germany. She read widely. Most of the notable Slovak personalities of the day frequented her home, and through them she learned of the political and cultural currents coursing among the Slovak leadership. Marína also saw the pressures that were being brought to bear against her father, with whom she had an extraordinarily close relationship. Not only did she love M. M. Hodža deeply as a daughter, she also acted as his secretary, editor, and sometimes travel companion. At a tender age she knew much about the immense pressures that political engagement can present, and also the exhilaration of working for a momentous cause.

MARÍNA HODŽA WAS ONLY 19 when, in 1861, she received a letter from one of the important men of Slovak letters, Viliam Pauliny-Tóth.[3] At the time he was editing two influential Slovak magazines published in Budapest: *Sokol*, a monthly illustrated magazine of the arts and literature, and *Černokňažník*, a weekly magazine for humor and literature.[4] He was looking for a correspondent who could write reports about literary news and events of the Slovak heartland—perhaps Marína would agree to do this. She did, in a long, exuberant, and heartfelt letter dated January 25, 1862:[5]

> As regards your request for me to be a correspondent, I must confess that it filled me with not a little pride that you, honorable sir, see in me such abilities. I now almost have the desire to think such things about myself, but first, of course, I would have to fulfill your

expectations, and this I doubt, for the creations of my peculiar spirit will hardly withstand even a gentle critique.

This letter was the first in a series spanning about four years, letters full of news, vignettes of life in Mikuláš, outbursts of emotion, and, in the eyes of some readers, a growing (though never directly stated) love. Pauliny-Tóth responded with his views on the national struggle, the challenges of publishing in a censored world, and news of his family.

Pauliny-Tóth published the reports that Marína sent. They mostly reviewed the performances of the community theater of which she was a principal organizer and much admired actress, as well as occasional literary gatherings and other celebrations. The community theater was one of the great civic organizations of Mikuláš. While it often put on plays translated from German and other languages, the performances were always in Slovak and thus supported national efforts. Most of these performances were held in a tavern in Vrbica, which was filled to capacity by townspeople and villagers alike. The actors were drawn mainly from the town's more prominent families, always including the Pálkas and the Bellas. Here is an excerpt from part of Marína's critique of a performance of *The Spaniards in Peru* by August von Kotzebue,[6] a prolific German author:[7]

> Ján Pálka as Alonzo de Molina drew great applause for his fine performance. . . . Samuel Pálka as Las Casas, the Dominican monk, appeared genuinely dignified and admirable; he looked and acted as if he had truly just come from some some monastic cell, and was often interrupted by loud applause. . . . The Peruvian women, played by Žofia Pálka and Marína Strnisko, played their roles, only next time they could be a little bolder.
>
> Conspicuous as well was Elvíra, the niece of Pizzaro (Zuzanna Bella), who played her role excellently, as she always does. It was probably her best performance ever. Peter Bella as the courtier (as well as other performers) also pleased the audience with good acting and appropriate costumes [all costumes were provided by the actors and actresses themselves].

As Marína's letter shows, many of the roles were played by members of my family. Zuzanna Bella was my great-grandmother, and Peter Bella was Zuzanna's poet-brother (Chapters 15 and 22), the author of the hymn, "*Aká si mi krásna, Ty rodná zem moja,*" which was sung during the transfer of Grandfather Hodža's remains (Prologue). Ján Pálka was my great-grandfather (Chapter 15), a young man at the time of this performance; he and Zuzana married shortly thereafter

(Family tree 3, Appendix V). Samuel Pálka was Ján's younger brother, and Žofia Pálka the daughter of a more distantly related Samuel Pálka.

In those days an energetically acted play was high enterntainment and would draw an audience without distinction of education and class. This particular play was not for entertainment only, however. Rather, it conveyed a potent political message to the audience. The play's hero, Bartolomé de las Casas, was a sixteenth century activist who struggled for the rights of the native peoples of Mexico and Peru, laboring then under Spanish rule.[8] Surely, many in the audience would have recognized the parallel to the situation of Slovaks under Magyar rule.

Marína's biographer, Peter Liba, described in this way her perception of the role of theater in Slovak national life:[9] "For Marína Hodža, theater was a means of arousing the nation from its indifference, its fearfulness—and also of awakening higher, more elevated and noble feelings." The authorities as well could see the effect of Slovak theater on the people, and they tried to curb it. Marína described what happened after the performance of *The Spaniards in Peru:*[10]

A party was supposed to follow the performance. Permission was initially granted by the viceišpán [the second-highest county official], but at the last minute it was withdrawn and the party was to be canceled. Following a renewed request, permission was again obtained but only under the condition that two armed constables would be present, at which the insulted audience became angry and dispersed. So the innocent party of our people—and it is these last two words, of course, that so annoy certain persons—was ruined by the arbitrariness and readiness to use power of one man, the viceišpán.

MARÍNA HODŽA ALWAYS SEARCHED FOR PRACTICAL steps that she, as a woman in male-dominated times, could take to support the national cause. One such step was founding a reading circle, the *Beseda dievčenská*, for the girls of Mikuláš.[11] The fifty-six girls held weekly meetings in which they read literature in the new literary Slovak (as well as some in Czech), presented their own works, and raised funds for Slovak schools. The members of the circle celebrated all Slovak holidays and national events. They attended the gatherings of the newly-founded cultural organization, *Matica Slovenská*, where Marína recited poetry, and collected funds for its support. In all this, they were entering the public arena, moving beyond the safety of their own circle and well beyond the social traditions in which they had been raised. Needless to say, the authorities were not pleased to see yet another expression of Slovak national spirit.

Through such actions, young Marína became perhaps the leading Slovak feminist of her day, even though the word "feminist" had not yet been coined. As time went on, she adopted the phrase "everything for the nation" (*všetko za národ*) as her personal motto. Now it was not only the father but the daughter as well who served as a thorn in the side of the Magyar and *magyarone* powers in Mikuláš.

May 1863 brought an event that would be central in Marína's life—the physical attack on her father, M. M. Hodža, and his friend, the teacher J. D. Makovický, by two of the local gentry (Chapter 20). She wrote to Pauliny-Tóth:[12]

> My dear friend,
>
> I write as I have never written before. I am shaking, shaking with inexpressible, never before experienced, pain, shaking with revenge. Yes, do not wonder, I shake with revenge!
>
> . . . But listen, friend, brother, son of a nation whipped into submission, persecuted, listen! Listen how the sufferings of a martyr tortured for years are crowned.
>
> [Here follows a detailed description of the attack].
>
> Oh, I shake! This thug, this human excretion, with his godless, accursed hand did not fear to touch the holy head of my dear father. O God, dear God!
>
> . . . O God, I can't even tell you how my poor father feels. I can't look long at his so noble face, now battered and aching by a thieving, murderous hand. His whole face is swollen, black and blue, wounded especially around the eyes, one of his teeth knocked out. The doctor was just here, saying he hopes that there is no real danger and prescribing only cold compresses until the morning.
>
> . . . I feel terrible, terrible storms within me, as I have never felt before. Am I not horrible, unrecognizable? Yes, I am horrible. In my father—dishonored, battered, in pain—is my whole nation dishonored, battered and in pain, and surely this nation will shout, "Revenge." And this I too shout, this I swear, to the murderers of my dear father, the murderers of my nation!

The local authorities stood by in silence, taking no action on the grounds that gentry were immune from prosecution. Two days later, on a Sunday, a crowd of several hundred gathered in front of the Lutheran church and proceeded from there a few blocks to the county seat on the main square, demanding that the imperial representative in County Liptov insure justice and punishment of the attackers. The Hodža sisters were in the crowd, as were many of the young women of Mikuláš. Once inside, Marína leaped onto a table and, raising her arms, called out to the crowd, "Swear revenge!" Many raised their arms with her and took that oath.

For this public protest, Marína was arrested and was to be jailed, but her sentence was commuted to twelve hours of house arrest. A modicum of justice was done: Despite their noble status, both of Hodža's attackers were jailed at least briefly.

THE ACCUSATIONS AGAINST HER FATHER were unceasing. Marína mentioned them occasionally in her letters, usually commenting that he remained unafraid. For the most part, she focused on her own work with the theater and the young women of Mikuláš, and on the reports that she faithfully continued to send to Pauliny-Tóth. Still, the tone of her letters grew darker. In another year, on August 18, 1865, she wrote a paean to the innocence that she was losing:[14]

> Well, it can't be helped. One gets older and that youthful freedom of the spirit leaves him—or if it doesn't leave him, he must willy-nilly choke it off—that flight so dear, so beautiful, so dream-like, so elevating, and yet so dangerous; that imagination, supposedly so damaging, that often takes the smallest, least significant thing and knows how to paint it brightly and interestingly. Those feelings, sparks, lightning bolts, tender, fragile flower buds, beautiful, so they say, but filled with vice and not suitable for this world—not practical!!!—unhealthy idealism. So you see, this is how one ages, desiccates. Strictness and that whole poor reality of this life and this world weigh tear by tear—and one desiccates. Less and less is it possible to play on those pain/love strings of the soul that seem to be sounding their last, or perhaps have already sounded their last, or perhaps never will.

She closed:

> Good bye, my dear friend. Warm regards to your wife. To you, once again and always, my heartfelt good bye, and my sincere request that you will always remember kindly, my dear and precious friend, your sincere admirer and friend, Marína H.

They never wrote to each other again.

Discouraged by the endless battles on the side of her father, who was being driven ever closer to defeat and despair, and feeling the overwhelming power of the authorities bent on destroying the national spirit that had been such a part of her being, Marína accepted a scholarship that would take her far away from home, to a recently-founded institute for the training of Lutheran deaconesses in Neuendettelsau, Germany.[15] She left home with some dread. By the time she returned in a year, in 1866, Hodža's enemies had finally succeeded. He had been suspended from his post as minister of the Lutheran church in Mikuláš, his suspension had been confirmed by the emperor, and the family had been forced to move out of the parish house. Despite her family's dismal circumstances and pressures from the authorities, Marína founded a school for girls in Mikuláš. Though she was the only teacher, many girls came and she reveled in the school's success.

It was her last great outpouring of love and energy for her people. When in 1867 Michal Miloslav Hodža finally elected exile, Marína closed her school and left Mikuláš with a heavy heart. She wrote to a friend:[16]

> Oh, it is hard to leave this place, especially since I have had to take leave of my school to which I was devoted with all my heart and which prospered all through the whole school year and far exceeded my expectations, despite all the intrigues of our enemies. . . .

> Having to abandon the work I have started and to have no prospects for the future is very hard for me to bear. . . .

With her mother and sister she tended to her father in Tešín for the last three years of his life. After his death in 1870, Marína, her mother, and her sister returned to Slovakia, each settling in a different place. Marína abandoned all of her former activities and made a meager living by sewing and teaching sewing classes. Six years later, at the age of thirty-three, she fell in love with a man a few years younger than herself. Marína Hodža and Filip Hladký, a lawyer, married, and by all accounts their marriage was a happy one. They were childless, but they raised one of Marína's nieces as their own. Sadly, Filip was drafted into the Austro-Hungarian army and returned from war in the Balkans with his health seriously undermined; he died in 1901 after they had been married twenty-five years. Marína herself died in 1920 at the age of seventy-eight. She lived to see Slovakia become free within the Czechoslovak Republic, but not long enough to see her revered father's remains brought home in state to Mikuláš in 1922.

Following Michal Miloslav Hodža's death 1870, there was no shortage of opportunities for Marína to engage with the national movement and with education and theater for women. The active and highly effective women's organization, *Živena,* had been founded in Martin in 1869. Theater companies thrived in several cities, and there were any number of publications for which she could have written. But Marína chose instead a self-imposed seclusion, devoting herself to her husband and to her unpretentious sewing.

On the days in June of 1875 or 1876 when the annual celebrations remembering the Memorandum of the Slovak Nation were being held (this memorandum, signed in 1861 in Martin, is still viewed as the single most important expression of Slovak national aspirations), she wrote to her then fiancée, her beloved Filip, this self-portrait:[17]

I feel a little guilty that this national day, which I once celebrated with such enthusiasm, matters so little to me now. Still, involuntary pictures from the past occasionally tug at my heart. I see myself, exhilarated and dressed in national costume, processing at the head of our "beseda ženská" under the red, white, and blue flag as we walked to the places where, with national rejoicing, we celebrated this national holiday and all the great events in the life of our nation! Carried away by the feelings of love for my nation, exhilarated, admired by so many Slovak souls—I was happy; every such day was a gift to me. And yet when, after all the farewells, I returned to my own self, I often felt a great emptiness, and knew not what was missing. . . . This is how it was in the dreams and illusions of my youth, completely dedicated to my nation. But then followed disappointments, bitter awakenings, and with these—above everything with the death of my dear father—my heart froze and turned against the miserable, ungrateful nation whose ingratitude broke the spirit of him who devoted and sacrificed his entire life to the national cause! A horrible pause followed in my life, but after it came a new and blessed life with you and for you, my only Filip. Only indeed, for everything else—all my love for my nation and all my sorrows—is as if it has fallen asleep, and all that remains in my soul is my love for you. . . .

Marína was truly her father's daughter; her whole being was about her nation and about her inner world. When she felt disillusioned about her nation, she withdrew from public life and lived only the quiet life of personal love.

CHAPTER 22

Bellas—Freedom Fighters and Poets

Mikuláš had long been one of the centers of Slovak national feeling and activity, but in the latter half of the nineteenth century, despite the pressures of an ever more forceful Magyarization, its economic power grew as well. The influence of the guilds was finally fading out, opening new opportunities for enterprising businessmen. More than that, following the Compromise of 1867, which transformed the Habsburg Empire into the Austro-Hungarian Empire (Appendix I), the Hungarian government embarked on a policy of actively supporting industrialization.[1] This policy included the development of a railway network that would link Hungarian cities with each other and also with the Austrian part of the empire and beyond. In 1872 the railway finally reached Mikuláš, en route between Košice in the east and industrial centers like Bohumín in Silesia in the west. With the railway came investors from Budapest and Vienna, providing capital that enabled local entrepreneurs to make the transition from manufactories to full-fledged factories. It also brought a wider world outlook to the educated strata of Mikuláš.

My great-grandfather Janko Pálka (1835-1904, Family tree 3, Appendix V), was a well-known figure in this emerging environment. While still working in his father's leather workshop, he was among the first of the local leathermen to set out to improve his prospects by learning the latest, increasingly industrial, techniques being used in distant lands, as far away as Bavaria. In 1876 he inherited his share of the business.[2]

As business opportunities expanded, Janko took good advantage of them. In 1882 he was one of the first in Mikuláš to introduce steam power into his factory. Unfortunately, the following year Mikuláš suffered the greatest of its periodic fires:[3]

> The wind blew fiercely and unceasingly, ripping out the burning shakes from the roofs while the flames lept from one part of town

to another. The sky was filled with burning roof fragments like flaming ravens that set one roof after another ablaze. There was nothing to do but to gather up the children and flee to Vrbica which the flames did not reach. . . . The fire was unstoppable. It did away with the factory of Stodola & Kováč in an hour and a half.

Janko Pálka's factory, too, burned. According to a contemporary account[4], " Of the famous leatherworks of Kováč & Stodola, Lacko Brothers, and Janko Pálka, equipped fully as well as are those of our largest cities, nothing was left except the soot-covered walls." But business was booming, and loans from Budapest and Vienna were available. Within just four years Janko managed to rebuild his factory, improve its power and machinery, and buy additional land. The other leatherworks recovered as well.

Over the years Janko kept making improvements;[5] as the twentieth century approached, his factory employed sixty men, twelve women, and twelve apprentices, and prepared 20,000 hides per year. Their work was good. It was exhibited in Budapest in 1885, in Versailles in 1900, and in 1890 won a silver medal in Vienna. He gained membership the Regional Association of Hungarian Industrialists, a rare position for a Slovak, and later he was elected to the association's board of directors.[6]

IN 1862, MICHAL MILOSLAV HODŽA PRESIDED OVER the marriage of Janko Pálka and Zuzana Bella, the daughter of his long-time suppporter Jozef Bella. Marína Hodža wrote to Viliam Pauliny-Tóth:[7]

> And now I am going to announce to you a new and truly joyful couple, Janko Pálka and Zuzana Bella, certainly known to you, both from the theater and as patriots. They are truly excellent souls, in the national cause as in every other respect, a pair that brings joy to all of our hearts. On November 26th we will go to the wedding.

Through this marriage two of the most prominent families of Mikuláš were united.[8] We already know Zuzana's father, Jozef Bella—furrier by trade, voracious reader of all things Slovak, mayor, prisoner in Debrecen, delegate to the emperor. Jozef Bella and his wife Mária Lang raised seven children, five sons and two daughters. They were an extraordinary group of siblings, counting two soldiers who fought in wars of liberation, three significant writers including two well-known poets, and two daughters who married into other notable families (Family tree 4, Appendix V).

Like so many of the other members of Mikuláš society, the Bellas were devout Lutherans who were very serious both about their religion and its meaning in everyday life, and about the Slovak national ideal. They raised their children accordingly. Here is how one of their sons, Ján Bella, recalled his childhood:[9]

Our parents, being industrious, pious, truth loving, and nationally aware, raised us in that same spirit. Our family praised the Lord every morning with song and prayer. On Sunday afternoon all of us in the household, including the servants, gathered around the table. After singing several hymns, we had to elaborate to our father points that we remembered from that morning's sermon. Then we read out loud a classical commentary [Sartorius's *Postilla*[9]] on the text for the day, each one of the boys reading one section. This helped us to read well. In the evenings of working days, we read from texts that taught us morals. The servants who listened also learned from this, especially when our father, from time to time, explained important points from the readings.

This honoring of morals and ideals was reflected in the lives of the Bella children, who responded actively to the social and political currents of the times. They were well aware of these currents for, in addition to the news that came in connection with the burgeoning leather business, an active press had earlier come into existence, and newspapers and magazines were available even in Mikuláš. They were heavily censored by the government, but even so news about the wider world was available. The reading public might have been small, but it understood that the multiple revolutions of 1848 had by no means been the end of the armed struggle for justice and national rights, and that the captive nations of the giant empires—Russia, Austria-Hungary, and the Ottoman Empire—were restive. Uprisings continued throughout the rest of the century, and their stories spoke to the spirits of two of the Bella sons.

In 1858 the eldest, Jozef Bella (1832-1876; trained as a furrier like his father) heard about the uprising of the Montenegrins against the Turks.[11] A restless spirit in any case, he left his wife and two young children in Mikuláš and went south to fight as a volunteer in the Montenegrin army. He returned home, but in 1863 an uprising broke out in Poland and Lithuania, which were then under Russian rule.[12] Jozef picked up his rifle again and went to fight with the Poles. Hoped-for military support from the Western powers did not materialize, and after two years of bloody fighting, the uprising was put down. Jozef survived the battles. He moved south again and spent a number of years in the Balkans. His love of the people there and their history is reflected in his epic poem about *Rajčo Nikolev*, a Bulgarian hero. When the Serbs and the Bulgarians rose up against the Turks in 1876,[13] Jozef heeded the call of the battle for freedom once again. He was killed at Aleksinac in southestern Serbia, the site of several major battles. *Rajčo Nikolev* and a number of his other poems were published posthumously in 1906-1907.[14]

Jozef Bella, the most adventurous of the Bella freedom fighters-poets. He left Mikuláš in 1858, fought in at least three wars for freedom, and died in southern Serbia in 1876. Archive of the Museum of Janko Král', Liptovský Mikuláš.

Jozef's younger brother, Daniel Bella (1834-?), was trained as a tailor,[8] but was also a soldier at heart. He fought in the Italian wars of independence, married a German woman in the Croatian capital of Zagreb, and worked as a minor official in the Croatian legation in Buda. Finally he became an officer of the Royal Guard in Buda, where he is thought to have died.

The three other sons made their marks as poets and writers, not as soldiers, but like their freedom-fighting brothers they, too, died far away from home. Their devotion to the land they left behind is evident in their poems. My own favorite poet is Peter Bella-Horal (1842-1919).[8] He followed his father's trade as a furrier, but became best known as a poet and translator. The Bella family's fur business failed in 1873, so Peter moved to Budapest, studied telegraphy, trained with the railways, and found employment as a minor railway official, first in Transylvania and then in Budapest, where he lived for the rest of his life. He married a German woman but tried to raise their only child, a daughter, as a Slovak.

He never returned to Mikuláš. As a poet he took the pseudonym Horal (man of the mountains) and wrote many lyrical poems that glow with his love and longing for home. A number of these were set to music by leading Slovak composers such as Eugen Suchoň[15] and Ján Levoslav Bella,[16]" and are even today part of Slovakia's choral repertoire. We met perhaps his best known poem, often sung as a patriotic hymn, in the Prologue: *Aká si mi krásna, Ty rodná zem moja . . ".* (How beautiful you are, O land of my birth . . .). It portrays the natural beauties of his beloved native place, County Liptov, but speaks to all Slovaks.

Peter Bella-Horal, to me the greatest of the Bella poets. He wrote the hymn, "Aká si mi krásna, Ty rodná zem moja," that is widely performed today, and was sung at the church services for Grandfather Hodža in Chicago and Martin. Archive of the Museum of Janko Kráľ, Liptovský Mikuláš.

I grew up with another of Peter Bella-Horal's poems, not realizing that one of my own ancestors had written it. It is a paean to his Slovak mother tongue. A few years ago, I found a beautiful recording of it by an American popular singer with Slovak roots, Ľuba Mason.[17] It is one of her most frequently requested songs, and she sings it in the purest Slovak. It starts like this:

Materinská moja reč, taká si mi milá,
ako by ma moja mať menom oslovila,
ako by ma ľúbajúc k srdcu privinula,
ako by ma žehnajúc Bohu porúčala.

You are as dear to me, mother language mine,
As if my own mother called me by my name,
As if she, loving me, pressed me to her heart,
As if she, blessing me, offered me to God.

In his lifetime, Ondrej Bella (1851-1903)[8] was the most highly recognized of the Bella poets. He served in a number of cities, including Pest, Graz, and

Prague, as a Lutheran chaplain in the Austro-Hungarian army, finally settling down in Krakow where he died. He never married. He started publishing poems even as a gymnasium student, often hiding behind pseudonyms. With a gift for languages, he translated into Slovak the works of Russian, Polish, German, and Hungarian writers, and even those of Henry Wadsworth Longfellow. Some of his own writings were ambitious and complex. At heart, however, he was a folk poet, reveling in the rhythms and sounds of the Slovak language spoken in the villages. Two collections of his short poems were published to great acclaim, one in 1880 in Pest, and the other in 1923, twenty years after his death, as part of the reading curriculum for Slovak schools. My copy of this little book[18] is inscribed by its editor to Grandfather Hodža, who was the Czechoslovak minister of agriculture at the time of its publication. The editor wrote: "Few of our poets immersed themselves as fully in the spirit of our folk song, or presented it as beautifully."

Ján Bella (1836-1924) wrote the memoirs about his father, Jozef Bella, from which I have quoted several times.[8] He was trained as a leather craftsman, but he left the trade and gained enough education to become a teacher in Lutheran schools, the author of school textbooks and annuals, a prolific author of magazine articles, and a poet. He settled first in Pest, where he worked with, among others, Viliam Pauliny-Tóth. Later he moved to Békéš Čaba, a notable Slovak settlement in the eastern Hungarian lowlands (see Appendix III), where he died.[19]

ALL THE BELLA BROTHERS, WHETHER SOLDIERS or writers, died far away from home. The two daughters stayed in Mikuláš to raise their families. Mária Bella (1839-1922)[8] married Ján Bauer from a family of bakers. She became a teacher and also, like most of her siblings, wrote poetry throughout her life, though not primarily for publication.

Her daughter, Ľudmila Bauer (1861-1948), married the leatherworker Jozef Stodola (1856-1938) whose three younger brothers—Aurel, Emil, and Kornel—were among the most remarkable Slovaks of their time.[20] (The Stodolas and the Pálkas were interlinked by marriages, at least seven of them over the generations. It makes for complicated family trees![21])

Zuzana Bella (1844-1932), my great-grandmother Pálka, had a long career in the important amateur theatre of Mikuláš and was one of Marína Hodža's closest friends (Chapter 21).[8] She was also gifted in other arts. As a girl she took drawing lessons and became quite accomplished. One of her sketch books is in the archives of the Museum of Janko Kráľ[22] and shows a level of skill that would be rare today. And, like her siblings, she wrote letters and poems throughout her long life.

She and Janko Pálka had three daughters and one son, Ján Ľudovít Pálka (1869-1935), my own Grandfather Pálka. In 1926, at the age of eighty-two, she wrote her son a poem for his birthday:[22]

> Hopes, Hopes! bright colored hopes,
> May your life, my son,
> Always reflect your hopes.
> May God give you health, and nights full of peace,
> The blessing of work and of bread abundant;
> Delight in your children, respite from your cares,
> Peace in your home, and a bit of joy too.
> For this every day I ask the Lord,
> (For heaven hears a mother's prayer)
> God full of strength! And faith warms my soul
> That He surely will grant your hopes, like my own.

She did not neglect her grandson, my father. In 1929, on his twenty-eighth birthday, she wrote him a letter that he kept all his life. He had it framed, and he had me hang it on his wall after my mother died:[23]

Janíčko, my dear grandson!

You know that I love you and that I wish you everything good from God. And so, on today's celebration of your birthday, I want to say a few sincere words to you.

Today you are entering the age in which every sensible and responsible man tries to step into true humanity, to establish his own hearth, in a word, to get married! Only, as the saying goes, the problem is that he who wants to have a satisfied soul has to find his own other half. With you, it is high time that you start to find your other half—and he who seeks, shall find!

There are still honorable Slovak homes where you can find a girl to your liking—kind, healthy, and sensible—but don't delay with this important step and don't stop looking until you find what you are seeking.

Janíčko, my dear grandson—I am slowly nearing the end of my life, but I ask God that I might live long enough so see by your side your other half, of whom I ask in my heart only that she be your truest friend and the angel of peace in your home, that she take joy in the success of your work, and if heavy cares fall on your shoulders that she not make them worse by her lamentations but rather sweetly look into your eyes and cheer you with these words:

Nič sa neboj, Janíčko moj, veď sme oba mladí,
čo nemáme, to mať môžme, len sa majme radi!

Never fear, Janíčko dear, we're still young , you know,
What we don't have now, we can have still, just let us love each
other.

God showers his blesings on homes such as these. I ask the Lord that
he listen to my prayers and fullfil my longings and hopes.

Later in 1929 Zuzana wrote this letter to her son, Grandfather Pálka, and her
grandson, my father, on the occasion of their joint name day. In Slovakia, the
day of the year identified with a particular name is always a day of celebration
for holders of that name, as important as their birthday. This is why Zuzana
made sure to write. A bride was still very much on her mind![22]

You two Jáns, both dear to my heart, are today celebrating the occasion of your name day, and I come to you with the sincere wish
that God give to both of you health and blessings for your work. I
also wish that our household may flower in the love of our family,
and that you, Janíčko, may as soon as possible find that which it
is your duty to find for the comfort of your father, so that on your
name day next year, you may be congratulated by your young bride
to the delight of us all. I wish this for you with all my heart, and
you, Janíčko, take it to heart. I believe that then you will find the
true meaning of your life, and the true joy and duty.

My great-grandmother did not quite live to see the wedding day she
yearned for; she died in 1932, and my parents weren't married until 1935. But,
perhaps by design, their wedding was on Ján's day.

CHAPTER 23

Ján Pálka and
His Utopian Socialism

My grandfather, Ján Pálka (1869-1935), is one of the most captivating characters I uncovered in my entire search through family history. In his business life he experienced highs and lows, passing from great wealth during World War I to bankruptcy during the Great Depression. More than this, however, he was a committed Christian and social thinker who brought his convictions into the operation of his business. His risky experiment in Utopian Socialism resonated throughout Czechoslovakia. Battered by predominantly external circumstances, the experiment failed. However, this failure brought no bitterness and did not change my grandfather's conviction about the rightness of what he had tried to do. He was also a very loving father. As he approached death in 1935, it must have done him good to see his eldest son, my father, marry so happily.

AS JANKO PÁLKA'S ONLY SON (Family tree 3, Appendix V), Grandfather Ján was slated to inherit the family business, and he methodically set about preparing himself for this responsibility. He excelled as a student in gymnasium, but that was not enough for him. An independent-minded spirit, he set about furthering his education on his own. At the age of twenty he set out on a journey of several years, finding work in Vienna; Zagreb and Rijeka (in today's Croatia, but then part of Austria-Hungary); and several places in Germany. His goal was to gain a European-standard education in the leather business by working in a series of different factories, much as, some years earlier, a journeyman would have trained to become a master by working with a series of different masters in their workshops.

In his memoirs[2] Grandfather Pálka gives a few glimpses of his adventures while he was so far away from home. For example, at one point he wandered on foot down the trails along a romantic stretch of the Rhine River, from Mainz to Düsseldorf, a distance of over 100 miles even on today's relatively straight highways. This included the Rhine Gorge, famous for its concentration of castles—some forty of them in various states of preservation and disrepair—and since 2002 a UNESCO World Heritage Site. He reveled in the beauty of the countryside, all the more because he was at the time immersed in the poetry of Heinrich Heine. He had come across Heine while listening to a concert of Schubert and Schumann *Lieder* in Vienna. The texts so captured his imagination that he promptly bought all of Heine's works and committed many of the love poems to memory. These lines of poetry, he writes, served him well when he started courting!

Young Ján's self-education program was not limited to on-the-job training and travel, music and poetry. He also read widely among the great Russian novelists (Gogol, Turgenev, Dostoyevsky, Tolstoy), whose writings often constituted social commentary, and also among natural scientists. The socialist thinkers, including Marx, influenced him deeply. It was said that he was the first in Mikuláš to study Marx in the original German.[3]

In addition to these secular works, he read the New Testament with intensity. For a time he stopped eating meat, smoking, and drinking alcohol. Soon, however, he came to a different conclusion:[4]

> Giving up all delights is not the foundation of a Christian life. However worthy such self-denial may be, a person can also live well and piously if he does not refuse all the delights and pleasures that life offers, and the strictest abstinent and vegetarian may live worse than he who does not disdain God's gifts—among which are a baked goose and a glass of fine wine—as long as his heart is filled with "God who is Love." But, moderation in all things!

ONCE HE RETURNED TO MIKULÁŠ, Grandfather Pálka's education in the family business began in earnest. Janko Pálka had earlier introduced steam-powered machinery into what had begun to resemble a factory (Chapter 22). Big paddles swirled the hides in their vats, and mechanical arms pulled them out of one solution and lowered them into the next. Leather drive belts that were sometimes 100 feet in length or longer and were themselves made in the factories of Mikuláš, distributed power from the single steam engine to all the various machines. Despite these improvements, the life of a laborer was tough, and young Grandfather Pálka experienced his share of it even though he was the owner's son:[5]

> In those days we worked from 5 o'clock in the morning until 7 o'clock in the evening,[6] as well as two hours on Sunday morning. Then the wages were distributed and everyone went to church.

Once or twice a week we worked overtime, from 8 to 10 o'clock at night. It was a hard life, and sometimes we really didn't even have time for a good night's sleep. I can't remember ever being late for work or skipping a day.

The laborers, in addition to endless days in the factory, worked their small fields and gardens. Most of them lived in villages that could be as much as an hour away. Their life was exhausting, so it is perhaps not surprising that so many of them turned to alcohol. Alcoholism had long been the plague of the villages, and under these new, partially industrialized circumstances, it was perhaps even worse. Liquor was strictly forbidden in the factories, but the taverns opened early and many laborers began their day with a tumbler of the cheapest brandy, bought on credit. Then it was brandy at lunch, on credit . . . brandy during the afternoon break, on credit . . . brandy after work, on credit. On Saturday, right after the wages were distributed in cash, it was time to pay the tavern-keeper. A good part of the wages earned with numbing labor would disappear. The next Monday the cycle would begin again.[7] Grandfather Pálka witnessed this depressing and demoralizing round playing out week after week, year after year, and it deeply affected his future life.

THE YEARS AROUND THE TURN OF THE CENTURY, when he was in his early thirties, were memorable ones in the life of Grandfather Pálka. In 1900 he married, successfully courting not a local girl but Darina Jurenka of District Myjava, the daughter of the very successful and highly respected banker, Samuel Jurenka (Chapter 15). It was still in the days when not the prospective groom but his representative, the *pytač* (the "asker"), went to ask the bride's father for her hand. Grandfather Pálka's *pytač* was his cousin and fellow-leatherman, Jozef Stodola. Stodola also served as the best man at the wedding in Myjava, and a draft of his flowery toast has been preserved. Here are a few of his words:[8]

> Dear bride, dear friend and groom! Into the bright wreath of our dear family have you, dear friend, woven a new and beautiful bud. A bud that will, bathed in mutual and faithful love, open into a graceful rose that will serve as a new ornament in our family. In the name of this family, absent here today, I welcome you, dear bride, into our family circle. Be assured that there too, under the mountains that reach the sky, there in our beautiful land you will find true family hearts that will gratefully embrace you. I lift my glass to the health of our newlyweds. May the merciful Lord grant that they may live in peace, joy, and pure love for one another. May every cup of bitterness be taken away from them.

The young Ján Pálka and his wife, Darina Jurenka.
Presumably taken close to their wedding in the year 1900.
Author's archive.

A year later, in 1901, the Pálka's first child, my father, was born. The birth of a couple's first child is always a special event, and my grandparents commemorated it by having a christening gown of fine white cotton, ornamented with pure white embroidery, stitched. It served all five of their children. Many years later, my mother carried this tiny gown with her on her escape from Slovakia to France so I could be christened in it (Chapter 2). The family kept it safe during the war and brought it home to Slovakia. Years later Aunt Ludinka, who had also been baptized in that gown, gave it to me. All of our grandchildren have worn it at their baptisms, and our younger daughter, Tanya, is now keeping it safe for the next generation.

In the year of his marriage, Grandfather Pálka was invited by his father, Janko, to become a partner in the family firm. When Janko died in 1904, Grandfather Pálka became the sole owner. He brought the energy of youth into the business. For example, he was the first in Mikuláš to use electrical power to drive his factory's machinery.[9] The steam-driven generator was on site, and the electricity it produced served not only the factory but also the Pálka apartment, which was adjacent to the factory building. Later he sold some of this power to the great book printer and binder of Mikuláš, František Klimeš, whose workshop was in the same building. Grandfather Pálka employed around eighty workers, much the same as his father had, but their productivity was now far greater. The Pálka leather factory was among the largest in Mikuláš and thus in the whole of Slovakia.

THE LEATHER BUSINESS BROUGHT WEALTH to the Pálkas. The national importance of this industry was widely recognized and appreciated among the Slovak intelligentsia.[10] In the Slovak counties there were far larger industries than leatherworking—first and foremost mining and smelting, but also lumber, textiles, paper-making, and others. All of these, however, were almost entirely in the hands of Magyars and Germans. Leatherworking, by contrast, was a Slovak business. The owners of most of the businesses were Slovaks. Further, when they needed credit, they obtained it from the few Slovak-held banks that existed at the time. Thus, this relatively minor industry represented a sizeable fraction of all Slovak capital in the Slovak counties of Hungary. Its greatest center was Mikuláš.

When resources were adequate, Grandfather Pálka invested in real estate, not only in Mikuláš but also in Bratislava and even in Vienna. In 1911 he purchased a remarkable property in Mikuláš in which the next generation of the Pálka family—my father, Uncle Miško, Aunt Ludinka, and Uncle Dušan—grew up. (The fifth sibling, Darina, died in infancy.)

The villa had been built just after the turn of the twentieth century by Emil Stodola, an attorney who later became an important national leader (Chapter 22, note 20).[11] Emil had maried Vincentia Polónyi, the daughter of a wealthy Slovak expatriate by name of Gabriel Polónyi who had settled in Bucharest. Polónyi was originally a *šafraník* like Andrej Pivko (Chapter 14). He made his fortune by establishing a highly successful store in Bucharest that sold general goods as well as women's clothing. Vinca wanted the design of the villa to echo the style favored by Romanian nobility, in part as a symbol of the sympathy of Slovaks for the struggle of the Romanians against domination by the Magyars. The villa was completed in 1906. Not long after, however, family fortunes faded. Emil and Vinca sold their beloved Villa Stodola and moved to Budapest. It must have given them at least some comfort that the buyer was Ján Pálka, not only Emil's cousin but a man with a Slovak awareness equal to Emil's.

In my family, this house was always referred as the "tower villa" (*vežičková vila*) because of a corner tower in which all the children had their rooms. Despite its ornate design, the villa was quite small and not really adequate for the large, multigenerational Pálka family, so Grandfather Pálka added a number of rooms as well as central heating, the first in Mikuláš. Set in the large and beautiful gardens was not only a cottage built in Slovak village style, but also a tennis court and even a running track, reflections of the sporting interests of the family. Inside were an elegant grand piano from the Viennese firm of

Villa my Pálka grandparents bought and enlarged, and in which my father and all his siblings were raised, in 1976, Communist banner hanging on the front. In the foreground our daughters Rachel and Tanya. Photo author.

Bösendoerfer, the European standard of the times, and a pool table. In this house Uncle Dušan composed his first popular songs, playing them on the piano and singing them for his mother, Darina. It was the site of many gatherings of the Slovak intelligentsia, as well as home base for my father's motorcycle excursions into the Tatras (Chapter 13), and the fun-loving environment in which my mother's friendship with Aunt Ludinka and her love of my father grew (Chapter 27).

Great-grandmother Zuzana Bella lived with her son's family for many years, for Janko Pálka had died in 1904 but she lived until 1932. She was a living link to the glorious past of Mikuláš, for had she and Janko not been married by Michal Miloslav Hodža himself? She had witnessed at close hand Hodža's persecution and ultimate exile. She had lived through the revolution of 1948, and her father Jozef Bella's captivity at the hands of Lajos Kossuth's Magyars (Chapter 19). She was only in her early thirties when the railroad first came to Mikuláš. In her youth she had been a prominent amateur actress and one of Marína Hodža's closest friends (Chapter 21), and all her life she wrote poems. She was a devout Lutheran, but she enthusiastically kept the company of Catholics and free-thinkers.[12] She loved her children and her grandchildren. Her only son, my Grandfather Pálka, adored her. So did both of my parents.

THE GRADUAL INDUSTRIALIZATION OF MIKULÁŠ and County Liptov was of central importance to its economic development, but it brought with it the whole host of social problems that accompanied the Industrial Revolution. By modern standards working hours were extremely long, fourteen hours per day (including two hours of breaks) and two hours of work on Sunday; wages were low; there were no provisions for sick leave or health care; and vacations were unheard of. Workers began to organize and press for better treatment. In 1890, Slovak workers started celebrating May 1 as their holiday.[13] This was only four years after annual May Day celebrations, calling attention to the conditions of the working class, were launched internationally, inspired by the violent "Haymarket affair" in Chicago.[14]

The first strike in Mikuláš was also launched on that first May Day in 1890.[15] The primary demand of the strikers was for shorter hours. Most of the leather factories of the town were affected by the strike, including those of Ondrej Pálka (the grandson of Ondrej the younger, Chapter 16) and Janko Pálka. The number of strikers varied greatly from factory to factory; the total for the town was reported to be 388, a substantial fraction of the 1,000 or so factory workers in the city. After three days, the factory owners started to negotiate with the strikers, and on the fourth day the local governmental authorities approved the agreement. Working hours were shortened by an hour; start time was now 6:00 a.m. instead of 5:00 a.m., closing time remained at 7:00 p.m. The prevailing total of two hours of break time—a half hour each for breakfast and afternoon snack, one hour for lunch—was preserved. Sunday work was discontinued. Workers could still be called in on Sundays and holidays, but would be paid overtime.

WORLD WAR I WAS THE PEAK PERIOD for the leather factories of Mikuláš.[16] The huge armies required boots, belts, and many other articles manufactured out of leather. In 1916, in the midst of the war, Grandfather Pálka cofounded a second business, the firm of Lacko-Pálka, that focused on leather for soles, while his own business manufactured the uppers for shoes and boots as well as drive belts for industrial purposes. The new factory was housed in the building vacated by the failed Stodola firm, remodeled and re-equipped to the highest contemporary standards. A separate company was formed to build and operate a branch line of the railway, so that raw materials and finished leather products could be transported more efficiently. Grandfather Pálka was a partner in this company as well. The demand for labor became so great that prisoners of war were used to supplement local manpower.

AT THE END OF THE WAR, GRANDFATHER PÁLKA was a wealthy and influential man. He did not take his success for granted, however. He was troubled by the poverty of his workers. Not only had he contended with strikes in which legitimate demands were made, he had continued his study of Marx. Moreover, from his youth he had been preoccupied with the question of what constitutes a good Christian life, particularly in the real world of business and politics. He was a strong financial supporter of the Lutheran church and held several lay positions in the church. He struggled to reconcile what he saw as the core teaching of Christianity—that we are all children of one loving God—with the social and economic inequities he saw all around him, including among his own workers. Here, from his *Memoirs,* is one of his contemplations on these issues:[17]

> What is an ideal? I read somewhere that an ideal is like a lantern that a man carries in front of himself on a pole and follows, always trying to reach it. I accept communism as an ideal in the sense that it calls for universal brotherhood in life and in work. The ideal is unattainable, just like the lantern that I carry in front of me on a pole. However, we can try to reach this ideal, and humanity, perhaps unconsciously, is moving in this direction. First there was slavery, then serfdom, and now the relationship of the earnings of the employer and of the worker. The injustice in this relationship resides in the fact that the worker does not receive the full value of his work, and he is therefore exploited by the employer. Let us give the worker the full value of his labor and if, for reasons beyond his control, he falls into poverty, let us take care of him [we, society, the state]. Then we will have taken a large step to toward the lantern ahead of us.

He put his beliefs on the line when, on September 20, 1919 he posted on the doors to his factory his first "Announcement to My Workers." This was a carefully crafted philosophical statement, the practical import of which was the establishment of profit sharing and shared decision making between himself as owner and his employees. In his *Memoirs* he describes how his wife, Darina, could not understand what he was doing and panicked at the prospect of having to take care of herself and the children while he was giving his fortune away.[16] At a critical domestic moment Milan Hodža came from Prague to visit. He listened to Grandfather Pálka, nearly ten years his senior, explain his intentions and plans, embraced him with enthusiasm and joy, and (at least according to the *Memoirs*) peace descended on the family.

Here is how his announcement opened:[18]

> As of today, I am changing the factory and firm heretofore owned exclusively by me into a corporation, and in what follows, I want

to indicate what thoughts, views, and motivations have led me to this action.

On the one hand, I have been led by the social question, in which I have always been interested. On the other hand, I have been led by the conviction that we must work industriously and energetically to create new values if we wish to maintain ourselves and our republic. . . . The ideal human society is most beautifully embodied in the teaching of Christ, that we should live as the children of one Father in heaven and in this way prepare the kingdom of God on earth.

Following a detailed explanation of what he finds of value in the works of Marx, and why he simultaneously rejects communism in practice, Grandfather Pálka goes on to say:[19]

I explain all this because I cannot agree that the nationalization of companies, recently often emphasized and demanded also in our country, would constitute a significant social reform.

With the nationalization of private companies, capital is simply transferred from private hands into the hands of the state, production becomes more costly because of the inefficiency of a large bureaucracy, and it has been proven that workers never work as hard for the interests of the company as does the owner himself.

However, while I see no special social reform in nationalization, I would see such a reform beautifully realized in an industrial association in which labor is united with capital in the person of the producer [worker]. . . .

Now Grandfather Pálka put forth what he had decided to do:[20]

1. The workers shall participate in each year's profit. The extent of participation will rise from 20% in 1920 to a maximum of 25% five years later. . . .

6. The working day shall be eight hours.

7. Every worker who has worked at the factory for 10 years without interruption shall receive 1 week per year of fully paid vacation; for 20 years, 2 weeks, and so forth . . .

8. A Board shall guide the business. It shall include three representatives elected by the workers.

9. Any worker who recommends an innovation or change that proves to be useful should inform the Board of this, and the Board shall determine an appropriate reward.

10. On May Day of each year the Board shall distribute the proceeds of the foundation of 25,000 crowns that I have established for the support of needy workers.

11. The Board shall also allocate scholarships from the 50,000 crown foundation I have established to support the studying children of my workers.

In short, Grandfather Pálka put in place profit sharing, shared governance, a sharply reduced work week, paid vacations, and rewards for on-the-job creativity. He also established foundations for the support of needy workers and especially for the education of workers' children. Modeled though these steps were on previous European social/economic experiments, notably that of Ernst Abbe and the Carl Zeiss company in Germany,[21] they were nevertheless astonishing ones for a self-educated and only moderately wealthy capitalist in a remote corner of Czechoslovakia to take on his own initiative, especially in economic times that, as we shall soon see, were becoming turbulent.

Grandfather Pálka, taken some time in the 1920s. Archive of Karol Pavlů.

The Pálka experiment attracted enormous attention throughout Czechoslovakia, in academic circles as well as in business and in government. My grandfather delights in quoting in his *Memoirs* from the many newspaper articles about his work that appeared at the time, including some in the immigrant press in America. He was invited to give a number of lectures around the country, including in Prague. One such lecture was at the national conference of the Union of Czechoslovak Students held in Liptovský Hrádok near Mikuláš. Many notables spoke there, including Alice Masaryk, the daughter of Czechoslovakia's founding president, as well as government ministers and professors. Upon their return to Prague, the students sent Grandfather Pálka a moving letter:[22]

> Dear Mr. Pálka,
>
> Allow us to thank you from the bottom of our hearts for coming to be with us, and for delivering such a deeply felt and interesting lecture about your worthy efforts. Rest assured that your words did not fall on stony ground.
>
> All participants of the conference agree that your lecture was the culminating point of our entire undertaking. . . . We hope that you will come among us again and that your work, which you have made your life's goal, will one day be crowned with well-deserved success.
>
> We wish you this with all our hearts, and hope for your further support.
>
> Václav Havel, chairman
>
> Jaroslav Kose, secretary

The Václav Havel who signed this letter was a member of a highly cultured, wealthy, and patriotic Czech family with a history of resisting Habsburg influence and supporting Czech culture and business.[23] He was active in student politics and was elected the first chairman of the Union of Czechoslovak Students in 1918, the year of the republic's birth. He was a strong supporter of President Masaryk (Chapter 26) and remained active in politics the rest of his life. His son, also named Václav Havel, is the man we know today as the foremost leader of Czechoslovakia's fight for freedom from Communism and as the country's first post-Communist president.

THE PÁLKA EXPERIMENT IN SOCIALIZATION that was so nobly conceived and attracted so much attention throughout Czechoslovakia (and strong opposition from all the other leather factory owners of Mikuláš save one), was initiated in 1919. By 1922 it was over, and the Pálka factory very nearly went out of business.

The main reasons for the failure were economic.[23] Boom times for the leathermen of Mikuláš started to decline with the end of World War I and the creation of Czechoslovakia, due to a combination of factors. First was the sudden loss of markets. For all their flaws, the Habsburg Empire and the Austro-Hungarian Empire constituted economic wholes of vast proportions. A business anywhere in the empire could count on the entire empire as a source of needed raw materials and as a market for its products. All this changed the moment Czechoslovakia was created. Suddenly, between this new state and a much-diminished Hungary there was not only a political boundary but an economic one as well; both Czechoslovakia and Hungary enacted protective tariffs. The railway lines that had been built during the last forty years of the empire were designed to link Slovakia primarily to Hungary and not to the Czech lands. These lines were now partially severed. In addition, even within Czechoslovakia itself Slovak businesses were forced to pay higher railway tariffs than did Czech businesses, so the transportation costs that Slovaks had to pay in order to function within the new Czechoslovak market rose abruptly. The Hungarian banks that had provided funds to Slovak businesses ceased giving them credit. Czech banks stepped in, but they were out for their own profit, and their conditions were harsh. And overshadowing everything else, Czech industry of all kinds was far ahead of Slovak industry. An estimated seventy to eighty percent of the industry of the Austro-Hungarian empire had been concentrated in the Czech lands, and it was highly efficient and well funded by the Czech banks. It was hard for any Slovak businesses to compete, and the leather factories of Mikuláš were no exception. Their production fell by over fifty percent between 1918 and 1922. Inventory accumulated. Workers had to be laid off. Some businesses closed altogether.

There were international factors as well. European economies in general were in a turmoil. Germany's was the worst—inflation soared until, in 1923, it exploded into a monstrous hyperinflation.[24] By November 5 of that year, a loaf of bread in Germany cost 140 billion marks. The hyperinflation was over mercifully quickly and spared other countries, but economic dislocations were apparent all over the continent, including countries in which the leather factories tried to sell their products. Despite heroic efforts, Grandfather Pálka's factory could not escape the economic conditions that affected the entire industry.[25] Even successful sales turned into losses: Pálka sold a large number of tanned hides in Hungary, but due to massive inflation the Hungarian currency was suddenly devalued to ten percent of its original value, and instead of a profit, the sale resulted in a loss. He had established his new business in 1919 with a capitalization of two million crowns. This capital was wiped out. He injected into the business an additional two million crowns out of his personal fortune, and that also was lost. The funds that were to be distributed to workers were lost. To survive the crisis and save a business that had lasted for ninety-seven years, Pálka provided yet more funds from his own savings. He barely made it.

The behavior of the workers added to the difficulties. Despite all the advantages they were offered, the workers did strike. An eyewitness account gives a vivid picture of the atmosphere:[26]

> . . . the workers barricaded themselves, and their wives brought them baskets filled with food, fresh clothing and slippers. The workers on the second floor hoisted the baskets on ropes and pulled them through the windows, and gave their wives quick instructions about what to do and what else to bring . . .

The strike reflected the widespread challenges with which the workers confronted Pálka.[27] The first group of three worker representatives on the board resigned because of a lack of support from their colleagues. (It was rumored, falsely, that they were now reaping huge personal gain because they were part of management.) One member of the second trio of representatives, a Communist, left for America, and a second quit after threatening Pálka that no new board members would be elected unless everyone's wages were increased. Courses in bookkeeping, offered to the workers so they could become more effective in shared business governance, were never well attended; by the end of the first year, attendance was zero. Substantial thefts occurred, including one valued at 100,000 crowns. Much of the antipathy to Grandfather Pálka's vision by his own workers was fomented by Communists. The Communist and far-left socialist press was predominently critical of Pálka, presumably because they did want an experiment in socialization to succeed when it was launched by an an outspokenly anti-Communist businessman.

Despite the failure of the experiment in "utopian socialism," the Pálka business itself survived and to some extent recovered. It maintained representation abroad—in London, Berlin, Vienna, Budapest, and Krakow. However, it faced one obstacle after another, most of them linked to fluctuations in the European and Czechoslovak economies, and to the general difficulties that Slovak industry faced in competing with Czech industry. The final blow came during the Great Depression. In 1929, Grandfather Pálka still employed 137 workers. In 1930 the number fell to 84, in 1931 to 37, and finally in 1932 to 19. Then the business that had started in 1827 was dissolved. The banks took over the factory. The *vežičková vila,* including even its furnishings and other contents, was sold to help cover the accumulated debts. Supported by their sons, my grandparents moved to an apartment in Bratislava. There they died a few years later, Ján Pálka in 1935 and his beloved Darina in 1942. They are buried in the Lutheran Cemetery in the heart of Bratislava's old city.

GRANDFATHER PÁLKA HAD ANOTHER LIFE besides his business. The interior religious life that had manifested in his youth by his short-lived decision to become a non-smoking vegetarian never left him. It was the foundation of the experiment in utopian socialism on which he staked his personal fortune. For decades he served the Lutheran church in senior lay positions, and he wrote frequently, both in religious and in secular publications, about his beliefs. In this domain, just as in business, he was a revolutionary.

He did not hesitate to challenge orthodoxy:[28]

> The Church teaches, according to St. Paul and Martin Luther, that not through good works, but only through faith in Christ can one be saved.

> Through what faith? What does it mean to believe in Christ? That He was born of a virgin, that after His crucifiction He descended into Hell, where He overcame the Devil, and that He then rose from the dead? That He is the second person of the Trinity? That He established the sacraments, for Catholics seven, for Lutherans two, and for Jews none? Or that after death he who believes all this will go to Heaven and he who does not will go to Hell?

> No! The salvation of humanity will come from a faith in Christ that knows this: *It is necessary to understand that the best way of life is the way He taught us, and that the only meaning of our life is to try to live according to the will of God as He, the living Jesus Christ, explained it to us. And His principal commandment is—Love one another.*

"Christ's love in the heart and common sense in the head" (*Kristova láska v srdci a zdravý rozum v hlave*) was the motto he wanted his own and all other churches to preach and be guided by. He had no patience for arcane dogma, no patience for placing antiquated teachings above the findings of science, and no fear of expressing his views in the framework of the church he loved and to whose welfare he devoted immense energy.

HE WAS A PRINCIPLED MAN in the public realm as well. In the period before World War I, he had been an active participant and a local leader in the Slovak national movement, speaking out particularly on behalf of Slovak students. He supported the establishment of Czechoslovakia, and he held the welfare of the republic very dear. As he looked around at the world between the two world wars, particularly at the situation in the Soviet Union, he saw the greatest single social, economic, and political danger to be Communism, and he saw that Communism was fed by the abhorrent conditions prevailing generally in Europe:[29]

> Poverty and discontent are great on all sides, in all nations. Europe, as it is today, following the Great War, has no future! Peace is not stable, war threatens to break out at any moment. The development of technology in railways, steamships, and airplanes has brought formerly distant nations close together. Today, if one travels a day or two, he crosses many borders as well as customs barriers by means of which daily necessities are rendered more expensive, that prevent or at least complicate the export and import of necessary materials and hinder the natural development of industry. . . . Every state or statelet maintains an army because it is afraid of its neighbors. What do these armies cost? Billions, hard earned by the taxpaying world. And what do these amies do? They arm themselves and invent yet further ways of killing people: machine guns, cannons, tanks, and poison gases that in the next war will supposedly wipe out everyone, from infants and women to the elderly.

He argued repeatedly for a United States of Europe, or at least an Economic Union of European States. From his ruminations on the relationship of scripture to daily economic and political life he developed a powerful defense of pacifism, arguing that not even self-defense is permitted by the teaching of Christ on love. The goal of both individuals and states should be to alleviate the conditions that lead to attacks, not to justify a violent response when attacks occur:[30]

> Christianity teaches and preaches, "Do not kill." It teaches that people should guide their lives by love and common sense. Then there would be no hungry who have to steal, and there would be none who are attacked and have to defend themselves with the sword.

By all accounts, Grandfather Pálka was a good man, a very good man. He died in 1935, so there are not many people alive today who knew him personally. Those who do, however, agree in their descriptions of him. He was gentle, said Aunt Soňa Kovačevičová, who as a child lived next door to the Pálkas

(Chapter 15). He worked hard for his beloved Lutheran church. He supported the theater and, perhaps surprisingly, participated in the naturist club whose members took their exercise out in nature and nearly naked. He did not join the *Cecha*, that gathering of town notables that was so dear to my own father (Chapter 13), but when he died, the annual report of the *Cecha*, usually written in a teasing tone, lauded him in all seriousness as one of their own, despite the opposition that so many of his business colleagues had shown him when he voluntarily socialized his factory:[31]

> Before I give my report it is my duty to mention that this past year we once again lost one of our honorary masters, a man who was kind and highly cultured, Janko Pálka the elder. It is hardly necessary to say what he meant to our organization. All of us who had the honor to meet with him frequently, here in the rooms of the *Cecha* or anywhere else, know that with him there was never a shortage of subjects for conversation. He always posed questions of general interest, whether the topic was politics, or economics, or the events of the day, and from his questions always developed a discussion that was interesting and captivating. He is no longer with us, and we miss him. . . . We will certainly keep and honor his memory.

CHAPTER 24

Hodžas—Four Generations in the Nation's Service

The Pálkas were a leather-working family for seven generations, beginning as poor, landless craftsmen and gradually becoming wealthy entrepreneurs. They used their resources to support the Slovak national cause and the Lutheran church. The Bellas started as peasants, then spread out into a number of professions: Several became soldiers in the service of freedom, or public servants; others gave Slovakia some of her best-loved poems. The Hodžas started as millers, but for four generations spanning well over a century, they brought forth patriots, Lutheran pastors, and national political leaders. It is this remarkable Hodža heritage that my mother especially wanted me to understand and to appreciate (Family tree 5, Appendix V).

THOUGH THE KNOWN HISTORY OF THE HODŽAS reaches further back (Chapter 14), we can think of Ján Hodža (1784-1861), the miller of Rakša, as representing the first generation of Hodža activists.[1] He may have been only a miller in a tiny village in the hills of County Turiec, but he made his mark on the burgeoning Slovak consciousness. He raised his five children—Ján, Michal, Ondrej, Jozef and Mária—to be self-aware Slovaks at a time when the road to advancement lay in adopting Magyar ways, and he supported them in getting an advanced education, something precious and rare for Slovak youth before the establishment of Czechoslovakia. In remote Rakša he tracked the emergence of the movement for national awakening. In 1848 he actively publicized the Petition of the Slovak Nation that had been formulated and signed in Mikuláš, and in which his son Michal Miloslav had played such an important role. When the revolution of 1848-49 came, Ján became a public agitator for the Slovak cause and was arrested and jailed by the Hungarian authorities. The leaders of the revolution were in their thirties; Ján was then 64.

JÁN'S SONS MICHAL, ONDREJ, AND JURAJ formed the second generation of Hodža activists, and Michal and Ondrej initiated the family tradition of entering the ministry. Michal we already know about; here are the stories of his two younger brothers.

Ondrej Hodža (1819-1888) followed in Michal's footsteps, attending the Lutheran Lyceum in Bratislava and gaining a fine theological education.[2] He served as Michal's chaplain for a few years in Mikuláš, and he, too, participated in the great events that took place there: he was a cofounder of Tatrín in 1844 and a signer of the Petition of the Slovak Nation in 1848.

In that fateful revolutionary year, Ondrej was called by the Slovak Lutherans of Sučany to become their minister. Bursting with national feeling, he immediately started holding public gatherings in the square in front of the Lutheran church. He explained the revolutionary new laws just adopted by the Hungarian parliament and accepted by the emperor (the March Laws), especially what the abolition of serfdom would mean for poor Slovaks. He openly called for equality for Slovaks, an idea that was anathema to the Magyar power structure. The local *magyarones* had Hodža arrested and taken to Martin, where he was interned. However, he refused to be silenced. Soon armed revolution broke out, and both he and his father Ján were arrested and taken in chains to Banská Bystrica where they were imprisoned for three months. They were released mainly because of the approach of imperial forces and intervention by imperial authorities.

During the revolution Slovak volunteers in County Turiec fought against Hungarian armies. The volunteers were led by Ďurko Langsfeld, Ondrej's close friend and a somewhat distant ancestor of the Emil Langsfeld in whose house we lived in Chicago. In reprisal, the Hungarian commander sent a detachment to Sučany to arrest both Langsfeld and Hodža. Hodža managed to hide. Langsfeld was caught and within two days cruelly executed. Hodža would probably have met the same fate had he been discovered.

After the revolution Ondrej continued as an activist-patriot-pastor. He was a vocal proponent of the new Slovak literary language. He stood firmly on the side of the Protestant Patent that would have given Slovaks a far greater voice in the affairs of the Lutheran church. He was member of the committee that formulated the Declaration of the Slovak Nation in Martin in 1861, and was also one of its signers. He was a cofounder of *Matica Slovenská* in 1863. He fought for the establishment of the Slovak-language gymnasia. By the time Ondrej died in 1888, he had experienced both the euphoria of rising Slovak national consciousness and the oppressive power of the escalating Magyar attempts to suppress that consciousness. Despite all persecution, he remained a stubborn Slovak nationalist his entire life.

Juraj Hodža (1824-1874) was the third son whom the ardent Slovak miller of Rakša supported in his studies. Today Juraj is far less frequently mentioned than Michal or Ondrej, but his life pattern was markedly similar to that of his brothers.[3] Like them, he initially studied theology. He was active in national student circles and assisted Štúr in the publication of his newspaper, the *Slovenské národnie noviny*. While still a student, he was a founding member of Tatrín in 1844, and also a participant in the drafting of the Petition of the Slovak Nation in 1848. (The Petition had sixteen signers; three of them were the Hodža brothers.) Later he became not a pastor but an attorney.

To see Juraj's heart at work, let us return for a moment to the heroic year of 1848. The Hungarian authorities saw the Petition of the Slovak Nation as a serious threat and immediately declared martial law and issued arrest warrants for the leaders, Josef Miloslav Hurban, Ľudovit Štúr, and Michal Miloslav Hodža. All three fled from Mikuláš, each traveling on his own.

Štúr was accompanied by Juraj Hodža[4]. The only way to the border with Moravia and thus to safety was down the narrow valley of the River Váh in which Mikuláš is situated, giving the advantage to the police and military. To make their way undetected, Štúr and Juraj Hodža hid in a covered farm wagon that took them from village to village. They were delayed in crossing the river because it was in flood. Once across, they dared to stop at an inn for food, only to discover that a search party had been there just ten minutes earlier. They finally reached Štúr's brother Karol, the Lutheran minister in the town of Modra near Bratislava, and took refuge in his parish house. Štúr sent Hodža to gather information and tend to his responsibilities at the newspaper. While Hodža was gone, another search party surrounded the parish house, but Štúr had already slipped out into the vineyard. Hodža returned with disquieting news, including the fact that guards on the Austrian border already had Štúr's description and were actively looking for him. Helped by Hodža and a handful of other brave men, Štúr set out by foot and wagon through the hills for the Moravian border. Using a false passport, he made it safely across.

History books simply say that Štúr, Hurban, and Michal Hodža escaped from Mikuláš to Prague where they were enthusiastically greeted as leading speakers as the great Slav congress. The closer story is that they risked their personal freedom and indeed their lives to make the journey across the border. The young Juraj Hodža risked the same.

In 1849 Juraj joined the Slovak volunteers to fight for freedom. After the revolution he was a signer of the Declaration of the Slovak Nation and a member of *Matica Slovenská*. Because of his outspoken Slovak activities, the Magyar and *magyarone* gentry blocked him from any but low-level bureaucratic positions for the rest of his life.

THE PART OF THE HODŽA LINEAGE that I have known personally begins in Ondrej's parish house in Sučany, the birthplace of both Grandfather Milan Hodža and his much older half-brother Ján Miloslav Hodža (Chapter 14). In 1878, the year that Milan was born, Ján was appointed as Ondrej's chaplain in Sučany, a post he held until 1887. Then, for the next 31 years, Ján served as the pastor. He was appointed as the senior of the Lutheran Church's Turiec Seniorate, and in this role accomplished something remarkable: despite all the pressures from the Hungarian government, during his tenure not a single Magyar-language school was established within the Seniorate. When he retired in 1918, Czechoslovakia was just being born.

In his later years, he was an active member of Milan Hodža's Agrarian Party. Ján Hodža's relationship with his famous younger half-brother was warm and supportive. Here is a letter he wrote on Milan's fiftieth birthday in 1928, while Milan was the Czechoslovak minister of education:[5]

> My dear brother! And our dear uncle and our godfather!
>
> You are celebrating your 50th birthday. . . . Today you are at the peak of your life. When you look behind you, what do you see? Constant hardship, struggle, work, and injustice. And what do you see before you? Mostly, I think, what you have already experienced. And for this reason I wish that God may grant you health and strength for work and, finally, victory in your efforts. Also, at least a grain of gratitude from those for whose good you have dedicated your life!
>
> With my warmest greetings, your devoted brother,
>
> Signed:
>
> The old Hodžas—Ján and his wife Berta;
>
> The young Hodžas—their son Miloš and his wife Oľga;
>
> The youngest Hodžas—their children, Ivan and Jelka.

Like the other pastors in the family, Ján Hodža was deeply loved by his parishioners. His memory persists to the present day, more than half a century after his death. I was in Sučany in 2006 for celebrations of Grandfather Hodža's life when I was approached by a vigorous older man with a furrowed face, ruddy complexion, and somewhat gruff manner. He recognized me as the honored guest. "Here," he said. "I have brought something for you. It is a letter from our Ján Hodža, written to my grandmother. She kept it safe, as did my mother. I want you to have it." It turned out to be a letter of condolence, written in 1930. Hodža comforts the family, blesses the departed, quotes psalms and hymns, is full of gratitude for the life that has just ended. It was truly a heartwarming message in a time of grief. No wonder the family kept it for seventy-five years.

When I was in Sučany again in 2007, I went to the Sunday services as I always do on my visits. As I was making my way out of the front pew, a beautiful, tiny, white-haired woman came up to me and introduced herself. She, too, had brought me a gift—a photograph taken at the golden wedding anniversary of Ján Hodža and his wife, Albertína, and kept in her family ever since. This memento, like the letter of condolence, had been treasured by the family for over seventy years. I feel profoundly honored to have received them as gifts.

THE HALF-BROTHERS, JÁN AND MILAN, were the third generation of Hodža activists and patriots. Ján had three sons, two of whom died early in life. The middle son, Miloš (1889-1969), followed the family tradition and became a Lutheran pastor, writer of hymns, and national activist. Milan's only son, Fedor (1912-1968), worked in national politics all his life, first at home and then in exile.[6] They were the fourth generation. Thereafter, the Hodža descendants turned to other fields of activity.

Fedor, Uncle Dišo (from his middle name, Ondrej—Ondriško—Diško) was a family favorite. From his youth he was witty and charming, a good enough student and an outstanding sportsman. He was a skier all his life, and as a young man climbed all over the Tatras and had several first ascents to his name. He was mobilized as an army officer in 1938 (Chapter 1), then followed his father out of Czechoslovakia.

Having trained in the foreign service, he immediately joined the Czechoslovak embassy in Paris, as well as collaborating with his father on developing the Paris-based Slovak National Council, the unsuccessful effort intended to be a counterweight to the Czechoslovak government-in-exile under Edvard Beneš.[7] After the fall of France, both father and son moved to London. Here their ways parted. Grandfather Hodža left for the United States, Fedor took a series of positions with the Beneš-led government, first in the ministry of foreign affairs and later in the ministry of agriculture.

Once back in Slovakia, Hodža threw himself into party politics.[8] The two dominant parties of pre-war Slovakia, Hlinka's Slovak Peoples Party (HSPP) and the Agrarian Party led by Milan Hodža, were both disbanded by government decree. The democratic wing of the war-time Slovak National Council, mostly Agrarians, then formed a new umbrella political organization, the Democratic

Party, into which they sought to draw not only old Agrarians but as many members of the HSPP as possible, as well as other parties. Their primary goal was to counter the pressure that the Communist Party was already exerting. The main leaders of this effort were Jozef Lettrich and Ján Ursíny, who had contributed so much to the organizing of the resistance and of the Slovak National Uprising. Fedor Hodža played an important role in the organization of this new Democratic Party and was elected its general secretary.[9] His main responsibilities were developing the grassroots structure of the party, its publicity, its strategy against the Communists, and the efforts of the party to ensure equal status for Slovakia in the reconstituted Czechoslovakia. His efforts contributed in a major way to the overwhelming success of the Democratic Party in the first post-war elections in 1946, when it gained over sixty percent of the popular votes as against thirty percent for the Communists, the only other significant party. However the Communists, defeated at the polls, soon launched an unrelenting attack, filled with fabricated accusations of treason, on the Slovak Democratic leadership (Chapter 9). It was but a prelude to their successful coup in Prague in February, 1948. As soon as the Communists were in power, Democratic lives were in danger.

The many Czech and Slovak political leaders who then fled from Czechoslovakia formed several organizations in the United States to publicize the terror that was taking place in their homeland, to put pressure on the U.S. government to stand up to Communist expansionism, and to keep alive the hope for a return to democracy.[10] These organizations unfortunately reflected some of the old political divisions: a centralist vision for Czechoslovakia vs. the insistence on parity between Czechs and Slovaks vs. calls for an independent Slovak Republic. Hodža was energetically engaged in several of these organizations and tried to reduce the frictions among them, not only in New York but also in Canada and in Paris.[11] In the process, he defended his father's key idea of the importance of cooperation and federation in Central Europe.

After many years he took an apartment in New York, in the same building as my Aunt Gláša. We saw him more often. He visited with close friends in Canada and found time to go skiing. Then, in 1967, he was diagnosed with lung cancer. Operations were not able to stop the progress of the disease. While the Prague Spring was crushed by Soviet tanks, his condition worsened. After his death in September, 1968, my mother wrote to the family in Martin:[12]

> I think I first knew that there was no longer any hope upon our return from England in July, when we found him still in the hospital.
> . . He was probably never fully aware of the events of August 20th [the Soviet-led invasion of Czechoslovakia that crushed the Prague

Spring], even though in July he was still following developments in Czechoslovakia very closely. . . . I remember August 20th especially well, because that evening I returned from visiting Diško shaken by his condition, and later that night came the news about the invasion. . . . Later, when I sometimes asked Diško whether I should tell him what's new at home, he always just shook his head. You know, he was one of those who believed that a gradual relaxation would take place and he was extremely interested in domestic developments. . . . He remained just as you remember him, gay, witty, content. He was truly a unifying force among our exiles.

His funeral was the first I ever attended in my young life. The church was filled with mourners of many political persuasions while his closest collaborators gave the eulogies. His ashes were placed in the mausoleum at Fernwood Cemetery outside New York City.

The four generations of Hodžas who served the Slovak national ideal paid a high price. Ján Hodža was jailed. Ondrej Hodža was jailed and was in danger of execution. Michal Miloslav Hodža was persecuted, physically attacked, and ultimately hounded into exile. Milan Hodža, as we shall see, was fined, jailed, threatened with execution, driven into exile, and while in exile sentenced to eighteen years imprisonment. Fedor Hodža barely escaped certain imprisonment or worse; he, too, died in exile. It is a century-long story that has drama, nobility, pathos, and also many human imperfections. Through it all runs a thread of dedication to the Slovak nation, and an unwavering belief in human decency and its political expression in the form of democracy. This is the story my mother wanted me to understand and never to forget.

CHAPTER 25

Milan Hodža—Rebel Journalist

To my mother, Milan Hodža was always *Tatuško*—Daddy. She was very proud of him. When I was growing up, she made sure that I would be aware of his accomplishments and his stature in Slovak political life. It is hard to remember the specific stories she told me, but I never lost the sense that he was a remarkable man, a leader who left a legacy of vision and accomplishment that has few equals in Slovak history.

This was not just a proud daughter speaking. In the view of historians, too, he was a central figure in Slovak history:

Hodža entered Slovak history above all as the first modern Slovak politician who, with his tactical flexibility, was able to react to the needs and spirit of changing times while pursuing clearly articulated goals. Programmatically he always exceeded the territory of Slovakia and he tried to conceptualize the Slovak Question [the proper political-economic-cultural role of Slovakia] in the broadest Central European context.[1]

Milan Hodža was not only the most influential Slovak politician during the interwar period, but first and foremost a conceptual thinker.... Hodža's approach to the solution of complex problems ... was conceptually unified, starting with attempts to implement the step-wise economic and political rapprochement of Danubian states, the internal political re-organization of the Czechoslovak Republic through increased regional self-administration, and finally to plans for the autonomy of Slovakia.[2]

GRANDFATHER HODŽA'S SWEEPING VISION, ambitions and political career, launched just before the turn of the twentieth century, were forged in Magyar-dominated Hungary at a time when the oppression of minorities, and perhaps especially of Slovaks, was both official government policy and the self-proclaimed prerogative of arrogant individuals in positions of power. The policy of increasingly oppressive Magyarization, which affected Grandfather Hodža personally, was staggeringly effective. Here is one overview of the economic situation:[3]

> The Slovaks were predominantly peasant and poor: 66% worked the land and, of these, 58% owned less than the bare minimum of acres for subsistence .... of the 758 families who owned large estates, comprising 36% of the land in Slovakia, only ten considered themselves Slovak. The Slovaks controlled less than one percent of the industrial capital in the Slovak territories, and a Slovak middle class did not, for all practical purposes, exist....

This is why the leatherworks of Mikuláš were so significant. They were only modest enterprises, and the wealth of their owners could not compare with that of the land-owning aristocracy or of the German, Magyar, Jewish, or sometimes Czech owners of the big mines, paper mills, textile plants, or other businesses that were springing up, but they were Slovak-owned and Slovak-operated. "Slovak entrepreneurs at this time [the late 1800s] enjoyed their greatest success in Liptovsky Svaty Mikulas, where six factories grew out of the local tanning shops, employing about 500 workers.[4]"

Under the pressure of intensive Magyarization by the government and miserable economic conditions, the thirty years between 1880 and 1910 saw almost a quarter of all Slovaks adopt a Magyar identity and almost another quarter emigrate, primarily to the United States.[5] When Hodža was growing up, Slovak leaders were justifiably worried about the very survival of the Slovak nation.

During this dark period, the small stratum of stubborn Slovak nationalists most often found their centers of education, debate, and mutual support in private homes, and especially in the parish houses of small-town clergy.[6]

> In the 30s through the 90s [of the nineteenth century] our nationally-minded forefathers drew their spiritual strength exclusively from romantic poetry and religious books. They lived in a patriarchal manner. They sang from the *Tranoscius* [*Cithara sanctorum*, Chapter 18], and read from the Kralice Bible [the great Czech translation of 1613], the poems of Kollár and Sládkovič, the *Národnie noviny*, the poems and novels of Vajanský. Every valley had one or several such centers where nationalists gathered occasionally, debated, and encouraged one another. For the most part these were poor parish houses, where poets (in those days everyone wanted to be a poet) read their first efforts or critiqued what had just come out in a book or in the *Národnie noviny*.

Young Milan's mother, Klementína, had grown up in such a home, the parish house of her father, Ján Plech, in Liptovský Sv. Peter, not far from Mikuláš. The parish house of Milan's father, Ondrej Hodža, in Sučany was a similar hotbed of Slovak self-education and activity. Men like the great writer Svetozár Hurban Vajanský and especially Matúš Dula, for many years the chairman of the Slovak National Party, came often, and their discussions lasted late into the night. In this setting, young Milan imbibed the Slovak national spirit of his parents and their friends.

A precocious child, Milan captivated the visitors, pehaps Dula most of all:[7]

> The late Matúš Dula . . . always stoppped at the parish house, and when he saw young Milan he immediately started up a conversation with him. "So, how are you, Valibuk [a well-known figure in Slovak folk tales, literally one who topples oak trees]?" "Oh, uncle, just so-so." "You aren't sick, are you?" Dula asked. "Oh no, its just that mommy had a headache yesterday and daddy is not feeling well," was young Milan's self-assured reply, even though he was only three years old at the time. Dula could spend hours with him and predicted a bright future for the lad.

> When he was five years old he sometimes went with the poor young boys helping in the church up to the choir loft where he could observe his father and his uncle preaching. Once he put on his mother's skirt as a minister's robe, put paper glasses on his nose, grabbed the first book he could find and started to "preach" to his comrades, imitating father and uncle and quoting whole sentences from their sermons.

Milan's beloved father died in 1888, when Milan was only ten. At the funeral service, the church where he had served for so long was was filled with mourners. The Hodža family, including Milan, stood at the front beside the coffin. The pastor, a personal friend, came from neighboring Mošovce to deliver the eulogy. He spoke about Ondrej's passion for the upliftment of the Slovak people. He recalled how Ondrej had followed his brother, Michal Miloslav, who had contributed so much to the development of the Slovak literary language. He explained that forced Magyarization was wrong, especially within the Lutheran church, because Luther himself had established the language of the ordinary people as the right language for conducting services and for reading the Bible.

Suddenly, the service was interrupted. Here is an eyewitness account, reported by the *Národnie noviny* of August 2, 1888:[8]

On the 1st of August in Sučany we buried the retired pastor of Sučany and senior of County Turiec, Ondrej Hodža, our outstanding fighter, worker and sufferer. Very many mourners gathered, because Hodža was famous far beyond the boundaries of his church or his seniorate, and everywhere he was honored and respected as an untiring, inspired minister and a pure patriot who had no fear and never hid his feelings. We thought that such a universally respected man would be buried in quiet while all who gathered mourned. But that did not happen. The overseer [*slúžny*] of the District of Martin, Attila Ujhelyi, came, but not as an inspector of the church, nor as a Lutheran, but as a policeman who came to disrupt the service. This man dared to interrupt the sermon of Pastor Dobrucký by walking from his place in the pew, down the center of the church, right up to the pulpit where he called out to the pastor in Magyar in front of the whole thousand-member congregation: "I am the chief overseer and I forbid you to speak any further."

The outraged congregation filed charges against Ujhelyi, but the authorities sprang to his defense and no penalities were imposed.

Milan Hodža as a boy with his mother, Klementína Plech.
Author's archive.

LATER THAT YEAR, JUST MONTHS AFTER experiencing this desecration of his father's memory, ten-year-old Milan left the security of his home in Sučany for gymnasium. Like so many aspiring Slovak students, he moved from school to school—Banská Bystrica in today's Slovakia, Šoproň in Hungary, and finally Sibiu in Romania.[9] Later, his fellow students recalled how everywhere Milan went, he was recognized as an outstanding student, a natural leader, and an irrepressible Slovak nationalist. His stance as a Slovak rebel was revealed even at this early age.[10] In Banská Bystrica he was reprimanded for writing to his mother in Slovak rather than in Magyar. In Šoproň for two years in a row he remained silent during the singing of the Hungarian national anthem at the great national celebrations of March 15 (Chapter 19). For this he was expelled.

Milan concluded his gymnasium education in a German-language school in Sibiu in Transylvania, which is today in central Romania. This proved to be a time and place of personal flowering. The greatest cultural force in the region were Germans who had migrated from Saxony centuries earlier.[11] Unlike the Magyars, they were quite tolerant of the national aspirations of an energetic Slovak teenager, as they had been earlier when other young Slovaks had come to study in Sibiu because the Magyar-controlled government had closed all Slovak secondary schools. Here Milan perfected his German and read the classics of literature in Magyar and German. He threw himself into sports—especially soccer, which was the latest fashion in athletics—and he became an excellent swordsman. Milan had come to Sibiu a bright but slight and bookish boy; he left a physically strong and self-reliant young man.[12]

These experiences during his student days proved to be formative. Sibiu was the main center of the Romanian national movement in Transylvania, much as Martin was for the Slovak national movement in Upper Hungary. Milan studied the Romanian language and literature, formed close connections with Romanian students, and spent time in the homes of Romanian patriotic families. From that time on, developing working relationships with non-Magyar nations, including the Romanians, was a hallmark of his political thinking and activity.

Even today, he is well remembered in Sibiu. In 2002, the then-president of Slovakia, Michal Kováč, and his wife made a state visit to Romania. When they arrived in Sibiu, they were proudly shown Hodža's academic record, maintained in the leather-bound register of the gymnasium. President Kováč was kind enough to have a photocopy made for me, which he gave me as a surprise at a luncheon following the ceremonial interment of Grandfather Hodža's remains in the Slovak National Cemetery. Scanning the handwritten entries, we can see that in various semesters young Hodža received marks of "excellent" or "good" in Magyar, German, Latin, Greek, history, geography, mathematics, science, and religion. His papers were declared to be neatly written. Despite his past record of political independence, his behavior was considered to be good.

The Hodža family fairly overflowed with Lutheran pastors. Milan, however, forged his own path. After graduating from gymnasium in 1896, he registered for law at the university in Budapest and soon passed the first-level law examinations. He quickly recognized, however, that he was simply not excited by the complexities of the law. Instead, he read in several languages the leading works in many fields—Slavic studies, philosophy, literature, sociology, and history, both economic and cultural. In this way he acquired an exceptionally broad conceptual foundation for his future work. In addition to reading, he was an enthusiastic participant in political debates among many students of the non-Magyar nationalities—Romanians and Serbs as well as his fellow Slovaks. These students formed a new organization, the Union of Non-Magyar Students (*Združenie národnostných študentov*) and elected Hodža as president. His leadership of this multi-national group foreshadowed some of the roles he would play on a larger stage later in his life.[13]

THROUGHOUT HIS GYMNASIUM YEARS, Hodža had been an enthusiastic contributor to, and later editor of, student newspapers published in Magyar. Now, in 1897, he started to write for a Slovak language weekly, *Slovenské listy*, that had just been established in Ružomberok, a short distance downstream from Mikuláš. Its owner and editor was Karol Salva, an outspoken Slovak patriot from County Liptov, who had for a decade been publishing important Slovak books, as well as magazines for teachers and for children, the first Slovak women's magazine, and others. (Salva's own life story was remarkable, ending sadly in Cleveland, Ohio[14]). With *Slovenské listy* he added an overtly political publication to his extensive catalogue.

Slovenské listy was a breath of fresh air on the Slovak scene, bringing columns with local news and stories with local color. It was also the first real outlet for the pen of young Milan Hodža, its Budapest correspondent. Hodža forcefully called for Slovak political activism, and publicly challenged not only the outrages committed by the Magyars but also the passivity of the current Slovak leaders, including the man who had so cared for him when he was a child, Matúš Dula.[15]

During the summer of 1898 Salva was thrown in prison for two months for his writing. Needing someone to take his place as editor of *Slovenské listy*, he turned to Hodža, and so the fiery young journalist came from Budapest to Ružomberok[16]. Not far from Ružomberok was the tiny town of Tri Sliače (today Liptovské Sliače), the home of a man with whom Hodža was to share a long and complex relationship—the outspoken and charismatic Andrej Hlinka (Chapter 1). Hlinka, too, wrote for *Slovenské listy* and came almost every morning to Salva's crowded print shop, often finding Hodža sleeping in a side room after working much of the night. Hodža, in turn, often visited Hlinka in Tri Sliače.[17]

The two differed in many ways. Hodža, for instance, while born into a family that produced several generations of notable Lutheran pastors, never let sectarian religion have a public face in his work. He valued Christian ethics, but he was thoroughgoingly ecumenical in his approach to religion and more than anything he was a progressive intellectual.[18] In contrast Hlinka, fifteen years his senior, was a Catholic priest with fervent and conservative religious and social views that formed the underpinning of his political platform. As Czechoslovakia evolved, Hlinka and Hodža often took different positions, and their respective parties competed fiercely with each other. Early in their lives, however, they collaborated not only as newspaper contributors but also in their support of the organization of the new Slovak People's Party, an important regional bank, (*Ľudová banka* in Ružomberok), and a newspaper (*Ľudové noviny* in Martin)[19]. Moreover, during the crucial period during World War I, when the Austro-Hungarian Empire was facing defeat and disintegration and the future of Slovakia was being hotly debated, both Hodža and Hlinka came to see union with the Czechs as the best opportunity for Slovaks finally to move out from under Magyar domination. They were truly warriors in a common cause.

While in Ružomberok, Hodža had his first enounters with Magyar-administered justice. Arrested twice and investigated a third time for various political misdeeds—one marked by joining in the singing of *Hej, Slováci* in the streets of Ružomberok and another by his aggressive (though cautiously formulated) writing in *Slovenské listy*—he escaped lengthy imprisonment but had to pay fines that were substantial for a penurious youth just past his twentieth birthday.[20]

Later in 1897, another new Slovak publication appeared—*Hlas*—and it too voiced discontent both with the policies of the Magyar-dominated government and with the passive Martin center. It followed many of the ideas of Tomáš Garrigue Masaryk, the future founding president of Czechoslovakia (Chapter 26). Hodža admired Masaryk's writings and began to write for *Hlas* as well.[21]

IN 1901 IN BUDAPEST, HODŽA FOUNDED his own newspaper, *Slovenský denník*.[22] This was the first daily newspaper ever published in Slovak, but its birth was premature, and it folded after only a year when Hodža entered obligatory military service. Undeterred, in 1903 he founded *Slovenský týždenník* (*Slovak Weekly*), which served as his political voice for the next thirty-five years.[23] The key role *Slovenský týždenník* played in Slovak politics has been summarized in this way:[24]

Týždenník was a political newspaper; therein lay its great merit. The Slovak national movement, small as it was, had a sufficient quantity and quality of authors, poets, and theoreticians. They spoke to, and stimulated each other, but had little that was relevant to offer to the majority of the people. The *Národnie noviny*, for instance, was important as much, and quite possibly more, for Slovak intellectual and literary development as it was for political. . . . [The men] associated with this paper were patriots *par excellence*, but they were unable, and to an extent, unwilling to lead the Slovak people towards political mass activism. *Týždenník* served to fill the void. Not only politicization, but participation by the masses were the goals to which *Týždenník* was dedicated.

Within a few years of its founding, its circulation reached 14,000, the largest of any Slovak publication. This far exceeded the 400 to 500 copies the *Národnie noviny* published and rivaled the circulation of the larger Magyar newspapers, despite the fact that Magyars were far more numerous and that Slovak publications were not permitted to be sold in public. Slovak newspapers and magazines could only be delivered to homes, and at that, the delivery men were often subjected to harrassment.[25]

In keeping with his activist views, in his first editorial Hodža introduced *Slovenský týždenník* with these words:[26]

We believe that, if we Slovaks are to amount to anything, we must depend on no one and on nothing else but our own efforts and our own wisdom. We will always remember that a happier era in politics and in general advancement will flower for Slovaks only when they become economically strong and independent.

This coupling of the national and cultural aspirations of Slovaks with their economic advancement was characteristic of Hodža throughout his career. Though some of the planks of the platform he soon announced in *Slovenský týždenník* were specific to the political situation of Slovakia at the time, his focus presaged the political philosophy he would put forth throughout his life. He fervently believed that education represented the key not only to personal advancement but to the future of the whole nation, and he fumed at the fact that in Slovakia literacy was low and technical eduation virtually non-existent. He also fought for universal voting rights and the secret ballot. In Austria-Hungary voting was highly restricted on the basis of education, financial resources and ownership of land, with the result that only some six percent of the male population was allowed to cast a ballot. Voting was public, not secret, and elections were frequently accompanied by bribery and intimidation. Under these conditions, the political advancement of Slovaks and other minorities was unthinkable.

HODŽA NOT ONLY PRESENTED A COHERENT political platform in *Slovenský týždenník*, he also wrote incisive and biting analyses of political events. In 1904, for instance, Count István Tisza, the Hungarian prime minister and an arrogant Magyar, wrote a letter to the editor of a Magyar newspaper, noting that a new Slovak monthly had started publication and that it was very cheap and clearly aimed at the poorest strata with the goal of spreading the seditious doctrine of pan-slavism.[27] Fortunately, Tisza wrote, these wretched little Slovaks do not know how to read very well. Hodža, outraged, wrote an editorial in *Slovenský týždenník* in reply:[28]

> . . . Just read this: "Fortunately, they don't read very well." Those Slovaks. But what is this, you ask. Don't we pay taxes for schools? Don't we believe that he who knows the most is the best off? And especially with reading; that's something that every child needs to know in these hard times. Who dares to write that it's "fortunate" when we don't read very well? . . . Fortunate for whom? For ourselves? Hardly. For the nation? Surely it cannot be denied that the first requirement for an individual and for the country to flower is education. So whose fortune would it be if Slovaks really didn't know how to read and did not read? Oh yes, it would be good fortune, great fortune for those "gentlemen" [Hodža's ironic epithet for the Magyar ruling classes] and their government, and for their rule over us. Do you see how kind those patriots are who care for our welfare with such great feeling: it's fortunate that you can't read!

> . . . Now do you see why our "gentlemen" get mad when you vote for a Slovak candidate? Of course, because a Slovak candidate wants to have Slovak schools. Now do you see why they make Slovak editors run from one court of law to another? Hell, why not, when the Slovak editor gives his people everything that the miserly government and its "gentlemen" denies them—he gives the Slovak people a Slovak publication, he gives the Slovak people a Slovak conviction. Wolves in sheep's clothing circle you this way and that. . . . They all promise you [the sky], but not one of them gives you the Slovak language; not one of them gives you that one thing without which the Slovak nation is like an orphan without its mother, like a field without its harvest, like a church without its altar and like the cross without Christ. The truth is, they are afraid to give you your Slovak

language, because she is the way for the Slovak people to know the truth. They are afraid, because she is the foundation for the people to be their own masters. . . .

In his newspaper writing, Hodža used simple and vivid language that would appeal to the villager, whom Hodža passionately wanted to become an informed political actor. He was the first "investigative reporter" in Slovak journalistic history, writing about debates in the parliament, about legislation, about economic conditions and policies, about curruption and political intrigue. Over and over he showed how the Slovak people were being cheated, coerced, deprived of their rights, and held in subjugation. For this the Hungarian government made him pay.

Magyar officials tried to halt critical political reporting by bankrupting the voices that the government did not want to hear. Repeated court actions against writers and editors resulted in substantial fines and jail sentences for them, and the court proceedings themselves cost money. The charges were vague but serious: agitation against the Magyar nation, insulting a government official, or insulting the emperor. Much Slovak political writing could be forced by the authorities into at least one of these categories.

In 1909 Hodža announced in *Slovenský týždenník,* with more than a little pride, that the paper had been levied 5,700 imperial crowns in fines during a single week. The court cases came so thick and fast that in one issue he wrote laconically: "A whole week, and no fines!" In two years during this period, the paper had to bear 53,000 crowns in legal costs and fines. *Slovenský týždenník* accumulated more fines than all the other leading Slovak newspapers combined.[29] With this huge drain on resources, finances were often so tight that the costs of printing one week's edition were barely covered by the sales receipts of the previous week—there were no reserves whatever. The paper survived on its many subscriptions and on donations made quietly by the few Slovaks who could afford to do this, including some who had emigrated to America.

HODŽA'S FEARLESS WRITING CAUGHT THE ATTENTION of a wide public, including the progressive and self-aware Slovaks of the Lower Lands (Appendix III) who had started their own monthly, the *Dolnozemský Slovák (Slovak of the Lower Lands),* published in Báčsky Petrovec. In 1905 Hodža was invited to give a speech in Petrovec, and the crowd of thousands that gathered to hear him, including Serbs as well as Slovaks, gave him an enthusiastic reception.

After this speech, the Slovaks nominated Hodža as their candidate in the upcoming parliamentary elections, and the Serbs accepted.[30] The story of his campaign and election has become almost the stuff of legend.[31] Hodža personally visited every town and village in the district many times over, making speeches and holding discussions in Slovak, Serbian, German, or Magyar as needed. This was a far cry from the then usual practice of a few formal pronouncements in the main towns. His campaign organization visited virtually every voting household. When election day finally came, the excitement of the people was described in this way in *Dolnozemský Slovák:*[32]

> It was still night when the voters of the more distant villages prepared to depart for Kulpín [the seat of the electoral district]. In the darkness of night the villages came alive, carriages rumbled through the streets, and the voices of good people who with a clear conscience set out to to perform their most beautiful national duty were heard. . . . Cries for Hodža resounded and the carriages of our voters disappeared from our villages streets.

Remember that voting rights were restricted to a handful of men who were qualified by education, financial resources, and, most important, land ownership. Hence, the few eligible voters were almost like delegates for their communities.

> When the first carriages reached the voting area, the sun was just rising. More and more voters' carriages came, until by seven o'clock the area allotted to us was full. The voters from Petrovec came on foot, with Milan Hodža and Miloš Krno[33] in the lead. . . . The procession was made even more colorful and imposing by the large number of carriages from Kysáč, St. Futog and Begeč who went before them. From Petrovec to Kulpín there was one unbroken line of our voters. Along the way the crowd sang out our national songs, which rose to the heavens.

> In the meantime Mihajlovič's voters came too, some of them already showing the effects of brandy. [Mihajlovič was the official government candidate, and brandy the favored form of bribery.] . . . the soldiers kept interfering with us, while the Mihajlovič voters could come and go as they pleased.

> . . . All of our villages, Slovak and Serbian, voted in the most perfect order, so no one could find any excuse to use a weapon, bayonet, bullet or rifle against us. All the voters stayed together in exemplary order, and when it was their turn to cast their ballots, they voted quietly. . . .

> When dusk was settling, the outcome of the balloting was certain. The voters of Petrovec stood by the ballot box like a fortress wall.

While they voted, which took five hours, the government flunkies spread out into the nearby villages and dragged anyone they could still find to vote for Mihajlovič. With this trick they were able to secure another sixty-seventy German voters. This was their last gasp. When these stragglers had voted, our side still had a majority of two hundred votes . . . Our people, who had come to cast their ballots in enormous numbers, sang our national songs, which resounded jubilantly in the endless dark of night. Everywhere, a thousand voices cheered "*Živio Milan Hodža!*" *Hej Slováci* shook the windows of the voting room.

Finally, at 11:30, the president of the electoral commission announced to the gathered crowd that Milan Hodža had been elected as the representative of the electoral district of Kulpín. He had not even finished speaking when the crowd thundered, "*Živio Milan Hodža!*" Then Hodža, in a brief but pointed speech, thanked the Serbs and Slovaks for the trust they had shown him in electing him the representative of two brotherly nations.

AND SO, THE YOUNG JOURNALIST WAS NOW THRUST squarely into the rough and tumble of politics, a member of a tiny elected minority[34] trying to stem the tide of Magyarization before it was too late. Parliament was dissolved in 1906 and new elections were held in which Hodža was once again elected from the district of Kulpín. Until the elections of 1910, he represented his adopted population of Slovaks and Serbs, pressing for universal manhood suffrage, the rights of minorities, and policies for the economic upliftment of the peasantry. He also helped to form a Parliamentary Nationalities Party in which the Slovak, Serb, and Romanian deputies worked together on a common agenda. In this step we see another lifelong theme of Hodža's, the emphasis on the active cooperation of East and Central European nations for mutual support, advancement, and strength.

Parliamentary deputies were supposed to have immunity from prosecution for political statements. Hodža, however, continued to function as editor of *Slovenský týždenník* even while he served in parliament, and his writings were inflammatory enough to the Magyars that his immunity was lifted by action of parliament a number of times. Not only was he fined repeatedly, in 1907 he was held in Vacovo prison for two months. Many other Slovak activists were sentenced to Vacovo, and time served there later came to be seen as a badge of honor.

Parliament met in Budapest, so Hodža naturally maintained his old student apartment there. He frequently traveled back to the Lower Lands to keep in

Milan Hodža around the time of his years in the Hungarian parliament, 1905-1910. Author's archive.

touch with his constituents, and from time to time he returned to his home town of Sučany, mainly to visit his mother and his half-brother, Ján, who had taken their father Ondrej's place as the Lutheran pastor. There he came to know Irena Pivko, the third daughter of the well-to-do farmer and merchant Ondrej Pivko and his wife, Zuzana Pivko, née Majtáň (Chapter 14). Milan and Irena became firm companions. Irena was studying at the Magyar academy for teachers in Bratislava. (There were no Slovak-medium secondary schools of any kind—Magyar was the only option unless one left the country.) When she finished her training, she could easily have found a plum teaching position in a Hungarian state school in which Magyar was the medium of instruction. Instead, she studied Serbian, passed the necessary language examinations, and went to teach in a Lutheran church school in Stará Pazová, a Slovak town not far from Kulpín. Like Milan, she returned to Sučany fairly often, and they would meet en route in Budapest and travel together. Although their relationship was clearly growing, it did not meet with her parents' approval. As Irena, my Grandmother Hodža, recounted:[35]

> We were both from Sučany, and that is where we met. When I finished my studies at the teaching academy in Bratislava in 1905, Milan started to be very interested in me. Pastor Štetka was courting my sister, and Milan came with him to our house to court me. But my mother did not approve of our relationship. Milan was already politically very active and—you know how it was in Hungary then—he

was constantly facing politically motivated lawsuits. He was already a member of Parliament—he was first elected in December of 1905—and he was publishing *Slovenský týždenník*, in which he attacked both the Magyar government officials and the emperor himself. So he faced repeated lawsuits for agitation. My mother used to tell me that he would spend most of his life in prison and would never be free of fines for his political activity. But that did not scare me off. Just the opposite, in my eyes and in my heart these challenges made him even greater. My mother worried about me in the way that mothers always worry about their daughters. She saw nothing bad in Milan; it was only because of his political activity that she worried about my future. So, Milan began coming to our house less often. I obtained a teaching position in a church school in Stará Pazová (a small town of about 7,000 inhabitants of whom only 1,000 were Serbs, the rest were Slovaks). When I came home from Pazová, I traveled via Budapest where I almost always met with Milan. We loved each other, and it was hard on us that my mother did not much like the relationship. Once I fell a little ill. When I came home from Pazová on vacation, my mother got scared and told me, "Well, I see that love is making

Grandmother Hodža with friends in Stará Pazová, 1905. Left to right: costume from Stará Pazová, Serbian costume from Hercegovina, Grandmother Hodža, Serbian costume from Serbia. Author's archive.

you sick; so, go ahead and marry Milan." It goes without saying that I recovered very quickly, and the wedding was on October 5, 1909.

The newlyweds settled in Budapest. Irena began to work, no longer as a teacher but as her husband's secretary and collaborator, as well as a gracious hostess for the many Slovaks who visited Budapest. Among these was her sister Mária (Aunt Mária of Benice), whose wedding to Cyril Pivko took place in the Hodžas' apartment.[36] Soon children came. In 1910 she traveled back to Sučany and stayed with Milan's mother, Klementína, while she gave birth to my mother, also named Irena. In 1912 Fedor, Uncle Dišo, was born in Budapest. Aunt Gláša was not born until 1920, when the family had already moved to Prague, following the establishment of Czechoslovakia.

Based in Budapest and at home in many of the corridors of power in the Hungarian state, the young, brilliant, intense, fearless, and ambitious Milan Hodža would soon find new outlets for his energies, new opportunities to help his visions for Slovakia move closer to reality.

Grandmother Hodža holding my mother. Budapest, c. 1911. Author's archive.

Milan Hodža at the Birth of a Nation

When Grandfather Hodža was re-elected to parliament in 1906, he joined a record number of non-Magyar deputies—twenty-three. While this represented an unprecedented electoral success, these twenty-three deputies had no hope of actually passing any legislation in a parliament of over 400. The proceedings in the parliamentary chamber could be raucous—my mother told me that Grandfather Hodža often got hoarse and even lost his voice from trying to make himself heard above all the shouting. It would take a long series of increasing electoral successes to divert the Magyars from their ultra-nationalist policies. Was there another way?

PERHAPS. IN VIENNA EMPEROR FRANZ JOSEPH, on the throne since 1849, was old and tired. His son, Rudolf, had committed suicide, and the new heir-apparent was the emperor's nephew, Archduke Franz Ferdinand. And Franz Ferdinand had a fresh perspective on the empire. He considered the Compromise of 1867 that had created the dual Austro-Hungarian state to have been a catastrophe for the House of Habsburg, and he feared that the surging Magyars would try to destroy even this form of Habsburg power. For this reason, he was very interested in opposition voices being raised on Hungarian soil. (For a brief review of this history, see Appendix I.)

Among the opposition leaders was the Romanian Aurel Popovici who in 1906, the year of Grandfather Hodža's re-election, published a carefully worked out proposal for the re-organization of the empire based on its many nationalities; he called his book *The United States of Greater Austria.*[1] The basic idea had been in circulation at least since the days of the revolution of 1848, but new circumstances now made it timely. Prompted by Popovici's study, Franz Ferdinand collected around himself a think-tank of theoreticians and politicians who were seeking ways to re-organize the empire, diminish Magyar power, and improve the prospects of their own nations. Historians have come to call this the Belvedere Circle, after Franz Ferdinand's Belvedere Palace in Vienna. Soon Hodža was invited to join.[2]

The relationship between Franz Ferdinand and Grandfather Hodža stemmed at least partly from one of the most famous events of this period of Slovak history, the so-called tragedy at Černová, at the heart of which was Andrej Hlinka.[3] The village of Černová was Hlinka's birthplace, and he had inspired the construction of a new Catholic church there. It was to be consecrated in late 1907, and the villagers wanted their beloved son Hlinka to officiate. However, Hlinka had been suspended from his position as a Catholic priest and sentenced to two years' imprisonment as punishment for his political activities in the elections of 1906. The *magyarone* bishop insisted that four other priests perform the consecration. When the priests reached Černová, the villagers tried to stop their coaches by massing in the street, whereupon the overseer (*slúžny*) ordered his gendarmes to open fire into the crowd. Fifteen villagers were killed, seventy were wounded, and later thirty-eight were jailed. The event caused an uproar all over Europe.

In the Hungarian parliament, Hodža filed an interpellation, a formal request for the minister of the interior, Count Gyula Andrássy, to justify what had happened.[4] Passions ran high. As Hodža started to outline the events at Černová, shouts arose, "You lie!"

"I'll bring you eyewitnesses," said Hodža.

"False witnesses," came the shouts. "It's all the fault of *Slovenský týždenník*!"

Hodža was interrupted after nearly every sentence by the shouting of the Magyar deputies. Finally he posed his formal questions to Count Andrássy, who rejected them all and took the opportunity to attack *Slovenský týždenník* once again. The following day, on the urging of the Romanian Alexander Vaidu-Voevod, who was Hodža's colleague in the parliament and already a consultant to Franz Ferdinand, Hodža received his first invitation to an audience with the archduke.[5]

Hodža came prepared with a written analysis of the events at Černová. He also took advantage of the archduke's anger to ask him to intervene on behalf of Hlinka, and Franz Ferdinand responded by writing a personal letter to the pope.[6] The archduke increasingly valued Hodža's insights into Hungarian politics, as well as his ideas for the future organization of the empire, and continued to invite him for audiences and ask for written analyses. This seems remarkable, inasmuch as the key points of Hodža's democratic and Slovak-centered political platform (Chapter 25), which he reiterated at every opportunity, were anathema to a thoroughgoing royalist like Franz Ferdinand. Not only that, Hodža had published a number of editorial attacks on the Archduke himself in *Slovenský týždenník*. Nevertheless, it was said that Hodža soon became the most influential member of the Belvedere circle. In turn, Hodža placed more and more faith in the benefits that Slovaks would gain when Franz Ferdinand finally assumed the throne. He expressed these hopes repeatedly on the pages of *Slovenský týždenník*.

Hodža's direct dealings with the archduke, which came to be known as Belvedere politics, were widely discussed in Slovak political circles. Despite the benefits this relationship might bring, it created unease among some other Slovak leaders. Past reliance on the emperor, as during the revolution of 1848, had been sadly misplaced. Why should it be any more successful now? Further, to some of Hodža's contemporaries and competitors for leadership, and even some of his personal friends, private conversations in the Belvedere Palace smacked of personal maneuvering on Hodža's part.[7] Many modern historians, however, accord his approach great importance, both because it represented one of the few concrete possibilities for substantially improving the prospects of Slovakia and because it had a catalyzing effect on the entire Slovak political scene. One of the principal Hodža scholars of the Communist era, who was actually often critical of Hodža, went so far as to compare it to the great Slovak National Awakening:[8]

> [Belvedere politics] was not mere "high politics," serving Hodža's personal taste. It had a positive, energizing influence on the entire Slovak political scene. When formulating an overall evaluation, a comparison with the movement for national awakening of the mid-nineteenth century comes forcefully to mind.

In the spring of 1914, Hodža, his wife, and their two children—my mother, then four years old, and Uncle Dišo, only two—went home on one of their many family visits. They stayed in Benice with Grandmother Hodža's sister, Aunt Mária, and often traveled the short distance to Sučany to visit Milan's mother Klementína and his half-brother Ján. As Ján recalled many years later:[9]

> Milan came over from Benice one morning, and we sat down on the bench in front of the parish house. I asked him if he had heard the news. "What news?" he replied. "Yesterday they assassinated the archduke." He froze and remained silent. After some time he raised his head and cried out twice, "Terrible! Terrible! Within two months our monarchy will be up for grabs!"

On June 28th, 1914, Archduke Franz Ferdinand and his wife had been shot to death in Sarajevo, the capital of Bosnia and Hercegovina, by an extremist Serbian nationalist. There was shock throughout the empire and concern elsewhere in Europe. Matúš Dula remarked to Ján Hodža:[9] "In all this, I am most sorry about Milan. With the burial of the prince he also buried his hopes for the future of Slovakia."

Hodža wrote a long, laudatory, and moving obituary in *Slovenský týždenník*. It began with these words:[10]

Unheard-of sorrow gripped the hearts and stunned the senses of the oppressed of Hungary. . . .

And it closed, in typical Hodža fashion, with a call for strength and resolve on the part of the oppressed, and for a new path into the future:

Our strength is in ourselves. If it cannot be manifested in the form which he and we imagined, it will be expressed in another way, but it will not die. We must nurture it and enhance it without tiring and without fear.

AGGRESSIVE CIRCLES IN THE AUSTRIAN government took advantage of the assassination to make manifestly unacceptable demands on Serbia. Only a month later, claiming that Serbia's response had been inadequate, Austria-Hungary declared war. World War I began with nationalist euphoria throughout the empire. Soon, Germany, Austria-Hungary, Bulgaria, and the Ottoman Empire (Austria-Hungary's long-time adversary, see Appendix I) were fighting together as the Central Powers, ranged against the rest of Europe and, in 1917, the United States. By the time the war ended in 1918, an estimated sixty-five million men had been called to arms, eight-and-a-half million were dead, twenty-one million were wounded. Civilian casualties reached 6.6 million.[11]

When the armies of the Austro-Hungarian Empire were mobilized, Hodža, too, was ordered to report. He re-wrote his will and proceeded to join his unit in the city of Trenčín. Kornel Stodola (Chapter 22, Note 20), living in Vienna, wrote in his diary:[12]

August 9th. Hodža was here. He was called up. We went to buy things he would need—medicines, bandages, and similar things. I brought him some chocolate and went with him to the station. He was peaceful. When he was getting into his carriage, he said, "Don't worry, Kornel. We'll see each other again." I admired the strength of his spirit. After all, he has a wife and children. From my heart I wished him good luck, that he would return safely. I stood on the platform until the train moved out of sight, and then I left the station with a heavy, aching heart.

Milan Hodža as a soldier in World War I. 1915. Author's archive.

The day after he arrived in Trenčín, Hodža was arrested and taken to prison in chains.[13] A number of serious charges were lodged against him: not only the subversive character of a number of his editorial pieces in *Slovenský týždenník*, but also espionage, agitation, and organizing an uprising against the government. Conviction on these charges would carry a mandatory death sentence. His status as a former member of parliament was no help. His captain told him to prepare to be shot the next day.

Even under wartime conditions, however, basic due process prevailed in Austria-Hungary, and no execution could take place without conviction by a military court. Hodža was taken for trial to Bratislava. Again Stodola:[14]

> *August 13th.* Bad news. Samo Zoch wrote me from Modra that yesterday he saw how they were taking the arrested Hodža to Bratislava guarded with bayonets. I immediately started to intervene on his behalf with all the leading personalities known to me.

Hodža served as his own attorney. The presiding general could find no convincing evidence of the most serious charges—espionage and organizing for an uprising—and declared Hodža innocent, though dangerous and therefore to be kept under surveillance.[15] The matter of provocative writing in *Slovenský týždenník* would be part of a civil trial later. Shortly he was relocated to Veszprém, a purely Magyar city not too far from Budapest, where there would be no opportunity for political activity. One of Hodža's first assignments, however, gave him an opening. Inasmuch as there were no Slovak-speaking clergy in Veszprém, he was assigned the task of delivering words of farewell and blessing to Slovak soldiers who were being sent to the front. Ever the rebel, he regularly ended his talks by declaring, "May Slovaks live!" "*Nech žijú Slováci!*" Encouraging Slovak consciousness, especially at a time of war, could have been considered treason, but Hodža got off lightly—once the authorities realized what he was doing, he was simply assigned to other tasks.

In the meantime, the police raided Hodža's apartment in Budapest and confiscated all his correspondence with Czech leaders and organizations as proof of his anti-state activities.[16] It became part of the evidence in his civil trial, at which he was sentenced to eighteen months' imprisonment, to be served as soon as the war was over. His sentencing was clearly politically motivated, for it occurred at a time when prime minister Tisza was granting clemency in all other court cases against editors in Hungary.[15]

While her husband was being drafted, arrested, tried, sentenced, and moved from place to place, Grandmother Hodža was in Budapest tending to the children. My mother recalls clearly how other youngsters taunted her, shouting that as soon as the war was over her father would be going to prison. Soon, Grandmother Hodža took the children home to Slovakia. They lived again with Aunt Mária on the farm in Benice. However, my mother was now of school age, and there was no school in Benice, so she was sent to her grandmother Klementína in Sučany. Here is how she recollected this time many years later:[17]

> We loved each other dearly, my grandmother and I, but I must have been a handful for her. I can still see myself pouting and protesting as she combed and braided my hair in the morning. My grandmother died after my first school year, and I went back to the farm. My mother, who was a qualified teacher, tutored me herself during my second school year. The lessons always began with a religious hymn. This was terrible, for I never could carry a tune.

HODŽA WAS IN EFFECT A POLITICAL EXILE in Veszprém for a year. Then, in 1915, Kornel Stodola succeeded in having him transferred from Veszprém to Vienna. Stodola had become the nucleus of a group of Slovaks and Czechs who met secretly to discuss the war and its meaning for the future, particularly for Slovakia. Hodža quickly became the acknowledged leader of this group, and through it a central figure in the re-orientation of national policy that would shape Slovakia's future for decades: away from the struggle for equal rights within Hungary and toward political union with the Czechs in a single state.[18]

The leading man of these meetings was definitely Hodža, although a number of other outstanding people were there. . . . At these meetings I admired his oratorical gifts. No one knew better how to present his speech according to the needs of the moment, clearly or in a veiled way. When he wanted to be understood, then his lecture was clear, understandable to everyone. When, however, he did not want to commit himself on a subject, and how often that was necessary in our uncertain circumstances, then with admirable finesse he found words that meant nothing and still left the impression that they had expressed everything. . . .

I'll never forget the picture in our dining room. The distinguished faces sitting around the table. Among them Hodža in a casual pose, always with a cigarette in his hand, speaking in classical German. His remarks always formed an organic whole. The personalities about whom he spoke appeared to us fully formed. Listening to him was a delight.

How could a handful of men meeting in an apartment or a cafe in Vienna play a major role in the shaping of a new Czech-Slovak Republic? They did not officially represent any party, and they had no political base of their own. They had no authority to negotiate with anyone, and they did not as a group sign any documents. And yet, here is how a recent detailed study summarizes their influence:[19]

Under wartime conditions, the Martin-based leadership of the Slovak National Party could not compete with the Vienna group which, starting with the summer of 1915, entirely logically took the leadership of Slovak politics into its own hands. On the other hand, the natural, sometimes almost patriarchal authority of the Martin center . . . continued, which revealed itself in the decisive negotiations about the direction of Slovak politics [held in Martin] in 1918. Until that time, however, Milan Hodža and his companions in Vienna represented the actual, if not the official heart of Slovak politics. Starting with frequent contacts with Czech politicians in 1917, this headed toward the creation of an independent Czecho-Slovakia.

For one thing, they were in Vienna where the latest war news and political gossip was available to them—a far cry from the isolated towns of Slovakia. For another, the Slovak National Party was again in the grip of its own policy of passivity. Most of all, however, the strength of the group stemmed from its activist membership, representing Romanians, Serbs, and Germans as well as Slovaks and increasingly Czechs. Committed Slovaks visited from home—my own Grandfather Pálka was among them. Without a political organization but also unfettered in their actions, the men in Vienna could think broadly and spring into action when the time was ripe.

The Czech participants (including many who would soon become leading figures in Czechoslovakia) leaned particularly heavily on Hodža for his expertise on political and economic conditions in Hungary and his knowledge of the leaders with whom future negotiations would probably need to be held. These conversations had an immediate political effect, for they significantly influenced the increasingly pointed demands that Czech deputies in the Austrian parliament were making for the establishment of a new state that would include Slovakia.[20]

If Slovakia was to become an active partner in the Czechoslovakia that was taking shape in the minds of a handful of leaders, a mechanism for the expression of Slovak political will had to be developed. At the onset of the war, the Slovak National Party had once again adopted a policy of deliberate passivity—to remain quiet, expressing only nominal support for the Hungarian government and for the emperor, but also making no demands until the outcome of the war should become clearer. Even Hodža agreed, as Stodola records on the day of Hodža's departure to join his regiment in Trenčín just as the war was breaking out:[21]

> Already a week ago I suggested to Hodža that our Slovak National Party should issue some sort of statement. He replied: "We will demonstrate better by remaining silent."

Now, however, the tide of war was clearly turning in favor of the Western powers, and it was time to return to action. In June of 1917, Hodža had declared in dismay that in Slovakia it was deathly still.[22] In 1918, to break this stillness, Hodža started pressing the Slovak National Party, already a broadly constituted umbrella organization, to establish a Slovak National Council that would speak on behalf of Slovaks of all political persuasions.[23] Similar calls came from the Czech side.

As the tide of war swung decisively in favor of the Western powers and the disintegration of Austria-Hungary seemed ever more certain, the momentum for a new state of Czecho-Slovakia began to build.[24] In the fall of 1918, events started to follow one another at a dizzying pace. On October 18, the Czechoslovak National Council in Paris, already recognized by France, Great Britain, and the United States, declared itself the provisional government of a new

Czecho-Slovak Republic. A Czech delegation came from Prague to Vienna for hurried consultations with the Stodola circle there. The Czechs then split into two groups, one heading to Geneva for a meeting with the Czechoslovak National Council, and the other to Prague. On the same day, October 28, 1918, the delegates in Geneva debated the legal structure of the new joint state and the Czech National Council in Prague proclaimed the establishment of Czechoslovakia. On October 29 newspapers in Vienna and Budapest reported that there had been demonstrations in Prague, but government censors deleted any mention of the declaration of a Czecho-Slovak Republic.[25] Other communication was slow. Thus it happened that, when Slovak representatives gathered in Martin on October 30, they did not know that a Czecho-Slovak Republic had been declared in Prague and that one of their own, Vavro Šrobár, had signed the declaration on behalf of Slovaks. Their actions, therefore, were completely independent. In the morning of October 30, the Slovak National Council that had finally been appointed provisionally a few days earlier was officially confirmed in the rooms of the Tatra Bank on the main square of Martin, while the Hungarian gendarmerie surrounded the building. In the afternoon the great Martin Declaration, through which Slovaks withdrew from Hungary and joined Czechs

My father as a volunteer in the First Regiment of Slovak Liberty, 1918. Author's archive.

in a new state, was signed and a message to that effect was sent to Prague.[25] The self-proclaimed new nation quickly won international recognition. When World War I ended, Czechoslovakia was represented at the peace conference in Versailles by the foreign minister designated by the Czechoslovak National Council, Edvard Beneš.

IN THE MINDS OF THE STATESMEN GATHERED in the grand halls of Versailles, the war was over and there was a new state in Europe—Czechoslovakia. On the ground in Slovakia, however, the situation was chaotic. Hungarian troops occupied most of Slovakia's territory. Despite the proclamations made in Prague and in Martin, and the international recognition of the Czechoslovak National Council in Paris, Hungarian officials were making every effort to retain Slovakia within Hungary. Grandfather Hodža was sent to Budapest by the new Czechoslovak government to lead negotiations for the withdrawal of Hungarian troops. His conduct of these negotiations proved controversial, but they met their main goal: Hungarian troops left Slovakia and pulled back to Hungarian territory.[26]

Local Slovak militias, led primarily by Czech officers, were hurriedly organized to maintain order as the Hungarian troops withdrew. Such was the First Regiment of Slovak Liberty in which my father enlisted.

He was seventeen and still in the midst of his studies in Vienna when he was caught up in the momentous events that brought Czechoslovakia into existence. Here is how he recalled this time:[27]

> The revolutionary events of 1918 almost caught me in Vienna. I had been studying there since 1915 when I was expelled from all Hungarian schools as an incorrigible Pan-Slav. These were hard times. Because of the war, there was a shortage of food in Vienna, as there was in all other large cities. We ate bread made of corn flour, salted fish from Germany, dried vegetables, and some sort of turnips. Instead of cigarettes the shops sold *Hindenburg Tabakersatz*, Hindenburg tobacco substitute.

> In the fall of 1918 this situation reached its peak. The school was closed, first on account of the Spanish flu epidemic, and later because of a shortage of coal, the *"Kohlenferien"* [coal holidays]. For this reason my brother and I did not travel from vacation back to school in Vienna until October 27th. Our train took us as far as Leopoldov, where we were to change to the express from Budapest to Vienna. The platform was overflowing with soldiers who were returning home or deserting, mainly from the Itaian front.... They

finally announced that the trains from Budapest to Vienna were not running, that Budapest was in flames, and that there was an uprising in Vienna. It was several hours before we could board a train in the direction of Žilina and Košice. We noticed that many obviously important Slovaks were boarding the train, and finally learned that they were traveling to Martin to sign a declaration. This was the famous Martin Declaration by which Slovaks committed themselves to a joint Czech-Slovak Republic.

It took 16 hours for the train to reach Mikuláš. When we got there, the station was lit up and a crowd was standing on the platform waving flags. I thought they were Hungarian flags. Without waiting for the train to stop, I jumped out, leaped over the railing, and grabbed one of our employees who was holding a large flag. I slapped him, and yelled, "How dare you demonstrate with a Hungarian flag?" He just looked at me and said, "But young sir, please look, this is not a Hungarian flag, it's our Slovak flag." I apologized immediately, and in a moment the crowd, with the two of us in the lead, headed into town. We sang patriotic songs until we reached our house, on which was hanging the first Slovak flag in Mikuláš. Our mother had hurriedly stitched it during the night out of dyed bedsheets. Someone led the enthusiastic crowd in swearing their loyalty to the new Czechoslovak Republic on this flag. . . .

Then events erupted in rapid succession. It was necessary to take over the public buildings, offices, schools, and especially the post office with its telegraph and telephone. For this they sent two Czech corporals-technicians. One of them, named Zvoníček, was so short that when he mounted his bayonet on his Mannlicher rifle it reached over his head. . . . It was necessary to take care that the former Hungarian officials, teachers, and others would not damage or steal the furnishings. I was assigned to take over the gymnasium, now the Gymnasium of Michal Miloslav Hodža, which has just been finished and equipped. The principal was Dr. Mihály Habán from County Spiš [to the east of County Liptov], who was a bigoted *magyarone* even though his mother did not speak a word of Magyar. So Zvoníček and I set out to take over and seal the classrooms, laboratories, gyms, etc. Zvoníček took his Mannlicher, set his bayonet on it, and hung a couple of grenades on his belt. At the Tatra Bank I was given sealing wax and a metal seal. Thus outfitted, we set out to take over the gymnasium. The building was empty, but voices could be heard from the principal's apartment. We rang the bell, and the principal stepped out. The Czech immediately put his hand on the shoulder of the much taller Habán and ceremonially proclaimed, "I arrest you in the name of the Republic." Habán surely understood what was happening, but still he asked me in Magyar "*Mit mond az a katona, Pálka ur?*" (What is he saying, Mr. Pálka?) I explained to him in Slovak that he was under arrest, that he should not resist, that he should show us around the various rooms which we would seal, and that he would be personally responsible if any of the seals were broken. . . . Then we led him to the district court, where he was interned for a few days until the new principal arrived. The other schools and offices were also taken over by new people, mainly Czechs, since at that time there was a genuine shortage of Slovak staff and teachers.

Some days later my father joined a small group that was traveling to Eastern Slovakia to try to persuade people in rural regions to accept the new idea of Czechoslovakia. One of the group's members was Andrej Hlinka. At first, the response of the peasants who had come to the hastily organized meeting was lukewarm at best. Then it was Hlinka's turn to speak:

When Hlinka rose to speak, he used examples and references to the scriptures in such an inspiring way that, after the meeting, the people hoisted all of us up on their shoulders and carried us to the train station, singing patriotic songs all the way.

My father went on another such excursion, then joined the volunteer First Regiment of Slovak Liberty[28] and helped to patrol the border with Poland against smugglers. Soon regular Czech troops arrived in Slovakia, and after some time Czechoslovak legions from Italy and finally from Russia. In four months, when all foreign troops had withdrawn and Slovak territory was firmly under Czechoslovak control, the volunteer units were disbanded. My father packed his bags and returned to Vienna to finish his schooling.

There were other complexities in making Slovakia an integral and smoothly functioning part of Czechoslovakia. Ethnic Magyars held virtually all of the positions required to run an orderly society: They were the public officials, teachers, and judges; they staffed the railways, post offices, radio, and police (see Chapter 25, note 3). These thousands of men maintained their allegiance to Hungary, and many of them soon migrated to the now much-diminished Hungarian homeland. On the Slovak side, following a long period of deliberate ethnic suppression, the educated middle class was tiny and not adequate to take over the many positions the Magyars were vacating. As Slovak territory came under Czechoslovak control, many Czechs were sent to fill these positions. Furthermore, poorly educated Slovaks, especially in rural areas, had for generations known only the emperor as their ruler and Hungary as their homeland. They did not automatically feel an allegiance to the new state. A massive public education campaign about the formation of Czechoslovakia had to be undertaken.

As the turmoil in the new Czechoslovakia gradually faded, Grandfather Hodža moved his family from Budapest to Prague to begin a remarkable political career.

CHAPTER 27

Milan Hodža—Statesman of International Stature

With the war over and Czechoslovakia firmly established, the Hodža family settled permanently in Prague. From 1919 on, with only a few interruptions, Grandfather Hodža held ministerial appointments in a succession of coalition governments until the resignation of his cabinet during the crisis year of 1938:[1]

Minister for the Unification of Laws,[2] 1919-1920
Minister of Agriculture, 1922-1926
Minister for the Unification of Laws (again), 1927
Minister of Education, 1926-1929
Minister of Agriculture (again), 1932-1935
Foreign Minister, 1935-1936
Prime Minister, 1935-1938

Volumes have been, and continue to be, written about his activities and accomplishments during this long period of public service and political struggle.[3] Accolades continue to come his way: "The most significant Slovak politician and statesman in Czecho-Slovakia between 1918 and 1938 was Milan Hodza . . . ,"[4] ". . . a multifaceted personality—journalist, democratic politician and statesman, extraordinary Central European federalist and pioneer of the cooperation of Central European nations, public figure with natural ties to civil society. . . ."[5]

It is a complex story that cannot really be told in a few pages, and in any case it is properly in the domain of historians. Rather than trying to summarize the basic facts, I have selected a handful of episodes that contribute to a picture of the whole man, the rather enigmatic figure whose public life started with the righteous indignation that poured out of the pages of *Slovenský týždenník* during the days of Austria-Hungary, included years of national and international recognition but also controversy, and closed with a lonely death in a resort town on the coast of Florida. I can offer only a sketch, not a full portrait of the grandfather I never really knew, but even a sketch hints at the depth that a full portrait would convey (Plates 24,25).

Milan Hodža brought enormous commitment and self-discipline to his work. Uncle Miško Múdry (Chapters 4 and 5) interviewed Grandmother Hodža shortly after her husband's death. In her responses, she touched on this side of her husband's personality:[6]

> His home life was quite limited. He was always burdened by work, from his youth into his old age. Perhaps that is why I sometimes thought of him as a loner, or, better, a man who loved solitude so that he could devote himself to his thoughts quietly and without interruption. . . . He did not like noisy company. He did not drink, and he smoked only in his youth.[7] He stopped from one day to the next when he realized that smoking was not good for him. He went to bed early and got up early. He needed at least eight hours of sleep . . . . He was very precise about everything. He worked according to a schedule that he prepared in advance and wrote down in his notebook. In this notebook, he also jotted down ideas as they came to him. He used the shorthand that he had mastered in several languages. . . .

Grandmother Hodža first described her husband as a loner, then backtracked a little to emphasize that he was thinker who needed quiet to develop his ideas. And indeed, Hodža was among the foremost intellectuals of Slovakia. He had obtained a doctorate in philosophy and linguistics at the University of Vienna in the depths of World War I, while he was still a conscripted soldier of the empire and simultaneously the leading voice in Kornel Stodola's secret meetings.[8] Hodža's newspaper articles, speeches and assorted other studies were collected, edited, and published in the early 1930s in six volumes of some 4,000 pages.[9] They are so rich in conceptual framework and in theory that the modern intellectual historian Karol Kollár considers Hodža to be one of the two or three founders of the academic discipline of political science in Slovakia.[10] In addition to being a broadly educated and penetrating thinker, however, Hodža is universally regarded as an exceptionally able, practical, and flexible politician, ambitious and impatient for results.

EDUCATION AS THE ROAD TO PERSONAL FULFILLMENT and national upliftment was a lifelong passion for Hodža. Remember how he had thundered in *Slovenský týždenník:* "Who dares to write that it's fortunate when we don't read very well? . . . Surely it cannot be denied that the first requirement for an individual and a nation to flower is education. . . ." (Chapter 25).

Within months after Czechoslovakia was established, Hodža formally submitted a parliamentary proposal for the establishment of a university in Bratislava.[11] At the time there was no university anywhere in Slovakia, and advanced degrees could only be obtained in the Czech lands or in foreign countries. The required legislation was passed very quickly, just two weeks after Hodža made his proposal. The university opened its doors in 1921, as eight professors took their place—six Czechs and only two Slovaks. The Slovaks were Jozef Škultéty—literary historian, linguist, long-time editor of *Národnie noviny*, and president of the renewed *Matica slovenská*—and Milan Hodža.[12, 13]

Every student at today's Comenius University can be grateful to Milan Hodža for his or her higher education. But Hodža cared for the broad population of Slovakia, not just the intellectual elite. During his first term as minister of agriculture, for example, he established over a hundred agricultural elementary schools, as well as eleven technical schools, that specifically served the rural regions of Slovakia and Subcarpathian Rus'.[14]While he was minister of education, he established many more new schools—136 in Slovakia alone.[15] He was in this post for three years, so 136 new schools represents an average of nearly one school a week for three consecutive years. In a country as small as Slovakia, this was a veritable revolution, especially since many of the schools were in towns and villages whose children had never before had any access to education.[16]

Even when he was prime minister, and the pressures on him were enormous, Hodža supported the expansion of education, and took time out to participate in the ceremonial opening of new schools, including the elementary school I attended in Bratislava right after World War II. Schools at all levels, teachers, children, and aspiring adults—Grandfather Hodža cared for them all, as we shall see in the remarkable reminiscences recorded in Chapter 29.

FOR HODŽA, EDUCATION AND ECONOMIC REFORM were the two essential components of building a nation whose dominant component was the peasantry. Because farming practices were antiquated, he established a number of research institutes in fields such as forestry, livestock production, and veterinary medicine.[17] He saw to it that central governmental organizations for research and public education with their roots in Prague reached out to Slovakia, and he used these organizations to funnel substantial amounts of money and the services of technical experts to the rural Slovak hinterlands. He supported the organization of self-education societies, occasional practical courses held out in the rural areas, lending libraries, and numerous other programs for improving the educational level and technical competence of the peasantry.

Because Slovak farmers found it impossible to borrow money except in small amounts and at exorbitant interest rates, Hodža tried various ways to establish and support banks and other financial organizations explicitly designed to serve them. He started during his early years in Budapest,[18] but his greatest success was the Peasant Mutual Banks founded in 1924 during his first term as minister of agriculture.[19]

The first Peasant Mutual Bank was formed in October 1924, initiating a period of rapid expansion. By time the system was mature, in 1937, there were seventy-four, covering the whole territory of Slovakia, and the total membership had grown to almost 140,000, an enormous number for the times.[20] A significant fraction of the over six hundred million crowns deposited in these banks had never before left their hiding place in the peasant's humble cottage. Now the cautious and conservative peasant was not only depositing his money, he was sharing in the operation of the bank itself.[21] Peasant Mutual Banks were not only a financial success, they generated a major social transformation, especially in Slovakia's poorest regions, just as Grandfather Hodža had originally envisioned.

Hodža the intellectual visionary had conceived of the Peasant Mutual Banks. Hodža the practical politician had secured the necessary legislation and funding, and had found dedicated men to implement his vision while he himself stayed largely in the background.[22, 23]

To move national policy in the direction of support for the Slovak farmer, it was necessary to have political power. Reciprocally, to have political power based on the support of the masses, most of whom were peasants, it was necessary to have a party that attended to the needs of those peasants.[24] Over time, the all-Czechoslovak Agrarian Party evolved to meet this need.[25] In Slovakia this party, with Hodža as national vice-chairman, regularly received the second largest number of votes after Hlinka's Slovak People's Party. Its position in the Czech regions was even stronger, and its combined strength made it the dominant party in almost all Czechoslovak governing coalitions from 1922 to 1938.

It would not be useful here to enter into the intricacies of politics in Czechoslovakia, where there were many parties and alliances shifted in complex ways. Suffice it to say that the Agrarian party was the dominant national party, and that Hodža was its second in command and by far the most powerful Slovak representative.[26] This key position led to his many ministerial appointments and gave him extraordinary influence over political developments affecting Slovakia. Over a period of nearly two decades he focused this power on improving education, advancing the agricultural sector, and strengthening the position of Slovakia within Czechoslovakia. And, like any successful and ambitious politician, he tried to use his accomplishments to further his own career.

THE RELATIONSHIP OF SLOVAKIA TO THE CENTRAL GOVERNMENT based in Prague was already problematic when the country was founded in 1918,[27] and continued to be so throughout Czechoslovakia's existence. The problems were never fully resolved, and finally Slovakia and the Czech Republic separated peacefully in 1993.

During the twenty years of the First Republic, 1918-1939, three men dominated the Slovak political scene, and each held a distinctive view of this core issue. Vavro Šrobár, the principal leader of the old Hlasists, most fully espoused the ideal of a Czechoslovakia so completely united that Czechs and Slovaks were seen as but branches of a single ethnic nation (the doctrine of Czechoslovakism). Andrej Hlinka, charismatic and single-minded, quickly became the dominant voice among those emphasizing Slovak distinctiveness and demanding legislative autonomy for Slovakia. In the middle, with a complex position that evolved over time, stood Milan Hodža. During the 1920s the influence of Vavro Šrobár faded, and two men vied for the heart of Slovakia—Milan Hodža and Andrej Hlinka.

For Hodža, the best future for Slovakia was unambiguously within the broader framework of Czechoslovakia. He did not believe that Czechoslovakia could survive the autonomist pressures of Hlinka's party, and he tried to reduce the party's influence in any way he could. On the other hand, he saw all too well that the Czech-dominated central government did not take the real situation in Slovakia and the legitimate demands of Slovaks into account. He saw discrimination in taxes and tariffs, favoritism to Czech candidates for a huge array of bureaucratic appointments, and even the economic exploitation of Slovakia, to say nothing of a condescending attitude toward Slovak culture and aspirations. In contrast to Hlinka, however, he initially saw the solution not in an autonomy that threatened to break up the whole country, but rather in the increasing participation of Slovaks in the central government. However, this approach had only limited success, and as the years went by Hodža moved closer to the Hlinka position. Hlinka, autonomist though he was, always supported a united Czechoslovakia. However, when he died in 1938 his party was taken over by a far more radical faction that included avowed admirers of Hitler. Hodža's fears that autonomism would lead to a break-up of Czechoslovakia were amply confirmed (Chapters 1 and 6).

During his final years, struggling in exile and thoroughly disenchanted with the strongly centralistic stance of Edvard Beneš, Hodža adopted a platform that would have been difficult to distinguish from Hlinka's own: a largely autonomous Slovakia within a united Czechoslovakia. This can be seen in his writings and public pronouncements, but I also remember it well from conversations at home. There was no doubt whatsoever that my parents saw Grandfather Hodža first and foremost as a Slovak who battled against the Czech centralists, even though neither they nor he ever wavered in their allegiance to a united Czechoslovakia.

NO MATTER WHAT HIS SPECIFIC MINISTERIAL POST might be, Hodža always thought in broad, international terms. The concept of a "Federation in Central Europe" was a cornerstone of his thinking from the time of Austria-Hungary until his death. He worked for such a federation for many years and in many ways. In these efforts, he was not only ahead of his time in terms of what nations were ready to do, he was also unique among Slovak leaders. The late Pavol Lukáč, the young historian who was, more than any other single person, responsible for the transfer of Grandfather Hodža's remains in 2002, suggests an interesting perspective:[28]

> If we were to borrow the terminology of psychology, we could say that Slovak politics was frequently "introverted." It was focused on internal problems, and its political initiatives did not cross the boundaries defined by its own territory. Hodža's political thinking, however, demonstrates that there was in our politics also an "extroverted" component, leading to a Slovak self-conceptualization in a wider Central European or European context and requiring us to understand internal problems in close relationship to the international and global situation.

Hodža was free to think whatever he wanted about international relations, but translating his ideas into action was another matter. In the corridors of Czechoslovak political power, Edvard Beneš jealously and effectively guarded international affairs as his own domain. And for those many Slovaks whose political views were "introverted," being a "cosmopolitan Slovak" in itself aroused great opposition. Recall the obituary written in the American-Slovak newspaper *Slovenská obrana* (*Slovak Defense*) when Grandfather Hodža died in 1944 (Chapter 5). It extolled him for his fight against the Magyars, but it would not accept his presence on the international stage:[29]

> . . . he wandered far as a politician and statesman of European stature, far beyond the boundaries of his narrower homeland with which he identified himself through his ancestry, but which was too small for his political vision and for his personal ambitions. If he had devoted his extraordinary capabilities exclusively to the interests of this homeland, he would have become a great historical figure not only for his nation but for the whole world.

In what ways did Grandfather Hodža "wander far as a politician and statesman of European stature, far beyond the boundaries of his narrower homeland," the side of his work that elicits such admiration today? His exact proposals evolved over the years, of course, but the core of his idea was a federation of states stretching from the Baltic Sea on the north to the Aegean Sea on the south.[30] These nearly a dozen states would initially be bound together by trade agreements, including the relaxation of customs barriers. Over time the federation would evolve toward a system of governance in which each participating state would yield a little of its sovereignty in favor of strengthening the whole. Such a system would bring together over a hundred million people living in a mix of agrarian and industrial economies and become powerful enough to stand up to the pressures of Germany on the west and Russia on the east.

Even though Hodža's vision was not realized at the time,[31] it has received renewed attention in this era of the European Union. He belongs squarely to a stream of visionaries who saw Europe's brightest future in some sort of federation.[32] During the years surrounding World War II a number of notable leaders put forth federalist ideas, among them Aristide Briand, the foreign minister of France, and Winston Churchill[33]. The first concrete step was the implementation of a plan put forth by Robert Schuman, the foreign minister of France, in 1950. The Schuman Plan created the European Coal and Steel Community.[34] Precisely as Hodža had envisioned, this was an organization based on shared economic interests—it created a common market (i.e. it removed customs barriers) for coal, iron, and steel. The administration included a governing higher authority, a common assembly, and an independent judiciary; to it member governments yielded some of their own sovereignty. The European Coal and Steel Community was the direct antecedent of the European Union.[35]

Hodža is rightly regarded as one of the thinkers who anticipated, and actively sought to implement, multi-national federation—the greatest transformation in European political organization since the rise of nationalism. He was prescient concerning its broad outline, and in the idea that its best foundation would be an economic one. Actual historical development, however, has differed significantly from Hodža's vision: federation initially took root among the largest, most highly industrialized countries of Western Europe, not among the smaller, and until recently much more agrarian ones, of Central Europe.

Many leading figures have honored Grandfather Hodža for these efforts, both in writing and in public events. I have a vivid personal memory of one such event. In 1954, when I was just finishing elementary school, the International Peasant Union[36] honored the tenth anniversary of Grandfather Hodža's death with a celebration at the Carnegie Endowment International Center in New York. Of course, my parents and I attended. We sat in seats of honor in the front row of folding chairs that had been set up for the many guests. A few feet in front of us was the podium, flanked by an American flag and a Czechoslovak flag. Speeches honoring various aspects of Grandfather Hodža's work were delivered by a succession of distinguished political leaders, most of them exiles from various countries of Central and Eastern Europe. I tried to pay attention to the proceedings, but this was really challenging for a boy not yet in high school. What did make an impression on me, however, was a special message sent by John Foster Dulles, who was then the American secretary of state and a man about whom I heard in the news almost every day:[37]

> I am happy to join in paying tribute to Milan Hodža. He was a statesman whose practical understanding of the interdependence of nations was far ahead of his time. He is honored today for his constructive contribution to the cause of European unity and international understanding. May his vision of a union of sovereign and equal peoples in free association for mutual security and greater prosperity continue to inspire freedom-loving men on both sides of the Iron Curtain.

These words from U.S. President Dwight Eisenhower's secretary of state have been quoted many times in books and articles about my grandfather. They have a special meaning for me, however. Whenever I encounter them, I see myself sitting in the Carnegie Endowment's ballroom, listening attentively as they were delivered for the very first time.

Milan Hodža wearing medals honoring his international efforts. c. 1936. Author's archive.

The Hodža family in their garden, c. 1923. Left to right: Fedor (Uncle Dišo), Grandfather Hodža, my mother, Grandmother Hodža, Aglaia (Aunt Gláša). Compare with the siblings as adults in New York, p. 100. Author's archive.

In the years after my mother died and I was caring for my father, I was at his apartment almost every day. I took care of his correspondence, paid the bills, did all the things that were impossible for him to do because of his near-blindness. During one such visit he handed me a small wooden box, unfinished, just a plain, nailed-together packing box the size of a big, thick book. "Open it," he said. "They're mementos of your grandfather." Inside, I found a whole array of silver and enamel medals, brightly-colored sashes, and ribbons such as generals wear on their chests. They were the insignias of national orders: the French Legion of Honor, the Order of the Italian Crown, the Yugoslav Order of the White Eagle, the Polish Order of Polonia Restituta, and the Romanian Order of Faithful Service. A little research showed that they were the highest honors bestowed by these governments on non-citizens. I have not been able to identify exactly on what occasions my grandfather was given these honors, but surely they represent the high esteem in which he was held on the international stage.

Grandfather Hodža was no wishy-washy saint. In a political world that was every bit as power-driven as is today's, he was ambitious and ready to "play hardball," as the American expression goes. He used his influence and his access to money to push his agenda. He did not hesitate to try to sideline his competitors. His opponents and competitors attacked him for perceived political intrigue and corruption. The attacks, whether behind the scenes or through proxy battles in the public press, were sometimes vicious. On two occasions he felt obliged to take his adversaries to court for libel; he won both of his cases. When he left France for England, he was shadowed by the secret police of the Beneš-led Czechoslovak government-in-exile. Anti-Hodža stories were spread about a propensity that has characterized powerful and charismatic men for centuries—extra-marital affairs. At least one of these stories was true, and the woman involved was exploited by the Beneš group in London in their efforts to sideline Hodža politically, to an extent that seems to justify the term blackmail.[38]

THE MORE I HAVE STUDIED MY GRANDFATHER, the more aware I have become of his real complexity. Many saw him as a stern, self-controlled man with a penetrating intellect and a drive to action who did not allow himself the luxury of feelings:[39]

> Even during the time of Austria-Hungary, Hodža never belonged to those who attributed a special significance to the outward manifestations of national life—songs, costumes, superstitions. His nationalism, from his early years to the end of his life, was founded on realism, on active work for his people, on the understanding of the actual conditions they faced, and on the ability to grasp every problem and to make a decision. "Feelings are little developed in Hodža," wrote his life-long friend and biographer Anton Štefánek, and

After the hair stylist, c. 1925. Left to right: my mother, Aunt Vierka Štetková, Grandfather Hodža. Author's archive.

then added: "With his word and his pen he appealed to the mind of a person, not to his feelings. He thought and worked very concretely, in an evolutionary way. He hated the romantic revolutionary."

Within the family, however, he was seen as the loving father. This shows in everything my mother ever said or wrote. It is also clear in the reminiscences of others. He was godfather to his nieces and nephews. He never forgot a birthday. They remember his attentiveness and kindness. Many of them lived with his family while they studied in Prague. He was generous and caring, and even overprotective, as my mother wrote in her diary (Ch.2) and my grandmother confirmed:[40]

> He showed extraordinary care for the family. When he got married, he was already thirty-one years old. He cared so much for the children that he was actually anxious. If even the slightest thing happened to one of them, he would go for the doctor even at midnight. It was a bit extreme. Once, when she was five years old, our oldest daughter, Irene [my mother], made her way behind the stove that was standing in the corner. She didn't know how to come out. There was a fire in the stove, and she started to get hot. Milan got scared and was just about ready to get the mason to knock down the stove. But I knew that, if the child could get in, she could also get out. And so we pulled Irene out, and the stove remained standing.

He remained the doting father his whole life, as many stories attest. For example, on the wall of Aunt Zorka's house in Martin hangs a photograph taken in the early 1920s, most likely when Grandfather Hodža was in his first term as minister of agriculture. My mother was in her early teens. Her hair had always been kept in long braids that hung down below her waist, but now she was begging her mother to let her cut the braids and have her hair styled in the fashion of the day. Grandmother Hodža was unrelenting. "Your only sign of beauty, and you want to get rid of it! " was her curt response. But Grandfather Hodža, who usually kept out of the running of the household, knew perfectly well what his oldest daughter was yearning for, and one day he decided to act. Quietly, without saying anything to his wife, he took his daughter and her cousin Vierka, who was staying with the family while studying in Prague, to a hair salon. The stylist's scissors went to work. Snip—long strands of hair fell to the floor. More snips, until nothing was left of the braids at all. A part suddenly appeared where the hair had previously been pulled straight back. Then some curls. Ready for a fashion magazine! And to commemorate the occasion, Grandfather Hodža took the two girls straight to his favorite photo studio to have a portrait taken of all three of them.

During the summer the family was usually to be found in their mountain villa in Lomnica, while Grandfather Hodža continued to work in Prague and came for occasional visits. Here is an intimate letter my mother wrote from Lomnica to her busy father in Prague, another moving testament to family love. The letter is dated July 1933, while Hodža was in his second term as minister of agriculture. He was trying to deal with the devastating effects of the Great Depression on Czechoslovakia's largest economic sector.[41]

Drahý tatuško, Dear Daddy,

. . . As a respectful daughter, I consider it my duty to let you know that on the 13th of May I became engaged to Janko Pálka. Perhaps you will think that I should have told you this long ago, but you have been so busy with your work that I didn't want to disturb you with my personal affairs during those brief moments when you were able to rest. And besides, Mommy has known about it for about half a year, and her views certainly did not encourage me to confide in you as well. . . .

I don't know how you will look at this. . . . I realize that there are some justified objections, but they are all external in nature. . . . I can't even imagine that a more beautiful relationship than Janko and I have could exist between two people. It is hard to talk about it, we have such a truly deep mutual understanding, a sincere friendship, complete trust, and significant similarities in our personalities. . . . It would really be a great loss to cloud this relationship in any way. I know my parents well enough to be certain that they would never intervene with force in such an important matter, where the whole future of their child is at stake. . . . But even a passive resistance, like Mother started, can really hurt. I would only ask that you should be satisfied with my choice, that you would welcome Janko as a son in the same way that the Pálkas have welcomed me as a daughter. . . .

The Pálkas also did not know anything until this June. It was moving to see how glad it made them. If you, my parents, could also feel at least a little joy! . . . I will go into the future with joyous hope and with full faith, and I ask you both not to undercut me but to be my support. . . .

So, Daddy, I hope that you will not be angry at me when you read this confession, and that you will write back with at least a few words. . . .

Kisses from your daughter,

Irča

Grandfather Hodža's response has been lost, but it must have been immediate. Just four days after my mother's first letter was sent from Lomnica all the way to Prague, she wrote again:

Tatko môj zlatý, Dearest Daddy,

I don't know how I can possibly thank you for your loving words! They have lifted a heavy weight from my heart. I will not forget this for the rest of my life. Only now is my joy complete and without a shadow. Thank you from the depths of my heart. Yes, this is the way I always imagined the love and understanding of a parent for his child. Thank you, but words are so weak and inadequate.

Your daughter,
Irča

My parents were engaged in 1933. They were not married until 1935, when Hitler's pressure on Czechoslovakia was increasing and just a half year before Grandfather Hodža became prime minister. The wedding reception took place in the large, immaculately kept garden of the Hodža villa in Prague where Grandfather Hodža so dearly loved to walk. Family and friends came from near and far. And my mother never forgot that when the newlyweds were leaving for their honeymoon, her father came to see her off at the train carrying a big bouquet of red roses.

Hodža's caring side was not reserved for his family. Here, for example, is Ján Ursíny's eye-witness description of Hodža delivering the eulogy for his arch-rival but long-time friend Andrej Hlinka in 1938, surrounded by thousands of Hlinka's followers many of whom considered Hodža to be a traitor to the Slovak cause. This is what Ursíny saw:[42]

. . . I was with Hodža in Ružomberok at Hlinka's funeral. Although he was not much given to emotion, there were moments during his speech when his voice wavered, he almost couldn't speak, and there were tears in his eyes. They had a relationship as fighters-patriots.

Evidently the unusual bond between Hodža and Hlinka was a reciprocal one. One day in 2005, when I was sitting in the office of the historian Jozef Jablonický (Chapter 32), a man unknown to me wandered in casually. We were never introduced properly, but he must have known who I was because after rummaging in some papers for a while he turned to me and said, completely out of the blue: "When Hlinka was dying, Hodža wanted to come and see him, but it didn't work out. My father-in-law was at Hlinka's side at the end. He told me that Hlinka's last words were, '*Povedzte Milanovi, že som ho mal rád.*' 'Tell Milan that I cared for him.'" I was stunned. The man at Hlinka's bedside had been Alexander Mach, later the propaganda minister of the war-time Slovak Republic and one of its leading theoreticians and most pro-Nazi officials. Even acknowledging that the exact words attributed to Hlinka may have been altered as the story was handed down for many years until Mach's son-in-law told it to me, I am inclined to believe the essence and to see Hodža and Hlinka as great leaders of great heart—as men who had very different personalities and who saw the issues of their times differently, but who saw each other with respect and, indeed, with great caring.

MILAN HODŽA WAS A DYNAMIC FIGURE all of his life, and that life was played out virtually exclusively in the public arena and often with great controversy. This was hard for the family, especially for Grandmother Hodža. Yet, listen a final time to her words about her husband:[43]

> He was a good man, a very good man. He never hurt people, not even in political life. He did not attack his opponents personally. He knew neither jealousy nor hatred. All this made him even greater for me. I am proud of the fact that even in exile, which weighed heavily on him and which became all the more difficult because of unwarranted attacks on him because of his views on the Czech-Slovak relationship, he defended his position on substantive grounds and never attacked at a personal level.
>
> Finally I want to say, that it is not easy to be the wife of a politically active man in such a small nation as we Slovaks are. It requires many personal sacrifices and often also financial deprivation. It is not easy, but it is a matter of pride and duty for every Slovak woman who marries a publicly active man to understand him and to support him in his work. I believe that I eased my husband's work for him. Now, that he is no longer with us, the pull for home is even greater. If God allows, we would like to transfer his remains to his native town of Sučany, the place where his dear mother is buried. And I, too, would like to spend the remainder of my life there at home, in our Slovakia, together with our children. Dear God, let this be.

And so the story that we began when Milan Hodža's remains were finally transferred home to his beloved Slovakia, fifty-eight years after his death, is now complete. We have looked back in time over some 250 years—from the era of the craft guilds in the Habsburg Empire; through repeated cycles of oppression, exhilaration, and exile; through personalities including humble peasants, craftsmen, leatherworkers, devoted churchmen, entrepreneurs, and some of the finest figures in Slovak history. I have been amazed to watch it develop in my own awareness, and grateful that I have been able to learn it and tell it. What remains is to recount how the story continues to unfold in Slovakia today.

PART III

MY SLOVAKIA TODAY

Part III returns to my own experiences. Since the fall of Communism, I have visited Slovakia often, and I relish the close family contacts, new friendships, echoes of the past, and hopes for the future that I have found there. From these many experiences I have once again focused on the stories of heroes, but I also tell about the place my father loved above all others. Through these stories, I offer you glimpses of what Slovakia means to me today.

CHAPTER 28

My Father's Place

For many reasons, returning to Slovakia is always an emotional experience for me. It is a country in which I am known in a different way than I am in the United States—not just as an individual, but as a member of a family that has a place in national history. When I engage with people and places that were important to my parents and grandparents, I feel a sense of connectedness with these earlier generations. Even my knowledge of the Slovak language, so widely admired, stirs emotions—I am deeply grateful that I have this knowledge, but also feel that I need to live up to expectations, and that is not always easy.

My life has been changed profoundly by my many encounters with my original homeland. For this reason I now offer you glimpses of today's Slovakia as I have experienced it, and hope that you will share with me some of my delight.

FOR MY FATHER, MIKULÁŠ and the surrounding region of County Liptov were always home, unambiguously home, no matter on what shore fate might have tossed him up (Map 3, Appendix II). It was beautiful, too, in his memory. Many have called it the most beautiful place in all of Slovakia. And for some, the beauty of Liptov and the fate of the Slovak nation have gone hand in hand. So Marína Hodža, savoring springtime in Mikuláš, wrote in her letter to Viliam Pauliny-Tóth on the first of May in 1862:[1]

> I have talked and written so much that I have quite forgotten everything else, until the buzzing of an irritating bee reminded me that I am in the garden. I had thought that I might be anywhere, but the bee reminded me that I am not in Budapest, or in Martin, but in the garden on a bench. Before my eyes I see everything greening, I see the nearby hills and groves, I hear the birds singing—everything reminds me that it is May! And then a thought appears, and without thinking I voice it aloud: Dear God, will May come soon for my nation? Or will December weather rule here forever? . . . And still, from time to time the gentle breeze of May is felt, the sun blazes

for a moment and melts the snows and warms us so that we will not freeze in the bitter winter. And maybe, maybe, we will sing some day: May is here! The snow and ice have melted!

Liptov is still beautiful, in May and all year round. The hills and mountains rise from the valley, their slopes dotted with dark groves of trees set among fields and meadows glowing gold in the afternoon sun. The peaks hold snow until June, the summer cloudbursts bring new life. The towns and villages have expanded, but they still nestle gently in the landscape.

MY OWN LIPTOV IS PARTLY FROM THE PAST. I have some vivid mental snapshots of life in Mikuláš after World War II—skating in front of our house, skiing over lunch break, setting up my electric train set, walking to school, playing in our back yard—but these memories are few and fragmentary, a handful of highlights emerging out of a wonderful but inchoate haze in which are blended true memories, photographs, and stories repeated until they feel like reality. I have, however, been given a great gift that has helped bring vague memories back into vivid light. For the past decade and more I have had a living link to my distant past and a guide to the living present: my neighbor and best friend from the days of my Mikuláš childhood, Ivan Rázus.

Ivan reentered my life thanks to a writer by the name of Milan Város. One of Város's main efforts has been tracking down and publicizing the stories of Slovaks who left home, mostly under difficult circumstances.[2] In 1995 he discovered that the grandson of Milan Hodža lived in Seattle, found a way to contact me, and arranged to interview me while we were visiting Bratislava.[3] Shortly thereafter, a fine article appeared in the weekly magazine *Život* (*Life*).[3] *Život* is a widely-read publication, and it reached the home of Ivan and his wife Viera. As it happened, Ivan was soon to travel to Alaska to see his daughter, who was working there as a physical therapist and who had studied at the University of Washington, where I was a professor in the Department of Zoology. She found my e-mail address and wrote to me, explaining that her father would be passing through the Seattle airport in about a week; he would love it if we could meet there!

The airport in Seattle is large and can be quite confusing, especially to one whose English is limited. Ivan also had to pass through immigration and customs, so the two-hour time he had at the airport shrank to almost nothing. I caught up with him as he was standing in line to board the flight to Anchorage. There we were, fifty years after we had last seen each other, sharing a few minutes in the midst of a crowd of strangers. Ivan had brought me a gift, a book from the library of his father, who had been the printer and bookbinder of Mikuláš.[4] It was a handbound copy of Grandfather Pálka's memoirs. Much of Chapter 23 is based on this volume. I have visited Ivan and Viera almost every year since then, and he has truly been my living link to the place from which my father sprang and which nurtured me, too, though for such a very short time.

MIKULÁŠ LIES IN A VALLEY CRADLED BY MOUNTAINS on the north and the south, broad in the middle but narrow at the western and eastern ends where the mountain ranges come close together. Pastures and cultivated fields dominate the view. Villages, towns, and cities lie scattered in the landscape, from the floor of the valley up to high mountain passes. The weather is formed by the mountains—blue skies, puffy clouds and thunderheads, frequent but brief rains, abundant snow in the winter, clear air, and a crispness that is rare in the lowlands by the Danube. A land of green and gold and blue, white in winter, punctuated by the red tile roofs of houses and cottages dating back centuries. Only the concrete block buildings of the Communist era and small clusters of advertising billboards introduce a jarring note.

The city sits in the middle of the valley, at the head of a huge reservoir (Liptovská Mara) created by damming the River Váh in the 1960s. Near the western end of the valley lies Ružomberok, the home of Andrej Hlinka and of Karol Salva's *Slovenské listy*. East of Mikuláš lies Važec, beloved of Ján Hála. South of Mikuláš, in the valley called Demänová, lie Slovakia's most famous limestone caves, further up the valley her largest ski area, Jasná. The mountains are criss-crossed by hiking trails, and ski touring is a demanding sport here, especially on the exposed and barren upper slopes. No wonder that the Slovak Hiking and Skiing Club, over which my father once presided, got its start here.

Old cities in Central Europe almost always have a central heart in which the great public buildings of the past were built, often around a square or in the nearby streets. So it is in Mikuláš. The square is bordered by two-story burgher houses dating back several centuries, now beautifully restored and brightly painted. At one end of the square is the town hall, at the other the magnificent gothic Church of St. Nicholas, Mikuláš's Catholic church (Plates 26, 27).[5]

On the west side of the city square is a two-story gothic building that I have come to know well and love dearly—the Museum of Janko Král'[6]. Named after one of Liptov's best-loved poets, it is a regional museum whose displays document ordinary life and major events in Mikuláš and nearby areas over a timespan of more than 500 years. Its main entrance is through a gracefully arched, cobbled passageway. To the right is the doorway to the main exhibit space, where one of the major displays is on leatherworking. Generations of Pálkas appear in this display, in personal photographs as well as accounts of their businesses.

Through the passageway, out the garden gate, through the small door that leads into an adjacent building, and up a steep spiral staircase—worn with age and built for people a foot shorter than we are today—are the back rooms of the museum. Here is housed the archive, stacks of acid-free museum boxes in which are stored letters, photographs, diaries, obituary notices, newspaper and magazine clippings—a trove of physical records relating to the families (including the Pálkas, Bellas, and Hodžas) and organizations that have shaped the city and the region. The generous staff of the archive have helped me with my research numerous times.

A FEW BLOCKS EAST OF THE SQUARE is the Lutheran church (Plate 21). This was my family's church, and I have been fascinated to learn something of its history.[7] With the onset of the Counter-Reformation, Lutherans were subjected to considerable oppression, as we saw in Chapter 14. Among the many things they were not permitted to do was to build churches. At best, they could meet in simple prayer rooms. In 1781, Emperor Joseph II issued his Edict of Toleration that relaxed many of these restrictions. The Lutherans of Mikuláš reponded promptly and constructed a new church on what was then the eastern edge of town. (Though the edict permitted Lutheran churches to be built, it forbade them from fronting on the square or on a main street.) They collected the funds, hand-built the church in just two years (1783-1785) and named it the "Toleration Church" in honor of the emperor's patent.

Like most Lutheran churches, the Toleration Church is as unprepossessing today as it was when it was built: tall windows without stained glass, the stucco exterior painted a pale yellow, the door plain wood, and inside simple wooden pews with no cushions and virtually no ornamentation. The pulpit, the baptismal font, and the altar in front of which M. M. Hodža stood in 1866 when he took his impassioned leave of his congregation are all original (Plate 23). I remember the altar from my childhood, especially its oval form. It is ornate, but there are no other decorations in the church, just memorial plaques to important church leaders.[8] On the outside, the entry is graced by the two larger-than-life statues that Janko Alexy fought so hard to have installed, Juraj Tranovský on the left and Michal Miloslav Hodža on the right (Chapter 20, Plate 22).

ALONG THE RIGHT SIDE OF THE SQUARE in front of the Toleration Church is the parish house in which M. M. Hodža and his family lived, set up now as a memorial to Tatrín under the aegis of the Museum of Janko Král'. Along the left side is an art gallery named after Peter Michal Bohúň, an extraordinarily fine painter who left a legacy of glowing, highly realistic portraits of many of the leading personalities of the period of the Slovak National Awakening and the Revolution.[9] In Bohúň's day the building was the Lutheran girls' elementary school of Mikuláš. Bohúň served there as a teacher while Michal Miloslav Hodža was the pastor; he taught most of the Lutheran girls of Mikuláš, including my great-grandmother Zuzana Bella. I was a student there too, though my time was limited to the second and third grade in 1948 and 1949. In the beginning I walked from home a few blocks away holding my mother's hand, still unsure of my place in this new setting. Once I became more comfortable, I just walked with my friend Ivan. We were in the last generation of students at the school, for under Communist rule church schools were abolished, and this eighteenth century building was given a new facade and, at Janko Alexy's urging. converted to its present use as an art gallery.

A number of the gallery's holdings have a special meaning for me. On the second floor hang Bohúň's portraits of Ondrej Pálka and his wife, Zuzana (Plates 18 and 19). Around the corner used to hang Bohúň's celebrated portrait of Michal Miloslav Hodža, reproduced in most books of Slovak history (Plate 20); it has now been returned to its institutional owner, the Slovak National Gallery in Bratislava. And the Bohúň gallery has a strong collection of paintings by Zolo Palugyay, Miloš Bazovsky, and Janko Alexy, my father's friends and companions on many excursions into the Tatras (Chapter 13).

THE PEOPLE OF MIKULÁŠ ALL HAVE THEIR FAVORITE SPOTS in the countryside, and Demänovská Valley, just to the south of the city, is one of the most popular. In a small area there are amazing limestone caves, opened to the public in the 1920s; trails for gentle walks through the forest of the valley floor; and Slovakia's greatest ski area, Jasná, rising in two stages from the valley to the crest of the Low Tatra Mountains.[10]

The Low Tatras are not craggy like the High Tatras, but the wind blows fiercely on their wide open slopes, the valleys fall deep between the peaks, the distances from shelter to shelter tax even the seasoned hiker, and storms can appear within minutes. It is grand hiking and ski touring terrain,[11] but the services of Mountain Rescue, in which Ivan served for many years both summer and winter, were organized for good reason. The slopes and valleys were also favorite haunts of my parents. When I was a boy they took me there, of course, especially into the caves where I saw stalagmites and stalactites and huge, fancifully ornamented natural columns for the first time.[11]

My father supported the construction of a hut in the upper reaches of the valley, alongside the small lake called Vrbické pleso. This was a project of the Slovak Hiking and Skiing Club (*Klub slovenských turistov a lyžiarov*), of which he was a long-time member and also an officer in the years before World War II. The hut served as a welcome base for skiers. Ski lifts were only a dream back then—gliding down meant first trudging up on the rudimentary equipment of the times. You only got one run a day!

Hut of Ján Pálka in Demänovská Valley, late 1930s. Archive of the Museum of Janko Kráľ, Liptovský Mikuláš.

My father's contribution to the construction of the hut was 20,000 Czecho-slovak crowns, then a very large sum, especially for a country still catching its breath after the ravages of the Great Depression. When the hut was completed and opened in the fall of 1938, the club named it the Hut of Ján Pálka (*Chata Jána Pálku*) in his honor. At some point it was renamed the Vrbica Hut (*Vrbická chata*). The new name too had a certain resonance, since the origins of the Pálka family were in the old village of Vrbica, now part of Mikuláš. Still later the hut became the home of the tavern Hell (*Peklo*) and was known by that name.

The story of the Hut of Ján Pálka has a sad ending. When I visited Ivan in 2009, he greeted me with a newspaper headline[12]: "*Pálkova aj Vrbická chata . . . sa sedemdesiatky nedožila*" (The Pálka or Vrbická hut . . . did not reach seventy). The wood of the hut had not been well maintained and was now damaged beyond any economically viable possibility of repair or reconstruction. After barely less than seventy years, the structure had been razed completely, and a new one was rising in its place. It echoes the style of the original, but those who knew the hut in its earlier days were not happy.[13]

ON FOUR DAYS IN JUNE THE VILLAGE OF VÝCHODNÁ, just off the main road some twenty miles to the east of Mikuláš, pulses with pent-up energy. For over fifty years now, singers and dancers representing towns and villages from all over Slovakia have come here to participate and compete in the largest of the country's numerous folklore festivals. There is no better place to see Slovakia's rich traditional culture on display.[14]

A procession through the village brings the performers to the amphitheater. On its two stages singers and dancers perform all day, in groups or solo. Off stage, impromptu singing is heard everywhere (Plates 29-32).

Children figure prominently in the festival at Východná, as well they should. How else but by the participation of children and youth, led by the example of adults of all ages, can a traditional culture survive in the face of television, video games, and a worldwide homogenization of musical styles? Janko Bulík's granddaughter, a former dancer herself, leads one of many such groups, and all three of her university-age sons perform. At Východná one feels that the crown jewels of the culture we have inherited from past generations are not only in skilled and loving hands, they are also being passed on to new generations who will hold them with equal enthusiasm and care.

North of Východná, in the direction of the rugged High Tatra mountains, lies one of the diminishing number of old-style sheep stations, a *salaš*. Not only do sheep graze here, but a range of products derived from sheep's milk is prepared.[16] They still have a prominent place in Slovak culture, as well as echoes in my own family. Hanging on the wall of my study is a beautifully carved wooden scoop, stained a dark walnut brown. On its outer surface the letters "J" and "P" are intertwined into a monogram in elegant relief. This scoop was given to my father by the employees of his factory as a wedding present, and it represents an aspect of the traditional culture of County Liptov. It is called a *črpák*, and it has only one use: to drink the first product of the fermentation of sheep's milk, called *žinčica*. A much-loved but short-lived drink, *žinčica* is traditionally only available at a *salaš*, and it is always drunk with a *črpák*, usually a larger but simpler one than my father's wedding gift. When Ivan once took me to drink *žinčica* at the *salaš* of Východná, he helped me experience yet one more facet of my father's place.

Still further east along the main highway is the village of Važec, my youthful father's favorite stopping place (Chapter 13). Hála's Važec burned to the ground in 1932. The village houses of today have sprung from the ashes of the old wooden cottages, and not many of their inhabitants till the fields any more—most of them commute to Mikuláš to work.

Hála is still present in Važec, however, although his voice is muted. His house is a gallery and museum,[15] and the old cottage in which he did all of his early work remains in the back, a reminder of what this village once was like. Unfortunately, in Važec there is also sad evidence of modern vandalism—all the paintings that were hanging in the Hála Museum were stolen some time ago. The museum was closed for several years while a new exhibit was prepared. It reopened in 2008, and visitors can once again see for themselves how a great heart, and skilled hand, portrayed the place that it loved more than any other.

IN ONE TRULY SPECIAL WAY, Mikuláš is a second home to me, for here is the house my parents built a few years after they were married and where they hoped to raise their family in the midst of the society they loved (Plate 28). It was a very modern structure for its day, designed by two of Czechoslovakia's premier architects.[16] After its confiscation by the Communist government in 1949, the house served a variety of purposes, including a nursery school; I have met many people who remember going there when they were children! For many years after the fall of Communism, it was the home of a support program for teens in trouble, The Pálka Center—Island of Hope. Today it once again belongs to our family, but it also serves Lutheran youth.

In her recollections of my mother, Aunt Vierka wrote about the early years of my parents' married life, describing them as the happiest they would ever experience, surrounded by fun-loving friends and having every prospect for a fine future.[17] These were the years my parents sought to bring back to life after World War II. They hired a landscape architect to make a design for the huge garden, and we sat around the dining room table while my mother explained all the symbols to me—how the architect had drawn in trees and bushes and flowers and an expanse of grass in the middle. The house was full in the autumn when everyone gathered in the kitchen to grind a spiced meat mixture directly into the prepared gut casings to make homemade sausages. Aunt Ludinka came from Bratislava and commandeered the kitchen to roast her coffee beans just before grinding them and making intensely black coffee in a copper coffee set from Turkey. Uncle Dušan came from Prague one time and encouraged me to be a composer like him. He gave me some lined paper on which I scribbled a few notes. When I was finished, he took my paper over to the piano where he played, so he claimed, the beautiful song I had just created. When Yvonne and I came to Mikuláš in 2009, for the first time in exactly sixty years I was able to sleep in this house.

SO THIS IS MY LIPTOV, MY INHERITANCE from my father, six decades and more after he had to leave it for good. There is still beauty in its landscape. Michal Miloslav Hodža is still a living presence. Traces of my father and the Pálka family are still to be found. I could not be born here, but I lay claim to the words of Peter Bella-Horal: "*Aká si mi krásna, Ty rodná zem moja*" (How beautiful you are, O land of my birth).

CHAPTER 29

Extraordinary Reminiscences

In June of 2005 I was sitting in a restaurant in Martin with my family, enjoying a meal after the most recent ceremonies honoring Grandfather Hodža (see Chapter 32), when my cousin Jelka pulled a letter out of her purse. "Here, Johnny," she said. "This is for you. The government secretary gave it to me earlier today."

The letter came from Mrs. Mária Klečková, who lived with her husband, Jozef, in the little village of Žiar, just to the north of Mikuláš. It was four pages long, written in a steady, clear hand, and it opened with a heart-warming story of childhood long ago:[1]

> Dear Family of Dr. Milan Hodža,
>
> Please forgive me, an 83-year-old woman, for sending you this letter. A few days ago I heard a radio interview with John Pálka, the grandson of Dr. Milan Hodža. In my memories I returned to my early childhood. I was ten years old when that wonderful, kind uncle [Milan Hodža] asked me to dance with him when I was a flower girl at the wedding of my sister, ten years older than I, who was marrying his personal secretary, Karol Folta. It was on the 8th of October 1932. . . .

In 1932 Grandfather Hodža was starting his second term as minister of agriculture of the Czechoslovak government and focused on helping pull the country out of the Great Depression. Despite his heavy commitments in Prague, he continued his way of suddenly appearing in people's homes and families and leaving behind lasting memories and important life changes. Imagine the distinguished minister of agriculture, vice-chairman of the powerful Agrarian Party and soon-to-be prime minister, freshly arrived from the far-away capital city, with all seriousness and courtesy asking the ten-year-old flower girl for a dance. A year later, when the young married couple's first child was born, Hodža came for the christening. The grateful parents named their son Milan in his honor.

Grandfather Hodža loved children, had great faith in young people, and held an unshakeable belief in the empowering value of education. He helped Aunt Mária's sister become a teacher and her older brother with his higher education in Prague. In fact, with Hodža's prompting all six siblings went on to obtain a higher education, something nearly unheard-of for Slovak families in their humble circumstances, as Aunt Mária's letter explains:

> My sister was a school teacher at a school that had been founded by Dr. Milan Hodža. He introduced this young teacher to her new profession with great ceremony because he considered it to be extremely important. In the eastern parts of Slovakia [where the family then lived] it was necessary to put forth great efforts to raise the educational level of the people. . . .
>
> He [would] show us children, and there were six of us, the right way through life in the form of stories. He emphasized that the greatest wealth is knowing the truth. "Education is the pinnacle of human happiness!" He was constantly establishing schools. He also found people, mainly young ones, to staff the schools, and for them he was an outstanding psychologist. . . .

Despite the many demands on his time, my grandfather came many times over the years to visit the family. Once, when Mária's school was holding a celebration, he came specially so that he could hear her recite a poem, which she knew perfectly to the end of her life. Her Uncle Milan was, as she wrote, her first teacher:[2]

> Forgive me for writing to you in this way, but the recollections of my childhood are stronger than my will, especially when I can write to you as a thank-you to your grandfather. After all, he was my first teacher, before I ever sat at a school desk. I was delighted when he told stories to us children. Today, I know that he made them up himself, because they always related directly to our mischief. He knew everything we had been up to. He corrected us through his stories.

Aunt Mária's letter has almost a fairy-tale quality, with Grandfather Hodža a kindly prince, arriving on his charger and making everything right! But it also portrays a period of Slovak history that was genuinely full of opportunity and hope for the future. Yes, Slovakia was backward in many ways, and there were ongoing internal struggles for its rightful status within the Republic of Czechoslovakia. Successive economic crises deeply affected many people. Nevertheless, under the First Republic of 1918-1938 there were previously unheard-of resources to address economic, social, and educational problems, and there was political freedom such as Slovaks had never before experienced. Despite serious issues, the future looked very bright.

However, within a painfully short time tragedy struck. By the spring of 1939 Czechoslovakia was no more, and Hitler's power could be felt everywhere. My family was driven into exile, and Aunt Mária's family was forced to leave Eastern Slovakia and return to their original home in County Liptov, where they spent the war years. Following World War II, after hardly a breath of peace and normalcy, came Communism. In Aunt Mária's words:[1]

> The most fateful year of my life was 1949. They [the Communists] arrested my sister and her husband, the couple at whose wedding Dr. Milan Hodža danced with me. . . . The parents were convicted of treason. Karol [Karol Folta, the father] had three brothers in the U.S.A. with whom he corresponded. Trained by Dr. Hodža, he had a different world view than the political masters of the day. He was a representative of the Democratic Party and yearned for the nations of Europe to be united; he was ahead of his time. The court's sentence (I was in the courtroom) was death by hanging, and for his wife death by firing squad. (I fainted, my baby was born prematurely, but she is alive and is a grandmother, and I a great-grandmother.)

The arrest and death sentence had international repercussions. On November 9, 1949, *The New York Times* and *The London Times* reported Folta's arrest.[3] On January 2, 1950, numerous newspapers including both *The London Times* and *The New York Times* reported the death sentence. Karol's three brothers lived in Minneapolis, Minnesota, where they were personal friends of Hubert Humphrey, one of Minnesota's two senators and later a Democratic candidate for the vice-presidency. Humphrey intervened on Folta's behalf with the Czechoslovak ambassador in Washington.[4] The ambassador coolly replied that he had been unable to do anything, because he received Humphrey's appeal on January 3, but Folta had been executed on January 1.[5]

The suave ambassador was wrong, for the death sentences had been commuted. However, the fates of Folta and his wife were horrific:[1]

> For a year they were on death row. After a year his sentence was changed to life imprisonment and his wife's to 30 years, since she had their son Milan to care for. My brother-in-law served 15 years, my sister 10 years and 3 months. Both had cancer. The authorities sent them home to die at their request and perhaps also under

diplomatic pressure from the U.S.A. I cared for their son myself. Our parents died before their time from grief.

Milan's wish to be with his parents forever was fulfilled on the 31st of March of this year. I placed his urn in his parents' grave. My parting with my nephew, whose heart was full of love for God and for other people, inspired me to write you this letter. Please excuse me!

With all best wishes,

Mária Klečková née Baranová

WITH THIS LETTER BEGAN AN OCCASIONAL CORRESPONDENCE, a sharing of family stories, an exchange of greetings at Christmas. More details emerged.[6] Not only had Karol Folta been Grandfather Hodža's secretary, later he was involved in one of the secret anti-Nazi organizations operating within the World War II Slovak Republic. At one point the group was betrayed and he was arrested, together with Jozef Lettrich and a number of others. When Folta was released, he became active in organizing the Slovak National Uprising. At the end of the war, he was a member of the expanded Slovak National Council and an official of the Democratic Party. Like so many others, this dedicated Slovak patriot was part of Grandfather Hodža's legacy to the fight against the Nazis.

After the coup of February 1948, the Communists tried to persuade Folta to join the party.[7] When he refused, the persecution began. His business was confiscated, and he felt his life was in danger. Like us, he succeeded in escaping to America, but he had to leave his family behind. Later, he made a desperate attempt to get them out. He arranged for guides to take his wife and his son, Milan, across the border. Folta himself returned from America to meet them at the barbed wire. Imagine him crawling forward from the woods on the Austrian side, ready to take his beloved wife and son by the hand to freedom. Instead, the worst fear of all escapees was fulfilled—he was betrayed. Instead of his family he was met at the border by the ŠtB. Subsequently his wife, as well as his two brothers, were also arrested. When the death sentences of the Foltas were commuted to long prison terms, they were assigned to forced labor in the uranium mines. The radiation to which they were exposed in the mines is the likely cause of the cancer they both contracted. The secret police followed the entire family until the fall of Communism in 1989.

DESPITE SPENDING HALF OF HER LIFE under the oppressive and also aggressively atheistic Communist regime, Aunt Mária was an intensely devoted Lutheran, even a mystic. In one of her letters to me she described visions she had during a near-death experience, when her heart failed one day during a church service.[2]

> It was Sunday. I was in church, sitting in my favorite place from which I had a good view of both the altar and the pulpit. Next to me was my son, a urologist; his wife, an internist; and my favorite grandson. We stood to listen to the word of God. . . . My eyes went cloudy and I fell under the pew. I did not know that I had fallen; rather I felt that I was flying over a beautiful, indescribable land, illuminated with a warming light in all the colors of the rainbow. I felt good, blissful. I heard festive singing. . . .

> I saw myself as a young girl who was standing by a large cross and wanted to stroke the feet of Lord Jesus, but I couldn't reach and started to cry. The cross stood not far from the railway hut in which my father worked as a dispatcher. There he met with your grandfather [Milan Hodža]. They understood each other very well. They wanted to build a new world. A world of peace, truth, and joy, so that we children would feel safe and happy in such a world. Both of them were very watchful, responsible. My brother-in-law joined them, as the personal secretary of Dr. Hodža. He left, troubled. Then I saw that he was being led to the gallows. I felt pain and asked for mercy. The gallows turned into a cross. . . .

The letter continues for several pages, the words of a woman whose deep Christian faith sustained her for a lifetime, and whose life was touched deeply by her contact with Grandfather Hodža many decades ago.

In 2006 I met Aunt Mária in person. Žiar is only a few minutes by car from Mikuláš. Even though it is a tiny village, addresses are not always easy to recognize, and it took Ivan and me some time to find their house. We were greeted by her husband of more than sixty years, Jozef, a retired engineer and professor. Their son, the urologist; his wife, the internist; and their son, Aunt Mária's favorite grandson, were with us. Sitting together we spent several happy hours telling family stories, mostly from the distant past. We walked through their wonderful garden, which was glowing with spring flowers. When we parted, Aunt Mária gave me a gift, a notebook that is part of the spiritual journal she kept year after year since her youth. She kissed me, and I felt as if I had been blessed by a saint.

In 2008, Aunt Mária died. I will always treasure her letters, true testimonials to the human side of Milan Hodža and to the strength of the human spirit even under the worst of circumstances.

CHAPTER 30

A Hero from the Lower Lands

Experiences of World War II came up often in the conversations of my childhood. We might be talking after dinner, just my parents and I, or there might be a group of Slovak friends who had come to visit, and reminiscences would naturally start to come forth. Many times, I remember, one of my parents would start a story with the phrase, "*nebohý Janko Bulík*" (the late Janko Bulík), and a faint hush would pass through the room. Not that people would actually stop talking, but for a moment there was a distinct, though ineffable, feeling of respect or awe that even a child like I, who knew nothing about Janko Bulík, could sense. Now, I think I understand the reason for this hush.

MEMBERS OF THE BULÍK FAMILY were among the prominent citizens of Kovačica, one of the major Slovak settlements in the Lower Lands (Appendix III), from the time of its founding.[1] Janko Bulík was brought up in an atmosphere of Slovak national self-awareness, and he carried this sense of Slovak pride all his life. Simultaneously, after the establishment of Yugoslavia following World War I, he was a genuine Yugoslav patriot. As a young man he was an outstanding athlete—he held the Yugoslav national record in the 100-meter dash and was slated to represent his country at the 1924 Olympics until an injury forced him to withdraw. Later, he was an officer in the Yugoslav army.

By the 1930s Bulík had become a prominent political leader in the Slovak community in Yugoslavia. In 1934 he was invited to speak on behalf of Slovaks at the Day of Czechs and Slovaks Living Abroad (*Deň zahraničných Čechov a Slovákov*) held at the Czechoslovak parliament. Here is part of what he said:[2]

> Slovaks today number around 3,400,000 souls. Of this number, only about 2,300,000 live in Czechoslovakia. Nearly a third, 1,100,000, live beyond the country's borders, scattered around the world. This fact testifies to the difficulties faced by the Slovak nation in the past. Poverty and oppression resulted in a mass exodus from Slovakia, so much so that Slovak patriots feared that the Slovak nation would bleed to death.

But behold, Providence decreed that in the defining moment, when freedom was taking birth and the Czechoslovak Republic was being formed, it would be precisely this part of the Slovak nation, living beyond the borders, that would decide the nation's fate. It became the spokesman of the whole nation, and contributed the most in blood and treasure to national liberation. This was true first and foremost of American Slovaks....

The nation represents a greater value than does the state, because states come and go according to the distribution of power, but the nation lasts forever. The Czechoslovak Republic did not create the Czechoslovak nation. Just the opposite, all parts of the nation, scattered around the world, with their joint efforts created the CzechoSlovak Republic....

He had an unshakeable sense of loyalty to his Yugoslav homeland, but he was true to his Slovak roots and to the new Czechoslovak Republic, and he worked tirelessly to nurture the bonds between the two.

Janko Bulík's activities and interests were many.[3] He was a successful lawyer. He led the establishment of *Matica Slovenská* in Yugoslavia and was its first president. He was active in the administration of the Lutheran church. He helped establish Slovak schools, notably the great gymnasium in Petrovec (Appendix III). And, he had strong ties to Milan Hodža.

Hodža had quite a following among the Slovaks of Yugoslavia[4], partly because of his historic elections from Kulpín in 1905 and 1906, but particularly because of his leading role in the agrarian movement. The Slovak farmers of Yugoslavia were progressive in their outlook on agriculture, and they were eager for technical information, new varieties of seeds, improved machinery, banks that would serve their needs, and so forth. All this had been integral to Hodža's efforts from the beginning, and he maintained significant popular support in the distant Lower Lands even through World War II. Bulík was a leader in this regional agrarian movement, giving public talks in the Slovak villages and meeting with local groups of farmers. He saw in Hodža the leader who best understood and addressed the needs and aspirations of Slovak farmers, whether in Slovakia or in the Lower Lands.

WITH THE RISE OF NAZI GERMANY, Bulík became a dedicated anti-fascist, and he was well-placed to put his political views into action.[5] His entire education, including law school in Belgrade, had been in Yugoslavia. Many of his fellow students and close friends were now in positions of authority in the government, and he drew upon these connections with skill and courage. Bulík's law office became the hub of the anti-Nazi activities of Slovak and Czech exiles in Yugoslavia. He helped them with financial support, lodging, and the vital official permission to stay in the country. He also helped large numbers of Jewish refugees, especially from Prague, travel through Yugoslavia en route to Israel. A personal introduction or well-placed telephone call from Bulík overcame many obstacles that no newcomer from Czechoslovakia, particularly a Jew, could possibly have dealt with on his own. Bulík undertook all this at great personal risk; the pro-Nazi elements in the Yugoslav government were strong.

Bulík helped both Slovaks and Czechs, and he helped supporters of both Hodža and Beneš.[6] He was unhappy about the ethnic, political, and sometimes religious divisions that existed in the resistance efforts of the exiles. However, his own primary allegiance he gave to Hodža. He saw Hodža as the greatest Slovak leader of the time, and he felt that the Slovak ex-prime minister Hodža should stand on equal footing with Czech ex-president Beneš in the shared fight against the Nazis. To this end, Bulík traveled several times to Paris to deliver materials to Hodža and take messages from him back as far as Prague. Both in Prague and in Slovakia Bulík helped organize the faction of the resistance that was led by and loyal to Hodža.[7] He was so deeply involved in the resistance that he finally closed his law office in Belgrade and moved to Kovačica. He buried a large number of documents relating to the resistance in a hiding place on the family property; they were retrieved after the war by a unit of the Czechoslovak military.[8]

It was in this context that Janko Bulík escorted my mother out of Slovakia just before my birth and secured for my father the forged Yugoslav passport that we depended on so heavily while we moved from place to place in France (Chapters 2 and 3). And it was likewise in this context that Vladimír Žuffa and my father visited with the Bulík family in Kovačica many weekends in 1940, including the memorable Easter Sunday described in Žuffa's memoirs and recorded in the photographs that haunted me for so long (Chapter 13). My parents were forever grateful to Janko for the help that he gave them. The way they spoke about him, however, conveyed more than simple gratitude. The story that follows, I believe, explains why.

IN 1941, JANKO BULÍK WAS BETRAYED by a double agent and arrested in Belgrade by the German secret police.[9] The Gestapo then went to Kovačica, marched into the Bulík house, and, while looking for documents, wrecked it. They tore apart the furniture, took up floorboards, and carted away all of the books in Bulík's large library. Whatever papers they could find, they confiscated, including the several passports Bulík had used in his secret activities. Thereafter, his family had to report at Gestapo headquarters every day.

Bulík himself was held and interrogated first in Belgrade. When he refused to reveal anything about the resistance or the people involved in it, he was sent to Prague where more "skilled" interrogators dealt with him. We have an eyewitness account of what this meant:[10]

> They interrogated him twice every day. Day after day. They were obviously not satisfied with his responses, because after every interrogation they forced him to carry a heavy rock up and down the closely guarded stairs to the top floor of the building. He carried it until he collapsed.

> They used a special Gestapo whip on him. . . . When he finally collapsed unconscious, or if he hesitated despite the whip, they carried off his body like a sack, threw him on the cement floor, sprayed him with cold water, and threw him freezing into his cell.

> But Janko Bulík kept silent. The proof is that nobody was ever arrested on the basis of his testimony. Not in Slovakia, not in the Czech lands, not in Yugoslavia—nowhere were his words used against even a single person who was interrogated by the Gestapo or by a state inquisitor. . . .

They could not break Bulík in Prague, so they shipped him off to Mauthausen. According to bland official records, he died there of pneumonia on January 30, 1942, not long after his arrival. Prison records, however, were routinely falsified for political convenience—many Jews who were known to have been killed in the gas chambers were similarly listed as dying of pneumonia. The reports that reached the family about what really happened to Bulík in Mauthausen are sketchy but consistent.[11]

On the edge of exhaustion and imminent death himself, Janko had the nerve to protest to the authorities about the inhuman treatment of prisoners he saw all around him. He was repeatedly tortured to extract information about his resistance activities, but he again refused to give any meaningful information or to betray anyone. In frustration, the German authorities had him thrown to a pack of trained attack dogs who tore him to pieces. This, I believe, is why I always felt a fleeting hush in the room when my parents spoke about *nebohý Janko Bulík*, the late Janko Bulík.

The story of Janko Bulík is not very widely known; you will find it only in a few of the books devoted to the resistance and the Slovak National Uprising, and now in the proceedings of a symposium held in his honor in Kovačica. Nonetheless, his heroism has received some important public recognition: In

1992 he was awarded the Order of Tomáš Garrigue Masaryk by President Havel, and a memorial has been placed in his honor in the Slovak National Cemetery in Martin. In my eyes he is a true hero, and this national recognition is the minimum that is owed him.

THERE IS MUCH MORE TO TELL. Remember the photograph (page 126) taken in front of a village house in Kovačica—adults in back, and in the front a young boy standing proudly with his pistol? This boy was Janko Bulík's son, ten years old at the time. In 2005 I was sitting with the historian Jozef Jablonický (Chapter 32, Plate 40) at the Slovak Academy of Sciences in Bratislava, talking about his area of expertise, the Slovak resistance in World War II. I was trying yet again to find clues about my father's activities in the resistance. From Jablonický I discovered that Janko Bulík's son, then in his seventies, was living in Eastern Slovakia! I tracked down his telephone number and arranged to visit him in the little town of Pozdišovce, on the outskirts of Michalovce in far eastern Slovakia, not far from the Ukrainian border. He welcomed me with open arms and told me story after story, both about his father and about himself.

He was named after his father, Ján, and was known to everyone as Jano. As a child Jano had lived with the family in Kovačica, because his mother had died in childbirth and his father was working in his law office in Belgrade and among the Slovak villagers of the region. With his father's death in Mauthausen, Jano was orphaned. After the war, a group of the men with whom his father had worked closely in the resistance, and all of whom we have met before (Janko Lichner, Jozef Lettrich, Ján Ursíny, Vladimír Žuffa, and my own father), were convinced that Janko Bulík would have wanted his son to seek a new life in Czechoslovakia. With the family's permission, they smuggled Jano from Serbia to Slovakia, disguising him as a deckhand on a freighter traveling up the Danube. Once he had been gotten safely into Slovakia, he was well taken care of, living with the Žuffa family and others in Bratislava.

Jano told me this story in some detail as we sat together on a couch in his living room. Suddenly, with a glint in his eye, he asked me, "Did you know that your father wanted to adopt me?" Grinning from ear to ear, he went on to tell me the story. My father cared for Jano deeply and tried to persuade him to accept adoption into the Pálka family, which would have brought him many immediate advantages. However, being an independent-minded young man by this time and just getting settled in his new country, Jano declined. Just before our family escaped in 1949, my father urged Jano to come with us across the border to freedom, but again he declined. After we were settled in New York, my father tried a third time, offering to find a way for Jano to escape and join us, but he declined yet again. He preferred to stay at home, where he went to medical school, married, raised his children (all of whom I have met), and practiced medicine for the rest of his life.

I am an only child. My parents lived through great adversity and did their best to shield me from the worst they had experienced, in part by simply not talking about it. But some of what they did not tell me would have thrilled me. In my sixty-sixth year, long after my parents' deaths and following the lead of just a handful of photographs in a family photo album, I discovered from Jano Bulík that I very nearly had an adoptive brother, the son of a hero whose very name brought a faint and fleeting hush to my parents' conversations.

JANO BULÍK HAD ONE MORE SURPRISE FOR ME. Plans were starting to be made for a big celebration in Kovačica, commemorating the life and work of Kovačica's greatest hero, Janko Bulík.[12] Jano would arrange for me to be invited to attend as an honorary participant.

Naturally, I was thrilled when the invitation came, and I made a special trip to Slovakia for the occasion (Plate 42). The Bulík family were driving on their own from Pozdišovce, while I joined a sizeable group of other Slovaks at our rendezvous point, the main bus terminal in Bratislava. We loaded into a small caravan of cars and vans and set out on our seven-hour journey across the rolling Hungarian plain.

I had expected Kovačica to be a picture-book village, with wooden cottages and narrow, winding lanes. Not so. Kovačica was planned and built as a town, with wide, tree-lined streets arranged in a grid pattern.[13] Most of the houses are of masonry construction, ranging from modest to grand. The population has been around 7,000 for a long time and is still predominantly Slovak. The language of instruction in the public schools is Slovak, and the local radio station broadcasts mostly in Slovak. The economy is based on agriculture, but it is supplemented by the earnings of hundreds of women who work as housekeepers in Belgrade, about an hour away by train. There is a thriving artistic culture including a music school for the children. The many fine Kovačica painters, who have developed a distinctive primitivist style, are famous throughout southeastern Europe and even show in Paris. The town center of Kovačica teems with galleries and museums showing their work.

We were lodged with local families and treated to all of our meals. Dinners started around ten o'clock in the evening, after the day's events, and went on until well past midnight. One of Kovačica's several folk music ensembles always played. I knew many of their songs from my own childhood and could happily sing along with everyone else.

THE CENTRAL PART OF EACH DAY was a scholarly symposium at which facets of Bulík's life were explored.[14] The session was opened and closed by singers from Kovačica's Lutheran church, mostly singing *a capella* so their beautiful voices could be heard in all their purity. They sang wonderful church hymns, but it was their final song that will always sound within me.

When I was very little, probably not more than four, my mother taught me a simple song that began with these words:

> *Po nábreží, koník beží, koník vraný,*
> *Skadial' že si, šuhajíček, mal'ovaný,*
> *Skadial' som, stadial' som,*
> *Slovenského rodu som,*
> *Duša moja.*

> Along the riverside a black horse runs,
> Where are you from, my handsome lad,
> Wherever I am from, there I come from,
> A Slovak by birth am I,
> My beloved.

I had sung this song, all of its verses, hundreds of times in my life, especially while my parents were still alive. Now I heard it performed by two sisters with bell-like voices of the greatest purity, in remote Kovačica, at the end of a full day of lectures about my family's hero, Janko Bulík. Before I knew what was happening, everyone stood and started to join in. I, too, sang, but only a little because I was struggling to hold back tears. We stood because, I later discovered, *Po nábreží, koník beží*, this simple folk song, had been adopted long ago by *Matica slovenská* as its hymn, and an audience always stands out of respect. The hymn was being sung that day because the day's lectures had been devoted to Janko Bulík, and Bulík was the founder of *Matica slovenská* in Yugoslavia in the early 1930s. As the sisters sang, and all of us with them, I did not know this history. I only felt my mother with me once again, and the tenderness with which she made sure that I would not forget.

THE CELEBRATIONS CLOSED ON A SUNDAY with services in the Kovačica Lutheran church. Early that morning, throughout the town people were streaming in the direction of the church, the men in suits, most of the women in traditional village dress, and all of them carrying in their hands hymnals that contained, I realized, a score of hymns written by Michal Miloslav Hodža. I made a point of arriving earlier than these crowds so I could spend some quiet time in the church. This was the very church in which my father and Vladimír Žuffa had received communion when they stayed with the Bulík family at Eastertime of 1940 (Chapter 13). Of course I yearned to see it.

The church of Kovačica is huge, much larger than I had expected. When I entered, sunlight was streaming in through the tall windows, flooding the interior so that the dark wood of the pews glowed in the morning light. It was almost empty then, so I was able to walk around the vast inner space without disturbing anyone. I felt as if I had reached the goal of a personal pilgrimage. I was now in the very place where my father had been nearly seventy years ago, separated from his family and newborn son and in danger of his life. I saw the pulpit from which Pastor Janiš had delivered his homily on the self-sacrifice of Slovak resistors. I stood at the altar rail where my father and his companions had knelt while receiving that Good Friday communion. Once the church began to fill, I sat in one of the pews, closing my eyes to more fully experience the poignancy of this moment. Suddenly, a voice from behind me cut through my reverie as a man called out, "Let us sing hymn number. . . ," and then filled in some number. He sounded the note, and the congregation, close to a thousand people, began to sing in full voice. When the hymn ended, another man stood and called out another number, and the congregation sang again until the very walls seemed to shake. So it went until the organ sounded the Introit to mark the beginning of the service itself. This was the wonderful old way of gathering for worship, rarely to be found in the twenty-first century.

JUST BEFORE OUR DEPARTURE FROM KOVAČICA, there was an informal buffet luncheon. When the meal was finished and most people had left, I noticed one of the organizers of the celebration helping to clear a table and singing to himself. The song sounded familiar, so I walked over to where I could better hear it. He was singing "Išiel som od milej" (I went from my sweetheart's house), a waltz that was written in Prague by my uncle Dušan Pálka and was, among all his compositions, one of my favorites. I joined in, and the organizer and I sang together to the end of the song. I asked him how he had come to know it, and he replied that it was part of his repertoire of Slovak folk songs. It delighted me to realize that Uncle Dušan's waltz had taken root so deeply in Slovak culture that, even in the outpost of Kovačica, it was perceived as simply a part of the folk tradition.

With the luncheon over, we visitors from Slovakia went to our waiting van and cars, the folk musicians gathered once again to play and sing farewell, and we set out for Bratislava with our hearts filled to overflowing. As for me, the Lower Lands had become a reality rather than a place in my imagination; a vital chapter in my father's life story had come alive in a way I had never dreamt it could; and Janko Bulík, an almost mythic hero to our family, had started to feel like a person I once had known myself.

CHAPTER 31

Ján Langoš and The Institute of the Nation's Memory

For forty years under Communism, secrecy ruled. Secret agents were everywhere, ready to report on their fellow-citizens. Interrogations and court proceedings were carried out in secret. World events were reported only through the filter of the Communist Party, otherwise they were kept secret. History was rewritten to suit Communist ideology, and anything not approved for publication by the censor remained secret. Parents kept their memories and their political views secret from their children for fear that they might inadvertently be revealed in school and result in punishment, expulsion, or worse (Chapter 9).

After freedom dawned, it was natural for people to want to peer into the dark corners of the past and reconstruct the life stories of their parents and their loved ones, and even their own stories, which they might never have fully comprehended. This was not a matter of just personal curiosity. Rather, the whole society had a need to come to terms with the secret actions of the past.

To that end, the government of Slovakia established the Institute of the Nation's Memory, *Ústav pamäti národa* (ÚPN). This stark and direct statement proclaims the ÚPN's mission:[1]

> [It is] the obligation of our state to make available the secret activity of repressive [state] organs during the period of unfreedom, 1939-1989, and to assign responsibility for the subjugation of the nation; murders; enslavement; robbery and humiliation; moral and economic decline accompanied by judicial crimes and terror toward the holders of dissenting views; the destruction of traditional principles of property law; misuse of upbringing, education, science and culture for political and ideological purposes; all this

as the expression of our conviction that he who does not know his past is destined to repeat it, and that illegal actions by the state against its citizens must not be protected by secrecy and must not be forgotten. . . .

THE BASIC SOURCE OF INFORMATION about the subversion of traditional values and processes for the ideological purposes of the state during the Communist period is the voluminous but nevertheless incomplete archive of the State Security, *Štátna Bezpenosť* (*ŠtB*). This archive contains reports by paid agents, by volunteer informers, and by state prosecutors; transcripts of depositions obtained during interrogations; confiscated materials; records of court proceedings; correspondence—altogether, a mind-numbing collection of physical evidence demonstrating how the unchallenged power of the state was directed against its citizens.

Of singular interest today is the identity of those who served the ŠtB. The ÚPN has published numerous lists of informers and agents at all levels, and these lists contain the names of many hundreds of people who are prominent in public life today—in business, in politics, in education and in both the Catholic and the Lutheran church. It is not always clear whether the actions recorded in the archive were taken out of personal conviction, for personal gain, or under threat. What is undeniably clear is that the ŠtB penetrated society completely, and that no one was safe from its prying eyes and ears. Further, it is clear that those who, for whatever reason, served the ŠtB are part of today's Slovakia. More than a few of these agents and informers of the past now hold public positions requiring public trust. After the ÚPN's lists were published, some resigned, some claimed that the lists were inaccurate, and others conceded that they had worked for the ŠtB but asserted that their actions were harmless or coerced. This issue of agents and informers is alive in each of Central Europe's post-Communist nations, be it Hungary, Poland, the Czech Republic, or any other. The pervasive legacy of Communism cannot be eradicated in one generation.

In such a situation it is not surprising that there were many obstacles to the establishment of the ÚPN. In the year 2000, then President Rudolf Schuster vetoed the enabling legislation. Formerly a high-ranking Communist official himself, he argued that the intended public disclosures would open old wounds and inadvertently strengthen the contemporary Communist Party. The parliament overrode his veto by the overwhelming vote of eighty-two to ten, and in 2002 (the year of the ceremonial transfer of Grandfather Hodža's remains) the Institute of the Nation's Memory, the ÚPN, was finally established.

A POLITICAL STEP SUCH AS THIS, facing the determined efforts of entrenched interests to derail it, must have equally determined proponents. One man in particular stood behind the creation of Slovakia's ÚPN—Ján Langoš.[2] He was born in 1947, the year before the coup that brought the Communists into power for just over forty years. Thus, Langoš grew up entirely under a system that was designed to blunt any sense of individual political freedom or responsibility. By training he was a physicist, and he could easily have kept to a narrow professional track. He was, however, one of those who refused to close their eyes to the realities of the Communist system and one of those who were never intimidated. For many years he belonged to the intellectual anti-Communist underground, taking part in the publishing of illegal writings known as *samizdat*, and for this he was interrogated by the ŠtB. A lifelong devout Catholic, he also worked with the Catholic underground. He joined the revolutionary movement *Verejnost' proti násiliu* (Public against Violence) that in Slovakia led the struggle to bring Communism down. After the Communist dictatorship fell, Langoš became free Czechoslovakia's first minister of the interior. This was the ministry under which the secret police operated and, backed by progressive legislation, the new minister immediately set about ridding the new system of its old agents.

With the dissolution of Czechoslovakia in 1993, Langoš became the chairman of Slovakia's reconstituted Democratic Party, the successor to the party forged during the resistance movement during World War II primarily by men who had gotten their start in political life under the influence of Milan Hodža. He served in the Slovak parliament. He wrote the statute that laid the ground for the ÚPN, and in 2003 he became its first director. Under his leadership, the ÚPN became among the most open and effective of such organizatons in post-Communist Central Europe. In a few short years the institute catalogued its vast holdings of documents from not only the Communist era but also the Slovak Republic of World War II; made this catalogue available on the internet; devised a procedure for releasing the documents to family members and appropriate research workers; and, most controversially, published the lists of ŠtB agents and informers so that the whole of Slovak society could know through whom the tentacles of state power had penetrated into their private lives. It is a remarkable accomplishment, and bringing it about took, above all, tremendous courage.

IN 2005 I SUBMITTED A REQUEST to the ÚPN for the release of any documents pertaining to Grandfather Hodža, Grandmother Hodža, my father, my mother, or myself. After all, my grandparents and my parents had been under the close scrutiny of both the totalitarian regime of World War II and the Communist regime thereafter, with Grandfather Hodža convicted of treason by the Slovak Republic and my father jailed by the Communists, so there had to be relevant documents sitting somewhere. As for myself, I wondered whether my name might not have been picked up from the interviews I did as a child with Uncle Miško Múdry on Radio Free Europe, or during our family visit in 1976. In due course I received a formal letter, signed by Ján Langoš himself, explaining that a search of the ÚPN archives had revealed only documents pertaining to my father, and that those would now be released to me.

I was scheduled to pick up a copy of these documents on June 16, 2006, and because this entailed meeting with a specific member of the small ÚPN staff, my cousin Irča and I went one day early to confirm the appointment. The office of the ÚPN was located in the middle of bustling Bratislava, along one edge of the Square of the Slovak National Uprising, in the middle of a row of nondescript, semi-modern office buildings. There was a sign above the door that read simply *Ústav pamäti národa*, the Institute of the Nation's Memory.

As we walked toward this unexceptional building we could see even from a distance that the place was in turmoil. An enormous black flag hung desolately from one of the upstairs windows. When we stepped through the doorway we saw people somberly striding this way and that, in seeming disarray. The receptionist was in tears, but managed to tell us that early that morning word had reached the staff that the founder, director, and main source of inspiration of the Institute of the Nation's Memory, Ján Langoš, was dead. He had been killed in a high-speed car crash at a highway intersection in Eastern Slovakia.

We returned the following day at our appointed time and, despite the shock that had struck the ÚPN, I received the promised documents from the files of the ŠtB. They contained records of my father's arrest, the charges against him, the order releasing him from prison, and a thirty-four-page transcript of his interrogation. All my life I had believed that my father had been accused of being an American spy and of hiding a secret radio transmitter in his basement. Nothing of this nature appeared in the case against him, nor were there any questions about it in the transcript of the interrogation. Rather, he faced the serious charge of treason and a series of other accusations, as we have seen in Chapter 27. For the first time, thanks to the courageus efforts of Ján Langoš and the ÚPN, I had reliable evidence, not faulty memories, of what happened when the ŠtB took my father away from home in the ninth year of my life.

THE ÚPN TAKES VERY SERIOUSLY its mission of ensuring a national memory—a memory that is not hidden but public. To this end the institute periodically publishes its key findings, puts out a journal, and hosts conferences. It has also erected a strategically located monument. This monument lies below the ruins of the fortress of Devín, a short distance to the west of Bratislava. Devín holds a distinctive place in Slovakia's sense of its own past. Štúr led his Young Slovaks to this citadel, perched high above the confluence of the River Morava and the Danube. During Communist times, uncounted Slovaks came to stand atop Devín, gaze across either river, and see Austria. The landscape they saw was the Russian Zone, to be sure, but Austria represented freedom. As well, the Morava, which is a much smaller river than the Danube, was a preferred crossing for thousands fleeing the Communist regime. Along its banks—where in the middle of the night families in rowboats and desperate single men often simply swimming struggled to gain the opposite shore undetected—the ÚPN and the Confederation of Political Prisoners of Slovakia have erected a monument, *Brána slobody* (The Gateway to Freedom.) The concrete faces of this monument are pockmarked as if damaged by bullets; the arch holds a twisted representation of the Iron Curtain; and on the innermost face is this text:

Brána slobody—*Gateway to Freedom* —*at Devín near the confluence of the rivers Morava and Danube. It commemorates the vast numbers of men, women, and children who lost their lives or were imprisoned because they tried to leave Communist Czechosovakia for freedom in the West. It also publicly acknowledges the more than two million Germans and Magyars who were forcibly expelled from Czechoslovakia immediately after World War II, no matter how they might have conducted themselves during the war. Photo author.*

In memory of citizens forced out of their homeland:
  Carted off to Soviet gulags, more than 20,000
  Deported after the year 1945, more than 2,200,000[3]
  Refugees from Communist oppression, more than 180,000
  Imprisoned for attempting to cross the border, almost 80,000

In memory of men and women killed attempting to reach freedom:
  The Communist regime shot, killed with mines and electrical
  current, and in other ways murdered in their attempt to cross
  the Iron Curtain on the borders of Czechoslovakia, in the years
  1948-1989:

And here hundreds are listed by name.

I was among the 180,000 fortunate ones, but my parents or I could easily have been among those imprisoned, shot, or otherwise murdered in our attempt to reach freedom.

THE DAY AFTER LANGOŠ'S DEATH, while Irča and I were in the offices of the institute, the international service of Czech Radio published in English an obituary featuring the thoughts of Fedor Gál, a long-time political activist, fellow-dissident under Communism, and co-founder of Public against Violence. His sober words reflected the high admiration he had for his dear friend:[4]

For Ján Langoš, the problem of Communism, totalitarian regimes, and the question of national memory was a mission. That he managed to establish the Slovak Institute of the National Memory was an incredible feat. In this work he encountered very strong opposition. His making public the ŠtB documents on the internet caused a wave of negative response, not to mention much litigation. As a result, Ján Langoš had many enemies, and I think that, in essence, he was a lonely person. Of course, he had a number of great friends, but his public work carried risks, and he committed himself to it fully.

Great work requires unyielding determination, a clear mind, and a great heart. Langoš had all three, and the work he performed deserves ongoing public recognition. Days after his death, the first such recognition was bestowed on him, the Prize of Milan Hodža. This award, presented in the name of the prime minister of Slovakia, had been given for the first time only the year before, in 2005 (Chapter 32). The final selection from among the nominees for 2006 was being made just as the death of Ján Langoš was announced. The awards committee immediately withdrew all other nominations and recommended unanimously that the Prize of Milan Hodža for 2006 be awarded to Ján Langoš, *in memoriam.*

The Langoš family was at his funeral in Bratislava at the time the public presentation of the Prize of Milan Hodža was to be made in Martin, so I was asked to accept the award on their behalf. A few days later, in the depth of their grief, they made time to meet with me in the offices of the ÚPN. It was a great satisfaction and honor for me that I could deliver the Prize of Milan Hodža to the family, in recognition of what Ján Langoš, their husband and father, had accomplished in a life dedicated to political freedom and public service—service that had directly impacted countless lives, including my own.

CHAPTER 32

Celebrating Milan Hodža

The return of Milan Hodža to his native land—executed on a grand scale, full of pageantry, and laden with emotion—was a celebration such as I will probably never experience again in my lifetime. It confirmed everything essential that my mother had told me about my grandfather: that he holds a unique place in Slovak history, that he was deeply loved by many people, and that he deserved to rest at home, not in exile. And, coupled as the event was with Slovakia's drive for membership in the European Union, it felt like it also heralded a particularly bright future for Slovakia itself[1].

GRANDFATHER HODŽA WAS ABUNDANTLY CELEBRATED during his lifetime as well, especially on the occasion of his fiftieth and sixtieth birthdays. He turned sixty in the pivotal year of 1938, when Czechoslovakia was in danger of its life as a nation and he was its prime minister. Congratulations poured in from all sides, books were written in his honor, he was awarded honorary doctorates by Charles University in Prague and Comenius University in Bratislava, his home town of Sučany staged a celebration, the Days of Milan Hodža.

Communities from around the country sent gifts reflecting the respect and affection in which Hodža was held, nowhere more than in the poorest regions of Slovakia and in regions inhabited by the Magyar, German, and Rusyn minorities whose interests he had consistently defended. The most astonishing of these birthday gifts, lost after World War II but vividly remembered within the family, was a silver wreath from Subcarpathian Rus'. The wreath was composed of hundreds of small silver leaves, and on each leaf was engraved the name of a Rusyn village.

Several important birthday mementos still survive,[2] notably albums containing hand-painted certificates by which towns and villages bestowed honorary citizenship on Grandfather Hodža. The album from District Giraltovce in County Šariš opens with this moving statement that recalls the history of Slovakia under the Magyars, the positive changes under Czechoslovakia, and the work of Milan Hodža:[3]

Twenty years ago, after a long period of hopelessness, the chains fell from our calloused hands. Today, as we look around us, we see the generous fruits of political freedom and democracy. In our land, Slovak souls beaten down by slavery have come alive to greater education, economic progress, and Slovak national consciousness.

As we look with joy and pride on the two decades of the Republic that have passed, we remind ourselves of the centuries of national bondage. Your heroic actions stand before our eyes like stars in a dark sky, the actions of an awakener of our people who sacrificed himself to bravely prepare a better future for the people of our district.

With the greatest joy we recall your blessed activity in District Giraltovce before the overthrow [of Austria-Hungary]. The villages of County Šariš will not forget *Slovenský týždenník* and your visits in the years 1906-1909 when, in the midst of deathly silence [referring to the political passivity of the Martin center], you sowed faith and the courage to act.[3]

On the occasion of your 60th birthday, as a sign of our faithfulness and gratitude and with sincere wishes for abundant strength for the execution of your office, our townships have elected you our first honorary citizen. We ask that you willingly accept this expression of our respect and love.

The 1st day of February, 1938.

Perhaps a bit overwrought by today's standards, statements such as these nevertheless reflected an important reality of their day—the memories of the days of oppression under the Magyars were still very much alive, and many Slovaks of widely differing backgrounds knew and were grateful for Hodža's role in helping to bring about a better day.

Another album comes from District Žarnovica in the mining region around Banská Bystrica. This district still had a substantial German population, and the greetings of many of its villages were written in two versions, German as well as in Slovak. A third is from Lučenec, a district close to Slovakia's border with Hungary that to this day has a significant Magyar population. Its certificates were also mostly written bilingually, in Slovak and in Magyar (Plate 37, Appendix VI). In his youth, Hodža had railed against Magyar rule but he held no personal animosity against Magyars as a group. After Czechoslovakia was established, he repeatedly visited regions in which Magyars predominated, he spoke there in his polished Magyar, he honored great figures in Magyar history. He worked hard to improve the way all minorities in Czechoslovakia were treated. For this, he was repaid with with respect even within Hungary, and he gained the affection of Magyars within Czechoslovakia.[4]

AFTER WORLD WAR II, and especially following the Communist takeover of 1948, the memory of how much Hodža had done for Slovakia and Czechoslovakia during his long career as a journalist, political leader, statesman, and intellectual rapidly faded, in part due to deliberate Communist falsification of history. The people who had known him, or had seen the fruits of his many efforts, grew older and died. Hodža continued to be a prominent presence on the pages of scholarly publications, but he disappeared from school textbooks and from the awareness of much of the Slovak population.

The Hodža name was eradicated from public view in many ways. One example I know well relates to the school I attended in Bratislava when my parents and I returned to Czechoslovakia after World War II. The school had been established in 1937 as the State Elementary School of Milan Hodža. Hodža came in person for its ceremonial opening; a wonderful newsreel of his arrival, speech, and departure has been preserved in the school archives. It was still known by this name when I was a student there in 1947. The Communists took power in February of 1948, and within two months, in April 1948, Hodža's name was removed from the school.[5]

Similar steps had been taken even earlier, under the Slovak Republic that formed in 1939. For example, Grandfather Hodža had long supported the development of a business school in the city of Trenčín, and in 1937 it was named the Czechoslovak Academy of Dr. Milan Hodža in his honor. However, Hodža was seen as an archenemy by the leaders of the World War II Slovak Republic, and almost as soon as they came into power they removed his name from the school.[6] Hodža, the democrat, was anathema to a totalitarian Communist regime; Hodža, the proponent of a united Czechoslovakia, was anathema to Slovak ultranationalists.

GRANDFATHER HODŽA DIED IN EXILE and his remains rested in the Bohemian National Cemetery in Chicago for nearly sixty years. He was remembered by only a relative handful of people—those who were old enough to remember his contributions during the days of Austria-Hungary and of the First Republic, and the families of his many admirers and collaborators. It was the efforts of academic historians and political scientists that gradually brought his important role in Slovak history to light once again.

Even under the Communists, scholars started to delve into Hodža's work and write about it extensively.[7] Immediately after the fall of Communism, as if unleashed after a long period of gestation, a number of studies on Hodža burst into print and public view. For example, Jozef Jablonický, who under the Communists had risked his personal freedom to uncover the activities of the democratic stream in the Slovak National Uprising (Chapter 6), organized the first academic conference on my grandfather. Its printed proceedings sold out quickly, and numerous other publications followed.[8]

In the mid-1990s a new scholar appeared on the scene—Pavol Lukáč. The more Lukáč delved into the life and contributions of Milan Hodža, the more he became convinced that for Slovakia's sense of its own history, it was not only appropriate but also important to bring Hodža's remains home. To seek support in this matter, he approached my family in Slovakia and even visited us in Seattle, and he made his case to his friends in the Slovak government.

While this seed was germinating within the government's inner circles, other steps were being taken.[9] A plaque in honor of Milan Hodža was unveiled on the wall of the Bilingual Gymnasium in his native Sučany. The Club of Slovak Culture in Prague commissioned its leadership to place a commemorative plaque on the exterior wall of the Hodža villa in Prague. The unveiling of this plaque in 2001 was a memorable occasion. The speakers included the Slovak prime minister Mikuláš Dzurinda and the Czech vice-premier Vladimír Špidla, as well as Pavol Lukáč. My wife and I were not able to come from the United States, but we had a family representative in our daughter Tanya, who was at the time serving in Italy as a nurse in the U.S. Air Force. She and her husband bundled up their two small children and drove from Venice to Prague to attend the ceremony. Dressed in her formal U. S. Air Force blues, attended by her handsome husband and with two beautiful children in tow, she was a major attraction.

A central outcome of this event was the definitive decision by Prime Minister Dzurinda to proceed with the transfer of Hodža's remains under the aegis of the government of Slovakia. The goal was to restore Hodža's legacy and his role in Slovak history to their rightful place in public awareness, and equally to highlight his ideas on a federation in Central Europe as Slovak contributions to the evolution of European political thought and organization. For these and other reasons, the ceremonial transfer of Hodža's remains was, in the words of the historian Pavol Lukáč,[10] "the return of a symbol."

THE RETURN OF A SYMBOL INTO PUBLIC CONSCIOUSNESS could not be accomplished in just a few days of ceremonies; it would require an ongoing effort to counteract the decades of official neglect. To this end, Prime Minister Dzurinda conceived of a new series of Days of Milan Hodža, celebrations to be held annually for a cycle of ten years. Their scope is substantial. The events open with a formal ceremony at the Slovak National Cemetery and the laying of wreathes and flowers on the grave in which my grandparents are buried (Plates 33, 34). This is followed by a major academic conference organized jointly by the Slovak Academy of Sciences and the Slovak National Library. The proceedings of the conference are published through the academy's press. The first three conferences were devoted to my grandfather,[11] while subsequent ones analyze the work of other major Slovak leaders who were his contemporaries.[12]

There is always an attempt to widen public participation in these celebrations. During their first year, 2005, there were two vehicles for this: an exhibition of historical photos and memorabilia, and a play written especially for the occasion.[13]

In succeeding years, outreach efforts have included pop music concerts on the main square in Martin, and more recently celebrations on the square of Grandfather Hodža's home town, Sučany. On the stage that is set up in front of the Lutheran church of Sučany (Plate 38) can be found something for everybody: plays and dances presented by school children, recitations of poetry, the introduction of government dignitaries, and music appealing to all tastes. One bright and sunny afternoon, for example, after I had added my own welcome to other brief speeches, I listened with pleasure to the Chamber Choir of Martin, a group that is highly regarded in Europe for its *a capella* singing of complex harmonies. The choir closed their performance with a piece I had come to know well since the church services in Chicago—Peter Bella Horal's *Aká si mi krásna, Ty rodná zem moja*. The choirmaster was both amazed and delighted to learn that a descendant of Horal's was the guest of honor!

To reach students in schools, Prime Minister Dzurinda suggested an essay competition for gymnasium students (Plate 36). The contest is organized through the Bilingual Gymnasium of Milan Hodža in Sučany, but it is national in its reach.[14] The essays are adjudicated by a panel that includes some of Slovakia's most distinguished historians, as well as representatives of schools and the press. Later, this highly successful program was expanded. The Elementary School of Milan Hodža in Bratislava organizes a parallel competition for elementary schools; the first round was carried out in 2008.[15]

The ceremonies close with a Sunday morning service in the Lutheran church of Sučany, the church served for so long by Milan's father, Ondrej, and after Ondrej's death by Ján Hodža, Milan's half-brother. It is customary in Slovakia to broadcast church services on the radio, the venue changing from week to week. In 2005, the first year of the Days of Milan Hodža, the honor of a broadcast fell to Sučany.

I HAVE BEEN DELIGHTED AND HONORED to participate personally in virtually all of these celebrations, and I have many exhilarating memories of them. For example, in 2007 I attended the concert held in Martin's main square. A stage had been erected in the square and festooned in the Slovak national colors of white, blue, and red. Hanging over the stage was a huge picture of Grandfather Hodža. A band that was a great local favorite had just stopped playing and left the stage. It was my turn to step into the brilliant lights and face hundreds and hundreds of animated young people, crowding together as far as the eye could see, cheering their favorite bands one after the other. My role was to remind them of the occasion of the concert—the celebration of Slovakia's annual Days of Milan Hodža.

Just minutes before I was to take the stage, I was sitting on one of the outdoor benches reviewing my notes. Much to my astonishment, the prime minister's foreign affairs adviser[16] spotted me from a distance and came to sit beside me. "I see you have your notes all ready," he said. "Well, I advise you to throw them all away and just speak from the heart. I heard you in Chicago. I know you can do it." Shocked, and with only five minutes to go, I put away my notes and started to rethink what I might say. Then my cousin Milan came to see what I was doing. "Talk to them in English," he advised cheerfully. "They're young, they all know some English, and when they hear you, they'll really pay attention."

With two minutes to go, I walked up the rickety stairs and took a seat at the side of the stage. As soon as the band stopped playing, the bouncy mistress of ceremonies called me to the microphone and introduced me with a joke that put me at my ease (Plate 35). I looked out over the huge crowd, stretching out as far as I could see. "I bring you greetings from America," I said in Slovak. I paused before my next sentence. To my astonishment, I heard a loud cheer! I welcomed the crowd again, this time in English. Another cheer. "When I speak in America, I always say that I am from Slovakia," in Slovak. A huge cheer. "Thank you for coming to honor my grandfather, Milan Hodža," in English." Cheer. "He died in America, but he is buried here in Martin," in Slovak. Cheer. "Thank you for coming to celebrate his memory." Cheer. In a few more moments my talk was over. The mistress of ceremonies thanked me and shook my hand before she introduced the next band. I took a deep breath, walked back down the stairs, and found my family. "It was great," Milan told me. "I heard them saying to each other, 'He's talking in English. Listen!' I told you it would work!"

And so I, a professor used to speaking to quiet academic gatherings in the United States, had for a moment entered into the ebullient world of popular culture in Slovakia!

A HIGHLIGHT OF THE DAYS OF MILAN HODŽA is the presentation of the Prize of Milan Hodža. The prize is awarded in the name of the prime minister of Slovakia; the winner is selected by the celebration's organizing committee. All the winners are distinguished figures in Slovak academic and public life. The first three we have already met.

In 2005, the inaugural prize was presented to Pavol Lukáč, the historian who worked more tirelessly and spoke more frequently and eloquently than anyone else both for the transfer of Grandfather Hodža's remains and for his restoration into the public consciousness of Slovakia.[17] The award was made *in memoriam,* for Lukáč had died shortly before, unexpectedly and at the young age of thirty-four. Our family had accepted him as one of our own. He was a visitor in our homes, a companion in our dreams. Even now, years after his death, we find ourselves remarking how we miss him, what a gap his death has left. It was fitting to award the first Prize of Milan Hodža to Pavol Lukáč, but no prize can replace a life (Plate 39).

In 2006, the prize was awarded to Ján Langoš, again *in memoriam,* for a life dedicated to casting light on the darkest chapters of Slovakia's history, and especially for the establishment of the *Ústav pamäti národa*, the Institute of the Nation's Memory. His work continues to resonate in the political life of Slovakia as the ÚPN once again becomes the focus of political controversy and as the Foundation of Ján Langoš awards its own prizes recognizing bold action on behalf of human rights.[18]

In 2007 the prize was awarded to Jozef Jablonický for his fearless research into the Slovak National Uprising and for his contributions to bringing back the memory of Milan Hodža. With his bushy gray beard and trademark jeans coat, Jablonický looks like a patriarch. He and I were hosted by the same family when we attended the celebrations in Kovačica, so I had the privilege of spending casual time with him every day. There I came to see that, like a true patriarch, he is a captivating spinner of tales. Most of them are about the Uprising and its human actors, great and small. They are based on meticulous archival research and countless hours of intimate conversation with those actors. His much-honored work represents a lifetime of brave commitment in the face of Communist attempts to silence him (Plate 40).

With such a distinguished roster of laureates, the Prize of Milan Hodža has become a truly coveted award.[19] The year 2011 saw an expansion of the concept underlying it. With the exception of Ján Langoš in 2006, all the awards heretofore had been made for distinguished academic work, albeit often with wider ramifications, a tradition that continues. In 2011, however, a second prize was created specifically for activity in the public arena—not political activity, from which the award remains deliberately distanced, but activity that promotes Hodža's ideals or contributes to the visibility of Slovakia on the international stage.

> The new Prize of Milan Hodža was awarded to an American in-stitution, the National Czech and Slovak Museum and Library in Cedar Rapids, Iowa. The NCSML focuses on the lives of immigrants to the U.S. from all corners of the former Czechoslovakia, both in its expositions and in its library holdings. Its building was opened in 1995 by Presidents Clinton of the United States, Havel of the Czech Republic, and Kováč of Slovakia. Since 2009 NCSML has been conducting an extensive Oral History Project on Czech and Slovak immigrants from 1948 onwards that is also being deposited with the Library of Congress; I am among the many interviewees.

> In 2012 the institutional Prize of Milan Hodža was awarded to Friends of Slovakia, an organization based in Washington, D.C. that is entirely dedicated to the goal of advancing Slovak-U.S. relations and making Slovakia more visible on the American stage. Work-ing closely with the Slovak embassy, it seeks to bring to American decision-makers a greater awareness of Slovakia, awards scholar-ships that bring Slovak students to the United States, encourages Slovak-American business interactions, and acts as a focus for Slovak-Americans who wish to serve their original homeland. Both NCSML and Friends of Slovaka truly serve the goal of bringing the best of Slovakia forward on the international stage.

The recognition that Milan Hodža has received since the end of the Com-munist era, starting with the attention paid him by scholars and culminating with the transfer of his remains and the institution of the Days of Milan Hodža, is remarkable. It is far beyond anything that we, his family, ever dreamed about, and we are forever grateful to all those who have made it possible.

Epilogue

The search for roots has become a vibrant part of the modern American landscape. Genealogical societies abound. Schoolchildren are often asked to construct their family trees. The idea that familial influences are transmitted for seven generations has become a cliché. We have come to understand that our origins and family history are not only fascinating, but also important to our own self-understanding.

I had such a perspective in mind when I started to work on this book. Its very first version was intended for our daughters and grandchildren, and was called simply *Johnny's Story*. It focused on me, my parents, and my grandparents rather than on more distant ancestors and historical context. However, as I found out more about my forebears—as I discovered unsuspected lives lived long ago, before there even was a Slovakia, and came to appreciate in a new way the struggles required to birth the very idea of a Slovak nation—I became convinced that I wanted to speak of the nation as much as I did the family. *Johnny's Story* turned into *My Slovakia, My Family*, and my intended audience grew to include the widest public that I could engage, both Slovak and American.

With the completion of the book came another notion, prompted by one of my enterprising Slovak cousins: for our family, reading a book about ancestors and homeland might be rewarding, but actually visiting the homeland and meeting the family of today would provide a visceral experience that no book could replicate. And so, in the early summer of 2012, ten years to the day after the ceremonial transfer of Grandfather Hodža's remains, our entire American family set out for Slovakia. We were eleven—two grandparents, two daughters, two sons-in-law, and five grandchildren—in all, three generations, ranging in age from thirteen to seventy-four. Especially for the grandchildren, it would be a personal introduction to one side of their own heritage (Plate 43, Appendix VI).

For part of our time we stayed in Mikuláš, in the house that my parents had built and that I had been forced to leave more than sixty years before (Plate 28). As we explored the country, there was something for everyone. Our oldest grandaughters enjoyed being treated as adults, sipping champagne from strawberry-decorated flutes while listening to Slovakia's greatest jazz trumpeter, fresh from New York, playing at a garden party at the *vežičková vila*, the ornate villa that had meant so much to my Pálka grandparents (photo, page 211). Our grandsons were thrilled by the World War II weaponry at the Museum of the Slovak National Uprising, the momentous event in which the followers of Grandfather Hodža had played such a central role. The athletes enjoyed scrambling to the summit of Mt. Chopok, the second highest summit in the Low Tatras, where my parents had loved to ski. The dancers were wowed by the great folklore festival at Východná (Plates 29-32). For the adults, perhaps the highlight was an afternoon spent with the granddaughter of Janko Bulík, the resistrance leader who was such a hero to our family. We feasted in the back garden; we reveled in the accordion and the tenor voice of one of our hostess's folk-dancing sons; and I got to talk on the telephone with her father, Jano Bulík, the adoptive brother I almost had. In Bratislava we enjoyed the Old Town, especially its whimsical public art (Plates 44-47). And on the last day everyone, without exception, delighted in being chauffeured around Bratislava in my cousin Karol's vintage Mercedes and Bugatti—perfectly restored, buffed, and polished (Plate 48) and eating a farewell dinner on the new promenade alongside the Danube, with a stunning view of the castle and the coronation Church of St. Martin (Plate 49).

It was fun. It was moving. It was exhausting. It was today's Slovakia, but with a full measure of ties to the past. My Slovakia had come alive for two more generations of my family. When I was a young teenager, my uncle gave me a book of photographs about Slovakia and inscribed it "To Johnny, so he won't forget." Now I wish the same for my own children and grandchildren—follow your passions wherever they may take you, but don't forget!

Acknowledgments

I have been helped in the preparation and writing of this book by many people. Some were family, some were friends, and others I did not even know before I started on my quest for family roots. The list is unusually long because *My Slovakia, My Family* appeared first in Slovakia, translated from the original English into Slovak and adapted for Slovak readers (*Moje Slovensko, moja rodina*, published in 2010 by Kalligram, Bratislava). It was then re-adapted for American readers, primarily by adding a considerable amount of background material, and edited once again.

I start with archives and museums: Archiv Národního muzea in Prague, Slovenský národný archív in Bratislava, Slovenská národná knižnica in Martin, Archív Matice slovenskej Martin, and most especially Múzeum Janka in Kráľa Liptovsky Mikuláš. The directors and staff of this museum helped me over the entire six-year period of my research, and I want to express my special thanks to them. The museum also gave me permission to reproduce the portrait of Michal Miloslav Hodža that was in their possession. In addition, the gallery of Peter Michal Bohúň in Liptovský Mikuláš allowed me to reproduce the portraits by Bohúň of Ondrej Pálka and of Zuzana Scholtz that are in their collection, and the Slovak National Gallery in Bratislava allowed me to reproduce the portrait by Bohúň of Michal Miloslav Hodža.

Numerous scholars have contributed in a significant way to the writing of this book. Foremost among them is my friend Mgr. Zdenko Ďuriška of the Biografický ústav of the Slovak National Library in Martin. Ďuriška has conducted extensive genealogical research on a series of notable Slovak families including the Hodžas and the Pálkas. He is currently working on a monographic study of the Pálka family that will soon be presented in book form. Without his work and active assistance I would not have been able to write about the older lineages of the Hodžas or the Pálkas. He gave me indispensable help all along the way, as well as critiquing the entire text.

In addition to Zdenko Ďuriška, the text was reviewed in its entirety by Dr. Peter Vítek, director of the Štátny archív v Bytči pobočka Liptovský Mikuláš, and by Prof. Susan Mikula, professor of history, Benedictine University, an expert on Milan Hodža. Selected chapters were reviewed by Dr. Stefan Auer of the Department of Politics and International Relations, LaTrobe University, Melbourne, Australia; Prof. James Ramon Felak of the Department of History, University of Washington; Dr. Alexander Maxwell of the School of History, Philosophy, Political Science & International Relations, Victoria University, Wellington, New Zealand; Dr. Nadya Nedelsky of the Department of International Studies at Macalester College; Prof. Emeritus Diethelm Prowe of the Department of History, Carleton College; Prof. Emeritus Norma L. Rudinsky of the Department of English, Oregon State University; and Dr. Jozef Šimončič, Professor Emeritus of History of Trnava University.

Finally, non-academic historians and genealogists helped me in very important ways: Ján Gálik and Ing. Branislav Borsuk of Myjava in connection with the Jurenka and Poláček families, and Igor Hodža with the Ursíny family. Dr. Vojtech Čelko of the Ústav pro soudobé dejiny of the Czech Academy of Sciences in Prague provided me many friendly and scholarly services, as did Dr. Miroslav Peknik of the Ústav politických vied of the Slovak Academy of Sciences who first introduced me to Dr. Jozef Jablonický.

My dear friend Ivan Rázus opened many, many doors for me in Liptovský Mikuláš where so much of my story takes place. I was rendered a special service by Dr. Martin Bútora, who had been the ambassador of Slovakia in the United States at the time of the transfer of my grandfather Milan Hodža's remains. He worked through the entire first version of the manuscript while it was still in English, and gave me very important suggestions for its improvement for Slovak readers. Finally, Dr. Patricia Krafcik, Evergreen State College, an expert on both Russian literature and issues of ethnicity in Slavic nations, reviewed the revised English manuscript and helped me with final story-telling touches. I am grateful to all these experts for helping me write a book that is factually as free of errors as possible and whose interpretations of historical figures and developments are balanced and in line with contemporary thinking. Whatever errors and imbalances remain, of course, are my responsibility.

A family history, almost by definition, draws heavily on the resources of the family itself. My work would hardly have been possible without the generous support of Aunt Zorka Frkáňová. She provided me with enormous amounts of material from the family archive that she and her sister Aunt Vierka Štetková maintained all through World War II, the Communist era, and up to the present day. I am not the only one to have benefited from her painstaking work—many another aspiring historian has found the path to her generous door. In addition, Uncle Zdeno Jurenka gave me my first insights into the history of the Jurenka and Poláček families, and my cousin Karol Pavlů and his wife Darina helped me reconstruct many Pálka family stories.

My narrative benefited enormously from the close reading of my friends, John Ashford and Marv Thomas, both of whom helped me be a better story-teller. The detailed editing of Margaret Bendet over many years helped me transform a collection of chapters into a unified manuscript written in smoothly-flowing language. My niece Michaela Chorváthová translated the hundreds of pages of manuscript from English into Slovak, and my cousin Irena Kuchárová edited the translation and worked with the editorial staff of the publisher, Kalligram. Adding to the family nature of the work, my cousin Jelka Bučková helped me at every step—arranging meetings, securing photographs, monitoring publications, and acting as an intermediary countless times. When it came time to prepare this English-language version, the staff of Kirk House Publishers provided expert publishing services and responded readily and creatively to my numerous requests and suggestions.

And finally, my beloved Yvonne patiently lived with my distraction for at least eight years. She read and critiqued every chapter and put up with one deadline after another. More importantly, she held our home together and endured not a little loss of companionship while I put my attention on research and writing. Over the years, she wrote two books herself. First came a wonderful story about dragons and children for young readers ages seven to eleven, illustrated with nearly a hundred of her brush-and-ink paintings in Japanese/Chinese sumi style. Soon thereafter she wrote and illustrated an instruction book on sumi for children. I thank her from the bottom of my heart for her patience and help, and especially for more than five decades of love and adventure together!

Slovak History in Brief

Though today's Republic of Slovakia was established only in 1993, Slovaks have a history that is traceable nearly 2,000 years into the past. Slavic tribes that included the ancestors of today's Slovaks arrived in the heart of Central Europe during the early centuries of the Common Era. Between about 500 and 1000 C.E., several Slav states rose and fell on territory that includes today's Slovakia. They are important in Slovaks' sense of their own history, but it is doubtful that any of them were yet Slovak in any modern sense, for national identities as we know them today developed only progressively. In the tenth century, large areas of Central Europe were conquered by new invaders, the Magyars, who established the far-flung Kingdom of Hungary there. From about the year 1000 C.E. until 1918, today's Slovakia was politically nothing more than a group of counties, situated in the mountainous north of the Kingdom of Hungary and inhabited by Slovaks. The latter part of this long period was marked by a struggle to develop and sustain a distinctive Slovak identity in the face of pressures for assimilation into Magyar society that grew increasingly intense from the eighteenth century onward. In 1918, the Slovak counties separated from Hungary and joined the lands of historic Kingdom of Bohemia to form Czechoslovakia. During World War II Slovakia declared independence, but this was a stillborn effort conducted by an authoritarian regime that included a number of Nazi sympathizers and was largely subservient to Hitler's Germany. After the war ended, Czechoslovakia was re-united. In 1948 the Communists took control, and for forty years the country languished behind the Iron Curtain. Communism fell in 1989. Soon, long-standing tensions prevailed and the Czech Republic and Slovakia separated peacefully. On January 1, 1993, Slovakia become a truly independent state for the first time in its history.

Here is the story of Slovakia told in a little more detail.[1]

Origins: To 500 C.E.

The entire area of Central Europe, including the territory of Slovakia, is rich in human remains and artifacts from the Paleolithic Era, the Neolithic, the Bronze Age, and later periods including that of the Celts. Graves have been uncovered, and the remains of dwellings and fortifications have been excavated. Exquisite, tiny figurines, decorated pottery, jewels, and weapons have been recovered and can be seen in national and regional museums as well as at the original excavation sites. All of these remains, however, represent a succession of civilizations that flourished and then died; they have no continuity with the present. For this reason, let us start our story with the roots of Slovakia's present civilization.

The nationalities of today's Europe, Slovaks among them, can be grouped according to the languages they speak: The Germans, Dutch, and Scandinavians (though not the Finns) speak Germanic languages, and English too has a strong Germanic foundation. The French, Italians, Spaniards, Portuguese, and Romanians speak Romance languages. The Poles, Czechs, Slovaks, and others in the west; the Slovenes, Croats, Serbs, Bulgarians and others in the south; and the Ukrainians, Belorussians, Russians and others in the east speak Slavic languages. Whether taken in terms of total population or of area, the Slavic nations, speaking a diversity of Slavic languages, are by far the largest constituent of the rich linguistic and cultural tapestry of the modern European continent.

The exact place of origin of the ancient Slavic tribes that spread out to populate this vast area and gave rise to such a diversity of related languages has been disputed for many years. However, a consensus view is starting to emerge. According to this view, the original Slav homeland was located in the plains between the Black Sea and the Baltic, in today's northwestern Ukraine, southwestern Belarus, and eastern Poland. During the early centuries of the Common Era these original Slavs, who were primarily a pastoral people, migrated eastward, westward, and southward, settled there, and ultimately became the dominant local population. However, their territory was repeatedly invaded and conquered, often by warrior peoples from further east. The Huns under Attila, and later the Tatars, are perhaps the most famous, but the Magyars, the ethnic Hungarians, will be the most important for our story.

Starting around the beginning of the Common Era, Central Europe was split by a well-defined military boundary, the *limes Romanus*, a string of fortifications built by the Romans that in its totality stretched for over 2,000 miles from the Black Sea to Hadrian's Wall in the British Isles. To the south was the highly ordered world of the Roman Empire, to the north the chaotic world of warring Germanic and Slavic tribes and the ruthless incursions of the Huns. The *limes* ran in part along the Danube, and there were important fortifications in the vicinity of today's Bratislava.

In the fifth century the Germanic tribes went°on the offensive and reduced the Western Roman Empire to little more than the area of today's Italy. Rome itself fell in 476 A.D. Instead of a new empire, however, disorganization ensued, and Slav settlement of the previously predominantly Germanic territories north of the Danube increased.

Early States: 500 to 1000 C.E.

It is not easy to reconstruct the various political formations that soon developed in Central Europe, or to match up their inhabitants with the ethnic groups of today. It appears, however, that among the early Slav states, and the first on Slovak territory, was Samo's Empire, formed in 623 C.E. and lasting until 685 C.E. At the peak of its short existence it covered a large region, centered in today's Slovakia and Moravia but including Bohemia and extending into parts of Germany in the northwest, Austria in the southwest, and Hungary in the southeast. King Samo was actually a Frank (a member of a group of Germanic tribes that controlled much of today's Germany), but he was elected by the Slavs of the region as their leader.

During the later 700s, about a century after Samo's death and the disintegration of his empire, a new center of power developed around what is now the city Nitra in southwestern Slovakia. The most famous leader of the Principality of Nitra was Prince Pribina, to this day a hero to Slovaks. Under his rule the territory of the state expanded and, most importantly, Christianity was introduced. Around 833 C. E. Nitra was partially conquered and effectively merged with the neighboring Principality of Moravia. The outcome was the Great Moravian Empire, the most important Slav state in this region until the establishment of Czechoslovakia. At its peak, the territory of Great Moravia far exceeded that of the later Czechoslovakia. Like its predecessors it was short-lived, disappearing by the end of the ninth century. However, during this period it produced a hero—Prince Svätopluk—and a critical moment in religious history, the arrival of the Byzantine missionaries Cyril and Methodius who created the first written Christian texts in a Slavic language, Old Church Slavonic.

Slovaks in the Kingdom of Hungary: 1,000 to 1918 C.E.

It is likely that by about the time of Great Moravia regional differences among the Slavs had become evident, and we can start to talk separately of the ancestors of today's Poles, Czechs, and others. Among these differentiating groups were the Slovaks, who had settled mainly on the southern slopes of the Tatra Mountains and nearby ranges and to a lesser extent on the plains farther south.

In the closing decades of the first millennium, Central Europe saw the influx of another people from the east—the Magyars. They spoke a distinctive, non-Indo-European language, and their original homeland is believed to have been in the region of the southern Ural Mountains. These were a warlike people with great fighting skills. They not only swept over the Slav peasantry, but were also prized as mercenaries by Germanic princes. Soon the Magyars brought the extensive plains of Central Europe under their control.

Progressively, especially with the defeat of the Great Moravian Empire, the territory of the Slovaks came to be dominated by the Magyars. According to tradition, on December 25, 1000 C.E., the Magyar chieftain, Stephen, who had converted to Christianity some years earlier, was crowned king by authority of the pope in Rome. He extended the borders of his kingdom, henceforth known as the Kingdom of Hungary, Christianized it, and, at least according to legend, ruled justly and wisely. He died in 1038 and was canonized in 1083. By that time the Kingdom of Hungary had become the greatest power between the Holy Roman Empire on the west and the Ottoman Empire on the southeast. However, its strategic location between two of the most powerful empires of the times, always vying for political and military advantage, exposed Hungary to constant external pressures.

In the pivotal year of 1526 Sultan Suleiman I, known in history as Suleiman the Magnificent, marched his well-armed and thoroughly disciplined army of some 65,000 men to the north and the west—from Istanbul to the great plains along the Danube—to wage war on the Hungarian king. Battle was joined in the broad fields near the town of Mohács in southeastern Hungary on a rainy day in June. Within a few hours some 14,000 of the young king's soldiers and 1,000 Hungarian noblemen were killed. The monarch himself drowned in a nearby swamp while trying to escape the slaughter. It was a black day for the Kingdom of Hungary, with consequences that were not reversed for centuries.

The remaining Hungarian nobility now took a momentous step. Despite sometimes violent conflict, they elected as their next king Ferdinand I of the House of Habsburg, who ruled large hereditary lands in Austria, southern Germany, and Silesia. In the same year, the nobility of Bohemia also elected him their king. Starting with these elections in 1526, the lands of Austria were united with the Kingdoms of Bohemia and of Hungary, and the Habsburg Empire came into existence. The House of Habsburg was to rule over these vast Central European territories for the next 400 years, until the map of Europe was redrawn at the end of World War I. It was in this context that the political history of Slovakia played out.

After being defeated by the Turks, the Kingdom of Hungary was reduced to its northwestern rim—largely today's Slovakia, a sliver of Hungary, and part of Croatia—known as Royal Hungary (Map 1, Appendix II). The Turks even took the Hungarian capital, Buda, so the seat of the Hungarian government was moved to Pressburg, situated on the Danube just forty miles downstream from Vienna. At the time, Pressburg was known both by this German name and by the Hungarian name of Poszony. Today, as the capital of Slovakia, it is Bratislava.

About 150 years later, in 1683, another Turkish army marched north and west. It lay siege to Vienna, hoping to bring the whole of Central Europe under the rule of the sultan. This time, however, it was the sultan's troops who were routed and retreated pell-mell. Not many years later, the Kingdom of Hungary reestablished its historic boundaries, stretching from the Tatra Mountains on the Slovak-Polish border in the north to the vicinity of Belgrade in the south, and from the border with Austria in the west to the far reaches of Transylvania in the east.

The capital of Hungary continued to be Bratislava, largely because of its proximity to the Habsburg Empire's seat of power, influence, and culture in Vienna. Eventually, it shifted back to Buda, though the kings and queens of Hungary continued to be crowned in Bratislava until 1830. The Slovak-inhabited territory, the main refuge of the entire kingdom during the Ottoman ascendancy, reverted to its original status as simply a group of counties within the kingdom. Collectively, they were called Upper Hungary (*Felvidék* in Magyar), but they had no distinctive administrative status. The region's Slovaks were predominantly peasants (both serfs and freemen) and craftsmen. There was a small Slovak intelligentsia, primarily clerics, and also a small group of Slovak nobility. The majority of the burghers were Germans; most of the aristocrats were Magyars. During the Reformation, most of the population became Lutheran, then during the Counter-Reformation most reverted to Catholicism.

The Rise of Nationalism

Dominant political power in the Kingdom of Hungary was always held by the Magyars, who had conquered the region and established the state, but on the state's territory lived large numbers of Slovaks, Serbs, Croats, Romanians, Germans, and other groups. The Magyars themselves represented less than half of the population. For centuries, ethnic distinctions were relatively insignificant. The Hungarian nation—the *Natio Hungarica* in the Latin of the times—consisted exclusively of the nobility. Most were Magyars, but it was their status, not their ethnicity, that identified them as Hungarians. The noblemen spoke Latin on formal occasions and their own languages at home. (Note the specific use of the term *Magyar* to refer to an ethnic group and *Hungary* to refer to the state in which the Magyars were dominant but which contained numerous other ethnicities as well. This distinction is of central importance to Slovaks, who for many years remained loyal to the Hungarian state while vigorously rejecting the attempts of the state to Magyarize them that were soon to appear on the scene.)

Starting in the mid-eighteenth century, a powerful new force arose in the consciousness of Europeans, including those of the Kingdom of Hungary—nationalism. No longer was the political allegiance of nobles exclusively to their king and of peasants to their nobles. Rather, the nation, and rights for the common man, became the focus. In 1848, revolution swept much of Europe, bringing down the monarchy of France and ultimately leading to the unification of Germany and of Italy. National tensions within the Habsburg monarchy escalated. In the face of the central power of Vienna, based on German culture and on the German language, Czechs recovered pride in their Czech identity and Magyars in their Magyar identity. Slovaks, too, experienced a great national awakening and the flowering of a sense of being a distinct people and taking pride in it. The Habsburgs emerged from the revolution of 1848 with their hold on the monarchy intact, but by 1867 the Magyars forced the transformation of the unified monarchy into a dual state, the Austro-Hungarian Empire, in which Austria and Hungary were equal partners.

Starting perhaps a century earlier, the Magyar ruling class of Hungary had embarked on a policy of Magyarization that was now applied with ever-increasing intensity. This policy was intended to convert the well-established multi-ethnic state into a state in which everyone regarded himself as a Magyar and all other national identities, and indeed languages, were lost. The story of Slovakia is largely the story of how this loss of identity was averted, how a Slovak national consciousness was cultivated, and, ultimately, how economic advancement and political power for Slovaks were won. Many members of my family, over many generations, contributed to this national story.

From Czechoslovakia to the Slovak Republic: 1918 to 1993

When World War I erupted in 1914, Austria-Hungary, by then a state torn by many internal dissentions, was allied with Germany and with its long-time adversary, the Ottoman Empire, as the Central Powers. Arrayed against them were the Western Powers including France, Great Britain, many of Britain's overseas territories including Australia, New Zealand, and India, and ultimately the United States. Russia's role was complex on account of the revolution raging there. After unprecedented bloodshed, the Central Powers were defeated. The map of Central and Eastern Europe was redrawn. Hungary lost two-thirds of its territory, a political decision that arouses bitter emotions among Hungarians even today. Romania gained Transylvania, and Yugoslavia and Czechoslovakia were created for the first time. In this process the Slovak leadership elected to separate from Hungary and join with the Czechs, forming the new joint state (Map 2, Appendix II). Members of my family played important roles in this pivotal decision, as well as in the building of the Czechoslovak state as a modern democracy.

The Czechoslovak Republic lasted twenty years, almost to the day. Unfortunately, it was subject to significant internal political tensions stemming both from its complex ethnic composition—including Czechs, Slovaks, Germans, Hungarians, and Rusyns—and to powerful external pressures, mainly from Nazi Germany but also from Hungary and even Poland. Nonetheless, it prospered economically and preserved its democratic foundations largely intact. Then, in September 1938, the Munich Agreement signed by Hitler's Germany, Mussolini's Italy, Britain, and France—without any participation by the Czechoslovak government—imposed the transfer to Germany of large areas of the Czechoslovak borderlands populated predominantly by ethnic Germans (Map 2, Appendix II). This decision paved the way for the break-up of Czechoslovakia; the establishment of the war-time Slovak Republic, nominally independent but in reality a German puppet; the direct takeover of the Czech lands by Hitler; and the onset of World War II.

The war saw the Slovak National Uprising, a large-scale revolt directed against the authoritarian Slovak Republic and against the German presence in Slovakia. The Germans put the uprising down, but it was a turning point in the history of Slovakia, pointing it away from an authoritarian direction and toward a democratic one. After the war Czechoslovakia was reunited, then taken over by the Communists in 1948. It remained a totalitarian Communist state and a satellite of the Soviet Union for just over forty years. The relatively relaxed period surrounding the so-called Prague Spring of 1968 was short-lived and was followed by a period of increased repression. In 1989, following the peaceful Velvet Revolution, the Iron Curtain finally collapsed. However, the old, pre-war tensions between Slovaks and Czechs could not be resolved, and Czechoslovakia's political leaders negotiated a peaceful separation, the Velvet Divorce. On January 1, 1993, the Czech Republic and Slovak Republic or Slovakia that we know today came into being (Map 3, Appendix II).

Maps

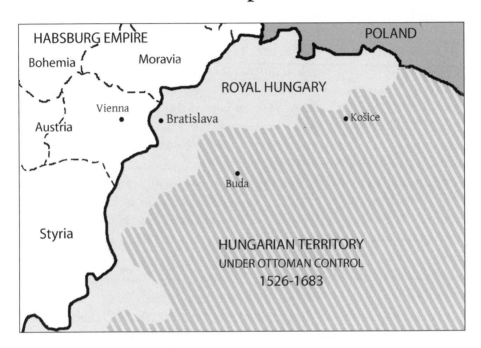

ROYAL HUNGARY, 1526-1683

1. The territory of the future Slovakia during the period of maximum Ottoman expansion in Europe, 1526-1683. The historic Kingdom of Hungary is shown in pale gray. The great majority of its area, shown striped and extending far beyond the borders of the map, was under Ottoman control for about a century and a half; sometimes this included even Košice, Slovakia's second greatest city. Only the small crescent of Royal Hungary (pale gray, unstriped) was uninterrupt-edly controlled by the Hungarian king. Its capital was Bratislava, then known as Pressburg (in German) or Poszony (in Magyar); most of its territory became today's Slovakia and Croatia. All maps based on Paul Robert Magocsi, *Historical Atlas of Central Europe, Revised and Expanded Edition*, University of Washington Press, Seattle, 2002.

CZECHOSLOVAKIA, 1918-1938

2. Central Europe has a complex history during which political units and boundaries have shifted many times (Appendix I). The western regions of Czechoslovakia—Bohemia and Moravia—constituted the core of the historic Kingdom of Bohemia established in the 12th century. They joined the Habsburg Empire in 1526, and were a major component of the Austrian portion of the Austro-Hungarian Empire from 1867 until the establishment of Czechoslovakia in 1918. The hatched area denotes the Czech borderlands that held a large German population. The eastern reaches of Czechoslovakia—Slovakia and Subcarpathian Rus' (in which the majority of the Rusyn population was concentrated)—were for centuries portions of the Kingdom of Hungary, within which they had no separate legal status. In 1918 they were joined with Bohemia and Moravia to form Czechoslovakia. Following World War II, Subcarpathian Rus' was transferred from Czechoslovakia to the Ukrainian Soviet Socialist Republic. At the same time, the boundary between Poland and Ukraine was moved westward; today, L'viv is one of Ukraine's major cities. In 1993 Bohemia and Moravia were separated from Slovakia, resulting in the establishment of the Czech Republic and the Slovak Republic or Slovakia.

SLOVAKIA, 1993-PRESENT

3. This map of today's Slovakia shows several of the cities that are important in the narrative of this book. Bratislava is the capital; several members of my family live there. Myjava is the family home of my paternal grandmother Darina Pálka neé Jurenka (Chapter 15, Appendix IV). Martin is the site of the Slovak National Cemetery where my maternal grandparents, Milan Hodža and his wife Irena Hodža née Pivko, are buried (Prologue), and the center of County Turiec from which all of my mother's side of the family stems (Chapter !4). It is a city of great significance in Slovak history. Liptovský Mikuláš and its immediate environs in County Liptov are the ancestral home of the Pálkas and Bellas (Chapters 15 and 22), and the place where my great-granduncle Michal Miloslav Hodža spent his working life (Chapters 18 and 21). Like Martin, it is prominent in Slovak history. Banská Bystrica, an old mining town, was the seat of the Slovak National Uprising during World War II (Chapter 6). Košice and Prešov in Eastern Slovakia were great centers of trade and learning.

The Slovaks of the Lower Lands

In the penultimate decade of the seventeenth century, just a few years before the first recorded Pálka learned how to soak and scrape hides and the legendary first Hodža taught his fellow-prisoners the scriptures and the first recorded Poláček helped organize the butchers of Brezová—just at the time, in short, when the roots of my family were becoming recognizable within the soil of what would more than two centuries hence become the nation of Slovakia—in faraway Istanbul the sultan's chief adviser, the Grand Vizier Kara Mustafa, conceived an ambitious plan.

At this time, the sultan ruled the entire southeastern quadrant of Europe.[1] Leopold I, Habsburg emperor in Vienna, was king of Hungary, but all that remained in his control was Royal Hungary, the slim northwestern crescent of the old Kingdom of Hungary that had once stretched east to the far borders of Transylvania and south to the edge of Belgrade (Map 1, Appendix II). Within this diminished territory the emperor was battling yet another rebellion among the nobles, and the shrewd sultan was supporting the rebels. Why not attack Leopold directly at his time of weakness, asked Kara Mustafa? Indeed, why not extend the sultan's rule to the emperor's seat in Vienna, and thereby add immeasurably to the glory of the Ottoman Empire?

Kara Mustafa's bold idea was accepted, and military preparations were set in motion. In 1682 troops of all descriptions and from all regions of the empire began to collect. When this army set out on its march north and west across the Hungarian plain, it numbered some 100,000 men. The Austrian ambassador to the Ottoman court, who traveled with the army, estimated that, as the sultan's troops ate their way across the land, 32,000 pounds of meat and 60,000 loaves of bread were consumed each day, and thousands of horses grazed the countryside. From the west, forces began to stream to the defense of Vienna, some 40,000 of them, both foot soldiers and horsemen. As the siege of the city became imminent, 40,000 Tatars arrived. Thus, in the space of about a year, a quarter of a million fighting men had descended on the small area in and around Vienna.

The dramatic story of the Siege of Vienna in 1683, and the successful defense of the city with the aid of Polish troops who arrived just as the final walls were being mined by the Turks, has been told many times.[2] The attacking Ottoman army was routed and fled in disarray toward the Balkans, pillaging as it went. And so the decline of the Ottoman Empire began.

The defeat at Vienna was the first of many for the Turks, and within a few years they were forced to pull back from their vast Hungarian territories to the vicinity of Belgrade, the capital of modern-day Serbia. This city had first been taken by Suleiman the Magnificent in 1521, who razed it and then rebuilt it. Belgrade prospered under continuous Ottoman rule for the next 150 years, but after that it was ferociously contested. It was captured by Habsburg forces in 1688, five years after the Siege of Vienna, and it traded hands three times in the next century. After each victory, the Ottomans substantially demolished it once again. The entire region around Belgrade, but particularly to the north and west, was devastated, so much so that when the Ottomans finally withdrew, the fields lay abandoned, countless buildings were destroyed, and village after village was deserted.

This was now border territory between the Habsburg Empire and the remains of the Ottoman Empire, and the emperor in Vienna wanted the region settled and protected.[3] Some years earlier he had established a military border zone in Croatia, staffed with Serbs brought in to serve as a special border militia. He now extended the military border far toward the Black Sea, and issued an invitation to peasants in his Hungarian domains to safely leave the lands of the nobles whom they had served for centuries, move to the border areas, and have access to fertile land to cultivate. In return they would serve in a militia designed to maintain the entire southern border of the monarchy against recurrent probing attacks by the Turks.

Many of the men who responded to the emperor's call, especially to the vicinity of Belgrade, came from the poorest regions of the kingdom, the Slovak counties of Upper Hungary.[4] Barely able to survive under the harsh conditions prevailing in the northern-most counties, with their hopelessly rocky soils and long, harsh winters, peasants had already been migrating out of this region for a century. They settled in the more benign regions to the south, forming Slovak enclaves in the nearby, predominantly Magyar lands. But now the situation was different. The emperor himself wanted peasants to move, and sometimes they could even have their own land—as much of it as they could cultivate. So families from the Slovak counties packed what few possessions they had. If they owned a wagon, they hitched their horse or bull to it, loaded up, and rode. If they didn't, they put a bundle on every back and walked.

The way was long, hundreds of kilometers across the Hungarian plains. Some migrant Slovaks stopped in what is now eastern Hungary and western Romania, others went on to the abandoned, wet fields and marshes lying between the rivers Danube and Tisa, the old principality of Vojvodina. Once they reached these depopulated borderlands, they settled in villages that had been abandoned for years. They built dikes to drain the marshes, and grew crops in far greater abundance than they could have done in their old homes in the Slovak uplands. But this was no paradise. Sometimes the fields flooded and the peasants lost their crops, sometimes the nobles who owned the land increased the rent, sometimes conditions got so bad that whole villages packed their few belongings and moved on once again. Nonetheless, the future was brighter than it had ever been before, so they sent word to relatives and friends to come and join them. In a year as many as 100 new families might appear in a village, each with many children, so that 500 or even 1,000 new mouths might suddenly need to be fed from the year's harvest.

This Slovak migration to and within the Lower Lands was not a one-time event; it continued for some two centuries. The settlements were established step by step. In Vojvodina the larger communities included Báčsky Petrovec and Kulpín in 1745, Stará Pazová in 1770, Kysáč in 1773, Slovenský Aradáč in 1786, Kovačica in 1802, and Padina in 1806.

As these Slovak settlements grew and prospered despite the difficulties, they remained determinedly Slovak. Typically, within two or three years a newly-established community sent back home for a Slovak teacher for the children. Then, as quickly as they could, they raised money, built a church, and sent back home for a pastor. (Most of the migrants were Lutherans escaping the oppression of the Counter-Reformation in addition to seeking economic opportunities that were beyond their reach at home.) In this way the Slovaks of the Lower Lands (the area of the old Kingdom of Hungary where today's Hungary, Romania, Serbia, and Croatia come together), the *dolnozemskí Slováci*, maintained close contact with the Slovaks of Upper Hungary.

This vigorous Slovak identity in the Lower Lands persists even today, well over two centuries and many generations after the first migrations began. Slovak is still spoken in the homes and is the medium of instruction in many of the schools; church services are conducted in Slovak; books and poems are written in Slovak; and on holidays you see people everywhere in traditional Slovak dress. The annual Slovak National Festival in Báčsky Petrovec, first conducted in 1920, today draws 15,000 Slovak participants from around Vojvodina and internationally.[5]

My own family had multiple ties to these communities, distant though they were from their home counties of Liptov and Turiec. One of the many Slovak teachers who served in the Lower Lands was Grandmother Hodža, then Irena Pivko. An independent-minded young woman, she left her native Sučany to study. She completed her education at the Institute for Teachers in Bratislava in 1905. In 1906, at the age of twenty, she took up her first and, as it turned out, only teaching assignment. It was in Stará Pazová, to the northwest of Belgrade, where she taught in the elementary school for three years. A photograph (page 242) shows her with three other young teachers, all dressed in national costumes.

Popular elections to the Hungarian parliament were introduced in the mid-nineteenth century, and the *dolnozemskí Slováci* were enthusiastic participants from the beginning. Kulpín and Petrovec elected one of the first Slovak representatives anywhere in the Kingdom of Hungary in 1869, Viliam Pauliny-Tóth (Chapter 21). In 1905 and 1906, while Irena Pivko was teaching in the elementary school in nearby Stará Pazová, the citizens of the Kulpín district elected her husband-to-be, the young and fiery Milan Hodža, to represent them in Budapest (Chapter 25).

Many years later, Janko Bulík from Kovačica and Belgrade helped my mother leave Slovakia (Chapter 2), provided my father with the Yugoslav passport that gave us indispensable cover in wartime France (Chapter 3), and was the lynchpin of the Slovak anti-Nazi resistance in Yugoslavia (Chapters 13 and 30). I myself have contacts with Slovaks in Kovačica and Kulpín that stem from my visit there in 2007 to honor Bulík, one of the most heroic men I have ever known about. Just as I was completing the writing of this book, I received an e-mail announcing that a bust of Grandfather Hodža had been placed on the main square of Kulpín. The Lower Lands, while far away from Slovakia itself, continue to mean much to my family.

APPENDIX IV

Pronunciation Guide

To an American reader, Slovak text looks mysterious, replete as it is with marks that the English alphabet does not use. However, the system of spelling is exceptionally rational and systematic, far more so than the quirky spelling we are used to in English. Every foreigner trying to learn English has wondered, why in the world is the "f" sound written so differently in the words *fit*, *stuff* and enou*gh*. Why do we write s*nee*r and d*ear* for the same vowel sound? Why is the *l* in wa*l*k silent? And so forth!

Presumably these irregularities have to do with the long history of written English and its acquisition of vocabulary from multiple other languages. The history of Slovak is very different. No single system for writing the language was adopted until the nineteenth century.

When a Slovak literary language was finally codified and widely accepted, the orthography—the system of letters used to represent the actual sounds of the language—was developed all at once by a trio of national leaders: Ľudovít Štúr, Jozef Miloslav Hurban, and Michal Miloslav Hodža; Hodža was my great-granduncle (Chapter18).

The system they put in place was modified shortly thereafter in the so-called Hodža-Hattala reform, and today's Slovak uses this revised form almost intact. It works extremely well.

Twenty-three of the twenty-six familiar letters of the Roman alphabet are used; *q, w, and x* appear only in foreign words. Modifications of the basic sounds are indicated by *diacritical marks* rather than by associating them with specific other letters. Here is how it works for vowels.

Any vowel can be sounded short or long. If it is short, it is unmarked. If it is long, it is marked by an accent mark over it. Two other diacritical marks are also used, as follows:

SHORT	SOUND	LONG	SOUND
a	up	á	argue
ä	Half-way between bed and bad		
e	bed	é	fair
i	bit	í	beet
o	sport	ó	long
ô	quote		
u	put	ú	snooze
y		ý	The difference between *i* and *y* is hard to hear and is not recognizable in all Slovak speech. It is maintained in spelling for historical reasons, but there are initiatives for eliminating the use of *y* altogether.

A consonant can be hard, soft, or in some cases long, marked with diacritical marks as follows:

HARD	SOUND	SOFT	SOUND
c	fits	č	*check*
d	dog	ď	*duration*
l	long	ľ	approximated by *ly*
n	now	ň	*news*
t	toe	e	*tune*
z	zoo	ž	*pleasure*

- In all cases the diacritical mark indicating softness is a little check mark. However, when used with tall letters, modern printed text simplifies it.
- The distinction between the hard *l* and the soft *ľ* can be hard for English speakers to hear. It is more pronounced in some regions of Slovakia, such as County Turiec, than in others, such as the region around the city of Trnava.
- *l*, *n* and *r* can also be long, indicated by *ĺ, ń, and ŕ*, marked just as in the case of long vowels. We do not use equivalent sounds in English words (except perhaps for b*rrr*), but they are easily made.
- *j* is always pronounced as a soft consonant. We would usually use *y* for this sound. The sound of our *j*, as in *jury*, would be spelled *dž*.

- One and only one modification of one consonant by a following conso-nant occurs: *ch*. In the alphabet it follows *h*, and is pronounced as the same combination in the German a*ch* or Na*ch*t.

- Like many other languages, Slovak does not use the sound of the English *th*. *t* is the closest equivalent.

Here is how a sample English sentence would be spelled using Slovak or-thography. Easy, right?: *Hír iz hau a sämpl Ingliš sentens wud bí speld júzing Slovak ortografy. Ízi, rajt?*

An excellent on-line pronunciation guide is available at: http://www.slav-ism.com/slovak/abc.htm.

Genealogy

My Maternal Great-Grandparents

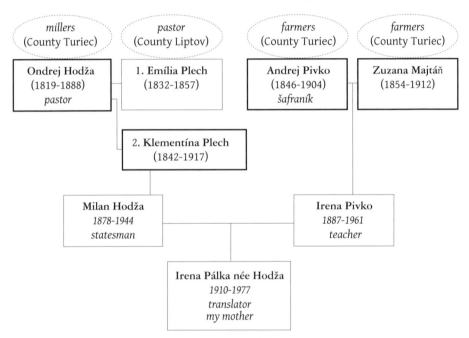

1. My great-grandparents on my mother's side—Ondrej Hodža, Klementína Plech, Andrej Pivko, and Zuzana Majtáň (all shown in bold)—had diverse occupations. Their ancestors lived in County Turiec and County Liptov, and they, too, made their living in a variety of ways.

The Four Pivko Sisters

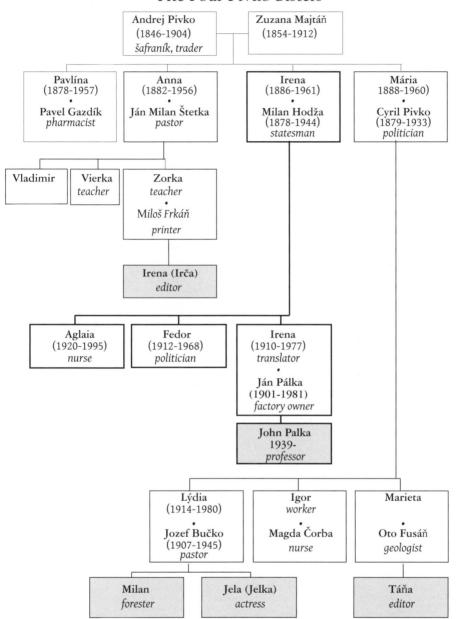

2. The four Pivko sisters, their prominent husbands, and their descendants. The cousins of my generation are shown shaded. They appear at various points in the narrative, especially Jelka as the daughter of the resistance hero Jozef Bučko (Chapter 6) and my companion on many occasions (e.g. Prologue), Milan as my consultant on addressing a crowd of young people (Chapter 32), and Irča who accompanied me to the Institute of the Nation's Memory (Chapter 31). Milan and I are seen as boys in the photograph on page 77 (Chapter 7), together with my paternal cousin Karol Pavlů (see also Epilogue).

My Paternal Great-Grandparents

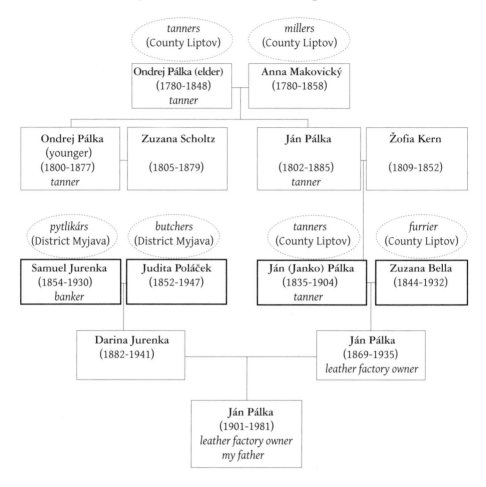

3. The occupations of my great-grandparents on my father's side—Janko Pálka, Zuzana Bella, Samuel Jurenka, and Judita Poláček (all shown in bold) and their ancestors as well—were as diverse as were those on my mother's side. The families lived in County Liptov and also in District Myjava in the borderlands with Moravia. Sometimes the family occupations were maintained for many generations; in other cases they changed abruptly from one generation to the next. The members of the great-grandparental generation were well-to-do; the generations before them were more modest, but highly respected in their communities.

The Bella Siblings

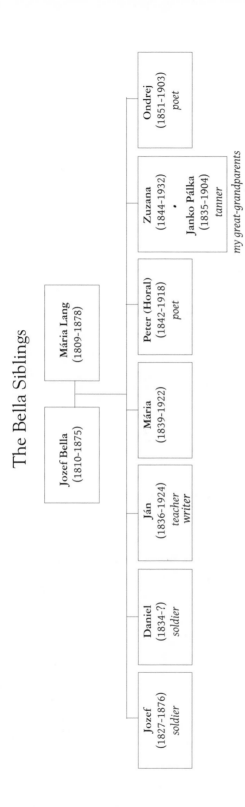

Jozef Bella
(1810-1875)

Mária Lang
(1809-1878)

Jozef
(1827-1876)
soldier

Daniel
(1834-?)
soldier

Ján
(1836-1924)
teacher
writer

Mária
(1839-1922)

Peter (Horal)
(1842-1918)
poet

Zuzana
(1844-1932)
·
Janko Pálka
(1835-1904)
tanner

my great-grandparents

Ondrej
(1851-1903)
poet

4. The remarkable Bella siblings. The men included two freedom fighters, a teacher-writer, and two poets. Despite an intense identification with Slovakia and her culture, all of them died on foreign soil.

Hodža Patriots and Activists

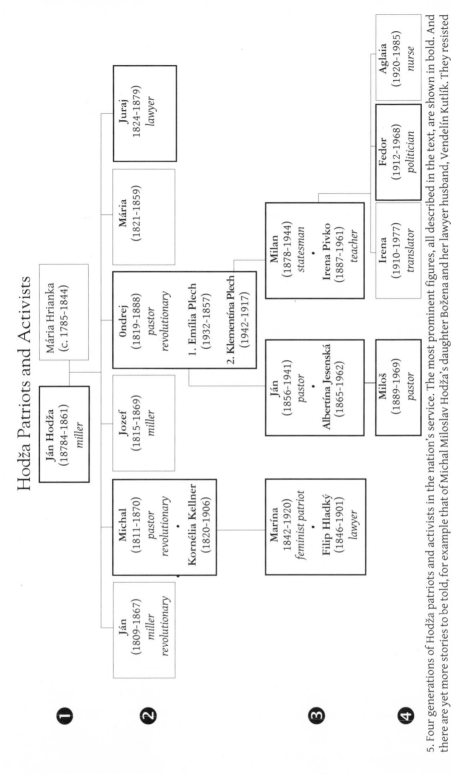

Ján Hodža
(18784–1861)
miller

Mária Hrianka
(c. 1785–1844)

❶

Ján
(1809–1867)
miller
revolutionary

Michal
(1811–1870)
pastor
revolutionary
•
Kornélia Kellner
(1820–1906)

Jozef
(1815–1869)
miller

Ondrej
(1819–1888)
pastor
revolutionary

1. Emília Plech
(1932–1857)

2. Klementína Plech
(1942–1917)

Mária
(1821–1859)

Juraj
(1824–1879)
lawyer

❷

Marína
1842–1920
feminist patriot
•
Filip Hladký
(1846–1901)
lawyer

Ján
(1856–1941)
pastor
•
Albertína Jesenská
(1865–1962)

Milan
(1878–1944)
statesman
•
Irena Pivko
(1887–1961)
teacher

❸

Miloš
(1889–1969)
pastor

Irena
(1910–1977)
translator

Fedor
(1912–1968)
politician

Aglaia
(1920–1985)
nurse

❹

5. Four generations of Hodža patriots and activists in the nation's service. The most prominent figures, all described in the text, are shown in bold. And there are yet more stories to be told, for example that of Michal Miloslav Hodža's daughter Božena and her lawyer husband, Vendelín Kutlík. They resisted Magyarization, worked with Slovak-minded students, and were cruelly persecuted. Their daughter Elena married Dr. Milan Ivanka, who was a prominent Slovak political leader in Czechoslovakia. She herself was a popular writer. The description of the memorable first encounter of her grandfather Michal Miloslav and his future bride Kornélia, quoted in the notes to Chapter 18, is her work.

Plates

1. *Plowing under the Tatras, oil painting by Ján Hála. This is one of Hála's many depictions of Slovak country life. My parents would have bought the painting directly from Hála after they were married in 1935 but before my mother left Czechoslovakia in 1939, most likely right after it was painted in 1937.*

2. Village girl, oil painting by Ján Hála (1937). Like the plowing scene on the previous page, this painting captures the Slovak village life and culture that Hála loved so much.

3. *Sleighride in County Liptov, oil painting by Jaroslav Věšín (1897). Like Hála, Věšín was a Czech painter who became very popular in Slovakia and often painted Slovak themes, even though he is best known for work he did in Bulgaria. My parents bought this painting from a close friend, who had commissioned it from Věšín himself.*

4. *Arrival at Bratislava airport. An honor guard carrying the flag-draped casket containing Grandfather Hodža's remains moves slowly past the short row of government officials and family. From right to left: Prime Minister Mikuláš Dzurinda, Minister of Culture Milan Kňažko, the prime minister's Chief of Staff Tibor Tóth, Yvonne, and I. The government airplane that brought the casket, the delegation, and us from Chicago home to Slovakia is in the background. Photo TASR/Vladimir Benko.*

5. *Funeral service at the Slovak National Cemetery in Martin. The flag has been removed from the casket (seen at the lower right), and ceremonially folded for handing to me. For me, receiving the flag from the captain of the honor guard was the emotional high point of the entire ceremony. Photo TASR/Jozef Durnik.*

6. Memorial service for Milan Hodža at the Lutheran church in Martin, where I spoke on behalf of the family. Photo Filip Lašut, Martin.

7. Unveiling of the monument erected to Milan Hodža in 1951 by the Sdruženie československých exulantov (Association of Czechoslovak Exiles). Author's archive.

8. Monument as seen in 2008. Photo author.

9. Birthday card I made for my mother in the early 1950s when I was around twelve, expressing the dual loyalties my parents tried so hard to instill in me. Author's archive.

10. Crossing Rohtang Pass, western Himalaya, shortly before the end of our first year in India, 1961. Author's archive.

11. Riding a camel at the home village of an Indian graduate student friend. Near Delhi, 1961. Author's archive.

12. *Young elephant, still being trained for temple service, delivering traditional blessings to new daddy. Mahout holds Rachel, two months old. 1965. Author's archive.*

13. *My mother visiting me in my first laboratory at the University of Washington, 1970. Author's archive.*

14. Uncle Dušan Pálka, Tanya, and I on Prague's Charles Bridge shortly after our arrival in Czechoslovakia in 1976. Author's archive.

15. Hiking in the Tatra Mountains (Modré pliesko) during our first visit to Czechoslovakia in twenty-seven years. Left to right: Tanya (age eight), Yvonne, Rachel (age ten). 1976. Photo author.

16. Rachel and Tanya wearing costumes (kroje) from Liptovské Sliače. Taken in my parents' apartment in New York City after our return from Czechoslovakia and England, 1976. Author's archive.

17. My father and I at a memorial ceremony for my mother, held at our home in Seattle. 1977. Author's archive.

18. Ondrej Pálka the younger. Portrait by Peter Michal Bohúň, 1860-1865. Kindly provided by the Gallery of Peter Michal Bohúň, Liptovský Mikoláš.

19. Zuzanna Scholtz, wife of Ondrej Pálka the younger. Portrait by Peter Michal Bohúň, 1860-1865. Kindly provided by the Gallery of Peter Michal Bohúň, Liptovský Mikoláš.

20. Michal Miloslav Hodža in his mature years. Portrait by Peter Michal Bohúň, 1866. Kindly provided by the Gallery of Peter Michal Bohúň, Liptovský Mikoláš, with the permission of the Slovak National Gallery, Bratislava.

21. *Lutheran church of Mikuláš with statues of Hodža and Tranovský flanking the entrance. Photo author.*

22. Statue of Michal Miloslav Hodža in front of the Lutheran church of Liptovský Mikuláš. Ladislav Pollák, sandstone. Photo author.

23. Church interior, including original pulpit and altar used by Hodža. Photo author.

24. Portrait of Milan Hodža. Oil, painter unknown.

25. *Portrait of Grandmother Hodža in national costume (kroj). Oil Painting by Nikolai Bogdanov-Belsky, one of Grandfather Hodža's favorite painters.*

26. *Catholic church of St. Nicholas on the square in the heart of Liptovský Mikuláš. Mikuláš grew up around this great church. Photo author.*

27. Old burgher houses, beautifully restored, on the main square of Liptovský Mikuláš. Photo author.

28. Villa my parents started to build in the late 1930s. It was finished during the first years of World War II while we were fleeing from the Nazis; we lived in it for barely over two years after the war. Photo author.

29. *Grand parade at Folklore Festival Východná 2012, flags in the lead: the Slovak flag on the left, the flag of the village of Východná in the middle, and the flag of the European Union on the right. Behind the latter is the banner of the folklore group Kriváň. It has pride of place because it is from Východná itself; scores of other groups follow. Photo author.*

30. *Crowds outside the amphitheater buildings at Východná. Photo author.*

31. *Solo dancer from the town of Detva in Central Slovakia. Detva is famous throughout the country for its colorful folk traditions. It hosts its own folklore festival, often just a week after Východná. Photo author.*

32. *Folklore group Vinica from the village of Myslava. Myslava is an industrial village now incorporated into Košice, the major city of Eastern Slovakia. It boasts two separate folklore groups and actively maintains ties with the descendants of numerous emigrants in the United States. Photo author.*

33. Laying of flowers on my grandparents' grave, Days of Milan Hodža 2005. At the foot of the grave stands then-premier Mikuláš Dzurinda. I stand at the head, and facing us are several members of my family. Photo Milan Bučko.

34. Laying flowers at the grave, 2008. Grandmother Hodža's sister Anna and her husband Ján Milan Štetka are buried in the adjacent grave. Photo Milan Bučko.

35. *Speaking to an enthusiastic crowd of young people at a pop concert during the Days of Milan Hodža 2006. Photo Milan Bučko.*

36. *Flyer announcing a ceremony at the English-Slovak Bilingual Gymnasium of Milan Hodža in Sučany at which the winners of the 2007 national competition, Hodža's Essay, are to be presented. Photo author.*

37. Hand-painted certificate awarding Grandfather Milan Hodža honorary citizenship in the city of Lučenec in celebration of his sixtieth birthday in 1938. It is written in both Slovak and Magyar, reflecting Hodža's ongoing support for national minorities. Archive of the National Museum, Prague.

38. Laying of wreaths at the bust of Milan Hodža that has been placed alongside his father's church in Sučany, Days of Milan Hodža 2009. Yvonne and I prepare to lay flowers on behalf of the family. Photo Milan Bučko.

39. *Author with Pavol Lukáč, the young historian who, more than anyone else, was responsible for the return of the remains of Milan Hodža to Slovak soil. We are celebrating this momentous event on the day of the final ceremonies at the National Cemetery in Martin in 2002.*

40. *The great historian Jozef Jablonický receives the Prize of Milan Hodža in 2007. Left to right: I, Jablonický, and Jelka Bučková, my cousin and daughter of the hero of the Slovak National Uprising, pastor Jozef Bučko (Chapter 6). Photo Milan Bučko.*

41. With Ivan Rázus, my childhood friend from Mikuláš who has served as my living link to the beautiful spots of County Liptov as well as the inner life of Mikuláš. Photo Yvonne Palka.

42. With Jano Bulík, son of our family's hero Janko Bulík (Chapter 30). The picture was taken in 2007 in Kovačica while we both attended celebrations honoring Janko Bulík. The white wall behind us is on the only remaining original portion of the house in front of which Jano was photographed with my father and a group of resistance organizers at Eastertime in 1940 (page 126). Photo in author's archive.

43. *Our whole American family visits Slovakia in 2012. This photo was taken in the Gallery of Peter Michal Bohúň in Liptovský Mikuláš, in front of Bohúň's portraits of my ancestor Ondrej Pálka and his wife Zuzana Scholz (Chapter 16, plates 18 and 19). From left to right: the Lochtefeld family—James, Vera, Gavin, Fiona, and our daughter Rachel; I with Yvonne; the Thomas family—our daughter Tanya, Mia, Carson, Chad. Photo Alida Hižnayová, who kindly gave us a tour of the gallery.*

44. *Presidential palace in Bratislava, the former residence of Count Grassalkovič, one of the high nobles of Hungary. The large open area in front of the palace, from which the photograph was taken, is Hodža Square, named after Michal Miloslav Hodža (Chapters 18-20). Photo author.*

45. Main Square of Bratislava, seen through the archway of the Old Town Hall that forms one of its sides. The square is a favorite meeting place, lined with old buildings, charming cafes featuring outdoor seating, and booths from which vendors sell souvenirs. It is also the venue for many public performances. Photo author.

46. On and near the Main Square of Bratislava are several whimsical sculptures. One of them is Čumil, the worker emerging from a manhole. Installed in 1997 as part of the reconstruction of Old Bratislava, it immediately became a favorite of locals and visitors alike. Here he is visited by our Lochtfeld grandkids, from bottom to top, Vera, Fiona, and Gavin. Photo author.

47. *Around a corner from Čumil is the newest of the statues, the paparazzo. He has found a fine subject in our granddaughter Mia Thomas, but is caught in the act by her watchful brother Carson. Photo author.*

48. *What could be more fun on a sunny Bratislava day than a ride in my cousin Karol's Bugatti? Author's photo of Carson Thomas.*

49. Evening view of Old Bratislava from the new restaurant-lined promenade along the Danube. The dramatically illuminated castle dominates the skyline, but St. Martin's Cathedral with its green tower roof is also striking. For centuries the coronation route of Hungarian kings led from the castle to the cathedral. For me, this view encapsulates today's Slovakia—despite ongoing debates about politics and economics, wariness about remnants of the Communist past, and a slim budget, this is a dynamic country that is trying to build its future on the foundation of its past.

Endnotes

Chapter 1: Prague, 1935-1938

1. Igor Lukes, *Czechoslovakia between Stalin and Hitler: The Diplomacy of Edvard Beneš in the 1930s*, Oxford University Press, New York and Oxford, 1996; Jindřich Dejmek, *Edvard Beneš, Československo a Mníchov: reality a mýty okolo osudového rozhodování z konce září 1938*. In: Jan Němeček, *Mníchovská dohoda, cesta k destrukci demokracie v Evropě*, Univerzita Karlova v Praze, Nakladatelství Karolinum, Praha, 2004.

2. Czechoslovak military planners understood these fortifications not as a means of defeating an overwhelmingly powerful German force, but as the foundation of a holding action. They were intended to stall the Germans until Czechoslovakia's own troops were fully mobilized. It was anticipated that the army would be forced to retreat eastward into Slovakia, and there it would fight until French troops came to its assistance and launched a counterattack. The maximum period Czechoslovakia could hold out alone against the Germans was estimated at only three weeks, and the anticipated, treaty-based intervention of France was therefore pivotal. The defense posture of Czechoslovakia, especially from a historical perspective, is well described by Miloslav Čaplovič, *Československá armáda a Slovensko v rokoch 1919-1939*. In: Milan Zemko and Valerián Bystrický (Eds.), *Slovensko v Československu (1918-1939)*, Veda, Vydavateľstvo Slovenskej akadémie vied, Bratislava, 2004.

3. The parliament elected Dr. Edvard Beneš as the country's new president only with Hodža's active support. The two men had different outlooks on many policy issues, and had also been political antagonists for many years, but Hodža had given his word to Czechoslovakia's founding president, Tomáš Garrigue Masaryk, that he would support Beneš, and he kept that word. The contemporary Czech historian and political comentator Pavel Kosatík has an interesting perspective on Hodža's action: *Uherský gróf v čele vlády*, Bradlo, no. 50/51, p. 8, 2008.

   > Supporting Beneš at this critical juncture might seem to be in conflict with the lifelong, relatively conservative thrust of Hodža's politics. He decided to give this support because his loyalty to the state triumphed over his party convictions. Certainly this was a key moment in Hodža's life: if, in 1935, he had enabled conservative forces in the Hrad [Prague Castle, the nerve center of Czechoslovak politics] to push through one of their own candidates, Czechoslovakia might have been able to avoid war with Hitler, and history might have been different.

4. Anna Krivá, *Zákon na obranu štátu a jeho vojensko-politické zretele*. In: Miroslav Pekník (Ed.), *Pohľady na slovenskú politiku*, Veda, Vydavateľstvo Slovenskej akadémie vied, Bratislava, 2000; Miloslav Čaplovič, *Československá armáda a Slovensko v rokoch 1919-1939*; Vladimír Zuberec, *Tragédia veľkého taktika*, Národná obroda, 10. decembra 1991.

5. The ethnic complexities of Czechoslovakia have been reviewed many times. I have relied primarily on the opening chapters of two studies: Paul Vyšný, *The Runciman Mission to Czechoslovakia, 1938*, Palgrave Macmillan, Houndmills and New York, 2003; and James Ramon Felak, *At the Price of the Republic: Hlinka's Slovak People's Party, 1929-1939*, University of Pittsburgh Press, Pittsburgh and London, 1994.

6. A particularly eloquent analysis of Slovak feelings and aspirations is given by Jan Rychlík, *Czech-Slovak Relations in Czechoslovakia, 1919-1939*. In: Mark Cornwall and R. J. W. Evans (Eds.), *Czechoslovakia in a Nationalist and Fascist Europe, 1918-1948*. Oxford University Press, Oxford and New York, 2007. James Ramon Felak, ibid., and Abby Innes, *Czechoslovakia: The Short Goodbye*, Yale University Press, New Haven and London, 2001, provide other balanced accounts.

7. Alena Bartlová, *Návrhy slovenských politických strán na zmenu štátoprávneho usporiadania ČSR v rokoch 1918-1935 a zapojenie HSĽS do vládnej koalície v rokoch 1927-1929*. In: Milan Zemko, Valerián Bystrický (Eds.), *Slovensko v Československu (1918-1939)*, Veda, Vydavateľtvo Slovenskej akadémie vied, Bratislava, 2004. James Ramon Felak, ibid.

8. Valerián Bystrický, *Milan Hodža a česko-slovenské vzťahy koncom 30. rokov*. In: Miroslav Pekník (Ed.), *Milan Hodža: štátnik a politik*. Veda, Vydavateľstvo Slovenskej akadémie vied, Bratislava, 2002. Available in English as Valerián Bystrický, *Milan Hodža and Czecho-Slovak Relations at the End of the 1930s*. In: Miroslav Pekník (Ed.), *Milan Hodža: Statesman and Politician*, Veda, Slovak Academy of Sciences Press, 2007.

9. What Henlein's real intensions were, at what moment in history, has long been disputed. A recent study that articulates the complex situation within the Sudeten German political sphere, and argues that Henlein himself only gradually moved toward being an agent for Hitler, is Mark Cornwall, *A Leap into Ice-Cold Water: The Manoeuvres of the Henlein Movement in Czechoslovakia, 1933-1938*. The historical and especially economic background to these complexities is analyzed by Catherine Albright, *Economic Nationalism in the Sudetenland, 1918-1938*. Both in: Mark Cornwall and R. J. W. Evans (Eds.), *Czechoslovakia in a Nationalist and Fascist Europe, 1918-1948*. Oxford University Press, Oxford and New York, 2007.

10. James Ramon Felak, *At the Price of the Republic: Hlinka's Slovak People's Party, 1929-1939*, pp. 183-185.

11. These are available online at the *London Times* archive, http://archive.timesonline.co.uk/tol/archive/

12. William L. Shirer, *Berlin Diary: The Journal of a Foreign Correspondent 1934-1941*, Alfred A. Knopf, New York, 1941, p. 97.

13. Sydney Morrell, *I Saw the Crucifixion*, Peter Davies, London, 1939, pp. 2-3.

14. Paul Vyšný, *The Runciman Mission to Czechoslovakia, 1938*. Jindřich Dejmek, *Nenaplněné naděje: Politické a diplomatické vztahy Československa a Velké Británie (1918-1938)*, Univerzita Karlova v Praze, Nakladatelství Karolinum, Praha, 2003.

15. Peter Neville, *Nevile Henderson and Basil Newton, Two British Envoys in the Czech Crisis 1938*. In: Igor Lukes and Erik Goldstein (Eds.), *The Munich Crisis, 1938: Prelude to World War II*, Frank Cass, London and Portland, 1999.

16. Paul Vyšný, *The Runciman Mission to Czechoslovakia, 1938*, p. 26.

17. Igor Lukes, *Czechoslovakia between Stalin and Hitler: The Diplomacy of Edvard Beneš in the 1930s*, pp. 139-140.

18. The intelligence reports on the basis of which the Czechoslovak government ordered the partial mobilization of its armed forces now appear to have been a sophisticated hoax, with the perpetrator still unidentified. Ibid., pp. 143-157.

19. James Ramon Felak, *At the Price of the Republic: Hlinka's Slovak People's Party, 1929-1939*, pp. 189-191.

20. See Note 8.

21. Sydney Morrell, *I Saw the Crucifixion*, gives many vivid examples.

22. Paul Vyšný, *The Runciman Mission to Czechoslovakia, 1938*.

23. Ibid., p. 148.

24. *Premier Hodža*. In: *The New York Times*, August 4, 1938. This piece credits Hodža with more influence than he actually had. For many years Czechoslovak foreign affairs were the jealously guarded domain of Edvard Beneš, first as foreign minister and later as president.

25. E.g. Paul Vyšný, *The Runciman Mission to Czechoslovakia, 1938*, pp. 237-238.

26. Ibid., pp. 310-316. Runciman's final report was submitted on September 21, 1938, in the form of two nearly identical letters, one to Chamberlain and the other to Beneš. It was several pages long, but a few words will show its tenor:

> Responsibility for the final break must, in my opinion, rest upon Herr Henlein and Herr Frank and upon those of their supporters inside and outside the country who were urging them to the extreme and unconstitutional action. . . .

> I have much sympathy, however, with the Sudeten case. It is a hard thing to be ruled by an alien race; and I have been left with the impression that Czechoslovak rule in the Sudeten areas for the last twenty years, though not actively oppressive and certainly not 'terroristic' [as often proclaimed by Hitler], has been marked by tactlessness, lack of understanding, petty intolerance and discrimination, to a point where the resentment of the German population was inevitably moving in the direction of revolt.

> . . . It has become self-evident to me that those frontier districts between Czechoslovakia and Germany where the Sudeten population is in an important majority should be given full right of self-determination immediately. If some cession is inevitable, as I believe it to be, it is well that it should be done promptly and without procrastination. . . . I consider, therefore, that these frontier districts should at once be transferred from Czechoslovakia to Germany. . . .

In his analysis, Vyšný adds: "The Runciman report amounted to one of the most hostile communications ever delivered from the representative of one friendly country to another."

27. Igor Lukes, *Czechoslovakia between Stalin and Hitler: The Diplomacy of Edvard Beneš in the 1930s*, pp. 221-228.

28. Ibid., pp. 230-231.

29. Jindřich Dejmek, *Edvard Beneš, Československo a Mnichov: reality a mýty okolo osudového rozhodování z konce září 1938*. Valerián Bystrický, *Slovensko a Mnichov*. Both in: Jan Němeček, *Mnichovská dohoda, cesta k destrukci demokracie v Evropě*, Univerzita Karlova v Praze, Nakladatelství Karolinum, Praha, 2004.

30. Igor Lukes, *Czechoslovakia between Stalin and Hitler: The Diplomacy of Edvard Beneš in the 1930s*, p. 231. The degree to which Beneš, and president Tomáš Garrigue Masaryk before him, dominated the politics of interwar Czechoslovakia was controversial at the time, and has recently come in for serious and sometimes scathing scholarly criticism. See, for example, Andrea Orzoff, *Battle for the Castle: The Myth of Czechoslovakia in Europe, 1914-1948*, Oxford University Press, Oxford, 2009, and Mary Heimann, *Czechoslovakia: The State That Failed*, Yale University Press, New Haven and London, 2009.

31. Igor Lukes, *Czechoslovakia between Stalin and Hitler: The Diplomacy of Edvard Beneš in the 1930s*, p. 231-232.

32. Syrový was a hero of the Czechoslovak legions formed in Russia during World War I, and had served as chief-of-staff of the Czechoslovak army (1927-1933) and later its inspector-general (1933-1938). In 1945, as soon as the war was over, he was arrested as a German collaborator. He was tried by the Communists, sentenced to twenty years' imprisonment, and released somewhat early. He never conceded any wrongdoing and continued to view Munich as a betrayal. http://en.wikipedia.org/wiki/Jan_Syrový.

33. Aunt Vierka and my mother were cousins: their mothers were sisters. See Chapter 14.

34. The brief text of the Munich Agreement is available on line at http://avalon.law.yale.edu/subject_menus/munmenu.asp.

35. Dorothy Thompson, a great journalist of the times, described the betrayal clearly in her radio broadcast of October 1, 1938:

> On Friday Czechoslovakia was disposed of by four men who in four hours made a judgment of the case in which the defendant was not even allowed to present a brief or be heard. .

.. Not one of the four men who thus arbitrarily disposed of a nation had ever set foot in Czechoslovakia. .... Not only is Czechoslovakia dismembered—what is left is destroyed as a democratic republic. It will be utterly impossible for the new state to exist, under the conditions created, as anything except a military and semi-Fascist dictatorship. .... Let us not call this peace. Peace is not the absence of war. Peace is a positive condition—the rule of law. This peace has been established on lawlessness, and can only maintain itself by further lawlessness. This peace has been established by dictatorship, and can only maintain itself by further dictatorship. This peace has been established by betrayal, and can only maintain itself by further betrayal.

http://www.otr.com/peace.html

With the passage of time a wide range of judgments about this pivotal event has been expressed. For a view that emphasizes the complexities of any military intervention on another country's behalf see, for example, Gerhard L. Weinberg, *Reflections on Munich after 60 Years.* In: Igor Lukes and Erik Goldstein (Eds.), *The Munich Crisis, 1938: Prelude to World War II.*

36. Erik Goldstein, *Neville Chamberlain, the British Official Mind and the Munich Crisis.* In: Igor Lukes and Erik Goldstein (Eds.), *The Munich Crisis, 1938: Prelude to World War II.* Frank McDonough, *Chamberlain and the Czech Crisis: A Case Study in the Role of Morality in the Conduct of International Relations.* In: Jan Němeček, *Mníchovská dohoda, cesta k destrukci demokracie v Evropě,* Univerzita Karlova v Praze, Nakladatelství Karolinum, Praha, 2004.

Chapter 2: Born on the Brink of War

1. Irena Pálková-Hodžová, *Rozpomienky na otca,* Naše Snahy 10,1944, pp. 21-22.

2. Ján Bulík, Personal communication, 2005.

3. Ivan Kamemec, *The Slovak Republic, 1939-1945.* In: Mikuláš Teich, Dušan Kováč and Martin D. Brown (Eds.), *Slovakia in History,* Cambridge University Press, 2011.

4. From the stories of Ludmila Pálka, my Aunt Ludinka.

5. Jan Kulkík and Jan Němeček, *Hodža versus Beneš.* Univerzita Karlova v Praze, Nakladatelství Karolinum, 1999.

6. Susan Mikula, *Milan Hodža and the Slovak National Movement, 1898-1918.* Ph.D. Dissertation, Syracuse University, 1974. Available through University Microfilms International, Ann Arbor, Michigan 48106, U.S.A. and London, England. p. iii.

7. Ján Jančovic, *Z kolísky na Dolnú zem,* Matica slovenská, Martin 2004, pp. 149-153; Personal communication, 2007.

8. Letter of Irena Hodža, dated July 9, 1939. Author's archive.

9. The American Hospital of Paris has a long and distinguished history. It was established in 1906. In 1913 the U.S. Congress passed an act giving the hospital federal status. During World War I its volunteer ambulance service was staffed by Americans and served over 10,000 soldiers. Its nursing school, which was in operation from 1914 until 1930, taught classes in English. During World War II it became a military hospital under the Red Cross. It has continued to modernize and expand up to the present, and in 2006 celebrated its centennial year. www.american-hospital.org.

10. After strokes incapacitated her, Grandmother Hodža was lovingly cared for by my aunts Vierka Štetková and Zorka Frkáňová in their home in Martin.

11. Diary of Irena Pálka née Hodža. Author's archive.

12. Originals kept in the family archive which was deposited in the Archive of the National Museum, Prague. Fond Milana Hodžu, 21/768.

13. The institutionalized persecution of Jews was formalized most completely in the so-called Jewish Codex that was promulgated on September 9, 1941 (See Chapter 6). It was the most restrictive anti-Jewish piece of legislation outside of Germany. Ivan Kamemec, *The Slovak Republic, 1939-1945.* In: Mikuláš Teich, Dušan Kováč, and Martin D. Brown (Eds.), *Slovakia in History.*

14. Archive of the National Museum, Prague. Fond Milana Hodžu, 21/766.

15. Many detailed chronologies of World War II and the events leading up to it are available. I have relied principally on two: the *Encyclopedia Britannica, edition of 1954*, and the web site of *The History Place*: www.historyplace.com/worldwar2/timeline/ww2time.htm#1940

16. Jan Hyrman, *The Free Czechoslovak Army*. www.nasenoviny.com/FreeArmyFranceEN.html

Chapter 3: Eluding the Gestapo

1. www.labaule.com/tourisme/histoire.php?lang=eng.

2. As in the preceding chapter, I have relied principally on two sources for the chronology of events related to World War II: the *Encyclopedia Britannica, edition of 1954*, and the web site of *The History Place*: www.historyplace.com/worldwar2/timeline/ww2time.htm#1940.

3. Diary of Irena Pálka née Hodža. Author's archive.

4. Irène Nemirovsky, *Suite Francaise*. Alfred A. Knopf, New York, 2006.

5. Diary of Irena Pálka née Hodža. Author's archive.

6. During World War II La Baule formed part of the protective stretch of coast leading to the nearby harbour city of Saint-Nazaire, home of one of the biggest U-Boat stations the Germans ever built. It not only serviced the German submarine fleet, but was also the only dry dock on the Atlantic capable of housing the German battleship Tirpitz, one of two Bismarck-class ships built for the German Kriegsmarine during World War II.

   La Baule and the surrounding areas were heavily occupied by the Germans throughout World War II. During the occupation a large number of Jewish residents and resistance members were deported to the concentration camps; in La Baule itself thirty-two Jewish men, women and children—the youngest of whom was three years old—were deported (with the assistance of the local French police) to Auschwitz where they all perished. Although there is a memorial in the Parc de la Victoire in La Baule to forty named war victims, there is no mention there or on any other memorial of the thirty-two Jewish deportees.

   Such was the importance attached the area by the Germans that their troops kept fighting in La Baule and Saint-Nazaire for nine months longer than in the rest of the department, eventually surrendering on May 11, 1945 (three days after the German unconditional surrender), making this one of the last liberated parts of France. This episode is called *Poche de Saint-Nazaire* from the French expression *poche de resistance*.

   http://en.wikipedia.org/wiki/La_Baule-Escoublac.

7. In 1953 my mother took a language class for foreigners at Columbia University in order to perfect her already excellent command of English. She saved all of the essays she wrote as homework for the class, and they are now in my archive. The account given here bears the title "A Danger I Escaped."

8. This account is based on my mother's stories as I remember them. There is a brief mention of our escape from Occupied into Free France in another essay assignment titled "A Letter to My Son." See also Chapter 12, pp. 113–114.

9. During World War II Portugal declared neutrality and Lisbon became a haven for refugees, particularly from Central Europe. Liberal policies allowed large numbers of Jews fleeing Hitler to pass through the country on their way to other destinations. The number of refugees from Germany alone exceeded 100,000. Lisbon also became a major center for espionage activities. http://en.wikipedia.org/wiki/Participants_in_World_War_II#Portugal.

10. www.aviation-history.com/boeing/314.html; http://en.wikipedia.org/wiki/Boeing_314.

11. www.clipperflyingboats.com.

Chapter 4: Immigrants in a New Land

1. Transcript of the interrogation of Ján Pálka by National Security (*Štátna bezpečnosť*), Bratislava, April 12, 1948. Photocopy released to me by the Institute of the National Memory (*Ústav pamäti národa*) on May 30, 2006. See Chapter 31.

2. Letter in author's archive.

3. The best-known member of the Langsfeld family of Sučany was Juraj (Ďurko) Langsfeld, a prominent Slovak leader in the revolution of 1848 (Chapters 19 and 20) who was captured and hanged by the Magyar authorities. The Emil Langsfeld who settled in Chicago was a distant relative. Information about the Langsfeld family courtesy Miroslav Miert of Sučany, 2002-2007.

4. Letter in author's archive.

5. Transcript of interrogation.

6. Dr. Michal Múdry-Šebík (1909-1978), known in our family as Uncle Miško Múdry, and his wife Jarmilka played a profound role in our life in exile. Our close friendship started in Chicago during World War II when Uncle Miško and my father found themselves working side by side on the assembly line at F & B Manufacturing, and we and the Múdrys saw each other almost every day. It continued in New York after our second escape from Czechoslovakia, both because he was my mother's boss at Radio Free Europe (Chapter 10) and simply because the friendship was so close. A lawyer by training, a long-time political organizer, and also a gifted actor, Uncle Miško was active in a number of Slovak emigrant organizations and worked with Grandfather Hodža as his personal secretary in the United States, the leading propagator of his ideas, and his biographer. In addition to numerous essays in the emigrant periodical *Naše Snahy* in New York, he was the author of two major studies, *Milan Hodža v Amerike* (Milan Hodža in America), Geringer Press, Chicago, 1949, and *Milan Hodža's Efforts to Federalize Central Europe*, published posthumously in Bohemia, Jahrbuch des Collegium Carolinum, vol. 20, p. 97-136, 1979. The Collegium, based in Munich, is a leading research institute for Czech and Slovak affairs.

7. Slovak National Archive, Bratislava. Fond Vladimíra Žuffu, established by his daughter, Naďa Micherová-Žuffová.

Chapter 5: Milan Hodža in America

1. The Lend-Lease program, initiated in 1941, enabled the United States to supply war materiel to Britain and other allies on a payment-deferred basis. It was a major step away from neutrality and toward active engagement in the battle against Germany and Japan. http://en.wikipedia.org/wiki/Lend-Lease.

2. The so-called Battle of the Atlantic lasted the full duration of the war period, from 1939 to 1945. http://en.wikipedia.org/wiki/Battle_of_the_Atlantic_(1939—1945).

3. A detailed chronological dissection of this conflict is presented by Jan Kuklík and Jan Němeček, *Hodža versus Beneš*, Nakladatelství Karolinum, Praha, 1999.

4. Hodža presented his views in detail in a book published in England during the war, Milan Hodža, *Federation in Central Europe*, Jarrold's Publishers, London, 1942

5. For analyses of Beneš's relationships with the Soviet Union and with Stalin himself see Igor Lukes, *Czechoslovakia between Stalin and Hitler: The Diplomacy of Edvard Beneš in the 1930s*. Oxford University Press, Oxford, 1996; Zbyněk Zeman and Antonín Klimek, *The Life of Edvard Beneš, 1884-1948*. Oxford University Press, New York, 1997; Colleen McCoy, *Policies and Consequences: Edvard Beneš and the Rise of Communism in Czechoslovakia*. Thesis, International Studies, University of Washington, Seattle. 1990.

6. When Slovaks came to the United States in the greatest numbers, in the decades surrounding the turn of the nineteenth/twentieth century, they formed numerous clubs and associations through which they could maintain their language and culture, obtain practical support including insurance, and generally give each other a helping hand. During World War I these groups were the main channel through which American Slovaks supported the formation of Czechoslovakia

(see Chapter 26). Religion was of central importance to the immigrants, and accordingly most of the organizations were either Catholic or Protestant (predominantly Lutheran). Their memberships were sometimes very substantial, numbering in the tens of thousands. See, for example, M. Mark Stolárik, *Immigration and Urbanization: The Slovak Experience, 1870-1918*. AMS Press, New York, 1989.

7. "Hope put in union of Central Europe." *The New York Times*, December 7, 1941.

8. The activities of Milan Hodža in the United States during the war years have received three comprehensive treatments. The classic was written by his close collaborator and program organizer, Michal Múdry, *Milan Hodža v Amerike* (Milan Hodža in America), Geringer Press, Chicago, 1949. A modern analysis is Pavol Lukáč, *Milan Hodža v zápase o budúcnosť strednej Európy v rokoch 1939-1944* (Milan Hodža in the Battle for the Future of Central Europe in the Years 1939-1944). Štefan Šebesta (Ed.). Veda, Vydavateľstvo Slovenskej akadémie vied, Bratislava, 2005. See especially Chapter 3, *Politická činnosť Milana Hodžu v emigrácií v USA a reakcie na jeho federalistické plány* (The Political Activity of Milan Hodža in the U.S.A. and Reactions to His Federalization Plans), reprinted from *Historickí časopis* vol. 51, no. 4, pp. 605-626, 1996. Most recent are two fascinating and closely analyzed treatments based on extensive source material from heretofore classified documents of the United States government: Roman Ličko, *Pod dohľadom spravodajských služieb: Americká vláda a slovenská otázka v USA v rokoch 1939-1945* (Under Surveillance by the Secret Service: The American Government and the Slovak Question in the U.S.A. in the Years 1939-1945).Univerzita Mateja Bela, Banská Bystrica, 2008; and Roman Ličko, *Nevítaný hosť: Milan Hodža v dokumentoch americkej vlády v rokoch 1941-1944* (Unwelcome Guest: Milan Hodža in Documents of the American Government in the Years 1941-1944). Univerzita Mateja Bela, Banská Bystrica, 2010. My account draws on all three sources.

9. For the text of *Europe at the Crossroads* and an examination of the history of this memorandum, see Pavol Lukáč, *K osudom Hodžovho memoranda* (On the Fate of Hodža's Memorandum), Střední Evrópa, vol. 62, pp. 81-91, 1996, and *Európa na križovatke ciest* (Europe at the Crossroads), Střední Evrópa, vol 62, pp. 92-100. The text of the memorandum, first published in International Peasant Union Bulletin, Jan.-Feb. 1954, pp. 14-18, is also included in Milan Hodža, *Federácia v strednej Európe a iné štúdie* (Federation in Central Europe and Other Studies), Pavol Lukáč (Ed.), Kalligram, Bratislava, 1997 (the Slovak edition of Hodža's primary work in English, *Federation in Central Europe*. Lukáč was unable to discover who in the American government had actually read Hodža's memorandum. The answer emerged in the secret documents analyzed by Ličko (Note 8). The memorandum was studied by officers of the OSS who reacted positively to it. However, it did not influence the major decisions of the United States government.

10. For recent analyses of this aspect of Hodža's efforts, see Slavomír Michálek, *Americký krajania a Milan Hodža (1941-1944)* (Slovak-Americans and Milan Hodža, 1941-1944), In: *Milan Hodža a integrácia strednej Európy* (Milan Hodža and the Integration of Central Europe), Miroslav Pekník (Ed.), Veda, Vydavateľstvo Slovenskej akadémie vied, Bratislava, 2006, and Ličko, 2008 and 2010.

11. This new information is detailed in Ličko, 2008 and 2010.

12. Múdry, pp. 37-40. The ambassador was Vladimír Hurban, the information chief Ján Papánek. Hodža and our whole family long suspected their underhanded activity, but proof has only come now in the documents uncovered by Ličko, 2008 and 2010. Beneš's own more open stance toward Hodža is noted by Kuklík and Němeček, 1999, p. 162.

13. Many accounts of Hodža's activity after his departure from Czechoslovakia, and particularly during his years in the United States, speak of his recurring health problems. A particularly thoughtful analysis of the relationship between his growing illness and his political activity is offered by Pavol Lukáč, *Posledné chvíle Milana Hodžu* (The Last Moments of Milan Hodža), OS (Fórum Občianskej spoločnosti), August 2000, pp. 8-11.

14. Múdry, p. 20

15. Michal Múdry, *Ku storočnici Dr. Milana Hodžu* (Toward the Hundredth Anniversary of Dr. Milan Hodža), Naše snahy, vol. 14, no. 1, pp. 9-10, 1978.

16. Dr. Irena Pálková-Hodžová, *Rozpomienky na otca*, Naše snahy, no.10, pp. 21-22, 1974.

17. I have had the pleasure of two extended conversations with Lad Zidek, from which some of my information is drawn.

18. *The New York Times*, July 4, 1944.

19 In an article published in the Czech newspaper *New Yorkské Listy* (*New York Letters*) and reprinted in Pittsburgh in the Slovak newspaper *Slovenský hlásnik*, Pittsburgh, July 6, 1944, Masaryk wrote:

> I knew Milan Hodža for nearly 40 years, and for this entire long period we remained personal friends even though politically we were not close. I valued this greatly in Milan Hodža, that he did not personalize the political differences that we sometimes had. During our last conversation, Hodža once again and very clearly repeated what I never doubted, that he stands fully behind [a united] Czechoslovakia and that he fully acknowledges Eduard Beneš as his president.
>
> During my last conversation with him I had, for the first time, the definite impression that I was speaking with a very sick man. He was tired, he had aged, and he showed what I might call a passive resignation to a cruel fate. That the end would come so quickly, of course, I never suspected. Today, when with these simple lines I say goodby to my old friend, I bid farewell to a Slovak patriot, an enlightened Czechoslovak, and a statesman. One more personal experience will bind me to Hodža's memory. He was prime minister in September of 1937, and as such he was present at the death of my father on my 51st birthday. Now I will go to Chicago to bow my head by his casket, which, for the time being, will be buried in the free soil of America. I'm sorry, I'm sorry, that Hodža did not live to return home to a liberated Slovakia, to which his heart was so very close.
>
> Good bye, Milan.

20. *Denní hlasatel*, Chicago, July 4, 1944.

21. The *Times of London*, June 30, 1944. I view this obituary, obviously written by an admirer of Hodža, as the best written at the time. Portions of it are quoted in Chapter 27.

22. *The New York Times*, June 29, 1944.

23. *Slovenská obrana*, vol. 21, no. 53, p. 4, 1944.

24. Dr. Irena Pálková-Hodžová, *Hájim pamiatku svojho otca, Dr. Milana Hodžu* (*I Defend the Memory of My Father, Dr. Milan Hodža*).

25. It has often been asserted that Edvard Beneš personally blocked the return of Grandfather Hodža's remains. I have no evidence either for or against this claim.

25. The event was widely reported in the Czechoslovak press. The actual certificate signed by President Václav Havel is in the author's archive.

Chapter 6: Slovakia Rises and Heroes Come Forth

1. Several extensive accounts of the events leading to Slovakia's independence are available in English. Among them are: Valerián Bystrický, *Slovakia from the Munich Conference to the Declaration of Independence*. In: Mikuláš Teich, Dušan Kováč and Martin Brown (Eds.), *Slovakia in History*, Cambridge University Press, Cambridge and New York, 2011; Stanislav J. Kirschbaum, *A History of Slovakia: The Struggle for Survival (2nd Ed.)*, St. Martin's Press, New York, 2005; and Anton Spiesz and Dusan Caplovic, *Illustrated Slovak History*, Bolchazy-Carducci Publishers, Wauconds, Illinois, 2006.

2. A fascinating and nuanced account of the details of the Slovak-German relationship is provided in Tatjana Tönsmeyer, *The German Advisers in Slovakia, 1939-1945: Conflict or Co-operation?* In: Mark Cornwall and R. J. W. Evans (Eds.), *Czechoslovakia in a Nationalist and Fascist Europe 1918-1948*. Oxford University Press, Oxford and New York, 2007.

3. A classic and comprehensive account of Hlinka's Slovak People's Party is provided by James Ramon Felak, *At the Price of the Republic: Hlinka's Slovak People's Party, 1929-1938*. University of Pittsburgh Press, Pittsburgh and London, 1994.

4. Independence has often been interpreted as a Slovak holy grail, and as such should have elicited widespread jubilation. However, Peter Pares, the British consul present in Bratislava at the time, gives a very different account: " The reception given to the declaration on Tuesday [14 March] by the people of Bratislava was lukewarm indeed. There were no manifestations of joy and the townfolk went about their normal business as if nothing had happened … a week after the declaration of independence the inhabitants of Bratislava are still unable to show great enthusiasm for the present state of affairs. The general impression is one of apathy or pessimism." Quoted in Kirschbaum, 2005, p. 190.

5. Ivan Kamenec, *The Slovak Republic, 1939-1945*. In: Mikuláš Teich, Dušan Kováč and Martin Brown (Eds.), *Slovakia in History*; Kirschbaum, 2005; Spiesz and Caplovic, 2006.

6. Tönsmeyer, 2007. Felak, 1994, describes the HSPP in this way: "Certain basic features characterized the HSPP ideologically throughout the interwar period. Above all, the party was nationalistic, autonomist, and Roman Catholic. The slogans 'For God and Nation' and 'Slovakia to the Slovaks' underscored these definitive traits." An incisive recent analysis of the role of religion in the governing philosophy of the Slovak Republic is given by Nadya Nedelsky, *The wartime Slovak state: a case study in the relationship between ethnic nationalism and authoritarian patterns of governance.* Nations and Nationalism 7(2), 215-234, 2001. See also Chapter 4 in Nadya Nedelsky, *Defining the Sovereign Community: The Czech and Slovak Republics*, University of Pennsylvania Press, Philadelphia, 2009.

7. A particularly cogent account of this evolution is given by Bystrický, 2011. A generally pro-HSPP account of the Slovak Republic and the Slovak National Uprising is given by Kirschbaum, 2005.

8. Quoted in Kamenec, 2011, p. 178.

9. Quoted in Kamenec, 2011, p. 183.

10. Felak, 1994; Tönsmeyer, 2007.

11. A detailed account of aryanization is given by Ľudovít Hallon, *Arizácia na Slovensku 1939-1945*, Acta Oeconomica Pragensia vol.15, no. 7, pp. 148-160, 2007.

12. Kamenec, 2011.

13. The deportations came to an end after about six months. Why exactly this should have been the case is still not very clear. Admirers of Jozef Tiso have argued that it was a brave and humanitarian action on his part, but most historians are very skeptical of this interpretation. Deportations were resumed after the German occupation of Slovakia in 1944.

14. Hallon, 2007.

15. Jan Kuklík and Jan Němeček, *Hodža versus Beneš*, Univerzita Karlova v Praze, Nakladatelství Karolinum, 1999, pp. 30-33.

16. Cited in Kuklík and Němeček, ibid, p. 32.

17. Jozef Jablonický, *Z ilegality do povstania*, Epocha, Bratislava, 1969. This landmark book was the first honest and detailed account of the Slovak National Uprising to be published in Czechoslovakia, and it remains unsurpassed in its scope, intellectual reach, and attention to human stories. Many of them are stories of men I remember from my childhood. As Jablonický writes in his Introduction, "After the events of February [the Communist putsch in 1948], a number of the best-known leaders of the defeated parties went into exile. I will name only a few: Dr. Jozef Lettrich, Dr. Matej Josko, Rudolf Fraštacký, Ing Kornel Filo, Dr. Ján Behárka, Dr. Samuel Belluš, Ing. Pavol Blaho and others." Almost all of them were frequent visitors to our little apartment in New York. The paintings that were so dear to my parents, and are to me today (Prologue), were painstakingly cleaned of accumulated New York soot by Janko Behárka.

18. Jablonicky, pp. 37-42. For my father's role in Lichner's escape, see Chapter 13.

19. Ján Ursíny came from a farming family that had intermarried with the Hodžas several times over two centuries. A leader in various rural uplift organizations even before he became active in Grandfather Hodža's Agrarian Party, he was one of the many talented young men whom Hodža gathered around himself, guided, and helped to place in positions where they could apply their

talents to the public good. Ursíny was a member of the central board of and a dominant figure in the Farmers Mutual Bank (*Rol'nícke vzájomné pokladnice*), which Hodža established during the 1920s (Chapter 27), and was active as well with other similar credit unions. Ján Ursíny, *Z môjho života*. Matica slovenská, 2000. See also Chapter 13.

Jozef Lettrich was born into the family of a forester. Like Ursíny, he was a protégé of Grandfather Hodža, a member of the Agrarian Party, and active in banking and farmers' organizations—he headed the legal office of the Farmers Mutual Bank (Chapter 27). Both Lettrich and Ursíny were jailed by the newly-established Slovak Republic in 1939. After their release, they became the main organizers of the movement that culminated in the underground Slovak National Council. Later Lettrich went into hiding because the Nazi-oriented government sentenced him to death. Vojtech Čelko, www.gymlet.sk/info/lettrich.html; Jozef Žatkuliak, www.sav.sk/zatkuliak_lettrich. pdf; www.osobnosti.sk/index.php?os=zivotopis&ID=1738.

Matej Josko was Ursíny's brother-in-law. After obtaining his law degree, Josko had become a newspaper editor. A committed supporter of a united Czechoslovakia, he joined the underground group organized by Ján Lichner. Most of the discussions were carried out in his apartment in Bratislava, despite the fact that the doorman of the building was outspokenly pro-Nazi. The initial six-member Slovak National Council was soon expanded to include representatives of other parties besides the Agrarians, and once the group exceeded ten, the meetings were moved to Josko's cottage in the country to avoid the attention of the doorman and the secret police. Stanislav Mičev, *Matej Josko, tajúplný Pinkerton*. In: Slavomír Michálek and Natália Krajčovičová (Eds.), *Do pamäti národa*, Veda, Vydavateľstvo Slovenskej akadémie vied, Bratislava, 2003.

Among the new members was Dr. Peter Zaťko, an outstanding economist, director of several economic organizations, and a parliamentary representative in the government of the Slovak Republic. He was also the Republic's director of the budget. One of Zaťko's closest allies was Dr. Imrich Karvaš, likewise an outstanding economist, professor and, under the Slovak Republic, director of the Bureau of Provisions and governor of the Slovak National Bank. In their official roles, the team of Zaťko and Karvaš successfully directed a prospering Slovak economy while minimizing its contribution to the German war effort. Some of their actions were truly audacious, for example transferring virtually all the gold reserves of the Slovak government to Swiss banks, where they would be out of the reach of the Germans and preserved for the use of post-war Czechoslovakia. In their secret roles, they diverted for the use of the resistance large quantities of medical supplies, food, technical equipment, boots, clothing, and other necessities, as well as huge sums of money. It was a courageous feat, and both economically and politically, an extraordinarily effective one. Peter Zaťko, *Národohospodár Peter Zaťko spomína*, Tranoscius, Liptovský Mikuláš, 1994; http://sk.wikipedia.org/wiki/Peter_Zaťko; Milan Karvaš, *Môj otec Imrich Karvaš*, Vydavateľstvo Rak, Budmerice, 2001; http://www.tyzden.sk/casopis/2008/4/na-vrchole-i-na-dne.html. For the roles played by Zaťko and Karvaš in earlier debates about the position of Slovakia within Czechoslovakia see Martin Vašš, *Národohospodári Imrich Karvaš—Peter Zaťko a slovenská otázka v tridsiatych rokoch 20. storoia*. Historický časopis 60 (1), 99-114, 2012.

20. In a massive, complex, evolving, and underground action, of course, there were many participants and struggles for influence and leadership. A nuanced picture of the full situation can be found in Jozef Jablonický, *Príprava a vznik Slovenskej národnej rady*, and Pavel Šimunič, *Povstalecká národná rada*, both in Miroslav Pekník (Ed.), *Pohľady na slovenskú politiku: Geopolitika, Slovenské národné rady, čechoslovakizmus*, Veda, Vydavateľstvo Slovenskej akadémie vied, Bratislava, 2000.

21. Jan Rychlík, *The Slovak Question and the Resistance Movement*. In: Mikuláš Teich, Dušan Kováč and Martin Brown (Eds.), *Slovakia in History*, Cambridge University Press, Cambridge and New York, 2011.

22. A modern account of the uprising itself is given by Vilém Prečan, *The Slovak National Uprising: the most dramatic moment in the nation's history*. In: Mikuláš Teich, Dušan Kováč and Martin Brown (Eds.), *Slovakia in History*, Cambridge University Press, Cambridge and New York, 2011. See also the classic volume by one of the uprising's principal leaders Jozef Lettrich, *History of Modern Slovakia*, Praeger, New York, 1955.

23. Anna Josko, *The Slovak Resistance Movement*. In: Victor S. Mamatey and Radomir Luža, *A History of the Czechoslovak Republic 1918-1948*. Princeton University Press, Princeton, 1973.

24. Ján Ursíny, *Spomienky na Slovenské národné povstanie*. Tranoscius, Liptovský Mikuláš, 1994, pp. 86-96.

25. Jozef Lettrich, *Odboj a povstanie*. In: Martin Kvetko and Miroslav Ján Ličko, Zborník úvah a spomienok o Slovenskom národnom povstaní. Stála konferencia slovenských demokratických exulantov, 1976. This article gives an exceptional picture on the Slovak National Uprising from the perspective of one of its principal leaders. A detailed account is provided by Jablonický, 1969, pp. 317-355.

26. Prečan, 2011.

27. Ibid.

28. Jablonický, 1969. See note 25.

29. Zora Frkáňová, *Koho dar nezvedie, hrozba neskloní: Martýr Jozef Bučko*. Tvorba, vol I (X), no. 5, p. 7; vol. IX(XII), no. 6, pp. 30-31. These articles, as well as the source materials for the remainder of this chapter, are from the personal archive of Jozef Bučko's daughter, my cousin Jelka Bučková. Many are collected in Zora Frkáňová (Ed.), *Jozef Bučko: Lebo mne žit' je Kristus—a umriet' zisk*. Evanjelický cirkevný zbor, Martin, 2010.

30. *Verím!* Editorial, Národnie noviny, December 24, 1941.

31. Quoted in ref. 29.

32. Ibid.

33. Letter dated August, 1945, from the state hospital in Trenčín and addressed to the Lutheran church office in Martin by Ivan Kolesár, Lutheran pastor and fellow-prisoner of Jozef Bučko.

34. Zora Frkáňová, 2010, p. 73.

35. Viera Štetková, *Povstalecký denník*, privately published.

36. http://en.wikipedia.org/wiki/Mauthausen-Gusen_concentration_camp.

37. Bučko's family collected these testimonials and kept them in its archive.

38. http://en.wikipedia.org/wiki/Ebensee_concentration_camp.

39. Eyewitness account by unnamed fellow prisoner.

Chapter 7: The Dream Is Shattered

1. "Apart from aerial bombardment and battles, great damage was caused by deliberate destruction by retreating German units. A third of the railway track was destroyed, and more than half the bridges. From 655 locomotives only 22 were usable. 93,000 houses were damaged or destroyed. The retreating army evacuated to Germany equipment from power stations and factories, as well as cattle and horses. Extensive areas were mined. The damage amounted to three times the annual income of Slovakia." Elena Mannová (Ed.), *A Concise History of Slovakia*, Academic Electronic Press, Bratislava, 2000, p. 274.

2. Igor Pivko, *Moje spomienky*, 1988. Author's archive. Abbreviated version published posthumously as *Igor Pivko, martinský evanjelik (1918-2001)* in Martinský Evanjelik, vol. 9, no. 2, 2002. pp. 27-29

3. Jelka Bučková, interview, 2004.

4. Ivan Bohuš, *Osudy tatranských osád*. Vydavateľstvo Osveta, Martin, 1982.

5. Every textbook of Czechoslovak, Czech, or Slovak history has an account of the coup that brought the Communists to power. They differ significantly in detail, interpretation, tone, and especially in how blame is assigned. Mary Heimann, in *Czechoslovakia, the State That Failed*, Yale University Press, New Haven and London, 2009, is far more critical of Czechoslovakia than I am willing to be, but the way she portrays this central event (pp. 165-176) shares many elements with my own perspective. A number of authors have addressed the formation and accomplishments of the Democratic Party. The most recent and comprehensive studies are Štefan Šutaj, *Slovenské občianske politické strany v dokumentoch (1944-1948)*, Spoločenskovedný ústav SAV Košice, 2002, http://www.saske.sk/SVU/downloads/publikacie/SOPS.pdf; and Marek Syrný, *Slovenskí demokrati*

'44-48: kapitoly z dejín Demokratickej strany na Slovensku v rokoch 1944-1948. Múzeum Slovenského Národného Povstania, Banská Bystrica, 2010.

6. Jozef Lettrich, Matej Josko, Fedor Hodža, and others fled and became active in various political groups in the West all dedicated to keeping the spirit of democracy alive for a Czechoslovakia that, they fervently believed, would be free again some day. Ursíny, Lichner, Žuffa, and others stayed home and paid the price—long-term imprisonment and sometimes torture.

Chapter 8: Under the Barbed Wire

1. Sister Cecilia and William Brinkley, *The Deliverance of Sister Cecilia*, Farrar, Straus and Young, NY, 1954.

2. www.gramarthof.com.

3. http://en.wikipedia.org/wiki/Hungerburgbahn and numerous other websites.

Chapter 9: Living and Dying in the Communist Nightmare

1. The villa in Lomnica was also taken over by the state, but in stages. For a few years, Grandmother Hodža had the use of one or two rooms, but finally it was confiscated altogether. She received a modest payment for her property, but it was placed into an account that was so rigidly restricted that she couldn't access the money.

2. Among the more detailed treatments of the early Communist era are Anton Spiesz and Dusan Caplovic, *Illustrated Slovak History*, Bolchazy-Carducci, Wauconda, 2006, pp. 234-255; and Jozef Lettrich, History of Modern Slovakia, Praeger, New York, 228-260. My account is based on these.

3. A vivid account of this tragic event is given by Madeleine Albright, *Prague Winter: A Personal Story of Remembrance and War, 1937-1948.* Harper, New York, 2012, pp. 395-400.

4. For an account of Czechoslovak purges and show trials, see Tad Szulc, *Czechoslovakia Since World War II*, Viking, New York, 1971, pp. 79-110.

5. After the war, Šmidke had become the chairman of the Communist Party of Slovakia; Novomeský had become minister of education. Husák held a number of leading positions in the Communist Party of Slovakia. He served as chairman of the Slovak Chamber of Deputies and in that position had been the principal architect of the Communist grab for power in Slovakia in 1947-48.

6. Zora Frkáňová, *Rodina Zory Frkáňovej, alebo neľahké cesty k dôstojnému životu.* Mosty 14 (12), 2005, pp. 4-5.

Chapter 10: ". . . So He Won't Forget"

1. In 1949 a group of visionary, powerful, and committedly anti-Communist men formed the National Committee for a Free Europe (NCFE). Among them were Allen Dulles, the director of the CIA, and Dewitt C. Poole, a former diplomat with expertise on Central and Eastern Europe who had for many years been probably Grandfather Hodža's closest contact in the State Department.

Among the several projects of the NCFE, Radio Free Europe (RFE), broadcasting to Central and Eastern Europe, and Radio Liberty (RL), broadcasting to the Soviet Union, grew to be the most significant. They were established in the belief that the Cold War was first and foremost a war of ideas, and that information was a key weapon in that war. Hence, they broadcast, in many local languages, programs about political and economic affairs, the arts, as well as human interest stories, primarily from behind the Iron Curtain. Funded heavily, though by no means exclusively, by the CIA, RFE/RL was closely supervised even though it gave its writers great leeway. The scripts of most broadcasts had to be translated from the local language into English so they could be reviewed by American authorities before they were aired. My mother's job was to translate from Slovak into English. http://en.wikipedia.org/wiki/Radio_Free_Europe/Radio_Liberty; www.rferl.org/.

In the year 2000 it was decided to deposit all the archives of RFE/RL, over 10,000,000 documents and 80,000 reels of audio tape, in the Hoover Institution at Stanford University where they are becoming available for scholarly research. www.hoover.org/publications/digest/3475896.html; http://hoorferl.stanford.edu/.

Today RFE/RL is headquartered in Prague. It broadcasts very little to Central and Eastern Europe, but a great deal to the countries of the Middle East and Central Asia. It has, for example, become the most popular radio station in Afghanistan.

2. Martin Kvetko and Miroslav Ján Ličko (Eds.), *Zborník úvah a osobných spomienok o Slovenskom národnom povstaní*, Totonto, Nový domov, 1976; and Jozef Jablonický, *Zborník o Slovenskom povstaní*, vol. 2 and 3, Naše Snahy, Toronto, 1980 and 1983. http://sk.wikipedia.org/wiki/Martin_Kvetko. Vojtech Čelko, www.gymlet.sk/info/lettrich.html; Jozef Žatkuliak, www.sav.sk/zatkuliak_lettrich. pdf. Jozef Lettrich, *History of Modern Slovakia*, Praeger, New York, 1955.

3. *Pamiatke Dr. Michala Múdreho-Šebíka*, Naše Snahy, Vol. 14, No. 6, 1978, pp.5-9.

4. *Slovakia*, Artia, Prague, 1953. A museum dedicated to the life and work of Karel Plicka has been established in the small Slovak town of Blatnica, not far from Martin.

    http://www.blatnica.sk/obecny-urad/muzeum-karola-plicku.html.

Chapter 11: Separating from the Past

1. Letter in the author's archive.

2. Perhaps the most distinguished of these is the Bronx High School of Science, boasting no less than seven Nobel Prize winners in physics among its graduates. www.bxscience.edu

3. There was a sense of humanitarian mission that you could feel at Cherry Lawn, and it is clear on the web site that continues to represent the school even though CLS itself closed in 1976: www.cherrylawnschool.org. Dr. Fred Goldfrank was a pediatric physician who left his career in medicine to teach children privately, and in 1915 founded Cherry Lawn. He once wrote an open letter about his educational philosophy that was later adopted as the Cherry Lawn Credo, and by tradition was read at every graduation by the graduate who had been at the school for the longest time. Here is an extract from it:

    I believe that it is happiness to do well whatever we do; to create anything that satisfies our creative instinct; to act so as to give pleasure to others; to live in accord with our own conscience; to love so that others will be benefited and none injured by our love; to work for the joy of work, expecting and receiving the financial rewards of our work as our due not our motive; to play, dance, sing, and read for the joy that is each of these activities. I believe that sorrow and joy come to each of us; that, though these are not evenly distributed, we learn in joy and in sorrow so to live that the world is better for our having lived, and that is our happiness.

4. www.swarthmore.edu

5. To us, Brad and Marion Smith were more than the directors of the Quaker Centre, they were the closest approximation to parents that we had at our wedding. Brad was a prolific author (22 books translated into 30 languages), among them *Portrait of India* (Lippincott, Philadelphia and New York, 1962), a funny, touching and profound account of his experiences in India; *Meditation: The Inward Art* (Lippincott, Philadelphia and New York, 1963); and the pamphlet *Dear Gift of Life: A Man's Encounter with Death* (Pendle Hill Pamphlet #142, 1965), meditations on life that he wrote while he was dying of cancer.

Chapter 12: Reconnecting

1. A wonderful though brief account of Uncle Dušan's life has appeared recently: Vojtech Čelko, *Radosť rozdávaná piesňami*, Slovenské dotyky vol. 14, no. 10, October 2009, pp. 8-9.

2. His elder son, also Dušan, made his living as a cartoonist for the newspapers, but before each cartoon was published, it was scrutinized carefully by a censor, even looked at with a mirror in

case the mirror image showed something that could possibly be interpreted as subverting the Communist cause.

3. We were in Czechoslovakia for only about three weeks, and village costumes take a long time to stitch. These were obtained for Rachel and Tanya by Darina Pavlů, my cousin-by-marriage. She was an ethnographer and had many contacts among people who carried on Slovakia's traditional culture. Seamstresses in the town of Liptovské Sliače were able to make the costumes on very short notice.

4. Kept carefully in my personal archive.

Chapter 13: Discovering My Father

1. Soňa Kovačevičová, *Liptovský Svätý Mikuláš: Mesto spolkov a kultúry v rokoch 1830-1945*. Tranoscius, Liptovský Mikuláš, 1993.

2. Soňa Kovačevičová-Žuffová, *Preskakovanie polienok*, Logos, Bratislava, 2001. pp. 18-21.

3. Jan Hála, *Tragedie dědiny*, Lidové noviny, July 24, 1931. Hála reprinted this essay as a pamphlet and published it privately as Jan Hála, *Památce starého Važce*, Važec na Slovensku, 1932.

4. Ján Hála, *Pod Tatrami*, Tranoscius, Liptovský Mikuláš, 1948.

5. Soňa Kovačevičová-Žuffová, *Preskakovanie polienok*, pp. 20-21.

6. Múzeum Janka Kráľa; Ľubica Rybárska, *O literárnej ceche*. In: *Múzejné starinky*, občasník Múzea Janka Kráľa v Liptovskom Mikuláši, Jún 2004, pp. 9-10.

7. Ivan Stodola, *Bolo, ako bolo, mozaika spomienok*, Slovenské vydavateľstvo krásnej literatúry, Bratislava, 1965. pp. 160-164. Stodola was my father's cousin: his grandmother, Ludmila Bauer née Bella, was the sister of my father's grandmother, Zuzana Pálka née Bella (see Chapter 22).

8. Mgr. Zdenko Ďuriška, Biografické oddelenie, Slovenská národná knižnica, Martin, unpublished manuscripts kindly provided to the author. See also Emil Kufčák, *Kožiarske závody v Liptovskom Mikuláši*, Kožiarske závody, Liptovský Mikuláš, 1972.

9. Letter in author's archive.

10. My sincere thanks to Dr. Peter Vítek, director of the Štátny archív v Bytči, pobočka Liptovský Mikuláš, for providing these documents.

11. Vladimír Žuffa, *Skok do neznáma*, Ladislav Takáč (Ed.). Vydavateľstvo Michala Vaška, Bratislava, 2004. This book was published privately by his daughter, Aunt Naďa Micherová-Žuffová, who gave me a copy in recognition of the close friendship of our fathers.

12. My father recounts the details of his wartime activities, particularly their financial aspects, in his deposition to the *Štátna bezpečnosť* during the time of his imprisonment in 1948. This deposition was provided to me by the *Ústav pamäti národa* (Institute of the Nation's Memory); see Chapter 31.

13. Among them were Jozef Rudinský and Ján Pauliny-Tóth. Rudinský was a Catholic priest, journalist, and follower of Grandfather Hodža who emigrated to the United States after many difficulties. He features prominently in the photographs from Kovačica. Pauliny-Tóth, the "Mr. Pauliny" whom my mother refers to in her harrowing account of our escape from the Gestapo (Chapter 3), was a Slovak diplomat and member of the Slovak National Party. He first collaborated with Grandfather Hodža in Paris, then became an active member of the Beneš-led government-in-exile in London. Interesting accounts of the wartime work of both of these men are given in Kuklík and Němeček, *Hodža versus Beneš*, Nakladatelství Karolinum, Prague, 1999. Rudinsky's work following his arrival in the United States is summarized in Miroslav Ján Ličko, *Ako chutí cudzina?*, Kalligram, Bratislava, 1999.

14. His adventures are recounted in the three edited volumes of his memoirs: *Skok do neznáma* (ref. 11); Ladislav Takáč (Ed.), *Len sa nikdy nevzdať*, Tranoscius, Liptovský Mikuláš, 2000; and Vladimír Žuffa, *Už sme torpédovaní*, Vydavateľstvo Michala Vaška, Bratislava, 2002.

15. Pavol Farkaš, starší, *Úryvky z histórie nášho sirotínca*. Very generously provided to me by Pavel Baláž, Matica slovenská v Juhoslávií, Mestný odbor Kovačica.

Chapter 14: The Deepest Roots of My Mother's Family

1. Paul Robert Magocsi, *Historical Atlas of Central Europe, Revised and Expanded Edition*. Univerity of Washington Press, Seattle, 2002. pp. 119-120.

2. Alena Bartlová and Ivan Thurzo, *Slovenský Perikles: Náčrt životnej cesty Milana Hodžu, prvého slovenského predsedu vlády ČSR*, Vydavateľstvo Spolku slovenských spisovateľov, 2008. Ivan Thurzo, a cousin to grandfather Milan Hodža, originally completed this book in 1937 in honor of Hodža's 60th birthday the following year. It portrays my grandfather's life in an unusually intimate way, relying on a good deal of oral and documentary history from the Hodža family and their friends. The manuscript had advanced to the stage of page proofs, but the political events of the time, leading up to the Munich Declaration of 1938, prevented the book's final publication. The proofs lay in the archives for 70 years. In 2007, at a conference dedicated to Hodža, the contemporary historian Vojtech Čelko called attention to their existence; his contribution was published as *Slovenský Perikles Milan Hodža*. In: Miroslav Peknik, (Ed.), *Milan Hodža a agrárne hnutie*, Veda, Vydavateľstvo Slovenskej akadémie vied, Bratislava, 2008. Alena Bartlová undertook to finally complete the publication process. Inasmuch as Thurzo's original version focused exclusively on Hodža's early life, she added her own text so as to bring to the public a narrative of Hodža's entire life and career. The heart of the book, however, remains Thurzo's intimate portrait of his famous cousin.

3. Zdenko Ďuriška of the Biographical Institute of the Slovak National Library, Martin, has for many years conducted detailed genealogical research on a number of leading Slovak families, the Hodžas and Pálkas among them. Much of my own book is drawn from his researches and publications. The genealogical information presented in the present section is drawn primarily from his study *Hodžovci v slovenských dejinách*, In: Miroslav Pekník (Ed.), *Milan Hodža a integrácia strednej Európy*, Veda, Vydavateľstvo Slovenskej akadémie vied, 2006. In this contribution, Ďuriška offers the most cogent available evaluation of the legend of the Hodža name. He considers it to be quite plausible, albeit not rigorously proven.

4. http://en.wikipedia.org/wiki/Rakša.

5. http://www.muzeum.sk/defaulte.php?obj=pamiatka&ix=pimmh.

6. Anton Štefánek, *Hodža: Osobnosť a práca*, In: A. Stefánek, F. Votruba a F. Šeďa (Eds.), *Milan Hodža: Publicista, politik, vedecký pracovník*, Českomoravské podniky tiskařské a vydavatelské, Praha, 1930, pp. 63-118. Also Samuel Cambel, *Štátnik a národohospodár Milan Hodža, 1878-1944*, Veda, Vydavateľstvo Slovenskej akadémie vied, Bratislava, 2001.

7. Bartlová and Thurzo, 2008, pp. 15-23.

8. Ján Ursíny, *Z môjho života*, Matica slovenská, 2000, pp. 9-14.

9. Milan Hodža of Rakša, personal conversation, 2007.

10. Elinor Pivko, *Benická vetva rodu Pivko*. In: *Genealogicko - heraldický hlas*, vol. 6, no. 1, pp. 20-30, 1996.

11. Zuzana Kmeťeová, *Slovak Folk Culture through Amateur Eyes*, www.sazp.sk/parabow/parabow2/index.html.

    Slovakia is an important source of familiar herbs including chamomile, peppermint, rosemary, and caraway, as well as oil-rich trees including several species of pine. These products were used in traditional medicine and dentistry, and their antimicrobial and anti-inflammatory properties are an area of modern research. There are no more *olejkárs*, but there are research laboratories investigating the properties of these ancient remedies using modern techniques. As for saffron, the great centers of production of this, the world's most expensive spice, are along the dry belt from Spain to Kashmir; Iran currently produces over 80% of the world's supply. However, there is a species of the crocus from which saffron is obtained that is native to the Slovak mountains. It was primarily this local material that the Slovak *šafraníks* distributed.

12. Béla Gunda, *Wandering Healers, Medicine Hawkers in Slovakia and Transylvania*, Southwestern Journal of Anthropology, vol. 5, pp. 147-150, 1949.

13. Vierka Štetková, notes from conversations with her mother Anna Štetková, daughter of Andrej Pivko and Zuzana Majtáň. Author's archive. Also Ondrej Hodža, Lutheran pastor of Sučany, notes in author's archive. See Family tree 2, Appendix V.

14. Vierka Štetková, notes, author's archive.

15. Ondrej Hodža, notes, author's archive.

16. Anna Pivko and Ján Milan Štetka had two daughters, my aunts Vierka and Zorka, both gymnasium professors (Family tree 2, Appendix V). The older, Vierka, was a fearless anti-Fascist during the Slovak Republic of World War II and participated in the Slovak National Uprising (Chapter 6). The younger, Zorka, is a long-time officer of the Club of the Friends of TGM and MRS (Tomáš Garrigue Masaryk and Milan Rastislav Štefánik) that promotes Slovak-Czech understanding, and the author of several books and articles that provide insight into the days of the Republic of Czechoslovakia and the guiding vision of its leaders. She has also been the holder of the Hodža family archive, an invaluable resource to historians and also to me as I have written this book.

Chapter 15: The Deepest Roots of My Father's Family

1. See for example Roman Holec, *Hospodárstvo*. In: Dušan Kováč (Ed.), *Na začiatku storočia, 1901-1914*. Veda, Vydavateľstvo Slovenskej akadémie vied, Bratislava, 2004; Anton Spiesz and Dusan Caplovic, *Illustrated Slovak History*. Bolchazy-Carducci, Wauconda, 2006. pp. 67-68, 176-181.

2. Emil Kufčák, *Kožiarstvo v Lipt. Mikuláši za feudalizmu*, In: Emil Kufčák (Ed.), *Kožiarske závody v Liptovskom Mikuláši*, Kožiarske závody, n.p., Liptovský Mikuláš, 1972. This is a comprehensive treatment of leatherworking in Mikuláš during the feudal period.

3. Emil Stodola, *Bolo, ako bolo*, Slovenské vydavateľstvo krásnej literatúry, Bratislava, 1965. pp. 11-12.

4. Emil Kufčák, *Vrbica a vrbický urbár*, Spoločenstvo bývalých urbarialistov a komposesorát, pozemkové spoločenstvo Vrbica—Liptovský Mikuláš, 2007. Liptov itself, with its rugged, heavily forested mountains, became the natural frontier between the expanding Kingdoms of Hungary and Poland, and was ceded by the Polish king to Stephen I, the founder of the Kingdom of Hungary, in 1018. See Ferdinand Uličný, *Od začiatkov do polovice 19. storočia*. In: Ferdinand Uličný, *Liptovský Mikuláš*, Credo, Bratislava, 2006.

5. Zdenko Ďuriška, *Pálkovci v slovenskom podnikateľskom a kultúrnom živote*, Unpublished manuscript. This study is the foundation for most of what I have written about the early history of the Pálka family.

6. Ján Drahotín Makovický, cited in Zdenko Ďuriška, *Otec mikulášskeho našinstva*, Tvorba 14 (23), no. 1, 2004. pp. 36-38.

7. Chronicle of the Pálka family started by Ondrej Pálka the younger. Museum of Janko Kráľ, Liptovský Mikuláš. Also cited in Zdenko Ďuriška, *Otec mikulášskeho našinstva*.

8. www.kralovalehota.sk/node/5.

9. Daniela Fiačanová, *Bellovská rodina osobností*. In: *Evanjelický posol spod Tatier*, 85, no. 8, 2004. p. 59; Bella, Jozef Pravoslav. In: *Slovenský biografický slovník, vol. 1 A-D*. Matica slovenská, Martin, 1986-1994. p. 193.

10. For genealogical information relating to the Jurenka family I am deeply indebted to Uncle Zdeno Jurenka of Bratislava (Chapter 8), and especially to Ing. Branislav Borsuk of Myjava who has been painstakingly researching the history of the Jurenka family for several years. I was privileged to be able to visit Myjava in 2009 and meet with three men who are dedicating their lives to keeping alive the history of the town and the region: Ing. Borsuk, Ján Gálik, and Peter Pavol Uhlík. They provided me with a wealth of information, in conversation and also in written materials.

11. Uncle Zdeno Jurenka kindly gave me a copy of the detailed Poláček genealogy prepared for family use by Ján Tvarožek Jurov in 1966.

12. Julius Bodnár, Ed., *Myjava*, Kníhtlačiareň Daniela Pažického, Myjava, 1911. Extract provided to me by Ján Gálik.

13. General Mills Museum of Milling History, www.angelfire.com/folk/molinologist/museum.html.

14. Ján Gálik, *Myjava v obrazoch histórie*, published with the support of Star, s.r.o., Myjava, 2010, pp. 181-186.

15. Branislav Varsik, *O čom mlčia archívy*, Slovenský spisovateľ, Bratislava, 1987. My friend Ivan Rázus of Liptovský Mikuláš gave me this book when I was on my way to visit Myjava in 2009.

16. Ing. Branislav Borsuk, letter in author's archive.

17. Ján Gálik, *Myjava v obrazoch histórie*, p. 167-175.

18. Ibid., pp. 181-186.

19. Tatiana Cvetková, *Myjavská banka*, BIATEC, vol.12, no. 10, pp. 28-29, 2004; *Päťdesiat rokov Myjavskej banky ú. spol. na Myjave a jej výročná zpráva za obchodný rok 1942*.

20. Ibid., p. 9

21. Ing. Branislav Borsuk, letter in author's archive.

22. The history of the Poláček family is detailed in Ján Tvarožek Jurov, *1664-1964, Rodokmeň Poláčkovcov (Tolarov)*, a copy of which is in the author's archive.

23. Uncle Zdeno Jurenka, personal conversation.

Chapter 16: Ondrej Pálka—"The Father of Our People in Mikuláš"

1. The Museum of Janko Kráľ in Mikuláš has a superb permanent exhibit on leatherworking in the region, spanning several centuries and including details on both guilds and individual families such as the Pálkas.

2. A very brief but illuminating overview of the long history of leatherworking is Pavel Viktor Žuffa, *Z histórie spracovania zvieracích koží*, in Emil Kufčák, *Kožiarske závody v Liptovskom Mikuláši*, Kožiarske závody, n.p. Liptovský Mikuláš, 1972.

3. Emil Kufčák (Ed.), *Kožiarske závody v Liptovskom Mikuláši*, includes a comprehensive treatment of leatherworking in Mikuláš during the feudal period.

4. Emil Stodola, *Bolo, ako bolo*, Slovenské vydavateľstvo krásnej literatúry, Bratislava, 1965. pp. 11-12. Stodola paints a vivid picture of the guild system and the life of guild members and their families. Much of the charm of the description lies in Stodola's tougue-in-cheek language, very hard to translate into English. For those who can read Slovak, here is a sample of his text:

    Neboli to nijaké fabričky, ale len dielne, "varštate," lebo cechové artikuly—a volený pán cechmajster ích s veľkou presnosťou dodržiaval—nedovolili poctivým pánom majstrom zamestnávať viac tovarišov a učňov, iba koľko ím to valné cechové shromaždenie odhlasovalo. A mohol pán majster vyrábať čo aj najkrajšie črievičky—veď niektorý z ních ako tovariš na vandrovkách zašiel až do Viedne—a mohli sa krásne panny pred dielňou aj do frontu postaviť, pán majster vyhovieť nemohol, lebo povolili mu najviac ak dvoch-troch tovarišov a niekoľko nezbedných učniskov. Cechová disciplína bola prísna. Napríklad v nedeľu a vo sviatky bolo povinnosťou nielen tovarišov a učňov, ale aj majstrov chodiť do kostola. Páni cechmajstri kontrolovali dochádzku a kto ju vymeškal, zaplatil do cechovej lády pokutu od medeného groša až po šestáky —podľa hodnosti. Podobné tresty zastihli ľahkomyseľného tovariša, ak sa pozabudol a vplyvom väčšieho kvanta pálenky správal sa ako "nerozumné hoviadko." Majstrom sa už nemohlo podobné prihodiť: nad nimi bdeli už prísne pani majstrové.

5. Emil Kufčák, *Kožiarstvo v Lipt. Mikuláši za feudalizmu*, pp. 19-20.

    Some of these certificates survive in the archives, their texts written in a Slovak so antiquated that it requires transcription and sometimes translation in order to be understandable to today's reader.

6. Emil Stodola, *Bolo, ako bolo*, p.12.

7. Zdenko Ďuriška, *Otec Mikulášskeho našinstva*. Also, Zdenko Ďuriška, *Pálkovci v slovenskom podnikateľskom a kultúrnom živote*, unpublished manuscript. These studies are the basis for the account I present here.

8. Emil Kufák, *Kožiarstvo v Lipt. Mikuláši za feudalizmu*, p. 35.

9. Zdenko Ďuriška, *Otec Mikulášskeho našinstva*.

10. Ibid.

11. Zdenko Ďuriška, *Pálkovci v slovenskom podnikateľskom a kultúrnom živote*.

Chapter 17: Nationalism

1. Peter Petro, *A History of Slovak Literature*, McGill-Queens University Press, Montreal & Kingston, London, Buffalo, 1995.

2. Much has been written on the history and theory of nationalism. Several on-line sources provide a useful entrée into the literature:

   www.nationalismproject.org; http://plato.stanford.edu/entries/nationalism; www.britannica.com/EBchecked/topic/405644/nationalism; www.fordham.edu/halsall/mod/modsbook17.html; http://en.wikipedia.org/wiki/Nationalism.

3. Several monographic studies give special attention to the case of Slovakia, sometimes compared with the Czech Republic. These include: Stefan Auer, *Liberal Nationalism in Central Europe*, Routledge Curzon, London and New York, 2004; Alexander Maxwell, *Choosing Slovakia: Slavic Hungary, the Czechoslovak Language and Accidental Nationalism*, Tauris, London and New York, 2009; and Nadya Nedelsky, *Defining the Sovereign Community: The Czech and Slovak Republics*, University of Pennsylvania Press, Philadeplphia, 2009.

4. Alexander Maxwell, 2009, and *Multiple Nationalism: National Concepts in Nineteenth-Century Hungary and Benedict Anderson's "Imagined Communities,"* Nationalism and Ethnic Politics 11: 385-414, 2005, gives extensive evidence that for a long time Slovak nationalists were first and foremost Hungarian nationalists, in the sense that they sought recognition and protection of Slovak rights within Hungary rather than political separation from Hungary. Slovak political separatism originated primarily during the revolution of 1848 and did not become definitive until World War I. Many other historians have articulated a similar view, if not so forcefully. See, for example, Dušan Kováč, *The Slovak political programme: from Hungarian patriotism to the Czecho-Slovak Republic*. In: Mikuláš Teich, Dušan Kováč and Martin D. Brown, *Slovakia in History*, Cambridge University Press, New York, 2011.

5. See, for example, www.fordham.edu/halsall/mod/modsbook17.html.

6. http://en.wikipedia.org/wiki/Reveille.

7. http://en.wikipedia.org/wiki/Taps.

8. Modern History Sourcebook: http://www.fordham.edu/Halsall/mod/1784herder-mankind.asp.

9. Elsewhere in the world, language has sometimes been seen as something yet more central—as the essence of revealed religion. Muslims consider Arabic to be so integral to the divine nature of the Koran that a translation is not possible—in a foreign language, the Koran ceases to be scripture. Many Hindus consider Sanskrit to have powers that no other language has—mantras, sacred phrases that invoke divine powers, can only be recited in Sanskrit. Their literal meaning survives translation, but their power does not. See Michael Sells, *Approaching the Qur'án: The Early Revelations*. White Cloud Press, Ashland, Oregon, 1999;. http://en.wikipedia.org/wiki/Qur'an_translations; James Lochtefeld, *The Illustrated Encyclopedia of Hinduism*, Rosen Publishing Group, 2001.

10. Oszkár Jászi, *The Dissolution of the Habsburg Empire*, University of Chicago Press, Chicago, 1929. Jászi was a foward-thinking and progressive intellectual who advocated European unification. At the end of World War I he served as minister of nationalities in the Hungarian government and advocated a reorganization of Hungary that would fully recognize the rights of the minorities. On this basis he tried, but failed, to entice the minority nations, including Slovaks, to remain affiliated with Hungary. This attempt included negotiations with Grandfather Hodža, who at the time served as Czechoslovakia's emissary to Hungary (Chapter 26).

11. Paul Lendvai, *The Hungarians: A Thousand Years of Victory in Defeat*, Princeton University Press, 2004.

12. It is useful to remember that the name Bratislava was not used at this time. The city was known both by its German name of Pressburg (Slovakized to Prešporok), and by its Magyar name of Poszony, i.e. in the languages of the two ethnic groups that held overwhelming political and economic power.

13. Lendvai., p. 194.

14. Ibid., pp. 191-205.

15. Pesti Hírlap, 26 June, 1842. "Bármerre tekintunk is Magyarországon, sehol sem látun ily tót nemzetiségre." Cited in http://en.wikipedia.org/wiki/Lajos_Kossuth.

16. Many have noted the irony that Lajos Kossuth was of Slovak ancestry, with family roots in County Turiec reaching back to the thirteenth century. See, e.g. http://en.wikipedia.org/wiki/Lajos_Kossuth and references therein. Eduard Chmelár, *Filozofia slovenských dejín (2), Zrodenie národa,* Slovo no. 38, 2007, points out that one of the chief organizers of the leading Slovak publication of the times, Štúr's *Slovenské národnie noviny,* was Juraj Košút, Lajos Kossuth's cousin. www.noveslovo.sk/clanok.asp?id=15700.

17. Slovaks were probably the most severely affected by Mayarization (see, for example, www.noveslovo.sk/clanok.asp?id=15700), but all ethnic minorities within the Kingdom of Hungary felt it to one degree or another. This included Serbs, Romanians, and others, even Germans. The Croats were in a stronger position, inasmuch as Croatia enjoyed partial autonomy within Hungary. Nevertheless, when revolution came in 1848, the Croats were among the fiercest opponents of the Magyars.

18. For a succinct overview of the evolution of the Slovak idea in the context of nationalism see, for example, Dušan Kováč, *The Slovak Political Agenda in the 19th and Early 20th Century: From Ľudovít Štúr to Czech-Slovak Statehood.* In: Sabrina P. Ramet, James R. Felak, and Herbert J. Ellison, *Nations and Nationalisms in East-Central Europe, 1806-1948: A Festschrift for Peter F. Sugar,* Slavica, Bloomington, 2002. A particularly incisive analysis of the Slovak National Awakening, with a special emphasis on language, is Peter Brock, *The Slovak National Awakening: an essay in the intellectual history of east central Europe,* University of Toronto Press, Toronto and Buffalo, 1976.

Chapter 18: Michal Miloslav Hodža and the Slovak Language

1. Slovo vol. 31, no. 2, p. 6, 2007. Sokol was founded in Prague in 1862 as a patriotic organization and part of the Czech national renaissance. American Sokol was established just three years later, in 1865, by Czech expatriates living in St. Louis, Missouri. http://en.wikipedia.org/wiki/Sokol; www.american-sokol.org/history.php. One of Sokol's chapters is the Czech and Slovak Sokol of Minnesota, www.sokolmn.org. The Hungarian authorities forbade the establishment of Sokol in Slovakia, but it became popular there after the formation of Czechoslovakia. This is why so many Sokol chapters in the United States have combined Czech and Slovak memberships.

2. A. Machek, *Naše písničky pro české svobodomyslné školy v Americe. 2. rozšířené vyd.* Sdružení českých svobodomyslných škol, Chicago, 1937.

3. Samuel's father had spent three years in the Czech lands and had steeped his son in the traditions of shared Slovak and Czech history and culture. For an extended account of Tomášik's life and work, see Rudo Brtáň, *Samo Tomášik (1813-1887)*, Matica Slovenská, Popularizácia klasického deditčstva, 1963.

4. Ibid., p. 13.

5. http://en.wikipedia.org/wiki/Hey, Slavs;

6. *Básně a písně Sama Tomášika České i Slovenské.* V Praze nákladem knihkupectví I. L. Kobra, 1888.

7. Kollár was the Lutheran pastor of Pest, and preached to his mixed congregation in both Slovak and German. His greatest poetic work, *Slávy dcera (The Daughter of Sláva,* Goddess of the Slavs*),* celebrated the greatness of all Slavdom. It was written in Czech, and it took its place alongside

the German works of Herder as a leading source of inspiration for young Slovak intellectuals. Šafárik served for twenty-four years as the headmaster of the Serbian Orthodox gymnasium in Novi Sad in the Lower Lands (Appendix III). Thereafter, he lived in Prague, where he held notable positions as a linguist and a scholar. He wrote several major treatises on the history of the Slavs and of Slavic languages, sometimes mythologized but nevertheless compelling for the times. Together, Kollár and Šafárik inspired an entire generation of Slovaks to the national cause.

The study of the history of language in Slovakia, and its relationship to Czech, is extraordinarily complex, and also related to shifting perspectives on the relationship among and classification of the Slavic languages collectively. In an earlier era even Grandfather Hodža weighed in on the question in his doctoral dissertation at the University of Vienna, which he self-published in 1920 under the title *Československý rozkol, príspevok k dejinám slovenčiny* (*The Czechoslovak Schism: A Contribution to the History of the Slovak Language*). In his defense of the historical prominence of a common Czech-Slovak language, he created a firestorm among his more nationalistically-inclined contemporaries. Excellent modern works include Peter Brock, *The Slovak National Awakening: An Essay in the Intellectual History of East Central Europe*, University of Toronto Press, Toronto and Buffalo, 1976; Alexander Maxwell, *Choosing Slovakia: Slavic Hungary, the Czechoslovak Language and Accidental Nationalism*, Tauris Academic Studies, London & New York, 2009; and Ľudovít Haraksim, *Slovak Slavism and Panslavism*, In: Mikuláš Teich, Dušan Kováč, and Martin D. Brown, *Slovakia in History*, Cambridge University Press, Cambridge and New York, 2011.

8. A particularly compelling analysis of the range of variation of spoken Slovak is presented in Alexander Maxwell, *Why the Slovak Language Has Three Dialects: A Case Study in Historical Perceptual Dialectology*. Austrian History Yearbook, 37, 2006, pp. 385-414.

9. Peter Brock, 1976; Alexander Maxwell, 2009.

10. I base my account of Hodža's life and work primarily on three important sources: Samuel Štefan Osuský, *Filozofia Štúrovcov. III. M. M. Hodžova filozofia*. Tlačou kníhtlačiarne Daniela Pažického, Myjava, 1932; the full-length biography by Ján Hučko, *Michal Miloslav Hodža*, Epocha, Bratislava, 1970; and a compendium of studies celebrating the hundredth anniversary of the great events of 1848, Július Lenko, Ed., *Zore nad Kriváňom, sborník o minulosti Liptova z príležitosti stého výročia Žiadostí slovenského národa v. Lipt. Sv. Mikuláši 10. mája 1848*. Vydal Prípravný výbor celoštátnych oslav 100. výroia "Žiadostí slovenského národa" a 30. výročia liptovskosvätomikulášskej rezolúcie v Lipt. Sv. Mikuláši, 1948.

11. Hučko, pp. 11-14. At the gymnasium Michal immersed himself in Latin, which was at that time the gateway to a continued education, and also in natural history. Banská Bystrica is in Slovakia's greatest mining region, whose production of gold, silver and copper was important on a European scale from the Middle Ages until well into the nineteenth century. Michal was especially captivated by the fossils that abounded there, unearthed (literally) by the extensive mining acivities.

The region of Banská Bystrica had been settled centuries earlier by Germans, who were brought in for their expertise in mining, and Michal came under the influence of a German professor who loved the Slovak language. This professor accepted one of the linguistic theories of the times, that Slovak was the closest of all the modern Slavic languages to the original Old Slavonic, and so was, in some sense, the mother-language of the Slavs. Young Michal left Banská Bystrica at the age of fifteen, thrilled by this vision of the historical importance of his mother tongue.

12. Ibid., pp. 14-22. Hodža was not primarily a trouble-maker, however, but a scholar. Even the Magyar-sympathizing rector recognized him as the school's finest student and asked him to stay for an extra year of studies. Hodža accepted, leaving Rožňava in 1829 at the age of eighteen.

Eager for more education, he registered at the Lutheran Collegium in Prešov, a city in Eastern Slovakia located on the ancient trade route from the Mediterranean to the Baltic and long a center of culture (Map 3, Appendix V). During Michal's time, the higher social strata of Prešov used German to communicate. The language of instruction at the Collegium was still Latin, but the dominance of German allowed Hodža to perfect his mastery of that language.

While in Prešov, Michal kept a journal, written in German and in Latin; the first entry was dated October 16, 1830. He copied quotations, summarized important readings, wrote commentaries, and occasionally recorded his personal thoughts. From this journal we learn, for instance, that he was much taken with the writings of the Jewish philosopher Baruch Spinoza, especially in regard to ethics. He worked hard to reconcile Spinoza's humanistic world view, in which God played an ambiguous role, with his own deep faith in Christianity. Most importantly, it was here that Michal was first inspired by the writings of Herder and Kollár.

13. Ibid., pp. 22-29. An astonishing roster of Slovak leaders obtained a secondary education at the Lyceum; today the list is prominently displayed on two huge panels framing the corner of the building.

14. Ibid., p. 26.

15. Ibid., pp. 34-35; 50-62.

16. Ondrej Palka, *Chronicle of the Pálka Family, Initiated by Ondrej Pálka the Younger*. Museum of Janko Král', Liptovský Mikuláš.

17. Hučko, p. 37.

18. Osuský, p. 15.

19. Ibid., p. 12.

20. Hučko, pp. 79-81; Osuský, pp. 24-25.

21. Hučko, p. 81-82. The writer Elena Ivanková, a granddaughter of M. M. Hodža and Kornélia, described this episode in very romantic language. See http://zlatyfond.sme.sk/dielo/1179/ Ivankova_Glosy/33#ixzz0z5cm7a8g.

> Michal Miloslav Hodža stands in the pulpit. A fortunate nation it is that has had sons like Hurban, Hodža, and Štúr. And a curse that in those times it did not understand them as fully as it should have. Young Hodža preaches, below a lovely girl listens to the sermon. Her head is bent, she is looking into her hymnal. Her wide green skirt is arranged on the pew, her dark jacket hints at the delicate form of her young body, a small cross hangs on a delicate chain around her neck. A gentle young girls of those times. . . The sermon comes to an end. The organ thunders. Children's voices squeal, the gates of the church swing open, the crowd presses to leave the church. The sun greets them. The people smile. 'The spring has come,' they say contentedly. 'Oh, and that new pastor, doesn't he ever have a voice!' exclaim the old women. The young pastor greets the girl at the door. The May wind plays around them. His broad, black cloak suddenly wraps around the girl as if the wind had a special delight in its action, and the girl stands ashamed, almost completely enveloped in the robes of the young man. . . He gazes at her. . . Embarrassed, she unwinds herself from the cloak. This was the moment when the young Hodža first saw his future wife.

22. For years Kornélia remained very conscious of the fact that she loved and had married a passionate Slovak while she herself had grown up in a German household. Both Hučko (p. 82) and Osuský (p. 29) cite a passage from a moving letter that Kornélia wrote to their daughter Marína twenty three years later, in which she still apologizes for her imperfect mastery of written Slovak while writing in wonderful Liptovian idiom not translatable into English:

> *Moje djeta nepozeraj kritičným očkom namoje listki čvo sa šetkiho, i zlohu i pravopisu, tíka, lebo ked bi si to počala Tvojim umelim okom posudzovat', velmi smješna bi Ti Tvoja mamička predchod'ila, nevid' v tom nič invo, len srdce a cit milujúceho materského srdca.*

> My child, do not look with a critical eye on the style and spelling of my letters, because if you did start to to judge in this way, your mother would seem to you very strange and funny. See nothing in this except a mother's loving heart.

23. Osuský, p. 29-30.

24. Many treatments of this crucial period are available. I have found Jeremy Brock, *The Slovak National Awakening*, to be particularly valuable. The goal of Štúr, Hurban, and Hodža was to develop a written Slovak that would be understandable to the ordinary person, just as the founders of *bernoláčtina* had done before. In contrast to the Bernolákists, however, they chose for their foundation the dialect spoken in the middle of Slovakia— especially the counties of Liptov, Orava,

and Turiec—as being the least influenced by neighboring Czech or Polish. Štúr, an expert linguist, would work on the grammar, while Hodža focused on orthography—defining how the letters of the alphabet and the several diacritical marks would represent the actual sounds of spoken Slovak, and formulating the rules of spelling. The study of Alexander Maxwell, *Choosing Slovakia*, 2009, is considerably more detailed, both with regard to the notions of nationality and nationalism current at the time and with regard to the use of language.

25. Hučko, pp. 82-106; Brock, pp. 47-54.

26. Brock, p. 50.

27. Hučko, 96-97. The original spelling proposed by Štúr quickly passed out of use and his *štúrovčina* never became a widely accepted form of Slovak.

28. Hodža became a particularly eloquent voice in the effort to reduce alcoholism in the villages, supporting temperance circles and devoting many of his sermons to the issue. One of these was later published under the title *Nepi pálenku, to je: nezabi*, (*Do Not Drink Brandy, Which Means: Thou Shalt Not Kill*.) In it, Hodža argues that the command "don't drink" is like God's commandment not to kill, because brandy kills the body and the soul of both the drunkard and his family. This and numerous other writings, and the growing success of his efforts to stem alcoholism, brought down the wrath of those who stood to profit from the sale of brandy, the tavern owners and the distillers. Complaints were lodged against Hodža, not only with the local authorities but even in distant German newspapers. Nothing illegal could ever be shown against him, but he had to defend himself from increasingly powerful oppposition. Osuský, pp. 31-32.

29. This includes the song that was to be chosen as the Slovak national anthem. Here is the story. While Štúr was still a professor at the Lutheran Lyceum in Bratislava, even before Tatrín met for the first time, the government had launched an investigation into his activities. The authorities could not prove that he had done anything illegal, but they dismissed him from his position nevertheless. His students were incensed, and twenty-two of them resigned in protest and prepared to leave city. During the turmoil, the protesters and their friends often met in local taverns, eating, drinking, singing, planning future actions, and often reading their own impassioned writings. During one such gathering, 23-year-old Janko Matúška presented a poem he had just written, set to the tune of a familiar folk song. Its first line was *Nad Tatrou sa blýska hromi, divo bijú* (There's lightning above the Tatras, thunder crashes wildly). The young patriots sang this song endlessly, and its fame spread to all the Slovak counties. Seventy-five years later, when Czechoslovakia was established, the first verse was adopted as part of the new country's dual national anthem, sharing this honored place with the first verse of the Czech *Kde domov můj* (*Where Is My Home?*). And in 1993, when Slovakia became an independent state, the first two of its original six stanzas were adopted as the new national anthem.

> *Nad Tatrou sa blýska, hromi divo bijú.*
> *Zastavme ích, bratia,*
> *ved' sa ony stratia*
> *Slováci ožijú.*

> There's lightning above the Tatras, thunder crashes wildly.
> Let us stop them, brothers,
> they will soon vanish,
> and Slovaks will arise.

> *To Slovensko naše posial' tvrdo spalo,*
> *ale blesky hromu*
> *vzbudzujú ho k tomu,*
> *Aby sa prebralo.*

> Our Slovakia has long slept deeply,
> but the the thunder's lightning
> is now rousing it
> to awake.

Hej, Slováci was written in 1834 by a twenty-one year old; *Nad Tatrou sa blýska* was written ten years later by a twenty-three year old.

Chapter 19: Michal Miloslav Hodža in the Midst of Revolution

1. The general history of the revolutions of 1848 is presented in many places; http://en.wikipedia.org/wiki/Revolutions_of_1848 is a convenient internet source. A clear and concise account from the Slovak point of view is available in Dušan Kováč, *Dejiny Slovenska*, Nakladatelství Lidové noviny, 1998, pp. 114-121.

2. Paul Lendvai, *The Hungarians: A Thousand Years of Victory in Defeat*. Princeton University Press, Princeton, 2003. pp. 215-221.

3. Milan Hodža, *Federation in Central Europe, Reflections and Reminiscences*, Jarrold's, London, 1942.

4. This history is told in many places. Ján Hučko, *Michal Miloslav Hodža*, Nakladateľstvo Epocha, Bratislava, 1970, tells it from the perspective of Hodža's life. See especially pp. 107-116.

5. Ibid., p. 109.

6. *Dokumenty slovenskej národnej identity a štátnosti. I.* Národné literárne centrum, Bratislava, 1998. p. 307-310.

7. There were only sixteen signers of the *Petition of the Slovak Nation*, but students arranged for the printing of 5,000 flyers with the full text and these were widely distributed.

8. Quoted in Ján Hučko, *Prvá Slovenská národná rada.* In: Miroslav Pekník (Ed.), *Pohľady na slovenskú politiku.* Veda, Vydavateľstvo Slovenskej akadémie vied, Bratislava, 2000.

9. Ján Hučko, *Michal Miloslav Hodža*, pp. 116-123. See also Miloš Janoška, *Sto rokov Liptovského Sv. Mikuláša.* In: Július Lenko (Ed.), *Zore nad Kriváňom, sborník o minulosti Liptova z príležitosti stého výroia Žiadostí slovenského národa v Lipt. Sv. Mikuláši 10. mája 1848.* Vydal Prípravný výbor celoštátnych osláv 100. výročia "Žiadostí slovenského národa" a 30. výročia liptovskosvätomikulášskej rezolúcie v Lipt. Sv. Mikuláši, 1948, pp. 57-67.

10. Daniel Rapant, cited in Hučko, p. 119.

11. The events are related in many writings. I have relied principally on Hučko, pp. 124-133.

12. Hodža went to Vienna, where he was well connected, and where he consulted with the leader of the powerful Croatian revolt, ban Jelačič. He wrote a *Manifesto to Slovaks* (*Hlas k národu slovenskému*), calling for armed insurrection against the Magyars and explaining why: The Magyars were unwilling to grant to Slovaks the very freedoms they had just won for themselves from the emperor; they jailed Slovak leaders or forced them into exile; other nationalities in Hungary were revolting, and now it was time for the Slovaks to take a stand as well. Hodža exhorted Slovaks to ignore the commands of the Magyar government, support their armed Slovak fighters with food and weapons, and remain faithful both to the Slovak nation and to the emperor.

    Shortly Hodža moved to Prague with financial and recruiting goals. While there he published a short book in German, *Der Slowak* (*The Slovak*), in which he elaborated the Slovak position, both from a historical viewpoint and with respect to specific recent, repressive actions on the part of the Magyars. In the meantime, Hurban traveled to partially autonomous Croatia and addressed its Diet in Zagreb, receiving both financial support and arms.

13. The history of the Poláček family is detailed in Ján Tvarožek Jurov, *1664-1964, Rodokmeň Poláčkovcov (Tolarov)*, a copy of which is in the author's archive.

14. A number of letters that Hodža wrote to his wife Kornélia from Prague and Vienna have been preserved. They reveal in a touching way the uncertainties he faced and the confidence he had in his personal safety. See especially Osuský, pp. 48-53.

15. Ibid., pp. 56-57.

16. Ibid., pp. 57-58.

17. Fighting took place throughout the Slovak counties of Upper Hungary, with imperial troops and Slovak volunteers sometimes fighting side by side. Prešov and Košice were taken by volunteer

forces. But no matter which way the war went, the imperial court remained extremely reserved toward its Slovak allies, always fearing what might happen if the Slovak taste for national identity went too far. Anton Spiesz and Caplovic, *Illustrated Slovak History*, Bolchazy-Carducci Publishers, Wauconda, 2006. pp. 119-120.

18. A vivid account of the events surrounding the writing and proclamation of the Petition of the Slovak Nation, as well as the events of the revolution, as seen from the perspective of the men and families of Mikuláš is presented in Július Lenko (Ed.), 1948. The arrest and jailing of the patriots of Mikuláš is described by Rudo Brtáň, *Z osudov liptovských národovcov v roku meruôsmom*, ibid, pp. 119-141. See also Ján Pálka, *Zápisky*, Vydavateľské oddelenie YMCA v Prahe, 1932, pp. 7-8.

19. Brtáň, in Lenko, 1948, p. 129.

20. Ibid., pp. 129-130.

21. Paul Lendvai, 2003, pp. 233-239.

22. Ján Hučko. In: Peknik, 2000, pp. 336-337.

23. Ján Hučko, 1970, pp. 148-150.

24. Daniela Fiačanová, Bellovská rodina osobností. *Evanjelický posol spod Tatier*, vol. 85, no. 8, 2004. p. 59. *Biografický lexikón Slovenska, vol. 1*, Slovenská národná knižnica, Národný biografický ústav, 2002, p. 318.

25. He and his wife, Anna Jurkovič, had nine children, including one of Slovakia's best-known writers, Svetozár Hurban-Vajanský.

26. The fates of the greatest Magyar leaders were likewise tragic. István Széchenyi fell into despair over the revolution and its aftermath and committed suicide. The Viennese authorities tried to mislead the public about the timing of his funeral, but 10,000 people showed up nevertheless, and some 80,000 took part in the funeral mass a few weeks later. Lajos Kossuth escaped the country, finally settling in Turin where he was followed by Austrian secret agents for the rest of his long life. Mainly because of his surrender at Világos, Magyar nationalists forever treated Artúr Görgey as a traitor and denied him even trivial civilian positions. Lendvai, 2003.

Chapter 20: Michal Miloslav Hodža: Poet-Prophet

1. Hodža's biographers have told the story well. See Ján Hučko, *Michal Miloslav Hodža*, Nakladateľstvo Epocha, Bratislava 1970; Samuel Štefan Osuský, *Filozofia Štúrovcov. III. M. M. Hodžova filozofia*. Kníhtlačiareň Daniela Pažického, Myjava, 1932. I did not have access to the handful of earlier studies.

2. Juraj Scholcz; see Osuský, 1932, pp. 13-19.

3. Ľudovít Karol Moesz, by profession a pharmacist and by conviction a *magyarone*; ibid, pp. 17-19

4. Hučko, 1970, pp. 64-78; Osuský, 1932, pp. 25-28.

5. Osuský, 1932, p. 26.

6. There were two distinct but closely related aspects to this battle. First, there was a resumption of the agitation to unify Slovak Lutherans and Magyar Calvinists. The political logic was simple. Slovaks formed a substantial majority of the Lutheran Church in Hungary; Germans were second; and the Magyar membership was small. The Calvinist church, however, was almost entirely Magyar, and its total membership was larger than that of the Lutherans. Were the two churches to be united, Magyars would have a numerical majority and would control the affairs of the combined church.

   The second aspect involved a patent issued by the emperor in 1859 that ordered a reorganization of Protestant churches in his Hungarian domains. The new organization would have reduced the influence of pro-Magyar elements. Under intense opposition from the Magyars, however, less than a year after the patent was issued, it was substantially weakened. Individual Lutheran congregations were given the right to decide whether they would be administered under the provisions of the patent or remain under the previous system.

Hodža saw in the patent the greatest step forward in centuries for his beloved church, and he made this cause his own. He lectured, explained, wrote, persuaded— in one-on-one conversations, at his home, in church, in public meetings. The opposition he faced was ruthless. In his own congregation, meetings became shouting matches, votes were blocked. While the ordinary members of the congregation were overwhelmingly in favor of the patent, a tiny minority of politically powerful *magyarones*—many of whom rarely attended services, and who refused to make financial contributions—forced its way. The Lutheran congregation of Mikuláš never adopted the patent. Hučko, 1970, pp. 165-169; Osuský, *Filozofia Štúrovcov*, pp. 86-111.

Hodža continued to agitate in favor of the patent. New formal complaints against the actions of the unyieldingly Slovak pastor of Mikuláš were lodged with church authorities. His opponents complained that he inappropriately read materials supporting the patent during services. They said that he was too often absent, neglecting his pastoral duties. They accused him of insulting the gentry, and they accused his supporters, including Ondrej Pálka and Jozef Bella, of irregularities in the handling of the church's finances. "This is the picture of the twenty-year functioning of Hodža," they wrote. "We cannot point to even a single act of his that has been beneficial to our church, for there is no such act." The noose was getting tighter. Osuský, 1932, p. 95.

7.   Hučko, 1932, pp. 173-178; Osuský, *Filozofia Štúrovcov*, pp. 111-120.

8.   It was alleged that not only had Hodža's trial been procedurally fatally flawed, but the signatures on a petition against Hodža had been extracted under threat:

> They forced the ordinary people to join them. It is well known, that they gathered signatures against the patent and against Hodža using deceit and force. They threatened their renters with eviction from their dwellings if they did not sign. Two rich men of Vrbica, Ján Miko and Michal Malek, who both betrayed the interests of their own nation, forced all their raftsmen, apprentices, and journeymen to sign against the patent. To gather more signatures, they forced even school children to sign. In a number of villages the gentry got the local men drunk, and while they were not in command of their senses they tricked them into signing by telling them that they were simply declaring that they were good Lutherans (Hučko, 1970, p. 176).

9.   Ibid., p. 180; Osuský, 1932, pp. 138-139.

10.   Osuský, 1932, pp. 139-140.

11.   Ibid., p. 155.

12.   Jur Janoška, *Storočná pamiatka narodenia Michala M. Hodžu*. Tranoscius, Liptovský Mikuláš, 1911. p. 5; *Tranovský evanjelický kalendár*, Tranoscius, Liptovský Mikuláš, 1923, pp. 85-90; Peter Vítek and Slávko Churý, *Politický, správny a právny vývoj*. In: Ferdinand Uličný (Ed.), *Liptovský Mikuláš*, published for the city by Credo, Bratislava, 2006. pp. 97-98.

13.   The statues come from the atelier of the sculptor Ladislav Pollák. I thank Dr. Peter Vítek for this information.

14.   Osuský, 1932, pp. 168-169.

15.   Ibid., p. 167.

16.   Ibid., pp. 175-286 contains a detailed analysis of Hodža's sermon themes, comparing his main ideas before and after the profound experiences of the revolution of 1848.

17.   Ibid., pp. 169-174.

18.   Many great writers have done this. Shakespeare is credited with having contributed some 1,700 words to English (http://www.shakespeare-online.com/biography/wordsinvented.html). Hodža did something similar for the Slovak language, especially in poetry. He composed long strings of words that create a turbulent flow of sound, an inspired attempt to convey the many nuances of a single meaning, and often it is hard to tell which words came from spoken Slovak and which ones he made up. Here is a short passage from his last poem (Osuský, 1932, pp. 171-172):

Nuž čo verím? Čo je sama viera,
Žrielo, vrielo a tok života,
Tá čo merí, meria, mieri miera
Vše, čo vesmír rúznom kolotá . . . .

So what do I believe? What is faith itself,
_____, _____ and the flow of life,
She who _____, measures, _____ _____
All that in the universe _____ whirls.

19. Ibid., pp. 356-385; Alexander Matúška, *M. M. H.*; Michal Eliáš, *Hodžova Matora*; Karol Rosenbaum, *Vieroslavín—Hodžov básnický testament*. All in: Michal Eliáš (Ed.), *K problematike slovenského romantizmu*, Matica slovenská, Martin, 1973.

20. Quoted in Miloš Janoška, *Sto rokov Liptovského Sv. Mikuláša*. In: Július Lenko (Ed.), *Zore nad Kriváňom, sborník o minulosti Liptova z príležitosti stého výročia Žiadostí slovenského národa v Lipt. Sv. Mikuláši 10. mája 1848*. Vydal Prípravný výbor celoštátnych osláv 100. výročia "Žiadostí slovenského národa" a 30. výročia liptovskosvätomikulášskej rezolúcie v Lipt. Sv. Mikuláši, 1948.

Chapter 21: Marína Hodža—Patriot-Feminist

1. The most important were three Slovak-language gymnasia (two Lutheran and one Catholic) and *Matica slovenská*, a cultural organization that embodied Slovak strivings for national identity. They lasted barely a decade—in 1874-75 the Hungarian government closed them all. It also confiscated all the resources of *Matica slovenská* even though they had been obtained through the small donations of the mostly penurious Slovak public, and, height of cynicism, used the proceeds to fund organizations dedicated to Magyarization. See, for example, Dušan Kováč, *Dejiny Slovenska*, Nakladatelství Lidové noviny, Praha, 1998, pp. 131-140.

2. Most of the material in this chapter is taken from the superbly annotated study by the literary scholar Peter Liba, *Listy Maríny Miloslavy Hodžovej Viliamovi Paulinymu-Tóthovi*, Matica slovenská, Martin, 1965. This book is another of the treasures I inherited from my mother.

3. *The Encyclopedia of Slovakia and the Slovaks*. Encyclopedic Institute of the Slovak Academy of Sciences, Bratislava, 2006.

4. *Sokol* was edited and published by Pauliny-Tóth from 1862 to 1869, initially in Budapest and later in the western Slovak city of Skalica. He edited and published *Černokňažník* from 1861 to 1864 in Buda, then later converted into a supplement for Sokol. Liba, 1965, pp. 41n-42n. Both magazines boldly served the Slovak national cause. Ibid., p. 7.

5. Ibid., p.40

6. August von Kotzebue was one of the most prolific and popular writers in the Europe of the time, authoring over 200 plays as well as numerous other works, some of which were extremely controversial. http://en.wikipedia.org/wiki/August_von_Kotzebue. *The Spaniards in Peru* was translated into English under the title *Pizarro, A tragedy in Five Acts* by Richard Brinsley Sheridan and published in Boston in 1799; the play has recently been reprinted in Germany from a 1923 edition.

7. Liba, 1965, pp. 51-52.

8. Las Casas has not been forgotten even today, as the extensive biographical piece in Wikipedia illustrates. For example,

> Las Casas played a significant historical role as an eyewitness to one of the most important eras in history. Las Casas made an abstract and copy of the diary Christopher Columbus kept of his voyages. He incorporated much of Columbus' writings, diary and log in his own history. Today, both the Columbus diary as well as the copy have disappeared but Las Casas' abstract has survived. It is an important source for the early period of Spanish Colonialism.
>
> He is commemorated as a missionary in the Calendar of Saints of the Evangelical Lutheran Church in America on July 17. In 2000, the Roman Catholic Church began the process to

beatify him. His work is a particular inspiration behind the work of the Las Casas Institute at Blackfriars Hall, Oxford (http://en.wikipedia.org/wiki/Bartolomé_de_las_Casas).

His life has also been the basis of socially-oriented street theater in Latin America (John Ashford, personal communication).

9. Liba, 1965, p. 24.

10. Ibid., p. 53.

11. Norma L. Rudinsky, *Incipient Feminists: Women Writers in the Slovak National Revival*, Slavica, 1991. Liba, 1965, pp. 18-19.

12. Liba, 1965, pp. 165-168

13. Cited in Liba, 1965, p. 29.

14. Ibid., pp. 276-277.

15. Founded in 1854, the Diakonie Neuendettelsau is still a thriving institution, now admitting men as well as women. Over 6,500 of its members provide social services, medical care and education, not only in Germany but also in other parts of Europe.

    http://www.diakonieneuendettelsau.de/index.php?id=654

    For an interesting account of the life of the founder of Diakonie Neuendettelsau and his impact on Lutherans in America, see Michael L. Sherer, *The Man Who Wouldn't Take No for an Answer*, MetroLutheran (Minneapolis), March, 2012, www.MetroLutheran.org; and http://en.wikipedia.org/wiki/Johann_Konrad_Wilhelm_Löhe.

16. Liba, 1965, p. 32.

17. Ibid, pp. 33-34.

Chapter 22: Bellas—Freedom Fighters and Poets

1. Roman Holec, *Slovensko v hospodárstve Uhorska—vývojové trendy a problémy*. In: Miroslav Pekník (Ed.), *Pohľady na slovenskú politiku*, Veda, Vydavateľstvo Slovenskej akadémie vied, Bratislava, 2000, pp. 61-80.

2. Zdenko Ďuriška, *Pálkovci v slovenskom podnikateľskom a kultúrnom živote*. Unpublished manuscript.

3. Ivan Stodola, *Náš strýko Aurel*. Mladé letá, Bratislava, 1968, p. 77.

4. Emil Kufčák, *Kožiarstvo od revolúcie 1848-1849 do roku 1918*. In: Emil Kufčák (Ed.), *Kožiarske závody v Liptovskom Mikuláši*, Liptovské závody, n.p., Liptovský Mikuláš, 1972, p. 38.

5. Ďuriška, unpublished manuscript.

6. Peter Liba, *Listy Maríny Hodžovej Viliamovi Pauliny-Tóthovi*, Matica slovenská, Martin, 1965, p. 63. Marína Hodža describes a younger Janko Pálka, hotheaded in his zeal for the Slovak cause:

    . . . . Janko Pálka, undoubtedly known to you, was accused as well. He supposedly dared to call Geduly "gebuly" in public, and to announce that if "gebuly" ever dared to come here, he, Janko, would be the first to throw a rock at his head. But Pálka is a fine man, and he held himself more than well . . . .

    The *magyarone* bishop Lajos Geduly was M. M. Hodža's most powerful opponent (Chapter 20); "gebuly" was a pejorative transformation of his name, based on the colloquial expression "gebuľa" for head.

7. Ibid, p. 121.

8. For a brief overview of this notable family, see Daniela Fiačanová, *Bellovská rodina osobností*. In: Evanjelicky posol spod Tatier, vol. 85, no. 8, p. 59 (2004).

9. Ján Pravdoľub Bella, Zápisky. Quoted in Rudo Brtáň, *Z osudov liptovských národovcov v roku meruôsmom*. In: Július Lenko, *Zore nad Kriváňom, sborník o minulosti Liptova z príležitosti stého výročia Žiadostí slovenského národa v Lipt. Sv. Mikuláši 10. mája 1848*, Prípravný výbor celoštátnych osláv 100.

výročia "Žiadostí slovenského národa" a 30. výročia liptovskosvätomikulášskej rezolúcie v Lipt. Sv. Mikuláši, 1948, pp. 119-141.

10. Ernst Sartorius was a German Lutheran theologian (1797-1859), very influential during the nineteenth century. His *Beiträge zur Apologie der Augsburgischen Confession* of 1853 is still available in paperback. A *postilla* is a biblical commentary.

11. http://wapedia.mobi/en/Danilo_I,_Prince_of_Montenegro.

12. Pitting the peasantry and the intelligentsia against the established aristocracy, and nations with proud individual histories against the hegemony of the Russian tsar, this uprising captured the support of free thinkers throughout Europe.

13. www.principlesofwar.com/scenarios/19thc/balkans/Serbo-Turkish War 1876.htm.

14. Jozef Bohuslav died when his son, Jozef Samuel Bella (1864-1946), was only twelve years old. After obtaining a medical degree in Prague, Jozef Samuel served for a while in Bratislava and among the Slovaks of the Lower Lands. Soon, however, he returned home to Mikuláš. Though a respected physician, he was also something of a town character, easily recognized by his shabby three-quarter-length coat and his tattered black doctor's bag as he went around on his many house calls. He died a bachelor after tending his patients with love and skill for fifty years. Ľuba Rybárska, *Jozef Samuel Bella (1864-1946)*, Múzejné starinky, Občasník Múzea Janka Kráľa v Liptovskom Mikuláši, June 2007, pp. 8-9.

15. Eugen Suchoň (1908-1993) is regarded as one of Slovakia's greatest composers. He set Peter Bella Horal's *Aká si mi krásna, Ty rodná zem moja* to music in 1932-1933. www.suchon.info/

16. Ján Levoslav Bella (1843-1946) was a native of Mikuláš, born into a Catholic family very distantly related to my ancestors, the Lutheran Bellas. Like Suchoň, he was one of Slovakia's most significant composers. http://en.wikipedia.org/wiki/Ján_Levoslav_Bella

17. http://www.lubamason.com/ It is available on her CD *Collage* under the title *Motherland*.

18. Ondrej Bella, *Výber z básní*. Matica slovenská, Martin, 1923.

19. His son, Metod Matej Bella (1869-1946), was raised in Békéš Čaba, studied law and theology, and became prominent in Slovak politics. In 1906 he was elected to the Hungarian parliament from the electoral district of Mikuláš. In the parliament, he joined Grandfather Hodža, who had been elected from the district of Kulpín in the Lower Lands (Chapter 25). He was active in the domestic political push to establish Czechoslovakia (Chapter 26). Later Metod Matej, a strong proponent of a united Czechoslovakia, held a variety of significant governmental posts and was active in Grandfather Hodža's Agrarian Party. At the same time he was a Lutheran pastor who devoted himself not only to pastoral care but also to the educational activities of the church.

20. A symposium devoted to the Stodola family, *Seminár Stodolovci v slovenskej kultúre*, was published in Biografické štúdie 26, 1999, 83-106. Available at www.snk.sk/?BS_26.

Aurel Boleslav Stodola (1859-1942) was a rarity among Slovaks—a highly acknowledged scientist and engineer. He spent most of his working life in Switzerland at the Technical University of Zürich (Eidgenössische Technische Hochschule), where even today annual lectures and a medal are given in his honor. From power plants to jet engines, the work of Aurel Stodola has influenced the whole modern world. www.lec.ethz.ch/about/history; http://web.mit.edu/aeroastro/labs/gtl/early_GT_history.html (The man behind the early gas turbine.) www.ethbib.ethz.ch/exhibit/stodola/index.html.

Ivan Stodola wrote a engaging biography of his uncle, *Náš strýko Aurel*, Mladé letá, Bratislava, 1968.

Emil Miloslav Stodola (1862-1945) was a lawyer, a sociologist, and above all a passionate Slovak nationalist in Mikuláš. He moved to Budapest where he became a noted and successful attorney, an important figure in the planning of the future Czechoslovak Republic, and a collaborator of Milan Hodža (Chapter 26). Later he was a leader of the Slovak National Party of Czechoslovakia which argued for the autonomy of Slovakia but on a different basis than Hlinka's Slovak People's Party. An exceptionally principled man, when the party became too nationalistic for his taste he resigned from it and left public life. Natália Krajčovičová, *Vzťah občianskeho a národného v názoroch a aktivitách JUDr. Emila Stodolu*, Acta Universitatis Palackianae Olomucensis 27, 1996, pp.

177-182; Natália Krajčovičová, *Občan nemá len jeden spoločenský rozmer, E. Stodola chápal samosprávu ako rozvinutejší a moderný stupeň správy*, www.civil.gov.sk/archiv/casopis/2002/21/2126mi.htm ; http://sk.wikipedia.org/wiki/Emil_Stodola.

Kornel Milan Stodola (1866-1946) was initially active in the family leather business. From 1911 to 1918 he lived in Vienna, and during World War I he hosted the meetings of a group of Czechs and Slovaka, including Milan Hodža, who were very influential in the establishment of Czechoslovakia (Chapter 26). Having acquired extensive training in economics, he held a number of leading business and political positions in the new country. Throughout his life he was an avid sportsman, excelling in climbing in the Tatras and helping to introduce skiing, which he had learned on one of his many trips abroad. http://sk.wikipedia.org/wiki/Kornel_Stodola; www.nbs.sk/_img/Documents/BIATEC/BIA03_02/stodola.pdf

21. Zdenko Ďuriška, *Legendy a skutočnosť*, Biografické štúdie 26, 1999, 83-106. Available at www.snk.sk/?BS_26

22. www.liptov.sk/muzea/kral.html, fond Bella.

23. Letter now in author's archive.

Chapter 23: Ján Pálka and His Utopian Socialism

1. A comprehensive genealogy of the Pálka family has been developed by Zdenko Ďuriška of the Biographical Institute of the Slovak National Library, Martin. An exhaustive monograph about the family is in preparation.

2. Ján Pálka, *Zápisky*. Vydavateľské oddelenie YMCA v Prahe. Tlačené v kníhtlačiarni Bratov Rázusovcov (predtým F. Klimeš) v Liptovskom Sv. Mikuláši. 1932.

3. Letter of Ferdinand Vyšný, Dokumentačné stredisko, Kožiarske závody. Now at Štátny archív v Bytči, pobočka Liptovský Mikuláš.

4. Pálka, 1932, pp. 20-21.

5. Ibid., p. 16.

6. This schedule was a holdover from the days of Empress Maria Theresa, who had decreed that working hours would be from 5:00 in the morning until 8:00 at night. This was a considerable improvement over common earlier practices! Emil Kufčák, *Kožiarstvo v Lipt. Mikuláši za feudalizmu*. In: Emil Kufčák (Ed.), *Kožiarske závody v Liptovskom Mikuláši*, Kožiarske závody, n.p., Liptovský Mikuláš, 1972. p. 28.

7. Ivan Stodola, *Bolo, ako bolo, mozaika spomienok*, Slovenské vydavateľstvo krásnej literatúry, Bratislava, 1965, pp. 18-21.

8. Slovenská národná knižnica—Archív literatúry a umenia, Signatúra: 112 Z 30.

9. Zdenko Ďuriška, *Reformátor a idealista*, unpublished manuscript

10. Roman Holec, *Podnikatelia a podnikanie na Slovensku pred rokom 1918*. In: Historické štúdie 41, 2000, pp. 165-174; a popular article on early Slovak entrepreneurs including the Pálkas is Jozef Ryník, *Aj Slováci vedeli podnikať*. In: .týždeň. 7, no. 12 (March 22), 2010, pp. 14-19.

11. Matúš Dulla (Ed.), *Slávne vily Slovenska*. Foibos, Bratislava, 2010, pp.105-108; Ferdinand Vyšný, *Vila Stodola v Liptovskom Mikuláši*, typescript found in the archive of Matica slovenská, Martin; Soňa Kovačevičová, *Ženy Stodolovskej rodiny v kultúrnom a spoloenskom živote*. Biografické štúdie 26, 1999, pp. 157-163.

12. Soňa Kovačevičová-Žuffová, *Preskakovanie polienok*. Logos, Bratislava, 2001.

13. Emil Kufčák, *Mesto prvomájových tradícií*. In: Emil Kufčák (Ed.), *Liptovský Mikuláš, Monografický zborník*. Stredoslovenské vydavateľstvo, Banská Bystrica, 1968, p. 215.

14. http://en.wikipedia.org/wiki/May_Day

   May Day can refer to various labour celebrations conducted on May 1 that commemorate the fight for the eight hour day. May Day in this regard is called International Workers'

Day, or Labour Day. . . . With the idea having spread around the world, the choice of May 1st became a commemoration by the Second International for the people involved in the 1886 Haymarket affair.

The Haymarket affair occurred during the course of a three-day general strike in Chicago, Illinois that involved common laborers, artisans, merchants, and immigrants. Following an incident in which police opened fire and killed four strikers at the McCormick Harvesting Machine Co. plant, a rally was called for the following day at Haymarket Square. The event remained peaceful, yet towards the end of the rally, as police moved in to disperse the event, an unknown assailant threw a bomb into the crowd of police. The bomb and resulting police riot left at least a dozen people dead, including seven policemen. A sensational show trial ensued in which eight defendants were openly tried for their political beliefs, and not necessarily for any involvement in the bombing. The trial lead to the eventual public hanging of four anarchists. The Haymarket incident was a source of outrage from people around the globe. In the following years, memory of the 'Haymarket martyrs' was remembered with various May Day job actions and demonstrations.

15. Kufčák, 1968, pp. 213-240.

16. Emil Kufčák, *Kožiarstvo od revolúcie 1848-1849 do roku 1918*. In: Emil Kufčák (Ed.), *Kožiarske závody v Liptovskom Mikuláši*, Kožiarske závody, n.p., Liptovský Mikuláš, 1972, pp. 43-45.

17. Pálka, 1932, pp. 33-34.

18. Ibid., p. 25.

19. Ibid., p. 27.

20. Ibid., p. 28-30.

21. Grandfather Pálka was by no means the only man considering these questions and possible solutions. Other European business leaders were thinking and experimenting along similar lines. The most famous and successful such experiment was the German optical firm of Carl Zeiss (www.cdvandt.org/carl_zeiss_stiftung.htm). Its founder, Prof. Ernst Abbe, was committed to social reform and had established the Carl Zeiss Foundation as early as 1889. The foundation was the recipient of the profits of the several Zeiss companies. These it allocated first for research and various cultural activities. The remainder went back to the companies to finance growth and employee benefits. The foundation also insured that working conditions in the Zeiss factories were uncommonly good for the times—eight-hour days, paid holidays, health benefits, profit-sharing, and a retirement plan. This successful model was an inspiration for Grandfather Pálka, though he had some reservations about Abbe's philosophical perspective.

22. Pálka, 1932, pp. 74-75.

23. John Keane, *Václav Havel: A Political Tragedy in Six Acts*, Basic Books, New York, 2000.

23. See, for example, Emil Kufčák, *Garbiarsky priemysel od roku 1918 do znárodnenia*. In: Emil Kufčák, (Ed.), *Kožiarske závody v Liptovskom Mikuláši*, Kožiarske závody,n.p., Liptovský Mikuláš, 1972.

24. See, for example, www.economist.com/businessfinance/displaystory.cfm?story_id=347363

25. Pálka, 1932, p. 72. Pálka summarized his misfortunes in much greater detail in a letter (dated April 23, 1930, addressee unknown) preserved in the Archive of the National Museum in Prague, 94/1; see also the recent analysis by Zdenko Ďuriška, *Reformátor idealista*, unpublished manuscript.

26. Iboja Wandall-Holm, *Zbohom, storočie*. Kalligram, Bratislava, 2003.

27. Pálka, 1932, pp. 65-68.

28. Ibid., pp. 142-143.

29. Ibid., pp. 106-107.

30. Ibid., p. 142.

31. *Zpráva notáriuša za cechovský rok 1935*. Archive of the Museum of Janko Král', Liptovský Mikuláš.

Chapter 24: Hodžas—Four Generations in the Nation's Service

1. Zdenko Ďuriška, *Hodžovci v slovenských dejinách.* In: Miroslav Pekník (Ed.), *Milan Hodža a integrácia strednej Európy*, Vydavateľstvo Slovenskej akadémie vied, Bratislava, 2006.

2. Ján Hučko, *Michal Miloslav Hodža*, Nakladateľstvo Epocha, Bratislava, 1970.

3. Alena Bartlová—Ivan Thurzo, *Slovenský Perikles, Nárčt životnej cesty Milana Hodžu, prvého slovenského predsedu vlády ČSR*, Vydavateľstvo Spolku slovenských spisovateľov, Bratislava, 2008.

4. Zdenka Sojková, *Skvitne ešte život, Kniha o Ľudovítovi Štúrovi.* Matica slovenská, Martin, 2006, pp. 128-130.

5. Photocopy in author's archive.

6. Jozef Lettrich, *Fedor Hodža nás opustil*, Naše Snahy, vol. IV, no. 5, p. 2, October, 1968, reprinted in Miroslav John Ličko, *Ako chutí cudzina?*, Kalligram, Bratislava, 1999.

7. Jan Kuklík a Jan Němeček, *Hodža versus Beneš*, Nakladatelství Karolinum, Praha, 1999.

8. A lucid overview of the complex political situation prevailing in Slovakia immediately after World War II is provided by Dušan Kováč, *Dejiny Slovenska*, Nakladalestv*í Lidové noviny, Praha, 1998. A more nationalistic perspective is found in Anton Spiesz and Dusan Caplovic, *Illustrated Slovak History: A Struggle for Sovereignty in Central Europe*, Bolchazy-Carducci, Wauconda, 2006. A detailed personal account is provided by Jozef Lettrich, History of Modern Slovakia, Praeger, New York, 1955.

9. Comprehensive accounts of party activities during this period are Štefan Šutaj, *Slovenské občianske politické strany v dokumentoch (1944-1948)*, Slovenská akadémia vied, Spoločenský ústav SAV, Košice, 2002: www.saske.sk/SVU/downloads/publikacie/SOPS.pdf; and Marek Syrný, *Slovenskí demokrati '44-48: Kapitoly z dejín Demokratickej strany na Slovensku v rokoch 1944-1948.* Múzeum Slovenského Národného Povstania, Banská Bystrica, 2010.

10. Miroslav John Ličko, *Ako chutí cudzina?*, 1999.

11. Two of the most important were *Rada slobodného Československa* (Council of Free Czechoslovakia) and *Stála konferencia slovenských demokratických exulantov* (Permanent Conference of Slovak Democratic Exiles). He was also active on the editorial board of *Naše Snahy*. Hodža's role in these organizations is detailed in ibid.

12. Viera Štetková, reminiscences, photocopy in author's archive.

Chapter 25: Milan Hodža: Rebel Journalist

1. Roman Holec, *Sedmohradsko—Slovensko—Milan Hodža*, Dilema, politicko-kultúrny časopis, 2003.

2. Valerián Bystrický, *Milan Hodža a česko-slovenské vzťahy koncom 30. rokov.* In: Miroslav Pekník (Ed.), *Milan Hodža, štátnik a politik*, Veda, Vydavateľstvo Slovenskej akadémie vied, Bratislava, 2002.

3. Suzanna Maria Mikula, *Milan Hodža and the Slovak National Movement, 1898-1918,* doctoral dissertation, Syracuse University, 1974. Available through Xerox University Microfilms, Ann Arbor, Michigan 48106, p. 24. Mikula continues (pp. 24-25):

> The intellectual and social conditions were nearly as depressing as the economic. The Slovaks did not have national educational opportunities. The only schools they had were the lower grades, and these were insufficient in number. Slovak middle schools, gymnasiums, and technical schools had been disbanded by the Magyars. The impact of the Magyarization drive is difficult to quantify. The peasants were relatively untouched, so long as they were content to remain poor, minimally educated, and inarticulate. A nation, however, cannot survive without an educated class, articulate spokesmen, and its own people in positions of authority. Here Magyarization was visible and effective. Thus among 46,449 people who had positions of civil authority in Slovakia, only 132 acknowledged themselves as Slovaks. Although there may have been others who considered themselves Slovaks privately, their public denationalization meant they were lost to the service of the nation. One of the most influential figures, next to the priest, among the peasants was the village and district notary, who collected taxes, conducted elections (which were by open balloting), and in general

oversaw the public affairs of the people. Of 5,313 notaries in Slovakia, only 38 were Slovaks. The number of nationally active Slovaks, who could be considered the Slovak intelligentsia, was very small, no more than one thousand families.

4. Anton Spiesz and Dusan Caplovic, *Illustrated Slovak History*, Bolchazy-Carducci Publishers, Wauconda, 2006, p. 180.

5. Elena Jakešová, *Spoločnost'*. In: Dušan Kováč (Ed.), *Na začiatku storočia, 1901-1914*. Veda, Vydavateľstvo Slovenskej akadémie vied, Bratislava, 2004, pp. 70-74. For those who stayed, economic conditions were harsh. Because of the industrialization of Hungary, including, at least to some extent, the Slovak counties, rural poverty was being replaced by industrial poverty. On May 1, 1890, the first major industrial strike in the Kingdom of Hungary took place. On Slovak territory there were actions in Bratislava, Košice, Bardejov, and Mikuláš. In Mikuláš, the army was called out to put down the strike. Emil Kufčák, *Mesto prvomájových tradícií*. In: Emil Kufčák (Ed.), *Liptovský Mikuláš, Monografický zborník*. Stredoslovenské vydvateľstvo, Banská Bystrica, 1968.

Despite increasing socio-economic dislocation, Hungary was on the ascendant. The government declared the year 1896 to be the Millenium Year—one thousand years since the Magyars under their chieftain Árpád swept in and conquered the Hungarian plain some time around 896 C.E. When eighteen-year-old Milan Hodža arrived in Budapest to take up the study of law in 1896, he would have encountered extraordinary sights. Fifteen years in the making, the Millenial celebration of Magyar glory was nothing short of spectacular and included many major public works. Here is a partial list, much of it familiar to today's tourist: Continental Europe's first underground railway; the Gallery of Fine Arts; the major part of the largest parliament building in the world (particularly ironic in view of the fact that the incredibly wealthy aristocracy still ruled with a firm hand, less than ten percent of the male population was allowed to vote, and intimidation, bribery and fraud were routinely employed by the government to keep elections under control); the Supreme Court building; the last section of the great boulevard of Pest; multiple bridges across the Danube; multiple conferences and congresses, some international in scope (for example, art historians, dentists, tailors, geologists, and others); around the country four hundred new primary schools, as well as many monuments and memorial tablets. Topping it all off was the Millenium Exhibition, with its 234 pavilions and 14,000 exhibits, ceremonially opened by the Emperor Franz Jozef. And this is only a sampling! Paul Lendvai, *The Hungarians: A Thousand Years of Victory in Defeat*, Princeton University Press, Princeton, 2003, pp. 310-319.

6. Anton Štefánek, *Hodža: Osobnost' a práca*. In: A. Štefánek, F. Votruba, F. Seďa (Eds.), *Milan Hodža, publicista, politik, vedecký pracovník*, Českomoravské podniky tiskařské a vydavatelské, Praha, 1930, p. 30. Štefánek was a long-time friend and collaborator of Milan Hodža and served for many years as Czechoslovakia's minister of education.

7. Alena Bartlová—Ivan Thurzo, *Slovenský Perikles, Náčrt životnej cesty Milana Hodžu, prvého slovenského predsedu vlády ČSR*, Vydavateľstvo Spolku slovenských spisovateľov, Bratislava, 2008, pp. 26-27. These anecdotal accounts are based on the reminiscences of Anna Styk, daughter of Juraj Hodža (Family tree 5, Appendix V) and thus Milan's older cousin, who helped take care of him during his childhood.

8. Quoted in Alena Bartlová—Ivan Thurzo, *2008*, p. 20; see also Július Žilka, *Z minulosti Sučian a ev. a. v. cirkvi sučianskej*, Prešov, 1933.

9. He was able to do this thanks to Aurel Plech, his mother Klementína's brother, a successful physician. Rejoicing in Milan's birth, Uncle Aurel immediately undertook to support the boy's education and held true to his word after Ondrej's death. Alena Bartlová—Ivan Thurzo, *Slovenský Perikles*, pp. 24-25, 30.

10. Anton Štefánek, 1930, p. 67.

11. Alena Bartlová—Ivan Thurzo, 2008, pp. 33-35.

12. Vladimír Fajnor, *Hodžove študentské letá*, pp. 631-635, and Anton Štefánek, *Hodža: Osobnost' a práca*, p. 67-68. Both in A. Štefánek, F.Votruba, F. Seďa (Eds.), *Milan Hodža, publicista, politik, vedecký pracovník*, 1930,

13. Alena Bartlová—Ivan Thurzo, 2008, pp. 36-39.

14. Salva's life story not only intersects with that of Milan Hodža, it also has close parallels to that of Michal Miloslav Hodža. Salva was born in 1849 in the town of Sielnica in County Liptov. He taught for over twenty years in Lutheran schools in Liptov, and was outspoken in his support of the Slovak cause. In 1887 he moved to Klenovec in County Gemer. Here he worked with the support of one of the great figures of Slovak public life, Štefan Marko Daxner (the principal author of the Declaration of the Slovak Nation of 1861), and formed a close working friendship with a Czech teacher, Karol Kálal. A decade later he and Kálal published a Slovak-Czech, Czech-Slovak dictionary, as well as other joint works. However, the upper echelons of the church hierarchy were filled with Magyars and *magyarones*, just as they had been in the time of M. M. Hodža. Over time, they gathered their strength to silence Salva. They found their opportunity when he published a vigorous article entitled "Every Slovak a human being" (*Čo Slovák to človek*) in response to insulting articles in Magyar papers comparing Slovaks to farm animals. He was investigated, and threatened with the loss of his position. The town sent a delegation with an appeal on his behalf to the general inspector of the church, and even to the prime minister, Koloman Tisza. Instead of listening, the prime minister dismissed them impatiently. "In Klenovec there are two sides. You represent one. The other is faithful to its [Magyar] nation and supports the actions of the authorities in the matter of the pan-Slav Karol Salva." Salva was ousted from his position as teacher and forbidden to hold any office at all in the Lutheran church.

    Now Daxner advised his friend to turn to publishing. Salva left home to learn the printer's trade in the Serbian city of Osiek. A year later he returned to County Liptov, settled in Ružomberok, and established a print shop. He published extensively: educational books, fiction and poetry from major Slovak authors, and magazines for teachers, for children, for peasants, and for the general public—anything to support Slovak upliftment. Between 1888 and 1909 he published 258 titles in around 750,000 copies, a very large number for the times. The magazine Home and School (*Dom a škola*), to which Czechs as well as Slovaks contributed, was one of the most important influences on Slovak education at the time. The annuals he published between 1883 and 1904 provided popular and welcome reading for poor, ordinary people. He started *Slovenské listy* in 1897. This venture proved to be financially unsustainable and closed in 1899, but throughout his publishing career he never failed to put forward the Slovak cause.

    During this long period he was constantly harassed and persecuted by the authorities, and faced unending financial difficulties. After over twenty years as a teacher and sixteen years as an undefatigable publisher, he had to sell his business to pay his debts. In 1909, at the age of sixty, he left home for Cleveland, leaving his family behind. In Cleveland he studied theology and became the pastor of a Slovak Lutheran congregation. He also continued his literary work, contributing to and editing Slovak publications and newspapers, notably *Amerikánsko-slovenské noviny* (American-Slovak News), the very first Slovak-language newspaper in the United States, founded in 1886, and *Slovenský Denník* (Slovak Daily). He died in 1913.

    Igor Tomo, *Slováci v zahraničí 17*, Matica slovenská, 1994; Národná osveta 10/2007, p. 5; Ľubica Bartalská, *Stodvadsať rokov slovenskej tlače v Amerike*, Knižnica, vol. 6, no. 8, 2005, pp. 21-24.

15. *Slovenské listy* stood in sharp contrast to the only Slovak newspaper to have survived the period of increasing Magyarization, *Národnie noviny*, published in Martin and representing the view of the Slovak leadership centered there. By the late nineteenth century this "Martin center" had watched one after another Slovak candidate for public office lose elections because of bribes, physical threats, and other manipulations by Magyars and *magyarones* (see, for example, Alena Bartlová—Ivan Thurzo, *2008*, pp. 44-45). Instead of putting their energy into political battles that seemed destined to fail, the leaders in Martin decided to focus on preserving and developing Slovak culture, particularly literature. *Národnie noviny* itself published much fine literature, but its readership was restricted to a tiny sliver of the Slovak population, the intelligentsia. Salva aspired to a much wider and more diverse audience for his *Slovenské listy*.

16. Alena Bartlová—Ivan Thurzo, ibid., pp. 39-41.

17. Alena Bartlová, *Andrej Hlinka*, Vydavateľstvo Obzor, Bratislava, 1991, pp. 14-15;

18. Miloš Kovačka, *Milan Hodža a krest'anstvo*. In: Miroslav Pekník (Ed.), *Milan Hodža a integrácia strednej Európy*. Veda, Vydavatel'stvo Slovenskej akadémie vied, Bratislava, 2006.

19. Alena Bartlová, 1991, pp. 16-18. Alena Bartlová—Ivan Thurzo, 2008, pp. 83-90.

20. Hodža's attorney at one of the trials was Pavel Mudroň, vice-chairman of the Slovak National Party and another frequent visitor to the parish house of Ondrej Hodža and a man who had known young Milan since his birth. Alena Bartlová—Ivan Thurzo, 2008, pp. 41-44.

21. *Hlas* was founded by two physicians, Dr. Pavel Blaho and Dr. Vavro Šrobár, both of whom had studied in Prague and had read Tomáš Garrigue Masaryk, a strong proponent of on-the-ground political work. Masaryk was an inspiration for a growing circle of active and committed young Slovaks, soon to be called Hlasists.

    See, for example, Karol Kollár, *Milan Hodža, hlasizmus a T. G. Masaryk*. In: Miroslav Pekník (Ed.), *Milan Hodža, štátnik a politik*, Veda Vydavatel'stvo Slovenskej akadémie vied, Bratislava, 2002.

22. Hodža had gained important training in journalism as the parliamentary reporter for the German-language newspaper, *Budapester Abendblatt* (Budapest Evening News). While a student in Šoproň, he had won an all-Hungarian award for his skill in stenography, the standby of journalists in the days before portable tape recorders. Now, as he sat in the gallery of the parliament hall, he mentally translated the Magyar-language proceedings into German, wrote them down in German shorthand, and was ready to go to press before any of his competitors. He also studied the technical side of publishing—page layout, typesetting, design of headlines, maintenance of subscription lists—everything that goes into the running of a newspaper. Anton Štefánek, 1930, pp. 75-80.

23. For an overall characterization of Hodža as a journalist, see Drahoslav Machala, *Milan Hodža v Slovenskom týždenníku*. In: Miroslav Pekník (Ed.), *Milan Hodža, štátnik a politik*, Veda, Vydavatel'stvo Slovenskej akadémie vied, Bratislava, 2002. For a comprehensive modern analysis, see Miroslav Pekník (Ed.), *Milan Hodža—politik a žurnalista*, Veda, Vydavatel'stvo Slovenskej akadémie vied, Bratislava, 2008. Hodža's journalism has also been the subject of a fine undergraduate dissertation: Anna Záborská, *Novinárske dielo politika Milana Hodžu*, bakalárska práca, Univerzita sv. Cyrila a Metoda v Trnave, 2008.

24. Suzanna Maria Mikula, 1974, pp. 65-66.

25. Anton Štefánek, 1930, p. 81.

26. Slovenský týždenník vol.1, no. 1 (April 7, 1903).

27. He was referring to *Zvolenské noviny*, published by Vladimír Fajnor.

28. *Slovenský týždenník*, vol II, no. 12 (March 18, 1904).

29. Miloš Hodža, *Slovenské evanjelictvo v utrpení*. In: Samuel Štefan Osuský, *Službe národu*, Štúrova evanjelická spoločnost' v Bratislave nákladom Vydavatel'ského a knihkupeckého ú. Spolku Tranoscius v Liptovskom Sv. Mikuláši, 1938, pp. 77-83.

30. Petrovec was the largest town in the electoral district of Kulpín, northwest of Belgrade. The Serbs and the Slovaks in Kulpín had long ago come to an unusual and mutually advantageous agreement: they alternated putting forward candidates for the Hungarian parliament, and then they supported each other's candidates. This meant that during one election year, both Slovaks and Serbs, irrespective of party affiliation, would vote for the Slovak candidate, and in the next election both groups would vote for the Serbian candidate. In 1869 they had jointly elected the Slovak editor Viliam Pauliny-Tóth (Chapter 21). Before Pauliny-Tóth entered the parliament, only one Slovak had ever served there, L'udovít Štúr in 1844, and he had gained his seat not by election but by appointment.

31. See, for example, Alena Bartlová—Ivan Thurzo, 2008, pp. 97-106; Ján Juríček, *Milan Hodža—Kapitola z dejín slovenskej, československej a európskej politiky*, Stimul, Bratislava, 1994, pp. 33-36

32. The original text was reprinted in full in a book in the possession Dr. Ján Bulík (Chapter 30). In the photocopy he kindly gave me, the bibliographic details of the book are unfortunately not visible.

33. Miloš Krno was a patriotic Slovak attorney who had enthusiastically supported Hodža's nomination as the candidate in Kulpín.

34. There was only one other Slovak deputy, Ferko Skyčák.

35. Michal Múdry, *Milan Hodža v Amerike*. Geringer Press, Chicago, 1949, pp. 216-217.

36. Igor Pivko, *Spomienky*, Martinský Evanjelik, Ročník 9, číslo 2, 2002, pp. 27-29.

Chapter 26: Milan Hodža at the Birth of a Nation

1. Aurel Popovici, *Die Vereinigten Staaten von Gross-Österreich. Politische Studien zur Lösung der nationalen Fragen und staatrechtlichen Krisen in Österreich-Ungarn*. Leipzig, 1906. http://en.wikipedia.org/wiki/United_States_of_Greater_Austria.

2. Jan Galandauer, *Belvederská epizoda v životě a paměti Milana Hodži*. In: *Milan Hodža, štátnik a politik*, Veda, Vydavateľstvo Slovenskej akadémie vied, Bratislava, 2002. Grandfather Hodža devotes the entire first chapter of his final work, *Federation in Central Europe, Reflections and Reminiscences*, Jarrolds, London, 1942, to Franz Ferdinand and his own interactions with the archduke. An extended treatment is also given by Suzanna Maria Mikula, *Milan Hodža and the Slovak National Movement*, Ph. Dissertation, Syracuse University. Available through Xerox University Microfilms, Ann Arbor, 1974, pp. 107-134. See also Ján Juríček, *Milan Hodža, Kapitola z dejín slovenskej, československej a európskej politiky*, Stimul, Bratislava, 1994, pp. 57-61, 74-77.

3. Juríček, 1984, pp. 49-51.

4. Ibid., pp. 51-55.

5. Ibid., pp. 55-61; Mikula, 1976, pp. 112-113.

6. Ibid., p. 56.

7. Ibid., p. 78; Mikula, 1976, p. 128.

8. Vladimír Zuberec, *Milan Hodža, politik a štátnik*, Zborník Slovenského národného múzea, História 34, Ročník LXXVIII, 1994, p. 86.

9. Ján Hodža, *Drobnosti zo života dr. Milana Hodžu*. Slovenská národná knižnica—Archív literatúry a umenia: 135 H 5.

10. Slovenský týždenník, vol. XII, no. 27 July 3, 1914).

11. Paul Robert Magocsi, *Historical Atlas of Central Europe, Revised and Expanded Edition*, University of Washington Press, Seattle, 2002.

12. Kornel Stodola, *Válečné roky s Milanom Hodžom*, Bratislava, 1938, p. 18.

13. Juríček, 1999, pp. 85-86.

14. Stodola, 1983, p. 19.

15. Juríček, 1999, p. 86.

16. While Hodža saw the reform of the Monarchy as the best mechanism for the advancement of the Slovak cause, he also saw great advantages in cultivating a strong relationship with the Czechs. He was sympathetic to the Hlasists. He tried valiantly to attract Czech capital to banks and other organizations that would serve Slovaks, particularly peasants (see, for example, Roman Holec, *Národohospodárske aktivity Milana Hodžu do roku 1918*. In: Miroslav Peknik (Ed.), *Milan Hodža, štátnik a politik*, Veda, Vydavateľstvo Slovenskej akadémie vied, Bratislava, 2002.) He intially rejected the practicality of a political union of Slovaks and Czechs, but he always gave it serious thought and, with the assassination of Archduke Franz Ferdinand, he was ready to accept it as the best way forward for Slovaks. Thus, there was plenty in his correspondence to substantiate the charge that he was engaged in Czechoslovak, anti-Magyar activity.

17. Irene Palka, *Episodes of My School Years*. Essay prepared for Columbia University class in English composition for foreign students, c. 1951. Author's archive.

18. Kornel Stodola, 1938, pp. 16-17.

19. Miroslav Pekník, *Milan Hodža a slovenská politika v predvojnových mesiacoch roku 1914 a v prvom období vojny*. In: Miroslav Pekník (Ed.), *Milan Hodža, štátnik a politik*, Veda, Vydavateľstvo slovenskej akadémie vied, Bratislava, 2002.

20. Zuberec, 1994, pp. 87-88. Thoughts of unification were also being entertained by other clusters of Slovak leaders. One group was in Budapest, where the principal leader was Emil Stodola, Kornel's brother (Chapter 22, note 20). Hodža, who visited Budapest fairly often, was regarded as the guiding voice there as well as in Vienna. Another group was based in Prague, centered around Vavro Šrobár and Hodža's close friend and collaborator, Anton Štefánek.

21. Stodola, 1938, p. 19.

22. Stodola, 1938, p. 53.

23. A handful of other voices, notably Ferdinand Juriga and Vavro Šrobár, were likewise urging the Slovak National Party to renounce passivity and establish a Slovak National Council. Soon the Slovak ice began to thaw. On May 1, 1918, the Social Democratic Party, the first to answer Hodža's call for a Slovak National Council, staged a boisterous demonstration in Mikuláš, the first political rally in Slovakia since the war began. There, under the leadership of Vavro Šrobár, a resolution was adopted demanding self-determination for the "Hungarian branch of the Czechoslovak nation." Interestingly for the course of history, both Hodža's *Slovenský týždenník* and the *Národnie noviny* of the Martin center, so often at odds with one another, reported that in Mikuláš *Slovaks* [not the "Hungarian branch of the Czechoslovak nation"] demanded self-determination. Vladimír Zuberec, 1999, p.88. Later in May the Slovak National Party held a meeting of its leadership at which Andrej Hlinka made one of his most famous pronouncements: "Let us say openly that we are for a Czecho-Slovak orientation. The thousand year marriage with the Magyars has not worked out. We must divorce." Alena Bartlová, *Andrej Hlinka*, Vydavateľstvo Obzor, Bratislava, 1991, p. 37.

24. As is well known, the greatest impetus for the new developments came from further away than Prague, Vienna, or Budapest. Tomáš Garrigue Masaryk, Edvard Beneš, and Milan Rastislav Štefánik worked together in France, and also in the United States and Russia, to persuade the Western Powers that forming a new state in which the fortunes of Czechs and Slovaks would be joined together was just. Important Czech and Slovak organizations in the United States supported the movement. The Cleveland and Pittsburgh Agreements were signed. Czechoslovak legions were formed, most notably in Russia. In January of 1918, President Wilson delivered a visionary speech to the Congress of the United States, dealing with issues of the great war and the coming peace. The tenth of its fourteen points declared: "The peoples of Austria-Hungary, whose place among the nations we wish to see safeguarded and assured, should be accorded the freest opportunity to autonomous development." In June, the Czechoslovak National Council, formed in Paris as early as 1916, was officially recognized by the government of France as the body entitled to speak for Czechs and Slovaks. The British government followed suit in August, the United States in September.

25. Dušan Kováč, *30. október 1918 a jeho muži*. In: Dušan Kováč (Ed.), *Muži deklarácie*, Veda, Vydavateľstvo slovenskej akadémie vied, Bratislava, 2000.

26. Marián Hronský, *Budapeštianske rokovania Milana Hodžu a prvá demarkačná čiara medzi Slovenskom a Maďarskom*. In: Miroslav Pekník (Ed.), *Milan Hodža, štátnik a politik*, Veda, Vydavateľstvo slovenskej akadémie vied, Bratislava, 2002. Marián Hronský, *Trianon: Vznik hraníc Slovenska a problémy jeho bezpečnosti (1918-1920)*, Veda, Vydavateľstvo Slovenskej akadémie vied, Bratislava, 2011, pp. 62-72.

27. Ján Pálka, manuscript in author' archive.

28. Miloslav Čaplovič, *Prvý pluk slovenskej slobody (november 1918—marec 1919)*. In: Historický časopis 43, no. 4, 1995, pp. 651-667.

Chapter 27: Milan Hodža—Statesman of International Stature

1. Grandfather Hodža's very first appointment was a relatively junior one, state secretary (undersecretary) in the ministry of the interior. One of his tasks in this capacity was to travel across the Slovak countryside, study the working and living conditions of the peasants, and report his findings

to Prague. Even a full year after the surrender of Austria-Hungary, the scars of World War I were still deep. Hodža was shocked at the acute food shortages he observed, particularly in villages that were remote from the railways, and he immediately set to work to alleviate them. Alena Bartlová, *Úsilie Dr. Milana Hodžu o prosperitu slovenského a československého rol'níctva.* In: Miroslav Pekník (Ed.), *Milan Hodža a agrárne hnutie,* (see below, Note 3), p. 80. This appointment has also been interpreted as Hodža's failed attempt to gain dominant influence over Slovak affairs. Xénia Šuchová, *Hodžove koncepcie administratívnej autonómie.* In: Miroslav Pekník (Ed.), *Milan Hodža a agrárne hnutie.*

2. At the end of 1919 Hodža was appointed as the first Czechoslovak Minister for the Unification of Laws. This was a ministry that dealt with the consequences of the divergent history of the Czech lands and Slovakia. Over many years, the Austrian and the Hungarian parts of the dual monarchy had developed different legal systems. These had been inherited by the two parts of the new Czechoslovakia, and now needed to be brought into alignment so that the entire country could operate under a single legal system. Hodža had been the first to articulate the need for this alignment, and as minister he established the mechanisms for identifying and implementing the necessary legal changes. Josef Fritz, *Dr. Milan Hodža a Unifikační ministerstvo.* In: Anton Štefánek, Františrek Votruba, František Sed'a (Eds.), 1930 (see Note 3); Alena Bartlová—Ivan Thurzo, *Slovenský Perikles* (see Note 3), pp.158-159.

3. Some of the full-length books devoted to Milan Hodža are the following:

   a. Alena Bartlová—Ivan Thurzo, *Slovenský Perikles, Nárčt životnej cesty Milana Hodžu, prvého slovenského predsedu vlády ČSR,* Vydavatel'stvo Spolku slovenských spisovatel'ov, Bratislava, 2008.

   b. Samuel Cambel, *Štátnik a národohospodár Milan Hodža, 1878-1944,* Veda, Vydavatel'stvo Slovenskej akadémie vied, Bratislava, 2001.

   c. Ján Juríček, *Milan Hodža, Kapitola z dejín slovenskej, československej a európskej politiky,* Vydavatel'stvo Stimul, Bratislava, 1994.

   d. Karol Kollár, *Milan Hodža: moderný teoretik, pragmatický politik,* Infopress, Bratislava, 1994.

   e. Jan Kuklík and Jan Němeček, *Hodža versus Beneš, Milan Hodža a slovenská otázka v zahrančiním odboji za druhé světové války,* Nakladatelství Karolinum, Praha, 1999.

   f. Pavol Lukáč, *Milan Hodža v zápase o budúcnost' strednej Európy v rokoch 1939-1944,* Štefan Šebesta (Ed.), Veda, Vydavatel'stvo Slovenskej akadémie vied, Bratislava, 2005.

   g. Michal Múdry, *Milan Hodža v Amerike,* Geringer Press, Chicago, 1949.

   h. Miroslav Pekník (Ed.), *Milan Hodža—štátnik a politik,* 3. vydanie, Veda, Vydavatel'stvo Slovenskej akadémie vied, Bratislava, 2002. English Edition - Miroslav Pekník (Ed.), *Milan Hodža—Statesman and Politician.* Veda, Slovak Academy of Sciances, Bratislava, 2007.

   i. Miroslav Pekník (Ed.), *Milan Hodža a integrácia strednej Európy,* Veda, Vydavatel'stvo Slovenskej akadémie vied, Bratislava, 2006.

   j. Miroslav Pekník, (Ed.), *Milan Hodža—politik a žurnalista,* Veda, Vydavatel'stvo Slovenskej akadémie vied, Bratislava, 2008.

   k. Miroslav Pekník (Ed.), *Milan Hodža a agrárne hnutie,* Veda, Vydavatel'stvo Slovenskej akadémie vied, Bratislava, 2008.

   l. Anton Štefánek, František Votruba, František Sed'a (Eds.), *Milan Hodža, publicista, politik, vedecký pracovník,* Českomoravské podniky tiskařské a vydavatelské, Praha, 1930.

   In addition, a number of dissertations have been devoted to Hodža, of which by far the most comprehensive is Suzanna Maria Mikula, *Milan Hodža and the Slovak National Movement, 1898-1918,* Syracuse University, 1965. Available through Xerox University Microfilms, Ann Arbor and London.

4. Anton Spiesz and Dusan Caplovic, *Illustrated Slovak History: A Struggle for Sovereignty in Central Europe,* Bolchazy-Carducci, Wauconda, 2006, p. 197.

5. Martin Bútora, *Hl'adanie najväčšieho,* týždeň, 25. júna 2005.

6. Múdry, 1999, pp. 220-221.

7. Aunt Vierka described Grandfather Hodža as a chain smoker (Chapter 1). Presumably this reflects the enormous pressures he faced in 1938.

8. His dissertation focused on the Slovak awakening of the nineteenth century. Perhaps because he was so deeply a political being—a *homo politicus*, as many have called him—his central thesis was that the establishment of the Slovak literary language was primarily a political act, not a necessary outcome of linguistic or cultural history. Published in 1921 as a 400+ page treatise called *Československý rozkol (Czechoslovak schism)*, it immediately created a controversy among other intellectuals (Václav Chaloupecký, "*Československý rozkol" v prácích Dra. Milana Hodži a Dra. Josefa Škultétyho*. In: Štefánek, Votruba, Sed'a (Eds.), 1930, and it continues to stimulate comment today (Ján Uher, *Milan Hodža a jeho Československý rozkol*. In: Miroslav Pekník (Ed.), 2002, English in 2007).

9. Milan Hodža, *Články, reči, štúdie. I. Aktivita a demokratizm v slovenskej politike od r. 1898 do r. 1906.* Novina, Praha, 1930. *II. Československá súčinnost' 1898-1919.* Novina, Praha, 1930. *III. Začiatky rol'níckej demokracie na Slovensku 1903—1914.* Novina, Praha, 1931. *IV. Cesty stredo-evropskej agrárnej demokracie 1921—1931.* Novina, Praha, 1931. *V. Slovenské rol'nícke organizácie 1912-1933.* Novina, Praha, 1933. *VII. Slovensko a republika.* Linografie, Bratislava, 1934. Vol. VI never appeared.

10. Kollár, 1999.

11. Miroslav Daniš, *Milan Hodža, profesor FF UK v Bratislave,* unpublished manuscript in author's archive, courtesy of doc. Daniš.

12. This uneven allocation of professorships has long been viewed as a glaring example of the inappropriate Czech domination of Czechoslovakia. Even the two Slovaks who were appointed could not be expected to exert a great collective influence on the university. For one thing, Škultéty was one of the most outspoken critics of Hodža's *Československý rozkol*. In addition, even in 1921 Hodža was deeply immersed in political life and many viewed him as an absentee professor. However, recent research into the archives of the university gives us a new appreciation of his contributions over the years. In addition to presenting extremely well-attended lecture series on modern European history from time to time, the records show that he was prominently involved in the establishment of several of the university's schools and departments, in appointments to the faculty, in cultivating strong relationships with Czech academics, in the construction of student dormitories, and in the allocation to the university's use of the hallmark building in whose main hall (the Aula) all major formal occasions are still conducted. This was typical of Hodža. He often initiated important undertakings, found appropriate people to lead them, and himself remained in the background.

13. In 2006, our family presented to the Department of History at Comenius University a collection of about two hundred volumes from the personal libraries of Grandfather Hodža and Uncle Dišo. These books had been preserved during World War II in Mikuláš, in a warehouse belonging to family friends (Zora Frkáňová, *Príhovor pri odovzdávaní hodžovských kníh FF UK v Bratislave,* typescript in author's archive). Most of them dealt with history, political science, and economics. The department was pleased and honored to receive them, and organized a reception and small academic symposium to commemorate the occasion. It was on this occasion that doc. Daniš first delivered his paper on Hodža as professor.

14. Ján Juríček, 1999, pp. 117-118; Alena Bartlová, *Slovák Dr. Milan Hodža na čele ministerstva pol'nohospodárstva*. In: Miroslav Pekník (Ed.), 2002, 2007.

15. Ladislav Šíp, *Dr. Milan Hodža jako ministr školství a národní osvěty*. In: Anton Štefánek, Františck Votruba, Františck Sed'a (Eds.), 1930.

16. At the same time, Hodža saw to it that education was also expanded in the already-advanced Czech regions of the Republic. Among the schools whose establishment he strongly supported was the Prague English Grammar School (a grammar school in the British sense of a secondary school or gymnasium), a visionary institution that reflected not only the cosmopolitan nature of this great city, but also Grandfather Hodža's vision of building strong and meaningful multi-ethnic and international relations. Its mission was "to turn out young people who are inspired with the idea of international solidarity." Instruction was in English, and a number of teachers

were brought from England and the United States. Czech, German and Jewish students studied together until the Nazis occupied Czechoslovakia in 1939 and shut the school down. The government re-opened it after the war. Given its ties to England and the United States, however, it was an immediate target for the Communists, and by 1953 it was shut down for good. www.radio.cz/en/article/86529

17. Alena Bartlová—Ivan Thurzo, 2008, pp. 174-178.

18. Roman Holec, *Milan Hodža a počiatky slovenského agrarizmu*. In: Miroslav Pekník (Ed.), 2008.

19. Cambel, 2001, pp. 95-116. In the Peasant Mutual Banks, funds were pooled by farmers living in a given region and loaned out again at minimal interest rates, far lower than those charged by commercial banks and a small fraction of the 50% commonly charged by local money-lenders. The government provided start-up capital and the first year's operating expenses. Immediate authority over the operation of each mutual bank was held by a local steering committee. Similar institutions existing in Western Europe since the nineteenth century may have been the inspiration for Hodža (Diethelm Prowe, personal communication).

20. At first glance this might actually seem a modest number, but let us look at it more closely. If an average farm family had five members (probably a conservative estimate), this number of depositors would represent 700,000 people living on farms. During this period, the population of Slovakia was around 3 million. Thus, around 25% of the entire population would have had money on deposit in these banks. Suppose that during this time the peasantry, the system's constituents, constituted half of the total Slovak population, or 1.5 million. Then the 700,000 people with family funds on deposit the the Peasant Mutual Banks would have represented around *half* of the entire peasant population!

21. It was an inspiring vision, but persuading a poor peasant to entrust his few crowns to any kind of bank was no small task. It required a man of special gifts. For this crucial task Hodža recruited Ján Cablk, whom he had known since the days of Austria-Hungary and who had been one of the members of Kornel Stodola's Vienna circle (Chapter 26). Cablk had a background in banking, so he could help with practical advice. His enthusiasm for the mission of the Peasant Mutual Banks was unflagging and contagious. Most importantly, however, he had an open spirit and endless empathy to which the villagers quickly responded. It was said by insiders that "What Hodža invented, Cablk implemented" (Cambel, 2001, p. 105). To support the whole effort, a central organization, the Union of Peasant Mutual Banks, was established to assist with administration, bookkeeping, monitoring of investments, and the like. At its head was Ján Ursíny, Hodža's relative from Rakša, his close lieutenant, and later one of the organizers of the Slovak National Uprising and of the Democratic Party during World War II (Chapters 6, 9, and 14).

22. The availability of low-interest loans made many things possible for peasants. For example, they could buy parcels of land made available through land reform (another area in which Grandfather Hodža was active from the founding of Czechoslovakia), or invest in equipment. Perhaps most importantly, however, it tided them over during the recurrent economic crises that struck Europe, including Czechoslovakia, during the inter-war years, and hit the poor Slovak farmer especially hard. Many thousands of farmers were able to hold on to their land because of the Union of Peasant Mutual Banks.

23. The Communists did away with this remarkable organization, which now lives mainly in the writings of scholars and the memories of oldsters. To those who have studied the economic development of Slovakia, however, it was a milestone. For example, in 2007, through the courtesy of Dr. Vojtech Čelko of the Institute of Contemporary History in Prague, I met Prof. Drahoslav Janik of the Institute of Economic History at Charles University. When I asked Prof. Janik what had been Grandfather Hodža's greatest practical contribution in his role as minister of agriculture, his unhesitating response was, "The Union of Peasant Mutual Banks. For this, a statue should be erected in his honor in every Slovak village!"

24. Grandfather Hodža was an erudite man who spent far more of his life moving in high society and in intellectual circles than he ever did on a farm. However, he understood the plight of the small peasant clearly, and he acted. In the words of Samuel Cambel, a leading Slovak historian of the Communist era who wrote an entire monograph on Hodža's work relating to agriculture and the peasantry:

It would be a long list indeed that would identify all the activities in which Hodža directly and personally, or through the ministry which he led, directly or indirectly touched the development of Slovak agriculture in its material and its spiritual aspects. He was fufilling his old dream, that the soil of Slovakia, cultivated and improved for centuries by the toil of its original Slav settlers, should return to their Slovak descendants.

Cambel, 2001, p. 86.

25. During his years in the Hungarian parliament, Hodža had tried to convert the long-established Slovak National Party based in Martin to an agrarian perspective. When that proved too slow a process he participated, together with Andrej Hlinka, in the establishment of a new party, the Slovak People's Party. Finally he struck out on his own and established the Slovak Peasants' Party. In 1922 this party merged with a corresponding Czech one to form the Republican Agricultural and Peasant Party (*Republikánska strana zemedelského a maloroľníckeho ľudu*), commonly known as the Agrarian Party. Xénia Šuchová, *Hodžova koncepcia administratívnej autonómie*. In: Miroslav Miroslav Pekník (Ed.), 2008.

26. Matej Hanula, *Milan Hodža—prvý muž agrárnej strany na Slovensku v 20. rokoch 20. storočia*. In: Miroslav Pekník (Ed.), *Milan Hodža a agrárne hnutie*, 2008.

27. Natália Krajčovičová, *Začleňovanie Slovenska do Československej republiky (1918-1920)*. In: Milan Zemko, Valerián Bystrický (Eds.), *Slovensko v Československu*, Veda, Vydavateľstvo Slovenskej akadémie vied, Bratislava, 2004. Vladimír Zuberec, *Milan Hodža, Politik a štátnik*, Zborník Slovenského národného múzea, História 34, vol. 88—1994, gives a good summary of Hodža's role in discussions concerning the Martin Declaration. See also Xénia Šuchová, *Hodžova koncepcia administratívnej autonómie*. In: Pekník (Ed.), 2008.

28. Lukáč, 2005, p. 127. Lukáč was by no means the first to offer this evaluation. Hodža was widely recognized for his international perspective many years ago, for example by R.W. Seton-Watson, a British historian who was an expert on Central Europe, a great defender of Slovaks on the international scene, and an advisor to the British Government:

Milan Hodža was the first modern Slovak politician to free himself of the narrow perspective of the Slovak struggle against the Magyars and to see his nation in the broader European context.

29. *Dr. Milan Hodža*, Slovenská obrana (Scranton, Pennsylvania), vol. 21, no. 53, July 4, 1944, p. 4.

30. Jiří Čurda, *Milan Hodža a jeho geopolitické názory*. In: Miroslav Pekník (Ed.), 2002, 2007.

31. Jan Rychlík, *Milan Hodža a príprava európskej integrácie*. In: Miroslav Pekník (Ed.), 2006. When Hodža assumed the prime ministership of Czechoslovakia in 1935, he also served as the foreign minister for a few months. During this short period he tried to implement his ideas, which became known as "Hodža's Plan," as a way of opposing Hitler's expansion. He traveled to many countries to make his case. However, it was too late.

32. Vladimír Goněc, *Milan Hodža v pohledu disciplíny "dejiny evropské integrace."* In: Miroslav Pekník (Ed.), 2006. The earliest of these in modern times was Count Richard Coudenhove-Kalergi, an Austrian nobleman who launched a movement called Pan-Europa which still exists and is easily found on the internet. Hodža was in contact with Coudenhove-Kalergi for many years, including the period of his exile; reciprocally, the count knew of Hodža's ideas, thought highly of them, and referred to them in his writings. http://en.wikipedia.org/wiki/Count_Richard_Nikolaus_von_Coudenhove-Kalergi;

http://rmmla.wsu.edu/ereview/59.2/articles/villanueva.asp;

http://en.wikipedia.org/wiki/International_Paneuropean_Union.

33. www.historiasiglo20.org/europe/anteceden.htm.

34. www.historiasiglo20.org/europe/anteceden.htm; http://en.wikipedia.org/wiki/European_Coal_and_Steel_Community.

35. www.historiasiglo20.org/europe/anteceden.htm; http://en.wikipedia.org/wiki/.

36. Alena Bartlová, *Podiel Dr. Milana Hodžu na medzinárodnej kooperácii agrárnych politických strán*. In: Bohumila Ferenčuhová (Ed.), *Slovensko a svet v 20. storočí*. Prodama, Bratislava, 2006.

37. Typescript in author's archive.

38. Kuklík and Němeček, 1999, pp. 105-106, 127; Dušan Segeš, *Hodža, peniaze, ženy a intrigi*. In: Valerián Bystrický a Jaroslava Rogul'ová (Eds.), *Storočie škandálov, aféry v moderných dejinách Slovenska*. Spoločnost' Pro Historia, Bratislava, 2008.

39. Cambel, 2001, p. 7.

40. Múdry, 1949, p. 221.

41. Archív národního múzea Praha 23/3. These materials were deposited in the archive by Aunt Viera Štetková and Aunt Zora Frkáňová who had hept them safe during World War II and the Communist era.

42. Ján Ursíny, *Z môjho života*, Matica slovenská, Martin, 2000, pp. 34-35.

43. Múdry, 1949, pp. 221-222.

Chapter 28: My Father's Place

1. Peter Liba, *Listy Maríny Miloslavy Hodžvej Viliamovi Paulinymu-Tóthovi*, Matica slovenská, Martin, 1965, pp. 55-56.

2. Milan Vároš, *Putovanie za krajanmi, 2. vydanie,* Vydavatel'stvo Format, Pezinok, 1997.

3. Milan Vároš, *Vnuk Milana Hodžu sa narodil v Paríži a je profesorom v Seattli: Odsúdený v Bratislave prekvapil Štátny department vo Washingtone*, Život, vol. 28, June 30, 1998, pp. 18-21.

4. Peter Brezina, *Tvorba a život živnostníka-knihára Pavla Rázusa*. Supplement to the magazin Knihália. Ateliér knihy Kohi Pap Skalica, 2001.

5. The Church of St. Nicholas was built during the early centuries of the Kingdom of Hungary. Documentary evidence for the church as we see it today reaches back to the 1200s, but this Gothic structure is built on the foundations of an older Romanesque church. How did elaborate churches come to exist in poor mountain villages? Initially by royal order. King Stephen, who had become a devout Christian, directed that throughout his realms groups of ten villages should pool their resources and build a church to serve all ten. The king himself would take care of the costly interior furnishings, and the bishop would provide the priest, books, and other necessities of everyday church life. These communal churches were built on sites that would be convenient for all ten of the villages they served, so they tended to be placed in a previously unoccupied spot somewhere near the middle of the village cluster. So it was with the original Church of St. Nicholas. When it was built, there was no town or even village of St. Nicholas. Rather, servants, peasants, and others who came to serve the church built their houses in its vicinity, and over time a new village appeared. Thus, this grand church, built by the men of the nearby villages of Vrbica (later the home of the Pálkas), Okoličné, and others, was the nucleus around which today's Mikuláš developed. Ferdinand Uličný (Ed.), *Liptovský Mikuláš*. Pre mesto Liptovský Mikuláš vydalo Credo, Bratislava, 2006. pp. 13-14.

6. www.muzeum.sk/default.php?obj=muzeum&ix=lhmjk.

   www.liptov.sk/muzea/kral.html.

7. A detailed history of Lutheranism in Slovakia is available in Daniel Veselý, *Dejiny krest'anstva a reformácie na Slovensku*. Tranoscius, Liptovský Mikuláš, 2004. For the Toleration Church of Mikuláš, see Daniela Fiačanová, *Evanjelický cirkevný zbor*. In: Uličný (Ed.), 2006.

8. Chief among these are Juraj Tranovský, Michal Miloslav Hodža, Juraj Janoška, and Vladimír Kuna. Janoška was a much-loved minister and bishop during the first part of the twentieth century, and was the chief organizer of the transfer of the remains of M. M. Hodža from Tešín to Mikuláš. Kuna was the minister during World War II and was passionately devoted to social causes. Among other practical actions, he greatly expanded the Lutheran orphanage. Under the eyes of the pro-Nazi Slovak regime and of the German Gestapo itself, he hid many Jewish children in the orphanage, passing them off as Lutheran children. In a famous incident, the police overheard a couple of the children speaking German with each other, as was customary in Jewish families. The quick-witted Kuna promptly explained that German was an obligatory subject in the orphanage's school, and

that the children were practicing their lessons. After the war, Kuna received an award from the State of Israel for his brave and resourceful actions.

9. www.muzeum.sk/default.php?obj=galeria&ix=gpmblm.

10. www.jasna.sk/ , accessible in English.

11. www.ssj.sk/jaskyne/spristupnene/demanovska-slobody/, accessible in English.

12. My—Liptovské noviny, October 14, 2008, p. 9.

13. Ibid. These are the words of Ján Hlavienka, who knew the history of the Hut of Ján Pálka intimately.

14. www.nocka.sk/vychodna.

15. The Hála Museum is an extension of the Museum of Janko Král' in Mikuláš.   www.muzeum.sk/defaulte.php?obj=mesto&ix=va.

16. Matúš Dulla (Ed.), *Slávne vily Slovenska*. Foibos, Bratislava, 2010, pp. 224-227; Martin Droppa, *Pálkov funkcionalistický skvost*. .týždeň, March 5, 2012, pp. 68-69.

    www.brno.cz/index.php?lan=en&nav01=2222&nav02=2220&nav03=2447&idosobnosti=19. The house he designed for my parents is reminiscent of his own villa in Zlín: www.zlin.eu/en/page/32294.bata-villas-and-family-houses-1/.

17. Viera Štetková, *Spomienky*. Author's archive.

Chapter 29: Extraordinary Reminiscences

1. Letter of Mária Klečková to the family of Milan Hodža, dated June 22, 2005. Author's archive.

2. Letter of Mária Klečková to the author, dated February 1, 2006.

3. *Prague Releases U.S. Embassy Aide*, The New York Times, November 9, 1949:

    . . .The government [in Prague] announced tonight the arrest of thirty-two more Czechoslovak citizens including two fomer members of Parliament, who were alleged to have been in league with 'a Western imperialist power' in Germany. Presumably this meant the United States. A third member of Parliament, alleged head of the ring, was declared still at liberty in Western Germany. He was identified as Dr. Michal Zibrin. The two former deputies arrested were Karol Folta and Jan Bendik. All three deputies are former members of the now-outlawed Slovak Democratic party. The announcement accused them of having bribed Czech refugees in German camps with cigarettes to spy.

    More Czech Arrests. Charges Against Former Deputies. London Times, November 9, 1949.

4. *Appeal Made to Prague. Senator Asks Czechs to Spare Life of Alleged Spy. The New York Times*, January 4, 1950.

5. *Put to Death as U.S. Spy. The New York Times*, January 11, 1950. Other remarks were attributed to Ambassador Outrata: Press Release, *Another American Spy??* http://dspace.wrlc.org/doc/get/2041/22955/b09f14-0223stext.txt

    We appreciate the fact that the United States are in a fortunate position where it is not necessary for them to penalize the crimes of treason, espionage, etc. by death in the time of peace. Unfortunately the position of small and dangerously exposed Czechoslovakia is naturally different, and the Czechoslovak government must, although reluctantly, resort to this extreme measure of justice. The case of Karol Folta is just one of such cases. Anyway, I do not see any reason for suspicion that Karol Folta did not get a fair trial.

    A few years later, Outrata himself was purged by the Czechoslovak Communist government.

6. Jozef Jablonický, *Z ilegality do povstania*. Epocha, Bratislava, 1969, pp. 60, 69, 249, 280, 281. See also *Situácia v Trnave v lete roku 1944*: http://aladin.elf.stuba.sk/~soula/mkd/md10-06.htm

7. http://mozaika.sme.sk/c/2445478/trest-smrti-pre-prastryka-karola-foltu.html This detailed account was given by Matúš Meščan on the basis of the recollections of his mother, Viera Meščanová, Karol Folta's niece. Her father Juraj, Karol's brother, was also arrested but was released after nine months of abusive interrogation.

Chapter 30: A Hero from the Lower Lands

1. Ján Marko, *Rovnianska rodina Bulíkovcov a jej podiel na verejnom živote*. In: *Odkaz predkov—Dr. Janko Bulík, vlastenec, demokrat a martýr*. Matica slovenská, Martin, 2007. *Kovačický proces*. Kovačica—Pančevo, 2002. Reprinted from a booklet published by the Kníhtlačiarsky účastinársky spolok, Martin, 1908, which was itself a reprint from the newspaper *Národnie noviny*.

2. Typescript from the personal archive of Dr. Ján Bulík, Pozdišovce; copy in author's archive. See also Marko, 2007, pp. 203-204 .

3. *Odkaz predkov—Dr. Janko Bulík, vlastenec, demokrat a martýr*. 2007.

4. Jozef Jablonický, *Ján Bulík a československý protifašistický odboj počas druhej svetovej vojny*. In: ibid.

5. Vladimír J. Žuffa, *Skok do neznáma*, Vydavateľstvo Michala Vaška, Prešov, 2004, pp. 29-122; Jablonický, ibid.

6. Žuffa, 2004, pp. 29-37, 42.

7. Jablonický, 2007, p. 113.

8. Zuzana Drugová, *Dr. Janko Bulík v spomienkach priateľov a syna*. In: *Odkaz predkov—Dr. Janko Bulík, vlastenec, demokrat a martýr*. 2007.

9. Jablonický, 2007.

10. Žuffa, 2004, p. 121.

11. Account given to me by Dr. Ján Bulík, Pozdišovce.

12. The celebrations in Kovačica actually had a dual purpose, to honor Janko Bulík and also an event known as the Kovačica Trial. In 1907, during the height of Magyar repression of minorities, Janko's parents were among the leaders of a protest against the imposition of Magyar-language church services in the virtually all-Slovak Lutheran congregation of Kovačica. For this Fero and Júda Bulík were prosecuted, tried, imprisoned, and fined in what came to be known as the Kovačica Trial. They and their fellow parishioners, deeply religious though they were, later continued their protest by refusing to hold baptisms and weddings in the church as long as it was controlled by Magyar authorities. They even buried their dead on their own. 2007 was the centenary of this event, and its celebration was coordinated with that of Janko Bulík. *Odkaz predkov - Kovačica pamätá*. Matica slovaská, Martin, 2007.

13. Ján Cicka (Ed.), *Kovačica 1802-2002: Zborník prác pri dvestoročnici mesta*. Miestne spoločenstvo Kovačica, Kovačica, 2002.

14. *Odkaz predkov - Kovačica pamätá*, 2007; *Odkaz predkov—Dr. Janko Bulík, vlastenec, demokrat a martýr*, 2007.

Chapter 31: Ján Langoš and the Institute of the Nation's Memory

1. www.upn.gov.sk/ This official web site of the ÚPN offers a great deal of fascinating material, including videotaped interviews with survivors of both periods of "unfreedom," the World War II Slovak Republic that was so much under Nazi control, and the Communist era. Portions of it are accessible in English. The mission statement quoted here is from the institute's founding legislation and is located under the heading O ÚPN (About) / Úlohy ÚPN (Missions).

2. www.njl.sk/.

3. Over 2,000,000 people, both Germans and Magyars, were forcibly transferred out of Czechoslovakia and into their ethnic homelands immediately after World War II. The background and complexities of this action are reviewed in Zdenk Radvanovský, *The Transfer of Czechoslovakia's Germans and its Impact on the Border Region after the Second World War*, and Štefan Šutaj, *The Magyar Minority in Slovakia before and after the Second World War*. Both in: Mark Cornwall and R. J. W. Evans (Eds.), *Czechoslovakia in a Nationalist and Fascist Europe 1918-1949*. Oxford University Press, Oxford and New York, 2007; See also Beth Wilner, *Czechoslovakia, 1848-1998*. In: Roger D. Peterson (Ed.), *Understanding Ethnic Violence: Fear, Hatred, and Resentment in Twentieth-Century Europe*, Cambridge University Press, Cambridge, 2002.

4. www.radio.cz/en/article/80156.

Chapter 32: Celebrating Grandfather Hodža

1. As Katarína Maxiánová points out (*Waking the Dead: Milan Hodža and the Slovak Road to Europe*, Slovak Foreign Policy Affairs, Fall 2003, pp. 65-73), there probably were immediate political considerations as well. In 2002, Slovakia was not only striving for membership in the EU, it was also in the midst of an election in which Prime Minister Dzurinda was campaigning hard for a second term for the governing coalition. EU membership was one of his party's primary planks, so the orchestrated revival of Hodža's memory played into the campaign. However, this only serves to highlight the lasting importance of Hodža's work. Were it not meaningful in today's world, it could not have been adopted by a political party to strengthen its own electoral campaign. In my personal view, whatever political motives there might have been, Dzurinda also has a genuine, personal admiration for Hodža and his legacy, perhaps even adopting Hodža as something of a model.

2. They are to be found in the Hodža collections of the Archive of the National Museum in Prague, where they were placed by our family.

3. Especially in 1906, Hodža came all the way from Budapest to campaign for a Slovak candidate for the parliament, Ľudovít Medvecký. This, as well as the honorary citizenship bestowed on Hodža, is noted in references to the region's history even today, for example http://sk.wikipedia.org/wiki/Giraltovce

4. József Kiss, *Slováci a Maďari podľa Hodžu*, OS, Fórum Občianskej spoločnosti, August 1994, pp. 74-75.

5. http://zsmh.sk/nasa-skola/historia-skoly.

6. http://oa-tn.edupage.org/about/?.

7. For example, Hodža figured prominently in the era's standard reference: Samuel Cambel (General Editor), *Dejiny Slovenska*, vol. 1-6, Veda, Slovenská akadémia vied, Bratislava, 1986. Vladimír Zuberec focused on Hodža and the agrarian movement more generally. Samuel Cambel, one of the era's most highly recognized historians and general editor of *Dejiny Slovenska*, wrote a memorable study of Hodža (*Štátnik a národohospodár Milan Hodža, 1878-1944*, Veda, Vydavateľstvo Slovenskej akadémie vied, 2001). It was his last work, and was published posthumously.

8. Jablonický organized this conference shortly after he was reinstated as the Director of the Division of Political Science of the Slovak Academy of Sciences. Held in 1992, it attracted nearly 20 historians and political scientists, not only Slovaks but also Czechs. The proceedings of the conference appeared as a slim, paperbound volume that quickly sold out. A second, expanded edition was published in 1994 and also sold out. The third, hardbound, edition, containing almost 400 pages contributed by 30 authors, was published in 2002 in honor of the transfer of Grandfather Hodža's remains; it appeared in English translation in 2007. A series of important monographic treatments of various aspects of Hodža's career and work appeared in rapid succession (Chapter 27, Note 3). A review of scholarly activity surrounding Milan Hodža is provided by Miroslav Pekník, *Milan Hodža vo svetle výskumu po roku 1989. Odkaz pre súčasnú politiku a otázka ďalšieho smerovania Dní Milana Hodžu*. In: Miroslav Pekník (Ed.), *Milan Hodža a agrárne hnutie*, Veda, Vydavateľstvo Slovenskej akadémie vied, Bratislava, 2008.

9. For a detailed review of the many early events honoring Milan Hodža, including their chronology and many of their most significant actors, see Vojtech Čelko, *Milan Hodža redivivus*, Odkaz, Listy Masarykovi spoločnosti, 22-23, září 2006, pp. 45-48.

10. Pavol Lukáč, *Prevoz symbolu*, Domino fórum, 15 augusta, č26, s. 8, 2002.

11. Miroslav Pekník (Ed.), *Milan Hodža a integrácia strednej Európy*, Veda, Vydavateľstvo Slovenskej akadémie vied, Bratislava, 2006; Miroslav Pekník, (Ed.), *Milan Hodža—politik a žurnalista*, Veda, Vydavateľstvo Slovenskej akadémie vied, Bratislava, 2008; Miroslav Pekník (Ed.), *Milan Hodža a agrárne hnutie*, Veda, Vydavateľstvo Slovenskej akadémie vied, Bratislava, 2008.

12. Pekník, 2008. Symposia devoted to Martin Rázus, Ferdinand Juriga, Ivan Dérer, and Anton Štefánek have been held thus far.

13. The exhibition, prepared by the National Library, was entitled *Milan Hodža—A Personality of European Stature* (*Milan Hodža—osobnosť európskeho formátu*) and was displayed first in Martin in

the spaces of the National Museum of Literature, and later in the great Toscan Palace in Prague. Peter Cabadaj, a literary historian at the Slovak National Library, was principally responsible for preparing the exhibition. http://slavni.terchova-info.sk/osobnost/peter-cabadaj/

The play about Hodža's life and work, *Hodža: A Lord in Peasant Garb* (*Hodža: Grandseňor v halene*), was written and produced by Róbert Mankovecký, the director of the Slovak Chamber Theater in Martin and a notable composer. The play was later filmed by Slovak Television and after its first broadcast was made available on DVD especially for use in schools.

14. See *Hodžova esej* on the web page of the Gymnasium: http://gbas.edupage.org .

15. See *Novinky*, then *Hodžov novinový článok* on the school's web page: http://zsmh.sk/

16. Milan Ježovica. He was deputy chief of mission at the Slovak embassy in Washington during the transfer of Grandfather Hodža's remains, and later moved to become Prime Minister Dzurinda's foreign affairs advisor. He has worked actively in the field of human rights.

17. Many of the works of Pavol Lukáč were collected in the posthumously-published volume *Milan Hodža v zápase o budúcnosť strednej Európy v rokoch 1939-1944* (*Milan Hodža in the Battle for the Future of Central Europe in the Years 1939-1944*), Štefan Šebesta (Ed.), Veda, Vydavateľstvo Slovenskej akadémie vied, Bratislava, 2005.

18. In 2009, the Prize of Ján Langoš went to Fedor Gál, friend and long-time fellow-activist of Langoš, and to the great spiritual and political leader of Tibetans in exile, H. H. the Dalai Lama.

19. In 2008 the prize of Milan Hodža was awarded to the Slovak National Library's Miloš Kovačka, for his extended efforts to present Hodža's contributions to the wider public and to illumine numerous chapters of Slovak history to which the nation can point with pride. Kovačka is, like Hodža, a son of County Turiec. A prolific writer and speaker with a ready smile and an eloquent turn of phrase, Kovačka upholds a vision of human greatness in the midst of difficult circumstances.

In 2009 the prize was awarded to Miroslav Pekník, Director of the Institute of Political Sciences of the Slovak Academy of Sciences, for his leading role in organizing the Days of Milan Hodža, for seeing into print so many of the monographs devoted to Hodža's life and work, and more generally for his many contributions to the scholarly analysis of the political development of Slovakia.

The laureate in 2010 was Vojtech Čelko, a Slovak historian who has worked for many decades in the Institute of Modern History of the Czech Academy of Sciences in Prague. A member of many binational organizations, Čelko has devoted his professional life to bringing forward the presence of Slovak political and cultural affairs in the Czech setting. Among many other things, he was the prime mover behind the placing of the memorial plaque on the Hodža villa that I described earlier.

The traditional Prize of Milan Hodža for 2011 was awarded to Zdenko Ďuriška, one of the leading genealogical researchers of the Slovak National Library. Ďuriška has devoted decades to studying a series of leading Slovak families, presenting both their complex genealogies and, perhaps more importantly, their contributions to Slovak national life. Among others he has worked on both the Hodžas and the Pálkas, and it is no exaggeration to say that without his painstaking research I would not have been able to write my own book.

In 2012 the world of Slovak historiography lost one of its luminaries, Marián Hronský. Hronský's greatest single effort was to illumine the struggles surrounding the setting of Slovakia's definitive boundaries at the the Treaty of Trianon in 1920, but he was a great voice for historical scholarship in general and an active participant in the Days of Milan Hodža. His colleagues honored his many contributions *in memoriam*.

Appendix I: Slovak History in Brief

1. I list here a sampling of books about Central European and Slovak history upon which I have drawn in preparing this brief account. It represents a range of interpretations of Slovak history, not all of which reflect my own. The selection is limited to English-language sources, focuses on publications since the year 2000, and is arranged alphabetically by author or editor.

P. M. Barford, *The Early Slavs: Culture and Society in Early Medieval Eastern Europe*, The British Museum Press, London, 2001.

Lonnie R. Johnson, *Central Europe: Enemies, Neighbors, Friends*, Oxford University Press, New York and Oxford, 1996.

Stanislav J. Kirschbaum, *A History of Slovakia: The Struggle for Survival*, Second Edition, Palgrave, New York and Basingstoke, 2005.

Carol Skalnik Leff, *National Conflict in Czechoslovakia: The Making and Remaking of a State, 1918-1987*, Princeton University Press, 1988.

Paul Lendvai, *The Hungarians: A Thousand Years of Victory in Defeat*, Princeton University Press, Princeton, 2003.

Robert Letz, Maria Kohutova, Viliam Cicaj, Vladimir Seges, Julius Bartl and Dusan Skvarna, *Slovak History: Chronology and Lexicon*, Bolchazy-Carducci, Wauconda, 2002.

Paul Robert Magocsi, *Historical Atlas of Central Europe, Revised and Expanded Edition*, University of Washington Press, Seattle, 2002.

J. P. Mallory, *In Search of the Indo-Europeans: Language, Archaeology and Myth*, Thames and Hudson, London, 1989.

Elena Mannová (Ed.), *A Concise History of Slovakia*, Academic Electronic Press, Bratislava, 2000.

Nadya Nedelsky, *Defining the Sovereign Community: The Czech and Slovak Republics*, University of Pennsylvania Press, Philadelphia, 2009.

Anton Spiesz and Dusan Caplovic, *Illustrated Slovak History: A Struggle for Sovereignty in Central Europe*, Bolchazy-Carducci, Wauconda, 2006.

Mikuláš Teich, Dušan Kováč, and Martin D. Brown (Eds.), *Slovakia in History*, Cambridge University Press, New York, 2011.

Appendix II: Slovaks of the Lower Lands

1. Jason Goodwin, *Lords of the Horizons: A History of the Ottoman Empire*, Picador, New York, 1998.

2. A detailed and thrilling account is given by John Stoye, *The Siege of Vienna*, New Edition, Birlinn, Edinburgh, 2000.

3. Charles W. Ingrao, *The Habsburg Monarchy 1618-1815*, Second Edition, Cambridge University Press, Cambridge and New York, 2000; Paul Robert Magocsi, *Historical Atlas of Central Europe, Revised and Expanded Edition*, University of Washington Press, 2002, p. 79.

4. Ján Sirácky, *Dlhé hľadanie domova, druhé, prepracované a doplnené vydanie*, Matica slovenská, Martin, 2002.

5. Ján Babiak, *Slovenské národné slávnosti I: Fakľa národného cítenia medzi dvoma vojnami*, Matica slovenská v Srbsku, Báčsky Petrovec, 2006.

Index